STRUCTURED READING

Eighth Edition

Lynn Quitman Troyka

Queensborough Community College,
The City University of New York

Joseph Wayne Thweatt

Southwest Tennessee Community College

PEARSON

Boston   Columbus   Indianapolis   New York   San Francisco   Upper Saddle River
Amsterdam   Cape Town   Dubai   London   Madrid   Milan   Munich   Paris Montreal   Toronto
Delhi   Mexico City   Sao Paulo   Sydney   Hong Kong   Seoul   Singapore   Taipei   Tokyo

Editor in Chief: Eric Stano
Editorial Assistant: Stephanie Brooks
Marketing Manager: Kurt Massey
Executive Digital Producer: Stefanie Snajder
Digital Project Manager: Janell Lantana
Digital Editor: Robert St. Laurent
Photo Research: IAS/Cecilia de Querol
Text Permissions: Glenview/PMG/Jen Roach

Project Coordination, Text Design, and
Electronic Page Makeup: Laserwords
Senior Cover Design Manager: Nancy Danahy
Cover Designer: Nancy Sacks
Cover Art: © Emilia Kun/iStock
Senior Manufacturing Buyer: Roy Pickering
Printer/Binder: R.R. Donnelley
Cover Printer: Lehigh-Phoenix Color/Hagerstown

Credits and acknowledgments borrowed from other sources and reproduced, with permission, in this textbook appear on the appropriate page within text or on pages 405.

Lexile® is a trademark of MetaMetrics, Inc., and is registered in the United States and abroad. The trademarks and names of other companies and products mentioned herein are the property of their respective owners. Copyright © 2011 MetaMetrics, Inc. All rights reserved.

Library of Congress Cataloging-in-Publication Data
Troyka, Lynn Quitman, 1938-
   Structured reading / Lynn Quitman Troyka, Joseph Wayne Thweatt.—8th ed.
      p. cm.
   ISBN-13: 978-0-20-524465-2
   ISBN-10: 0-20-524465-3
   1. College readers. I. Thweatt, Joseph Wayne. II. Title.
   PE1122.T76 2012
   808'.0427—dc23

                                                                    2012000902

7   17

Student edition: ISBN 10: 0-205-24465-3
ISBN 13: 978-0-205-24465-2
A la carte: ISBN 10: 0-205-24512-9
ISBN 13: 978-0-205-24512-3

www.pearsonhighered.com

Why Do You Need this New Edition?

If you're wondering why you should buy this new edition of *Structured Reading*, here are 9 good reasons!

1. **New!** For the first time, the book's interior design is in full color, bringing the material to life and making the reading experience more engaging.

2. **New!** Learning objectives have been added to the beginning of each chapter and reading selection, giving you a clear indication of what the main points are and what you are expected to learn. Now you have goals to keep in mind, which will help guide your reading.

3. **New!** We have added eight new reading selections for this edition of the text: Selection 3, " 'Freegans' Salvage Food from the City's Bountiful Garbage"; Selection 6, "Ugly and Lovable"; Selection 10, "Divorcing Couples Seek Solace in Ring-Smashing Ceremonies"; Selection 14, "Waging War on Wrinkles"; Selection 15, "The Danger of Hoarding"; Selection 23, "Guns in Kids' Bedrooms? Ohio Town Approves"; Selection 26, "Yes, Top Students Reap Rich Rewards, Even as Egg Donors"; and Selection 29, "Culture" in *Essentials of Sociology*. These new readings encompass a wide range of topics from dog abuse, to hoarding, to cultural issues. They come from a variety of sources, such as the Internet, newspapers, books, and textbooks to give you experience reading different formats.

4. **New!** We have expanded Chapter 10: "What Are 'The Author's Strategies?" It now includes sample paragraphs to illustrate an author's five purposes for writing as well as additional practice exercises on purpose and tone. In addition, we have expanded Chapter 2—"What Is the Reading Process?"—by incorporating material from the "What Is Reading On, Between, and Beyond the Lines?" from the previous edition.

5. **New!** We have combined Selection 30, "Reading Charts, Graphs, Illustrations, and Pictures" with Chapter 7, "How Can Maps, Outlines, and Visuals Help with Reading?" This section now includes more practice with reading charts and graphs, which will aid you as you develop your skills in Chapter 7.

6. **New!** We have added questions related to each reading selection in Parts 2 through 6 called "Thinking: Getting Started." These questions serve as a springboard for thinking and discussing prior to reading; these questions will help you engage in predictive reading.

7. **New!** In each of the reading selections, the more difficult vocabulary words have been **boldfaced** for the first time. This will help you identify words you need to understand and enable you to find the definition in the vocabulary list more quickly.

8. **New!** Images now accompany each reading selection to illustrate the subject of the reading and make it more engaging.

9. **New!** A Lexile® measure—the most widely used reading metric in U.S. schools— provides valuable information about a student's reading ability and the complexity of text. It helps match students with reading resources and activities that are targeted to their ability level. Lexile measures indicate the reading levels of content in *MyReadingLab* and the longer selections in the Annotated Instructor's Editions of all Pearson's reading books. See the Instructor's Guide in the Annotated Instructor's Edition of Structured Reading and the Instructor's Resource Manual for more details.

PEARSON

In tribute to our families—

David Troyka, Lynn's beloved husband (1924–2011)

and

Marilyn, Rob and Billie, and June Thweatt

Contents

* Indicates new selections to this edition.

Preface

In writing *Structured Reading*, Eighth Edition, we remained convinced that students learn best from guided, hands-on experience with complete, not partial, reading selections. We believe, too, that the best approach starts with detailed instruction in the separate skills areas that ensure movement to college-level reading abilities, followed by extensive, repeated practice with many complete reading selections that comprise five-sixths of this book.

In flight training, student pilots spend some instructional time in a training simulator. But within a short time, the instructors move students from the simulator to the cockpit of the airplane to give the students hands-on practice in flying the plane. Few passengers would fly with a pilot who had only simulator experience. Most want a pilot who has logged many hours of real flight time in the cockpit. Likewise, we want students to move quickly from the skills (the simulator) to actual reading (the cockpit) for extended practice. This method has worked well since the first edition of *Structured Reading* and is evidenced by its continued use by hundreds of teachers and thousands of students in the United States and Canada.

This new edition of *Structured Reading* builds on the techniques and strategies that have been the backbone of our previous editions. We've learned from our reviewers and teaching colleagues that Part One, which includes instruction in the separate college-level reading skills students need ("Central Theme and Main Ideas"; "Major Details"; "Inferences"; "Critical Reading"; "Reader's Process," and "Reader's Response"), is exactly what students are seeking from a reading textbook.

Our commitment to meeting the evolving needs of our students is also reflected in the topics of the reading selections. College students live in a world dominated by visual images, and gaining proficiency in reading these alternate texts is imperative in their efforts to become critical readers. As a result, we've expanded the chapter on reading charts, graphs, illustrations, and pictures. This is in addition to the eight reading selections we've replaced with new selections on more current, absorbing issues that students will find engaging.

Here are the new, major features of *Structured Reading*, Eighth Edition:

NEW TO THIS EDITION

- For the first time, the book's interior design is in full color, bringing the material to life and making the reading experience more engaging.

- Learning objectives have been added to the beginning of each chapter and reading selection, giving you a clear indication of what the main points are and what you are expected to learn. Now you have goals to keep in mind, which will help guide your reading.

- We have added eight new reading selections for this edition of the text: Selection 3, " 'Freegans' Salvage Food from the City's Bountiful Garbage"; Selection 6, "Ugly and Lovable"; Selection 10, "Divorcing Couples Seek Solace in Ring-Smashing Ceremonies"; Selection 14, "Waging War on Wrinkles"; Selection 15, "The Danger of Hoarding"; Selection 23, "Guns in Kids' Bedrooms? Ohio Town Approves"; Selection 26, "Yes, Top Students Reap Rich Rewards, Even as Egg Donors"; and Selection 29, "Culture" in *Essentials of Sociology*. These new readings encompass a wide range of topics from dog abuse, to hoarding, to cultural issues. They come from a variety of sources, such as the Internet, newspapers, books, and textbooks to give you experience reading different formats.

- We have expanded Chapter 10: "What Are 'The Author's Strategies?'" It now includes sample paragraphs to illustrate an author's five purposes for writing as well as additional practice exercises on purpose and tone. In addition, we have expanded Chapter 2—"What Is the Reading Process?"—by incorporating material from the "What Is Reading On, Between, and Beyond the Lines?" from the previous edition.

- We have combined Selection 30, "Reading Charts, Graphs, Illustrations, and Pictures" with Chapter 7, "How Can Maps, Outlines, and Visuals Help with Reading?" This section now includes more practice with reading charts and graphs, which will aid you as you develop your skills in Chapter 7.

- We have added questions related to each reading selection in Parts 2 through 6 called "Thinking: Getting Started." These questions serve as a springboard for thinking and discussing prior to reading; these questions will help you engage in predictive reading.

- In each of the reading selections, the more difficult vocabulary words have been **boldfaced** for the first time. This will help you identify words you need to understand and enable you to find the definition in the vocabulary list more quickly.

- Images now accompany each reading selection to illustrate the subject of the reading and make it more engaging.

- A Lexile® measure—the most widely used reading metric in U.S. schools—provides valuable information about a student's reading ability and the complexity of text. It helps match students with reading resources and activities that are targeted to their ability level. Lexile measures indicate the reading levels of content in *MyReadingLab* and the longer selections in the Annotated Instructor's Editions of all Pearson's reading books. See the Instructor's Guide in the Annotated Instructor's Edition of Structured Reading and the Instructor's Resource Manual for more details.

Here are highly useful supplements for our Eighth Edition:

• The *Annotated Instructor's Edition* (ISBN 0-205-24467-X) of our Eight Edition of *Structured Reading* provides answers to the exercises in the student edition, along with a 38-page "Instructor's Guide" found at the back of the text. The "Instructor's Guide" contains additional teaching strategies, readability levels for the thirty Reading Selections, and tips on using *Structured Reading* in either a classroom setting or a self-paced lab.

• An *Instructor's Resource Manual* (ISBN 0-205-24466-1) provides additional material for instructors as they prepare for class. This manual contains transparency masters, comprehension boosters, extra vocabulary exercises, and supplementary dictionary exercises. We have designed these materials to support instructors and lab tutors as they work with students. Available in print and for download from Pearson's Instructor Resource Center at no cost to instructors.

• *PowerPoint Presentations* (ISBN 0-205-24469-6) to accompany each chapter consists of classroom-ready lecture outline slides, lecture tips and classroom activities, and review questions. Available for download from Pearson's Instructor Resource Center.

• *MyReadingLab*, the most widely used online learning program in reading, is built on ease of use, a wealth of practice opportunities, and extensive progress tracking. It offers you skill remediation across four levels of difficulty, and it is the only site that improves your reading via two practice engines. "Reading Skills," modules of mastery-based skill practice, offer you exercise sets and feedback across 26 skill topics. "Reading Level," utilizing the Lexile® framework (www.Lexile.com), measures both your ability and text difficulty on the same scale, matching you with readings in your Lexile range and monitoring your progress.

Over the better part of a decade, *MyReadingLab* has been the most widely used online learning application for reading improvement, with almost 1 million student registrations across two- and four-year institutions. Pearson has published case studies and multiple surveys demonstrating how *MyReadingLab* consistently benefits students' mastery of key reading skills, reading comprehension, and critical thinking.

• The Test Bank for Developmental Reading (ISBN 0-321-08596-5) offers more than 3,000 questions in all areas of reading, including vocabulary, main idea, supporting details, patterns of organization, critical thinking, analytical reasoning, inference, point of view, visual aides, and textbook reading. Available for download from the Instructor Resource Center or from Pearson MyTest, a powerful assessment generation program that helps instructors easily create and print quizzes, study guides, and exams (www.pearsonmytest.com).

MyReadingLab™ For support in meeting this chapter's objectives, please go to MyReadingLab and work on your personalized learning path.

Acknowledgments

We never dreamed when we co-authored the Fifth Edition of *Structured Reading* in 1999 that we would continue to update and expand the text through the years and find fourteen years later that we have now completed the Eighth Edition. This edition holds special significance for both of us, since it marks the fourth edition we have authored. We first met at an English conference for college teachers over twenty-five years ago and have stayed in contact through the years because we share an unwavering commitment to students and their success in college, the workforce, and personal life. As developmental and first-year college level reading and writing teachers, we are dedicated to helping every college student achieve that success by learning to read skillfully, effectively, and with pleasure. In every edition since 1978, we have kept students in mind and have maintained the reading skills approach that we believe works best with students–complete, not partial, reading selections.

For their invaluable reviews of our Seventh Edition as we prepared the revision plans for this Eighth Edition we thank: Amy Blumenthal, Oakton Community College, IL; Palma Cortese, Massasoit Community College, MA; Sharon R. D'Agastino, Hudson County Community College, NJ; Donna Overstreet, University of Memphis at Lambuth, TN; Herman Pena, University of Texas at Brownsville and Texas Southmost College; Pat Pierce, Pulaski Technical College, AR; and Cynthia Spence, College of the Desert, CA.

We were privileged to work with an excellent team of professionals: at Pearson, Eric G. Stano, editor in chief, Developmental Reading and Writing; Stephanie Brooks, editorial assistant, Developmental Reading and Writing; and Joan Foley, production manager; at Laserwords Maine, Amy Saucier, project editor; and at Galileo Picture Services LLC, Cecilia de Querol, photo researcher.

On a personal level, Joseph Wayne Thweatt thanks his wife, Marilyn, for being his foremost encourager, indispensable sounding board, and proofreader as well as his long-time friends and former colleagues Charles and Sarah Demetriou, who offered willing assistance as they read, examined, and scrutinized each new reading selection for typographical errors and correct answers.

David Troyka, Lynn Quitman Troyka's adored husband of 47 years, passed away while this book was in press. Lynn owes him, more than anyone else, the inspiration and enthusiasm she brings to her teaching and writing. Lynn thanks Joe Thweatt, her co-author, for his years of fellowship and generosity of spirit; Ida Morea, her administrative assistant, for 18 years of loyalty and wonderful friendship; Bernice Joseph, David's treasured caregiver for the final three years of his life and now Lynn's excellent personal assistant; Kristen Black, Lynn's daughter, and Dan Black, her son-in-law, for their essential, loving presence in her life; and to Eric, Rachael, Nickyla, Nicholas, and Nehemiah Thomas for "adopting" her into their family of love and wisdom.

Joseph Wayne Thweatt

Lynn Quitman Troyka

Part 1

Skills for Reading

As a college student, why do you need a textbook called *Structured Reading?* After all, you already know how to read. Yet, a placement test score or an academic advisor says you need a course to show you how to read successfully at a college level. Our purpose in writing this textbook is to provide you with a concrete, structured method—with lots of opportunity for practice—that can ensure that you reach your goal.

Reading is a challenge for many people. As a college student, however, you're more advanced than the 90 million Americans who are unable to read well enough to function productively in today's world. Over 40 million adults cannot fill out a simple form. Another 50 million are unable to read newspapers or magazines. College students aren't in these groups. Rather, they need to master reading strategies needed for college success.

According to the North Central Association of Commission on Accreditation and School Improvement, there are six characteristics of good readers. Good readers understand (1) comprehension (able to make predictions, select main ideas, and recognize important details); (2) context (able to read between the lines to identify tone, setting, and the author's voice); (3) interpretation (able to use clues and evidence from the text to analyze problems and draw conclusions); (4) synthesis (able to read beyond the lines to apply and generate knowledge from outside the text); (5) conventions (able to make sense of words, grammar, and punctuation); and (6) evaluation (able to express opinions, ask questions, and challenge the text and the author).

Readers who use each of these six traits are, for the most part, reading **on the lines, between the lines**, and **beyond the lines** (explained in Chapter 2, Part 1).

In *Structured Reading*, we draw on excellent, convincing research about how adults improve their reading skills most efficiently. The best approach involves a structured system of skill building that is applied repeatedly to complete, whole reading selections. Part 1, the section you're now reading, explains the overall approach of *Structured Reading*, introducing you to the structured reading strategies that successful adult readers use. Part 1 also gives you much initial practice, with each skill presented separately.

Parts 2–6 of *Structured Reading* provide you with multiple opportunities to combine all the skills introduced in Part 1. After each of the 30 complete reading selections, you'll find structured questions that reinforce the strategies you've learned. The whole selections are representative of material that adults encounter in books, newspapers, magazines, and textbooks.

SETTING *YOUR* GOALS

Now that we, the authors of *Structured Reading*, have set our goals, we invite you to set yours. Please list below what you consider your strengths as a reader before starting your college-level reading class. Then, please list the areas in which you'd like to improve as a reader. These are your personal lists, so make them informal and honest.

WHAT ARE MY STRENGTHS AS A READER?

In what areas would I like to improve as a reader?

Chapter 1

What Is Your Personal Reading History?

LEARNING OBJECTIVES

- Analyze your reading background.
- Assess your current reading ability.

Everyone has a history of learning to read and of being a reader. By recalling the details of that history, people can come to understand their strengths and weaknesses as readers. Here's a questionnaire that prompts you to remember and analyze your reading history.

ACTIVITY A MY READING HISTORY

Think about and answer these questions.

1. Before you started to read as a child, did family members or other adults read to you? _____ If yes, did you enjoy it? _____ Why or why not? _____

2. What's your first memory of starting to read (if you recall your approximate age at the time, give it)? _____
_____

3. What's the title (or story outline) of one of the first books you read as a young child? _____
_____

4. When you were in school (Grades 1–12), did you encounter any difficulties with reading? _____ If yes, what were they? _____

5. What's the title (or story) of your favorite book when you were in elementary school? _____What did you like about it? _____

6. What's the title (or theme) of one of the best books you've ever read?

   _____

7. In general, as you were growing up, if you could choose between watching television or reading for pleasure, which did you choose? _____ Why? _____

8. What's your estimate of the number of complete books you were assigned to read in school? _____ Did you enjoy most of them? _____ Why or why not? _____

9. How often did you read for your own pleasure (fill in the table below)?

SCHOOL YEARS	almost daily	once a week	once a month	once or twice a year	never
Elementary					
Middle					
High					

10. How often do you currently read for your own pleasure? _____

    Do you read newspapers? _____ magazines? _____

    books? _____

11. Other memories or comments: _____

As you reflect on your answers, what do they suggest about your current reading ability? Your answers might hold a clue about why you're enrolled in a college-level reading class. For example, people who've had many reading experiences in childhood tend to be better adult readers. These people had many chances to practice regularly. If you didn't have

4

such chances, the reading class you're enrolled in offers you the chance to start catching up. Anything you do well requires continued, disciplined practice—whether it is participating in a sport, playing a musical instrument, or cooking a favorite dish.

MyReadingLab™ **What Is Your Personal Reading History?**
For support in meeting this chapter's objectives, go to MyReadingLab and select *Reading Skills Diagnostic Pre-Test*.

Chapter 2

What Is the Reading Process?

LEARNING OBJECTIVES

- Recognize the three phases in the reading process.
- Differentiate between reading *on*, *between*, and *beyond* the lines.

Reading is not just looking at words. Reading is a complex, diverse process. The reading process, like many other processes, involves a number of distinct, yet connected, stages. An often overlooked stage in the reading process is preparing to read—preparing both your mind and your surroundings—so that you are able to concentrate on the material. Another stage in the reading process involves your eyes (looking at the page) working together with your memory (accessing the store of information you already know). To learn new material by reading, you "hook" it to what's in your memory. Knowledge builds on knowledge. To build the knowledge base required in college, you need to marshal your self-discipline so that you actively engage with all interactions between your eyes and your memory. This chapter discusses three primary stages in the reading process and shows you how to make them an active part of your reading process.

CONCENTRATING DURING THE READING PROCESS

The ability to use the reading process skillfully takes concentration and self-discipline. Before you start a reading session, seek out places where, and times of day when, you'll not be interrupted or distracted by people or noise. Never mislead yourself into thinking you can concentrate adequately when you're in a room where people are talking, or the TV is on, or music is playing loudly, or when you're expecting a phone call. If you are uncomfortable with silence, as some people tend to be, experiment *honestly* with what gives you comfort: soft, nondistracting music, a clock that ticks reassuringly, or other options. If there's little private time where you live, schedule yourself to read in a quiet corner of the library or a spot in a park or public building with minimum human traffic. Check out which college classrooms are empty during off-peak class hours.

Aside from external influences on your concentration, internal factors can also get in your way. These include daydreams, personal problems, anxiety, and failure to stick with what you set out to accomplish. Concentration takes your total mental immersion in what you're doing. Developing an outstanding ability to concentrate is a major challenge facing college students. At all times, try to work with fierce determination to concentrate and focus with razor-sharp intensity. This is a learned ability. It doesn't come to most people automatically. The good news is that everyone can learn to concentrate and focus. You'll find that the more you practice, the stronger and more stubborn becomes your refusal to tolerate distractions, either external or internal.

One way to monitor your powers of concentration is to place a short stroke (vertical mark) on a sheet of paper each time your mind wanders. Doing this reminds you that you're not concentrating. At the end of the page or article, count the number of strokes you have accumulated. The next time you read, compete with yourself. Reduce the number of strokes you make per page or article. Soon, with practice, you can decrease the number of strokes.

Use the following paragraph to test your powers of concentration. Place a short stroke (vertical line) within the lines each time your mind wanders. Then, count the strokes as your baseline to measure your progress toward reducing the number of strokes as you read. The paragraph is from a student essay about the homeless in *Steps in Composition*, Seventh Edition, by Lynn Quitman Troyka and Jerrold Nudelman.

> The largest group of homeless people consists of families with children. To save on the cost of labor, many companies have downsized their operations or moved them out of the United States. The companies' stockholders may have benefited, but the companies' workers have not. For example, May and Joe Kalson, who lost their jobs when General Motors closed its factory in New York, had to live on welfare after their unemployment insurance ran out. But the payments did not cover all of their expenses. When the Kalsons no longer could pay their rent, they piled into their old Chevy and headed for Detroit in search of work in an automobile factory. But there were no job openings. Their first night in Detroit the family stayed in a homeless shelter, where some of their clothing was stolen while they slept. The Kalsons now sleep in their car. According to the U.S. Conference of Mayors, over half of all the homeless people in this country are families like the Kalsons.

PREVIEWING IN THE READING PROCESS

The overview of this chapter highlighted the idea that learning involves your "hooking" new knowledge to old. Because of this, you read best when you already know something about the topic at hand. Even a little helps. Thus, your first concern when beginning a reading selection is to determine your level of prior knowledge about the topic. To check your prior knowledge about a topic, use the technique called *previewing*. For example, would you go to a movie without knowing something about it? Most likely, no—unless you specifically want to be totally surprised. Perhaps you have heard people say good things about the movie, you have read a review of it, or you know one of the actors. If you have an idea about the movie, you can predict in a broad sense what to expect.

The same holds tenfold for reading. Before you read, you need some knowledge of what you're about to read. By engaging in the act of previewing, you establish all-important connections between what you already know and what's new to you. And once you have some basic information about the reading, you can begin to make predictions about that information. As you will see, the act of previewing and predicting will give you a platform on which to stand as you dive into the reading process.

To preview, do these three things (to yourself or aloud):

1. Based on your looking over the material, consciously predict what the topic and its development are likely to be about.
2. Ask yourself consciously what you already know about the topic.
3. Predict what your reading the material will add to what you already know.

It is also important to keep in mind that no one previewing method works for all material. Writers present material in a huge variety of ways. Here are guidelines for other approaches to try out—and to adapt to your needs and preferences.

- For an essay or article, read the opening and closing paragraphs, where main ideas are often found. Then, stop to decide what you predict the essay or article is about. Next, read the first lines of the paragraphs (as you become more skilled, you can skip some paragraphs if a few seem to cluster around one idea). Then, stop to revisit your first prediction and modify it, if necessary.
- For a textbook chapter, read the title, the first paragraph or introduction, the subheadings (often appearing in **boldface print** or *italics*), and the conclusion or summary. Then, stop to decide what you predict the textbook material will cover.

Students often avoid previewing and predicting because they aren't willing to take the time to do it. Yes, previewing and predicting take time, but the payoff is tremendous. Without previewing and predicting as you start each reading selection, you float in an open sea without oars and a compass.

The discipline for, and skill of, predicting as you read is so important that the next section discusses how effective readers continue to predict even after the previewing stage of the reading process.

PREDICTING IN THE READING PROCESS

Predicting is a continuous, active part of reading. This means that your mind is always ahead of where your eyes are on a page. You're actively wondering, guessing, and forecasting what's next. At the same time, you're actively deciding whether your predictions were correct or incorrect compared to what you found and adjusting future predictions in light of that. Practicing and polishing your predicting skills upgrade not only your comprehension but also your reading speed.

In working to read at a college level, you want to make conscious what is largely a preconscious human mental process. To master the art of predicting, you need to be aware of your thinking as you read. Stop occasionally to predict to yourself what you think will come next. As you move along, revise your predictions according to what you encounter. No one, not even the most skilled reader, always predicts accurately. The more you practice predicting, the easier and more useful it will become for you. If at first this activity slows you down, rest assured that you'll catch on soon.

Here's a description of the predicting process in action. It's based on Selection 5 in this textbook. Turn to it now, and keep your finger there so that you can flip easily to it as you read this paragraph. Immediately, you see that the title is "Darkness at Noon." In thinking quickly about those words, you can reasonably predict that the essay will be about (1) an eclipse of the sun; (2) a blackout caused by loss of electricity; (3) a tragedy of some sort; or (4) because each person's predictions are personal, anything else that comes to your mind. Next, read beyond the title and get a general impression of the essay through surveying—looking over—the piece. Then, scan the first and last few paragraphs, and you'll find that predictions 1, 2, and 3 are way off the mark. Adjust your thinking accordingly. Once you know what "Darkness at Noon" is about, you continue predicting as you go through the rest of the material.

In *Structured Reading*, each of Parts 2–6 begins with six questions called "Thinking: Getting Started." We have intended for these questions to prompt you to start your predicting process concerning the reading selections in each part. Use these thought-provoking questions as a springboard to thinking before you start your reading.

When you read a textbook, the process of predicting is central to your being able to study and remember information. The next chapter (Chapter 3) shows you how prediction operates as part of a structured reading and study technique. Often referred to as *SQ3R*, its first two steps (*S* and *Q*) involve active predicting during reading.

ASSESSING *YOUR* SKILL WITH PREDICTING

You might already be skilled in making predictions as you read. Or you might do well with only one aspect of making predictions. Choose a chapter (or a four- to five-page section of a chapter) in one of your text-books other than *Structured Reading* and apply the techniques of prediction in this chapter. Then, record below the title of the book and chapter (or section) you read, and write a brief summary of what you discovered about your skill with predicting.

APPLYING *YOUR* SKILLS

Reading **on, between**, and **beyond** the lines means reading closely. You can get intensive and extensive practice by reading closely all the exercises that follow each reading selection in *Structured Reading*.

Reading **on the lines** means understanding the stated meaning of the material. Here you look for the exact, literal meaning of what's written. In *Structured Reading*, three kinds of exercises have been designed especially to help you develop your ability to read on the lines: "Vocabulary" (explained in Chapter 4 in Part 1), "Central Theme and Main Ideas" (Chapter 5), and "Major Details" (Chapter 6).

Reading **between the lines** means understanding what's implied but not stated outright. When ideas are implied, you need to read between the lines to figure out what's not said directly, but is meant for the reader to realize nevertheless. To do this, look for these underlying assumptions or attitudes:

- Attitude toward you, the reader (respectful, condescending, playful, etc.), as reflected in the writing
- Assumptions concerning what you, the reader, are expected to know before you begin reading the material
- Attitude toward the topic (objective, biased, passionate, etc.)

To figure out authors' assumptions and attitudes, depend on how the authors express what they say. What words and phrases hint at something that's not stated? What alternatives of word choice were at the authors' disposal, and why did the authors choose the words used? Also, how do authors use evidence? Do they distort facts and information only to make their point? What line of reasoning do the authors use? Does the writer tell a story or make an argument? Your answers to such questions provide a portrait of the author's tone. Just as you can tell how people feel about a topic from their tone of voice, so can tone also emerge from the writing. In *Structured Reading*, a number of exercises have been designed especially to give you practice with reading between the lines: "Inferences" (Chapter 8) and "Critical Reading" (Chapters 9, 10, and 11).

Reading **beyond the lines** means you develop informed opinions about the subject being discussed in the material you're reading. To do this, come to your own conclusions based on what's been stated (on the lines) and what has been implied (between the lines). In *Structured*

Reading, "Reader's Response" exercises (Chapter 12) offer you opportunities to think and talk about your personal point of view about the subject of what you're reading. The subjects vary so that you can practice in diverse realms of thought.

In Parts 2–6, every reading selection in *Structured Reading* provides you structured practice with reading on, between, and beyond the lines. The entire purpose of *Structured Reading*'s exercises is *not* merely to test whether you've read a selection. That would be a simplistic waste of time. Rather, the purpose of all the exercises is to guide you along a structured path that leads to your being comfortable and skilled with reading at a college level.

The driving force behind the structure and content of the exercises is this: "If a person can't make a mistake, that person can't make anything." The learning moment is at hand if you choose a wrong answer to a question. Seize that moment! Figure out *why* your answer is wrong. If your answer is incorrect, examine your personal line of reasoning to figure out what you misunderstood. The exercises in *Structured Reading* are designed so that students learn as much, if not more, from an incorrect answer than from a correct one. Did the misunderstanding come from forgetting to read closely, with your full focus? Did the misunderstanding result from having missed what's implied but not stated?

Learning the reading habits and thinking strategies for college-level performance takes time. Don't get discouraged, and don't give up. *Structured Reading* challenges you to grow as a reader by deliberately asking you to stretch beyond what you're used to as your personal reading method. The ultimate goal is for you to make giant strides toward upgrading your reading ability.

MyReadingLab™ **What Is the Reading Process?**
For support in meeting this chapter's objectives, go to MyReadingLab and select *Active Reading Strategies*.

Chapter 3

What Is the Role of "SQ3R" When Reading to Study?

LEARNING OBJECTIVES

- Develop a reading strategy for textbook reading.
- Apply SQ3R to textbook reading.

SQ3R stands for *Survey*, *Question*, *Read*, *Recite*, and *Review*. It's a study technique to help you maximize your comprehension while minimizing your reading time. Learning how to use these principles will help you master textbook material—that is, retaining information over the long term, learning information to the point of recall, and understanding the facts and how they fit together. Try applying this five-step process to the textbook excerpts in this book (Selections 27 and 28). The investment of your time is worth the benefits. You'll notice improvement in your concentration, comprehension, and reading rate. The following box describes the SQ3R technique.

SQ3R for Studying

S = Survey Before you read closely, look over the title, headings, and subheadings. Look also at the captions under pictures, charts, graphs, or maps. Consciously predict what you think the topics will be.

Q = Question Turn each heading and subheading into a question using the *"five W's and one H"*: *who, what, when, where, why*, and *how*. By asking questions, you prepare your mind to read for the answer.

R = Read Read closely, keeping in mind the questions you've already asked about the material. Strive to hook any new material onto what you already know. Come to understand the material.

R = Recite After you've read two or more pages, go back to whatever headings, subheadings, or boldface words you used to form questions during the *Q* part of

---

SQ3R. Cover up the specific paragraphs, and in your own words, say aloud or to yourself what the material is about.

R = Review Look over the material again. Move somewhat slowly and take special notice of key spots: the title, main headings, subheadings, and important paragraphs. As you review, you might highlight key areas with a see-through marking pen—but be careful to highlight only major ideas. If you fill a page with highlighter pen, you need to work harder on separating minor material from key points. Next, think through whether your predictions made during your survey were correct. The review is intended to pull together all the pieces as if you're working on a jigsaw puzzle.

Following are a few paragraphs about the giant panda, from a publication of *The Healthy Planet*. Practice applying the SQ3R technique as you read it.

Evidence of the Giant Panda in Ancient Times

For more than three million years, the Giant Panda lived in remote, forested areas of China. Numerous fossil remains provide evidence that the mammal known to the Chinese as daxiong mao (dah-sh-WING, MAH-oo), which means "large cat-bear," lived in more than 48 different localities throughout China as well as one site in Burma.

The Giant Panda has appeared in Chinese books about literature, medicine and geography for more than 2,000 years. At one time, the mammal was hunted for its beautiful and unusual coat because superstitions thought it to possess the power of prediction and protection: It was believed that having a good night's sleep on a panda pelt indicated good fortune, while the pelt itself was thought to keep ghosts at bay. Today, the Giant Panda is the much respected national symbol of China.

An Appealing Pace of Life

A slow metabolism makes the panda an energy-conserving animal, which means it uses a minimal amount of energy to find its next food source. If it didn't have to, the panda would probably not move at all. In the wild, the Giant Panda will plunk itself down in the midst of a bamboo forest and simply pull at the shoots it can reach.

Using its unique wrist bone that acts as an opposable thumb, the panda can grasp bamboo. The animal peels the bamboo like a banana by holding it between its five fingers and its wrist knob. An especially tough esophagus helps the panda swallow the fibrous bamboo.

MyReadingLab™   **What Is the Role of "SQ3R" When Reading to Study?**

For support in meeting this chapter's objectives, go to MyReadingLab and select *Active Reading Strategies*.

Chapter 4

How Can I Improve My Vocabulary?

LEARNING OBJECTIVES

- Classify three types of context clues to increase vocabulary.
- Define unfamiliar words using structural analysis.

English is a rich language with over one million words. Yet, the average English-speaking adult has a vocabulary of only 40,000–50,000 words. And sadly, most of us use about 500 words in our everyday speech.

When you possess a large vocabulary, you can express and think about fine shades of meaning. You can think with precision. For example, unless you're a sailor, you probably refer to all the various lines on a sailboat as "ropes." *Ropes*, however, is a basic, generic term suitable only for armchair discussion. When the wind is blowing a gale, and the waves are covering the deck with solid sheets of water, you want to yell out to your crew something more specific than "tighten the rope." Sailors say such exact phrases as "harden the jib sheet," "ease the boom vang and rig a starboard preventer," or "mind the dingy painter while we back down on the anchor rode." Such phrases communicate clearly at a mature level. Whether you're reading, writing, or speaking at the college level about sailing or science, about football or philosophy, about literature or sociology, a strong vocabulary is essential.

As a young child, you learned words very quickly. You imitated adults and older children. When you grew old enough to start school, your vocabulary acquisition slowed down. By middle and high school, you had to work to enlarge your vocabulary. Teachers gave you vocabulary lists, perhaps ten words a week, and then tested you. Often what happened after the test was that unless you used the words, you forgot them. Now that you've reached college, your vocabulary has fossilized in a sense. The good news is that every adult, no matter what age, is capable of learning and using new vocabulary words. The simple truth is that you'll remember new words only when you make up your mind to use them as often as possible. Memorization without usage is ineffective.

USING CONTEXT CLUES

Success in college, and in certain jobs, depends heavily on vocabulary. One of the best ways to learn new words is to discover them in your reading. Push yourself to try to guess the meaning of a word from the way it is used in a sentence. This method calls for using *context clues*. With context clues, you try to determine the meaning of an unfamiliar word by looking for evidence in the sentence that contains the word, in the sentences that precede the word, and even in the sentences that follow the word. Context clues can be divided into four categories:

- Restatement context clues
- Definition context clues
- Example context clues
- Contrast context clues

USING RESTATEMENT CONTEXT CLUES

For a **restatement context clue,** look for a thought that's repeated in different words in the same or a nearby sentence. Sometimes, the restatement enlarges or limits the original thought. When writers repeat a thought, often taking the form of a synonym, you need simply to think about the shared meaning of the original and the restatement. For example, what does *fray* mean in the following sentence:

- He jumped into the **fray** and enjoyed every minute of the fight.

Perhaps a reader would guess that *fray* means either "fight" or "audience." After thinking of those two possibilities, the reader would note the words *jumped into* earlier in the sentence. Those words suggest an energetic entering, rather than a passive joining. *Fight* would be the correct choice.

Sometimes a restatement is set off by punctuation, which makes the reader's job easy. For example,

- Fatty deposits on artery walls combine with calcium compounds to cause **arteriosclerosis** (hardening of the arteries). [**Here the restatement appears in parentheses** *after* **the difficult word.**]
- The upper left part of the heart—the left **atrium**—receives blood returning from circulation. [**Here the restatement appears** *before* **the word in dashes.**]

ACTIVITY B   RESTATEMENT CONTEXT CLUES

Using restatement context clues, circle the best meaning for the italicized *words in the sentences below. (Answers on page 98.)*

1. In searching for food, homeless people often have to *scavenge* in dumpsters.

   Scavenge means   a. sleep.   b. hunt.   c. hide.

2. Sir Edmund Hillary and his climbing partner, Sherpa Temzing Norgay, were famous *alpinists*. In fact, they were the first to reach the top of Mt. Everest in 1953.

   Alpinists means   a. balloonists.   b. mountain climbers.
   c. parachutists.

3. An *adroit* boxer—one who can dodge, jab, and avoid being knocked out—is generally not the type of fighter a crowd wants to see.

   Adroit means   a. entertaining.   b. nervous.   c. skillful.

4. Era had the *audacity* to cut line in front of me in the school cafeteria. Then she had the nerve to ask me to loan her a dollar to pay for her lunch.

   Audacity means   a. impoliteness.   b. opportunity.   c. boldness.

5. At first, I was *dubious* whether I could complete the course. After the first major test, however, I was not as doubtful.

   Dubious means   a. unsure.   b. discouraged.   c. devastated.

6. The basketball players made a *simultaneous* jump for the ball. This concurrent movement resulted in a collision.

   Simultaneous means   a. at different times.   b. at the same time.
   c. at conflicting times.

7. We have informed the guests about the *postponement*. The ceremony will not take place until a later date.

   Postponement means   a. cancellation.   b. advancement.   c. delay.

8. I am glad you were able to *alleviate* Kathie's fear of airplanes. Your suggestions made it easier for her to fly.

   Alleviate means   a. lessen.   b. increase.   c. eliminate.

9. George Washington Carver was a famous *botanist*. He developed literally hundreds of uses for the peanut.

   Botanist means one who studies   a. animals.   b. plants.   c. fish.

10. On a movie set, *surrogates* often stand in for the real stars while technicians adjust the lights and camera angles.

    Surrogates mean   a. professionals.   b. amateurs.   c. substitutes.

USING DEFINITION CONTEXT CLUES

A **definition context clue** means that the word is formally defined in the same sentence. Formal definitions are direct and easy to spot.

- To say that my misunderstanding your instructions caused me **chagrin** would be like saying my daily appetite is satisfied by a grain of sugar. The Tenth Edition (2000) of *Merriam Webster's Collegiate Dictionary* defines **chagrin** as "distress of mind caused by humiliation, disappointment, or failure." Replace *distress* with *agony* and *misery* in that definition, and perhaps you can better imagine my feelings.

Some definition clues are less direct. For example, a difficult word might be defined by a detailed description rather than a formal definition. Descriptive definitions are less obvious than formal ones, but once you become aware of the descriptive approach, you can use them to your advantage.

- The most **overly aggressive** people I know are also the most successful in business. They possess great stores of energy, never hesitate to take the lead and make quick decisions, interrupt conversations, and tell others what to do.

Definition of "chagrin"—By permission. From Merriam-Webster's Collegiate Dictionary, 11th Edition ©2011 by Merriam-Webster, Incorporated (www.merriam-webster.com).

ACTIVITY C   DEFINITION CONTEXT CLUES

Following are 10 sentences, each of which defines the italicized word. Use the clues in the definition sentences to fill in the answers to items 1–10 that follow. (Answers on page 98.)

- *Polyester* is generally characterized as a wrinkle-resistant fabric.
- A *skeptical* thinker is one who questions beliefs or concepts.
- *Phi, theta,* and *kappa* are Greek letters meaning *wisdom, aspiration,* and *purity.*
- A street that curves and bends best describes a *sinuated* road.
- To feel *chagrin* is to be embarrassed or annoyed.
- A paragraph has *coherence* when the sentences are arranged in a clear, logical order.
- *Geriatrics* is the diagnosis and treatment of diseases associated with the elderly.
- A breed of powerful sled dogs developed in Alaska is the *malamute.*
- An *ambiguous* answer to a simple question is unclear because it can mean at least two different things.
- A person who talks without changing the pitch of the voice speaks in a *monotone.*

1. Your explanation of your actions is _____ because it can be taken in two ways.

2. I fell asleep listening to his _____ voice.

3. We need an expert in _____ to explain my grandparents' health.

4. A city apartment is no place for a dog as large as a _____.

5. My philosophy professor was _____ about whatever she read in newspapers.

6. I felt deep _____ when I realized that I had forgotten my best friend's birthday.

7. We couldn't understand the scientist's explanation of nanoseconds because it lacked _____.

8. The spot where the old country road goes up a hill and starts to _____ has been the site of many serious car accidents.

9. The Greek letter for wisdom is _____, for aspiration is _____, and for purity is _____.

10. Fabric made of _____ saves ironing time.

USING CONTRAST CONTEXT CLUES

A **contrast context clue** means you can figure out an unknown word when its opposite—or some other type of contrast—is mentioned close by.

- We feared that the new prime minister would be a *menace* to society, but she turned out to be a great peacemaker.

This sentence suggests that *menace* means *threat* because the contrast is that "she turned out to be a great peacemaker."

As you read, watch for words that signal contrasts. Such words include *but, however, nevertheless, on the other hand, unlike, in contrast*, and others.

ACTIVITY D CONTRAST CONTEXT CLUES

Using contrast context clues, circle the best meaning for the italicized *words in the following sentences. (Answers on page 98.)*

1. Even though Raleigh insisted that she hadn't passed a red light, the police officer's videotape of her doing so was *irrefutable* proof.

   Irrefutable means   a. undeniable.   b. unrealistic.   c. questionable.

19

2. After a ten-mile hike to reach Pike's Peak, I thought I would be *ravenous*. Yet, I was so relieved that the hike was over I couldn't eat a thing.

   Ravenous means   a. highly excited.   b. extremely lazy.
   c. very hungry.

3. The Marshes enjoyed their country house on Creve Coeur, and so they found it difficult to adjust to *urban* life in St. Louis.

   Urban means   a. expensive.   b. city.   c. secluded.

4. Unlike my wife, who does not approve of our children eating between meals, I *sanctioned* their eating fruit if it keeps them from crying.

   Sanctioned means   a. ignored.   b. approved of.   c. discouraged.

5. This week my bosses assigned me to the *tedious* task of proofreading every one of the ninety-four letters they wrote last week.

   Tedious means   a. envious.   b. complex.   c. boring.

6. Greg was *gregarious*, but his twin brother, Rory, was shy.

   Gregarious means   a. distrustful.   b. sociable.   c. outspoken.

7. An abridged dictionary, not an *unabridged* dictionary, has been shortened.

   Unabridged means   a. complete.   b. incomplete.   c. blended.

8. Although Michelle *somnambulates*, Veronica, her sister, never walks in her sleep.

   Somnambulates means   a. snores in her sleep.   b. talks in her sleep.
   c. strolls around while asleep.

9. Dee's whistle was *inaudible* to me; however, my puppy could hear it.

   Inaudible means   a. not seen.   b. not heard.   c. not recognizable.

10. Although a tuition increase of 15 percent has been approved, the college does not expect an *attrition* in enrollment.

    Attrition means   a. decrease.   b. growth.   c. renewed interest.

USING EXAMPLE CONTEXT CLUES

You are looking at an **example context clue** when an unfamiliar word is followed by an example that reveals what the unknown word means.

- They were *conscientious* workers, never stopping until they had taken care of every detail so that everything was done correctly and precisely.

The words *never stopping until*, *taken care of every detail*, and *done correctly and precisely* clue you to the meaning of *conscientious*. It means responsible, thorough, and reliable.

Often, an example context clue is introduced with signal words like *such as, for example, for instance,* and *including.*

ACTIVITY E   EXAMPLE CONTEXT CLUES

Circle the best meaning of the word shown in italics *in the following sentences. (Answers on page 98.)*

1. *Adversities*, such as poverty, poor grades, and a weak family background, can be overcome with effort.

   Adversities means   a. obstacles.   b. pleasures.   c. responsibilities.

2. Andrew had a reputation for doing *perilous* activities. For example, he loved to ride a racing bike without a helmet, climb mountains without a safety rope, and ride in a speedboat without a life preserver.

   Perilous means   a. thrilling.   b. dangerous.   c. remarkable.

3. *Pungent* odors, including those of perfume, room deodorizers, and household cleansers, can cause allergic reactions in some people.

   Pungent means   a. mild.   b. sharp.   c. weak.

4. An *obituary* generally includes the person's age, occupation, survivors, and funeral arrangements.

   Obituary means   a. death notice.   b. sermon.   c. will.

5. Brothers and sisters sometimes like to play a harmless *prank* on one another. For example, a sister might make up the idea that their mother wants the brother to do a messy household chore.

   Prank means   a. joke.   b. assignment.   c. request.

6. I could see by Carlos's *visage* he was upset. He had an angry frown on his face, and his eyes were wide with fury.

   Visage means   a. actions.   b. personality.   c. appearance.

7. *Pachyderms*, such as the rhinoceros, the hippopotamus, and the elephant, are mammals that live in Africa.

   Pachyderms means   a. sensitive.   b. hostile.   c. thick-skinned.

8. That mole on your arm is a dark color; you need to see a doctor who specializes in *dermatology*.

   Dermatology relates to   a. heart.   b. skin.   c. feet.

9. Servers in restaurants depend on customers to leave a *gratuity* for their services. Without tips, waiters couldn't make a living.

   Gratuity means   a. money.   b. compliment.   c. recommendation.

10. To avoid encountering fans, Mankind and The Rock of the World Federation Wrestlers agreed to a *rendezvous* at 12 midnight at Main Street and Broadway.

    Rendezvous means   a. exhibition.   b. match.   c. meeting.

USING STRUCTURAL ANALYSIS

Another strategy for understanding and learning new vocabulary involves using structural analysis. Structural analysis is using the parts of a word—roots, prefixes, and suffixes—to determine the meaning of a word.

Understanding the parts of a word is useful in defining unfamiliar vocabulary, although it is most effective when used in conjunction with the strategies for using context clues. Word parts, in the many combinations that you will find them, make up over 50 percent of the English language; so knowing the more common roots, prefixes, and suffixes can make a huge impact in your ability to expand your vocabulary. Here are some of the common word parts that you will encounter in the readings in *Structured Reading* and elsewhere.

USING ROOTS

Many words in the English language have their origins in Latin and Greek. These Latin and Greek roots allow you to know the basic meaning of many English words of which they are a part. Review the following list of common roots and notice the ways the root is used to form various words.

Root	Basic meaning	Example words
-anthrop-	human	misanthrope, philanthropy, anthropomorphic
-dem-	people	democracy, demography, demagogue, endemic, pandemic
-derm-	skin	dermatology, epidermis, hypodermic
-dict-	to say	contradict, dictate, diction, edict, predict
-duc-	to lead, bring, take	deduce, produce, reduce
-gress-	to walk	digress, progress, transgress
-ject-	to throw	eject, inject, interject, project, subject
-ped-	child, children, foot	pediatrician, pedagogue, pedestrian, pedestal
-pel-	to drive	compel, dispel, impel, repel
-pend-	to hang	append, depend, impend, pendant, pendulum

Root	Basic meaning	Example words
-philo-, -phil-	having a strong affinity for; love for	philanthropy, philharmonic, philosophy
-phon-	sound	polyphonic, cacophony, phonetics
-port-	to carry	deport, export, import, report, support
-scrib-, -script-	to write	describe, description, prescribe, prescription, subscribe, subscription, transcribe, transcription
-tract-	to pull, drag, draw	attract, contract, detract, extract, protract, retract, traction

USING PREFIXES

A prefix is a word part that is added at the beginning of a word to change the meaning. Review the list that follows and notice the many ways prefixes are used to create new words.

Prefix	Basic meaning	Example words
a-, an-	without	achromatic, amoral, atypical, anaerobic
anti-, ant-	opposite; opposing	anticrime, antipollution, antacid
auto-	self, same	autobiography, automatic, autopilot
bio-, bi-	life, living organism	biology, biophysics, biotechnology, biopsy
co-	together	coauthor, coedit, coheir
de-	away, off, reversal or removal	deactivate, defrost, decompress, deplane
dis-	not, separate	disbelief, discomfort, discredit, disrepair
ex-	from, beyond, former	exclude, exhale
fore-	before (in time or place)	forerunner, forecast

Prefix	Basic meaning	Example words
hyper-	excessive, excessively	hyperactive, hypercritical, hypersensitive
inter-	between, among	international, interfaith, intertwine, interject
ir-, in-, il-, im-	not	irregular, irreplaceable, illegal, imperfect
micro-	small	microcosm, micronucleus, microscope
mono-	one, single, alone	monochrome, monosyllable, monoxide
non-	not	nonessential, nonmetallic, nonresident
post-	after	postdate, postwar, postnasal, postnatal
pre-	before	preconceive, preexist, prepay
re-	again, back, backward	rearrange, rebuild recall, rerun, rewrite
sub-	under	submarine, subway, subhuman
thermo-, therm-	heat	thermal, thermometer, thermostat
trans-	across, beyond, through	transatlantic, transpolar

USING SUFFIXES

A suffix is added to the end of a word to change the meaning or to change the part of speech of a word. For example, by adding the suffix "-ion" to the verb *create* you will change it to *creation*, which is a noun. Observe the various ways the following common suffixes are used and the types of words they form.

Suffix	Basic meaning	Example words
-able, -ible	forms adjectives and means "capable or worthy of"	likable, flexible
-ation	forms nouns from verbs	creation, civilization, speculation, information

Suffix	Basic meaning	Example words
-fy, -ify	forms verbs and means "to make or cause to become"	purify, acidify, humidify
-ism	forms nouns and means "the act, state, or theory of "	criticism, optimism, capitalism
-ize	forms verbs from nouns and adjectives	formalize, jeopardize, legalize, modernize
-logue, -log	speech, discourse; to speak	monologue, dialogue, travelogue
-logy	science, theory, study	phraseology, biology, dermatology
-ment	forms nouns from verbs	entertainment, amazement, statement, banishment
-ty, -ity	forms nouns from adjectives	subtlety, certainty, cruelty, frailty, loyalty, royalty; eccentricity, electricity, peculiarity, similarity

After reviewing these lists, you may notice that many roots, prefixes, and suffixes are used in combination. For example, the word *dermatology* combines the root *derm* with the suffix *-logy* to form a word that means the study of the skin. It is useful to keep in mind that structural analysis is only one strategy for understanding unfamiliar vocabulary. Used in combination with the other strategies discussed in this chapter, knowing roots, suffixes, and prefixes will greatly expand your ability to decipher new words.

ACTIVITY F STRUCTURAL ANALYSIS

Use context clues and structural analysis and circle the best meaning for the italicized words in the sentences that follow. (Answers on page 98.)

1. Animals have been known to use *nonverbal* signals to let both other animals and humans know what they want.

   Nonverbal means   a. not loud.   b. with aggression.
   c. without sound.

2. Mike's behavior is *inconsistent* with who he is, and I will have a talk with him to find out why.

   Inconsistent means   a. unfriendly.   b. changeable.   c. odd.

3. The young man talked to everyone at the party *except* the woman he really liked.

   Except means   a. not included.   b. especially.   c. mostly.

4. The woman couldn't wait for the *disbursement* from the bank to arrive in the mail.

   Disbursement means   a. letter.   b. payment.   c. package.

5. After Lucy brought the dress back to the store with a ragged tear, it was not *salable*.

   Salable means   a. able to be returned.   b. able to be worn.
   c. able to be sold.

6. The two brothers shared the car, so they had a *rotation* schedule they both followed.

   Rotation means   a. rule.   b. consistent.   c. regular change.

7. After John *transferred* to the new high school, he was unable to make new friends.

   Transferred means   a. failed.   b. joined.   c. moved.

8. Rachel wasn't going to deal with a boyfriend who didn't believe in *monogamy*.

   Monogamy means   a. gift buying.   b. religion.   c. one mate.

9. There is no way a neat person like Jake will be able to *cohabitate* with someone as messy as Mike.

   Cohabitate means   a. to share.   b. to live with.
   c. to be friends with.

10. The cyclist stared after the speeding car in utter *astonishment*.

    Astonishment means   a. shock.   b. anger.   c. sadness.

LEARNING AND REMEMBERING NEW WORDS

So that you do not have to rediscover a new word repeatedly, you want to work at reviewing and remembering new words all the time. How can you learn to remember new words? A personal method of vocabulary study that fits your learning style will work. Here's a good method to try—or to adapt to be most effective for you.

Learning New Words: The PWRA System

P = Pick Look and listen for new words you would like to add to your vocabulary. Choose selectively so that you concentrate on the words that will serve you best.

➡

Each word that is new to you will require thorough, repeated study. Most people can learn about ten new words at a time.

W = Write Use a 3 × 5 index card for each word you want to learn. On the front side of the card, write the word. On the backside of the card, write the definition.

Below the definition, write an original sentence using the word. Here's a sample card for the word *avocado:*

avocado

Front Side

a pear-shaped tropical fruit

An avocado is sometimes mashed and combined with onion, lemon juice, etc. to make a dip.

Back Side

→

R = Review Stack your 3 × 5 cards so that you see each card only on the side showing the word alone. Look at the word and try to recall the definition on the back. After you have been through the entire stack, turn over the cards so that you now see the sides with the definitions. This time look at the definition and your sentence to recall the word on the other side. As you work through your cards, divide them into two stacks: "know" and "don't know." Then, review the cards in your "don't know" stack. This intensifies your concentration. Before you end your study session, go through both stacks of cards again.

A = Apply Once you have learned a word, apply it. Actively use the word in your speaking and writing. Push yourself to find occasions that allow you to fit in the word. To reinforce your mastery of the word, hold it in the front of your mind, thinking about its definition and appropriate use. Only when you're certain that you "own" the word—that is, it's in your active vocabulary—can you move it to your list for every-two-weeks or monthly review. If you've forgotten the word, put it back on your daily study list.

In *Structured Reading*, we give you actual dictionary entries for the more challenging words in each reading selection. They are from *Webster's New World College Dictionary, Fourth Edition*. Having the entries readily accessible gives you hands-on experience with a first-class dictionary. We designed this resource so that you can become familiar with dictionary entries. Dictionary entries can look more complex than they are. Take apart the sections of a dictionary entry:

- Pronunciation guide for the word
- Material at the beginning of many entries, which tells how to pronounce the word and the origin of the word if it's derived from languages other than modern English
- Sequence of definitions for words with more than one meaning (most-to-less frequently used? oldest use to newest? other?)
- Various forms the word can take, such as a noun that can be adapted for use as an adjective

Along with the complete dictionary entries, *Structured Reading* offers you various types of vocabulary practice exercises. They include context clues, fill-ins, multiple choices, and crossword puzzles. Working with vocabulary exercises in this textbook gives you hands-on opportunities to master your knowledge of words. Your goal is to "own" the new words.

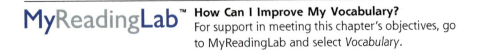

MyReadingLab™ How Can I Improve My Vocabulary?
For support in meeting this chapter's objectives, go to MyReadingLab and select *Vocabulary*.

Chapter 5

What Are "Central Theme" and "Main Ideas"?

LEARNING OBJECTIVES

- Determine the central theme of a passage.
- Locate the main idea of a passage.

In *Structured Reading*, the term **central theme** refers to what an entire reading selection is about. The term **main idea** refers to what a paragraph or group of paragraphs is about. To identify a reading selection's central theme and main ideas, you usually need to "read on the lines"—see Chapter 2 in Part 1. Sometimes, however, a central theme or the main ideas aren't stated outright. They're implied, which calls for you to "read between the lines," explained in Chapter 2. To figure out the central theme and main ideas of a passage, you need to read closely and give yourself the time to reflect on what you've read.

FINDING A CENTRAL THEME

The **central theme** of a reading selection is your answer to the question "What's the key point here?" A central theme is the key, the core, the significant message of a reading selection. To get to the central theme, try imagining this scene: A close friend stops by to visit you for a few minutes on the way to work. You invite him in and ask him to sit down. He glances briefly at the headlines on the front page of the newspaper lying on the floor. Not having time to hear all the details, he asks, "What's this about?"

The summary you give—neither too long nor too short—is a statement of the central theme, in this case of the newspaper article. For example, a good statement of a central theme would be "A high school coach is accused of receiving $200,000 for convincing one of his players to sign with a nearby college."

FINDING MAIN IDEAS

The **main idea** is the key message in a paragraph or several paragraphs. The main idea is the thesis, the topic, the subject of a subsection of paragraphs within a whole piece of reading. For example, what's the topic in the following paragraph?

> Many students believe teachers can prevent cheating. In other words, cheating would not be a problem if teachers took certain steps to prevent it. For example, students believe that cheating could be prevented if teachers announced tests early and the material to be covered on the test. They believe that in small classes teachers who work with students in a personal manner discourage cheating. Seating arrangements can also aid in combating cheating. They also believe that cheating could be prevented if penalties were made clear and firmly enforced. In short, cheating is perceived to be a teacher's responsibility, not a student's responsibility.

To find the main idea, do this: Locate one or two words that represent what the paragraph is about. In the preceding paragraph, the word is *cheating*. Using *cheating* as your key word, ask yourself *what* the paragraph says about cheating. The answer is the main idea: "Many students believe teachers can prevent cheating." (By the way, usually you need to state the main idea in your own words, even though here a quotation is appropriate.)

A good way to think of a main idea in a paragraph is to think about the design of an umbrella. Main ideas are "umbrella ideas." The main idea can be compared to the fabric covering an umbrella. All the major details are the supporting ideas—reasons, examples, names, statistics, and other material that support the main idea—and make up the metal spines of the umbrella. The diagram on the next page shows the relationship between a main idea and its supporting details.

Main ideas usually appear at the beginning of paragraphs, especially in textbooks, articles, and essays. Yet, many times, authors place the main idea at the end of a paragraph so that they can lead up to a small climax. Sometimes, writers put the main idea in the middle of the paragraph so that related material can surround it.

A main idea stated at the beginning of a paragraph is illustrated by the passage about cheating, shown earlier in this chapter. Here's a paragraph with the main idea stated in the final sentence. It's from "Dr. Ice Cream," in the *Washington Post*.

> Since Wendell Arbuckle retired, he has worked as a consultant—often traveling to ice cream factories to taste what they produce and evaluate it, much as tea tasters taste tea and wine tasters, wine. The tasting usually is done with two spoons, Arbuckle

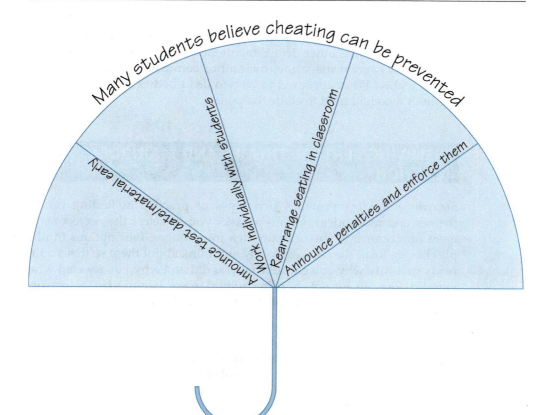

said, one for scooping the ice cream out of the package, the other for putting it into his mouth. Arbuckle said he usually stands over a sink, and spits out each sample without swallowing. "Sometimes I sample 90 batches a day," he said. "If I swallowed just a little bit of each one that would be too much." He evaluates the ice cream not only for flavor but also for texture as well, and gives advice on how to improve it.

Here's a paragraph with the main idea implied, not stated directly. It's from "Things Are Seldom What They Seem," in *Pageant* magazine.

Just because a body's in a hearse or on a body cart covered with a sheet in a funeral home doesn't mean it's dead, although the casual onlooker has every right to think so. However, policemen in Fresno, California, being of more suspicious mind, detected breathing coming from the bodies and arrested the two suspects they had been pursuing. Both were very much alive.

You need to "read between the lines" to determine when main ideas are implied, not stated. You want to identify the main point from the reasons, examples, and other details mentioned in the passage. In the paragraph from *Pageant* magazine, the author comments about appearance versus reality. What appeared to be two dead bodies were actually two fugitives who had tried to elude the police.

OBSERVING CENTRAL THEMES AND MAIN IDEAS IN ACTION

Structured Reading provides two types of practice in finding central themes and main ideas. One type asks you to select the correct statement of a central theme or main idea from among four options (multiple choice). Read the choices closely and think about them so that you're ready to justify why you chose what you did and why you rejected what you did. Reasons for not choosing an option are as important as reasons for choosing. Here's an example from *Black Belt* magazine:

> Lookout Mountain School for boys in Colorado is a school for boys who will not stay, voluntarily, at other places. They've been in trouble, in some cases deep trouble, with society. But the school, like other confining institutions, can't always offer total rehabilitation programs. The boys develop a certain amount of social retardation, being retained and confined. As one counselor puts it, "They can't function in society so they come here. Then we try to teach them to function in society." It's a tough job because, as he says, "The question remains: How can we teach them to function in society when they can't go out there?"

_____ 1. What's the main idea of this paragraph?
   a. Because Lookout Mountain School is a confining institution, it can't offer a total rehabilitation program.
   b. There's no attempt to rehabilitate the boys at Lookout Mountain School.
   c. Most boys at Lookout Mountain School are too "hardened" to be rehabilitated.
   d. Teaching delinquent boys to function in society is a tough job.

Answer: a

The second type of practice for finding central themes and main ideas is *open ended*. This type asks you to state a central theme or main idea in your own words. Here's an example from Rebecca J. Donatelle and Lorraine G. Davis, *Access to Health*.

For many smokers, the road to quitting is too rough to travel alone. Some smokers turn to nontobacco products to help them quit; products such as nicotine chewing gum and the nicotine patch replace depleted levels of nicotine in the bloodstream and ease the process of quitting. Aversion therapy techniques attempt to reduce smoking by pairing the act of smoking with some sort of noxious stimulus so that smoking itself is perceived as unpleasant. For example, the technique of rapid smoking instructs patients to smoke rapidly and continuously until they exceed their tolerance for cigarette smoke, producing unpleasant sensations. Proponents of self-control strategies view smoking as a learned habit associated with specific situations. Therapy is aimed at identifying these situations and teaching smokers the skills necessary to resist smoking.

In your own words, give the main idea of the preceding paragraph.

_____

_____

Answer: A variety of techniques is available to help smokers quit smoking.

PRACTICING WITH CENTRAL THEMES AND MAIN IDEAS

ACTIVITY G   CENTRAL THEME AND MAIN IDEAS 1

Read the following paragraphs and answer the questions that follow them. (Answers on page 98.)

From "Dealing with Unhappy and Difficult Customers," by Eric Tyson

(1) Some people say, "The customer is always right." In other words, even if a customer is being a jerk and trying to take advantage of you or is just being all-around difficult, you should bend over backward to please a customer.

(2) I don't buy this way of thinking. You should give the benefit of the doubt to customers because they can do lots of good for your business if you keep them happy and lots of harm if you don't. But some customers are a major pain in the posterior and impossible to please. Trying to keep them happy can be a time-consuming, costly process.

(3) Difficult people often don't have many friends so you probably won't get referrals anyway, and those customers they do refer to you may be as difficult as they are.

(4) If your business didn't do right by a customer, apologize, and bend over backward to make the customer happy. Offer a discount on the problem purchase or, if possible, a refund on product purchases. Also, be sure that you have a clear return and refund policy. Be willing to bend that policy if doing so helps you satisfy an unhappy customer or rids you of a difficult customer.

_____ 1. What's the central theme of "Dealing with Unhappy and Difficult Customers"?
   a. A business's customers are always right, so it's wise business practice to please them no matter how difficult they are.
   b. Some customers can never be pleased, no matter what you do, because they enjoy being unhappy and making others miserable.
   c. Business benefits when customers are happy, but getting rid of some difficult customers can help a business sometimes.
   d. Because of their never-can-be-satisfied personalities, difficult customers probably have few friends—or potential customers—to refer to you.

_____ 2. What's the main idea of paragraph 2?
   a. The author thinks that pleasing customers, even when they're difficult, is a bad idea.
   b. A business must give customers the benefit of the doubt, no matter how difficult they become.
   c. Unhappy customers can cause trouble for a business by spreading their opinions to other people.
   d. Keeping difficult customers happy can be a time-consuming, costly, frustrating process.

_____ 3. What's the main idea of paragraph 4?
   a. If your business has clear policies—with room to make exceptions—for handling complaints, most customers are usually satisfied.
   b. Clear policies for handling complaints help a business get rid of impossibly difficult customers without making the matter seem personal.
   c. Most businesses are better off without impossibly difficult customers, even if official policy says all customers must be satisfied.
   d. When a business can offer discounts and refunds, unhappy and difficult customers alike can be satisfied.

ACTIVITY H   CENTRAL THEME AND MAIN IDEAS 2

Read the following paragraphs and answer the questions that follow them. (Answers on page 98.)

From "Direct from Dell," by Michael Dell with Catherine Friedman

(1) Dell is the kind of company where everyone rolls up his sleeves and gets personally involved. We may be an $18 billion company, but our entire management team, myself included, is involved in the details of our business every day. This is, in fact, how we got to be successful: As managers, it's not enough to sit around theorizing and reviewing what those who report to us do. We frequently meet with customers and attend working-level meetings about products, procurement, and technology, to tap into the real source of our company's experience and brainpower.

(2) Why bother? It's a way to get close to our people, for certain. But that's not all. Our day-to-day involvement in the business helps us establish and allows us to maintain one of Dell's critical competitive advantages: speed. In this case, "staying involved in the details" allows for rapid decision making because we know what's going on.

(3) For example, when a problem crops up, there's no need for us to do more research or assign someone the job of figuring out what the issues are. Because we often have all the information at our fingertips, we can gather the right people in one room, make a decision, and move forward—fast. The pace of business moves too quickly these days to waste time noodling over a decision. And while we strive to always make the right choice, I believe it's better to be first at the risk of being wrong than it is to be 100 percent perfect two years late.

_____ 1. What's the central theme of this excerpt from *Direct from Dell*?
   a. Dell's managers stay involved in day-to-day issues so that they can make informed decisions.
   b. Almost everyone at Dell likes being part of an $18 billion company.
   c. The pace of most businesses today is slower than the pace at Dell, a fact that makes many people uncomfortable.
   d. Dell is successful because its managers do the theorizing and reviewing without having to consult its customers.

2. What's the main idea of paragraph 1?

_____

_____

_____

_____ 3. What's the main idea of paragraph 3?
   a. Problems are solved more easily when research has been completed.
   b. It's important for people to have information at their fingertips.
   c. Making decisions quickly is more valuable than making correct decisions.
   d. Today's rapid pace of business makes quick decision making important.

ACTIVITY I CENTRAL THEME AND MAIN IDEAS 3

Read the following paragraphs and answer the questions that follow them.
(Answers on page 98.)

From "Catfish and Mandala," by Andrew X. Pham

(1) The engine was running, but the sea had us in its palm. Our poor fishing vessel bobbed directionless, putting no distance between us and the mysterious ship in pursuit. The crew looked defeated. Mom muttered that it was terrible luck. First, the net fouling the propeller, now this. She said to Dad, "How could this be?" The calendar showed today to be auspicious. All the celestial signs were good—clear sky, good wind. She shook her head, looking at her Japanese flag, a patch of red on a white sheet, flapping noisily. Our hopes were pinned on that fraudulent banner.

(2) We waited. Time sagged. I counted the waves beneath our keel. There was nothing to do. The men's lips were moving, mumbling prayers. Eyes closed. Mom had her jade Buddha in her palms. Miracle. Miracle. Our boat seemed to plead with the ocean. Please send a miracle.

(3) It happened. The men stirred, but no one uttered a word. They looked hopeful, fearing that saying something might jinx whatever was happening. Another minute I could tell that the ship was veering away from us. They cheered. Tai instructed us to stay hidden, knowing that the ship had us in its binoculars. Mom was shaking with relief. Eventually, the ship went over the horizon and the men celebrated with a meal.

_____ 1. What is the central theme of this excerpt from _Catfish and Mandala?_
   a. A family hiding on a fishing vessel prays they will not be discovered.
   b. A family hidden by a boat's crew experiences several instances of terrible luck.

    c. People hiding on a fishing vessel are relieved when a crew from another ship chooses not to investigate them more closely.

    d. A ship's crew mistakes an illegal fishing vessel as Japanese.

_____ 2. What's the main idea of paragraph 1?

    a. The fishing vessel is not Japanese, even though it's flying the Japanese flag.

    b. The people hiding on the disguised ship are unhappy about their terrible luck.

    c. The people on the fishing vessel are strong believers in good luck and bad luck.

    d. The two examples of bad luck are the net fouling the propeller and a pursuing ship.

_____ 3. What's the main idea of paragraph 3?

    a. The men celebrate when a pursuing ship turns away.

    b. Tai, as the captain of the fishing vessel, gave the orders and everyone obeyed.

    c. The men stayed silent as the "miracle" happened before their eyes.

    d. The author's mother shook with relief when the ship went over the horizon.

ACTIVITY J   CENTRAL THEME AND MAIN IDEAS 4

Read the following paragraphs and answer the questions following it. (Answers on page 98.)

From "Fish for All Seasons," by Kitty Crider

(1) There is a lot of hoopla in the summer about wild salmon, especially the Copper River fish, which has had a highly successful marketing program in recent years. And it's a fine fish, to be sure.

(2) But the thing about salmon today is that it's like a strawberry. You can buy it fresh any time of the year, from somewhere. Salmon is no longer a seasonal item, found only in the wild. It's also farm-raised—in about 40 countries—and shows up on plates in the middle of the desert as well as near the coasts.

(3) Salmon illustrates how much the fresh-fish platter has changed in the past 10 years, primarily because of improved airline distribution and farm raising of more species. Fish that were once available only near their waters have become frequent fliers. And species that were only eaten in certain areas or months are being farmed in a variety of locations for year-round distributions.

1. What's the central theme for "Fish for All Seasons"?

   _____

   _____

_____ 2. What's the main idea for paragraph 2?
   a. Salmon is like a strawberry because both decay quickly.
   b. People almost anywhere can buy fresh salmon any time of the year.
   c. Salmon is farm-raised in about 40 countries.
   d. People can eat fresh fish, even in the desert.

_____ 3. What's the main idea of paragraph 3?
   a. All kinds of fresh fish can be flown to almost anywhere in the world.
   b. Fish farming in a variety of locations means year-round salmon distribution.
   c. Fresh fish can be found in the wild and on fish farms in 40 countries.
   d. Fast airline distribution and fish farming have led to increased availability of salmon.

MyReadingLab™   **What Are "Central Theme" and "Main Ideas"?**
For support in meeting this chapter's objectives, go to MyReadingLab and select *Main Idea*.

Chapter 6

What Are "Major Details"?

Major details support and develop a main idea. They emerge as you read "on the lines," a concept discussed in Chapter 2. Being able to tell the difference between a major detail and a minor detail is an important reading skill. Major details are the metal spines in the umbrella diagram shown on page 31. If you view all details as equally important, you'll become overloaded by details. To remember efficiently, you want to sort out the major details from the rest. Minor details can be interesting, but they're not basic to the understanding of the material you're reading.

FINDING MAJOR DETAILS

Differentiating between major and minor details takes practice. You can make such judgments only in the context of a complete reading selection. Depending on the framework in which the major detail is used, the same detail can be major or minor. For example, a person's age can be a major detail if the material is about the person's tragic, early death. On the other hand, a person's age can be a minor detail if the material is about the person's thoughts on global warming. Outlining (explained in Chapter 7) can help you figure out what's major, because it must be written on the outline, and what's minor, because it can be skipped without losing the main drift of the material.

Another way to identify major details is to look for words of transition such as *first, one, next, moreover, another, furthermore, in addition, also,* and *finally.* You are more likely—but not positively—looking at a minor detail when it follows words such as *for example, to illustrate, in particular,* and *for instance.* (For a complete list of words of transition, see Chapter 12 in Part 1.)

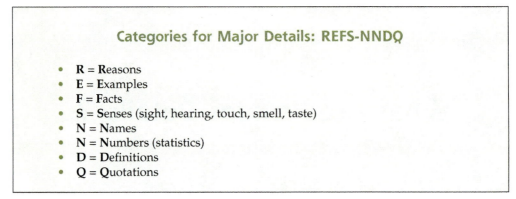

Categories for Major Details: REFS-NNDQ

- **R** = **R**easons
- **E** = **E**xamples
- **F** = **F**acts
- **S** = **S**enses (sight, hearing, touch, smell, taste)
- **N** = **N**ames
- **N** = **N**umbers (statistics)
- **D** = **D**efinitions
- **Q** = **Q**uotations

Yet another method for deciding what are major details is this formula: **REFS NNDQ** (hint: pronounce REFS, and name the letters NNDQ). Be aware, however, that this formula doesn't include the more obscure categories for major details.

Many writers depend solely on major details to imply the main idea of their material. For example, in the following paragraphs, details accumulate and build to give the whole picture. They explain why the doctor has recommended that his patient's leg be amputated. As you read this passage from *Mortal Lessons: Notes on the Art of Surgery*, by Richard Selzer, M.D., underline each detail.

> I invited a young diabetic woman to the operating room to amputate her leg. She could not see the great shaggy black ulcer upon her foot and ankle that threatened to encroach upon the rest of her body, for she was blind as well. There upon her foot was a Mississippi Delta brimming with corruption, sending its raw tributaries down between her toes. Gone were all the little web spaces that when fresh and whole are such delights to loving men. She could not see her wound, but she could feel it. There's no pain like that of the bloodless limb turned rotten and festering. There's neither unguent nor anodyne to kill such a pain yet leave intact the body.
>
> For over a year, I trimmed away the putrid flesh, cleansed, anointed, and dressed the foot, staving off, delaying. Three times each week, in her darkness, she sat upon my table, rocking back and forth, holding her extended leg by the thigh, gripping it as though it were a rocket that must be steadied lest it explode and scatter her toes about the room. And I would cut away a bit here, a bit there, of the swollen blue leather that was her tissue.
>
> At last we gave up, she and I. We could no longer run ahead of the gangrene. We had not the legs for it. There must be an

amputation in order that she might live—and I as well. It was to heal us both that I must take up knife and saw, cut it off. And when I could feel it drop from her body to the table, see the blessed space appear between her and that leg, I too would be well.

OBSERVING MAJOR DETAILS IN ACTION

Structured Reading provides you with three types of practice for finding major details. The first type asks you to decide if a listed detail is major or minor *in the context of the entire reading selection*. As you read the following example from *Read Magazine*, identify each detail and then decide whether it's major or minor. Be ready to defend your choice each time.

Where he lives, the air is so clean that sunsets are never red, not even purple. There's simply not enough dust in the atmosphere to break up the light. Instead, the purple evening sky is tinged with green from the forests below. Where he lives, the mountain slopes tumble downward from the sky, picking up trees as they go along and ending in the rush of a clear and unpolluted river. Eagles soar high above on the swirling air currents. Bighorn sheep bounce with sure hooves along the mountain peaks. Bears, deer, elk, and mountain lions roam the lower slopes. Where he lives is America, as it existed long before the coming of white settlers. He lives where Five Mile Creek flows into The River of No Return in a country named Light on the Mountains. He is one-sixteenth Apache but most of his forbearers came to America 300 years ago and kept moving westward in a search for freedom and elbowroom. Even his name is appropriate—Sylvan Hart. Sylvan comes from a Latin root meaning "forest," and a hart is one of nature's most elusive creatures, the male red deer.

_____ 1. Where Sylvan Hart lives, eagles soar high above on the swirling air currents.
_____ 2. Sylvan Hart lives in the rugged north central section of Idaho.
_____ 3. Sylvan Hart is one-sixteenth Apache.
_____ 4. Sylvan comes from a Latin root meaning "forest."

Answers: 1. Minor; 2. Major; 3. Minor; 4. Minor

TRUE, FALSE, or NOT DISCUSSED is a second type of exercise for Major Details. This type asks you to decide whether a listed detail is true, false, or isn't discussed in the material. To decide whether a major detail is *true* or *false*, read and reread carefully so that your concept of what the author wrote is clear. Only with close reading can you avoid jumping to the wrong conclusions. To decide whether an item is *not discussed* in the material, avoid allowing your mind to add in what's missing, no matter how much sense it makes. As you answer each question, be prepared to point to the source of each of your decisions.

Here's an example of a TRUE/FALSE/NOT DISCUSSED exercise for Major Details. It's from *Marketing: Real People, Real Choices* by Michael R. Solomon, Greg W. Marshall, and Elnora W. Stuart.

> Facebook is satisfying an unmet desire on the part of students to connect with and stay connected to other students in an electronic, easy-to-use, and fun format. The success also is related to influencers to whom students are exposed when deciding to participate in a social networking Web site. For example, reference groups are huge influencers when it comes to consumers deciding on which movies to see, what jeans to wear, or any number of other consumption decisions. As a result, if someone reestablishes a profile on Facebook and invites his or her friends to also develop a profile, the desire to be "part of the group" almost guarantees that those friends will use Facebook. In addition, self-concept is a very powerful motivator for some people. Since Facebook is an electronic networking site, it is possible for an individual to develop an online persona that is different from his or her in-person identity. Consequently, student users have the opportunity to develop a profile that transforms their in-person identity into the type of person they wish to portray. In some cases, they even develop more than one persona to appeal to different reference groups.

Decide whether each detail is true (T), false (F), or not discussed (ND).

_____ 1. Facebook is a social networking Web site.
_____ 2. Facebook has been known to reunite lost family members and friends.
_____ 3. Facebook allows students to create a personal profile.
_____ 4. Facebook does not allow an individual to develop an online persona that is different from his or her in-person identity.

Answer: 1. T; 2. ND; 3. T; 4 F.

FILL-INS are the third type of practice with major details. By filling in the missing words in a statement, your mind works to retrieve accurate information. As you work with fill-ins, be prepared to point to the material that led you to complete the statements the way that you did. (Consider a close synonym of the answer given to be correct.)

Here's an example of a fill-in exercise for Major Details. It's from a newspaper article published by United Press International.

Kim Jung-Sup's tragic man-against-mountain saga has made him a bitter man. He says he will find no peace until he conquers the Himalayan peak that killed two of his brothers. "I am a sick man, badly sick, sick with Mt. Manaslu," said the 42-year-old veteran climber. "I cannot fall asleep, haunted by the snow-covered mountain that keeps beckoning me. Unless it is conquered, I can never feel free." Kim has just returned home from his third unsuccessful attempt to scale the 26,915-foot-high Manaslu and was soaking his frostbitten feet in a bowl of medicated water. But his five-year battle against the mountain is not over, he said. He will try again next year. One of his two dead brothers still lies in a crevasse, his body in plain sight. The body of the other has never been found. Korean expeditions have lost 16 persons in Manaslu, including a Japanese cameraman and 10 Nepalese Sherpa guides.

Fill in the word that correctly completes each statement.

1. Kim Jung-Sup wants to conquer Mt. _____ in the _____ mountain range.
2. The mountain is _____ feet high.
3. Kim's battle against the mountain was unsuccessful _____ times.
4. Of Kim's dead brothers, the body of one has never been found, and the body of the other lies at the bottom of a _____ on the mountain.

Answers: 1. Manaslu/Himalayan; 2. 26,915; 3. three; 4. crevasse

PRACTICING WITH MAJOR DETAILS

ACTIVITY K   MAJOR DETAILS 1

Read the following paragraph and answer the questions that follow it. (Answers on page 98.)

From "Learn Horseback Riding in a Weekend," by Mark Gordon Watson

Learning how to behave with your horse is the first step towards building a good working relationship with him. A well-treated horse is trusting but a frightened horse can be very strong and dangerously unsafe. Always speak calmly. Horses are sensitive to tone of voice, so never shout. Avoid noises like road drills or motorbikes. Don't move suddenly or carelessly when around horses. Use persuasion to encourage your horse. Horses never forget a bad experience, but you can use their memory to your advantage, as they will also remember praise and rewards. Horses work best when they are in a happy environment and they like routine.

Fill in the word that correctly completes each statement.

1. Use a _____ tone when speaking to a horse.
2. Horses can become frightened by shouting and other loud _____.
3. Horses work best when in a routine, _____ environment.

ACTIVITY L   MAJOR DETAILS 2

Read the following paragraphs and answer the questions that follow them. (Answers on page 98.)

From "Diamonds" in "Mammoth Book of Fascinating Information," by Richard B. Manchester

(1) "Diamonds in the rough" are usually round and greasy looking. But diamond miners are in no need of dark glasses to shield them from the dazzling brilliance of the mines for quite another reason: even in a diamond pipe, there is only one part diamond per 14 million parts of worthless rock. Approximately 46,000 pounds of earth must be mined and sifted to produce the half-carat gem you might be wearing. No wonder diamonds are expensive!

(2) After diamond-bearing ore is brought up from the mine, it is crushed into smaller rocks no larger than one-and-a-quarter inches in diameter, and then washed to remove loose dirt. At the recovery plant, the ore is spread on tables covered with grease and sprayed with water. The water moves the rocks off the table, but the diamonds adhere to the grease. Then the grease is boiled off, leaving "rocks" of quite another sort.

Decide whether each detail is true (T), false (F), or not discussed (ND).

_____ 1. Out of 14 million parts of certain rocks, only a small part is diamond.

_____ 2. A diamond's worth is determined by how many carats it has.

_____ 3. No one has ever found a diamond larger than 1¼ inches in diameter.

_____ 4. Radioactive substances are used to separate the diamonds from the ore.

ACTIVITY M   MAJOR DETAILS 3

Read the following paragraph and answer the questions that follow it. (Answers on page 98.)

From "The Cake Mix Doctor," by Anne Byrn

> In addition to their shortening preparation time, cake mixes are a reliable friend. Cakes "from scratch" require some practice to pull off, and you fuss over the ingredients—the right flour, room-temperature butter. Yet, the doctored-up mixes are easily assembled using the dump method in which all ingredients are mixed in one bowl. And they bake up looking pretty, time after time. Plus, cake mixes adapt to new ingredients, be it a can of cherry pie filling or a handful of fresh strawberries. Tweak them with the right number of eggs and a suitable amount of fat and liquid, and they bake up not only into cakes, but also into bars, cookies, cheesecakes, crisps, pies, even a gingerbread house.

Decide whether each detail is Major *or* Minor *based on the context of the reading selection.*

_____ 1. Doctored-up cake mixes are easily assembled.
_____ 2. Baked cake mixes look pretty, time after time.
_____ 3. Pie fillings can be a can of cherries.
_____ 4. Cake mixes can be used to make bars, cookies, cheesecakes, crisps, and pies.

ACTIVITY N   MAJOR DETAILS 4

Read the following paragraphs and answer the questions that follow them. (Answers on page 98.)

From "Careers and Occupations," by Catherine Dubiec Holm

> (1) A variety of information is available on the Internet, including job listings and job search resources and techniques. Internet resources are available 7 days a week, 24 hours a day. No single network or resource will contain all information on employment or career opportunities, so be prepared to search for what you need. Job listings may be posted by field or discipline, so begin your search using key words.
>
> (2) A good place to start your job search is America's Job Bank <http://www.ajb.dni.us/>. America's Job Bank, run by the U.S. Department of Labor's Employment and Training Administration, provides information on preparing resumés and using the Internet for job searches, as well as trends in the U.S. jobs market and approximately 1.4 million openings. The Internet is completely unregulated, so if you come across a job offer that seems too good to be true, it probably is.

Fill in the word that correctly completes each statement.

1. Job listings are available at any time on the _____.
2. _____ from a field or discipline can help you search for information about jobs.
3. America's Job Bank is an Internet resource provided by the U.S. Department of _____.

MyReadingLab™ **What Are "Major Details"?**
For support in meeting this chapter's objectives, go to MyReadingLab and select *Supporting Details*.

Chapter 7

How Can Maps, Outlines, and Visuals Help with Reading?

LEARNING OBJECTIVES

- Construct concept maps or outlines to aid in comprehending a passage.
- Examine visuals to increase understanding of a passage.

Drawing maps and making outlines are two very effective ways for you to comprehend and remember what you're reading. Using the visuals that accompany a reading selection is another method to support you in determining the author's message and to further your understanding of the material.

MAPPING OF CONTENT

Mapping creates a visual diagram of a topic's major points and subpoints. Mapping, also called *clustering* or *webbing*, is a structured method to draw ideas on paper. This visual technique helps readers clarify what they are reading, comprehend larger chunks of material, and more easily remember what they have read. Maps demonstrate relationships between ideas by showing how they play themselves out spatially. The technique of mapping doesn't appeal to everyone, but try it a few times to get used to it. Then, you can decide whether to put mapping into your store of reading strategies.

To map, you begin at the center of a blank sheet of paper, which you can consider the center or nucleus. Draw a circle at the center into which you write the central topic of the article or essay. Next, drawing out from the center circle, make lines that spread out in various directions. End each line with a blank circle. In each of these new circles, write a main idea that's connected to the central topic of the material—this forms "branches" off the central topic. After this, work outward from each main idea by drawing shorter lines ending with circles into which you write supporting details for each main idea. As you work out from the center of the sheet of paper in all directions, you generate a growing, organized structure of what you're reading, which is composed of key words and phrases. Adapt this technique to what you're reading or rereading. Maps can be drawn in all sorts of patterns and shapes, so you can decide how you prefer to display it on a map.

ACTIVITY O   MAPPING 1

Read this paragraph twice. First, read it for its meaning. Second, reread it with an eye toward drawing a map of it.

Elephants are the largest animals that live on land. There are two chief kinds of elephants: African and Asiatic. African elephants live only in Africa south of the Sahara. Asiatic elephants live in parts of India and Southeast Asia. An African elephant is about the same height at the shoulder and rump. Its back dips slightly in the middle. However, an Asiatic elephant has an arched back that is slightly higher than the shoulder and the rump. The ears of an African elephant measure as wide as four feet and cover their shoulders whereas the ears of an Asiatic elephant are about half as large as those of the African elephant and do not cover the shoulders. The forehead of an Asiatic elephant forms

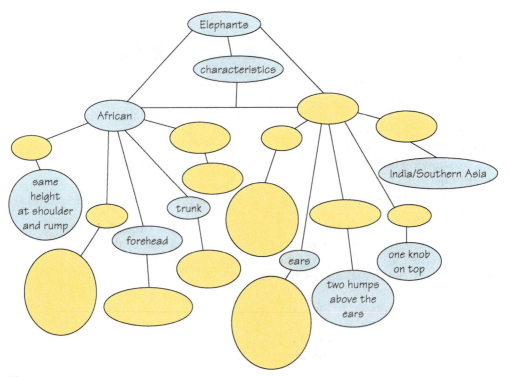

a smooth curve, but the Asiatic elephant has two humps on its forehead just above the ears. The trunk of an African elephant has two finger-like knobs of flesh on the tip whereas the trunk of an Asiatic elephant has only one fingerlike knob on the tip. The trunk provides a keen sense of smell, and elephants depend on this sense more than on any other.

Fill in this map of the paragraph about elephants. Some answers are provided to get you started. (Answers on page 100.)

ACTIVITY P   MAPPING 2

Read these paragraphs twice. First, read it for its meaning. Second, reread it with an eye toward drawing a map of it.

From "You Are How You Eat" by Enid Nemy

As for chocolate eaters, there are three main varieties, at least among those who like the small individual chocolates. A certain percentage pop the whole chocolate into their mouths, crunch once or twice and down it goes. Others pop the whole chocolate into their mouths and let it slowly melt. A smaller number hold the chocolate in hand while taking dainty little bites.

Peanuts and popcorn are a completely different matter. Of course, there are always one or two souls who actually pick up single peanuts and popcorn kernels, but the usual procedure is to scoop up a handful. But even these can be subdivided into those who feed them in one at a time and those who sort of throw the handful into the open mouth, then keep on throwing in handfuls until the plate, bag or box is empty. The feeders-in-one-at-a-time are, needless to say, a rare breed with such iron discipline that they probably exercise every morning and love it.

Candies like M&M's are treated by most people in much the same way as peanuts or popcorn. But there are exceptions, among them those who don't start eating until they have separated the colors. Then they eat one color at a time, or one of each color in rotation. Honestly.

Fill in this map of the paragraphs about eating methods. Some answers are provided to get you started. (Answers on page 100.)

Many people like to work at understanding ideas by using mapping techniques. These people report that mapping feels like drawing a picture. They let their hand glide across the page, capturing ideas within circles. Many "mappers," who often prefer not to write outlines, say that they relax and think better when they map. Many other people, however, feel that a map seems cluttered, unorganized, and difficult to use to identify the main and subpoints. They prefer to outline.

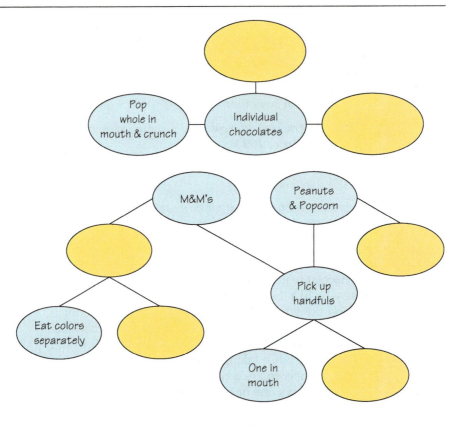

OUTLINING

Outlining is a structuring process that helps you organize, understand, and remember information. You might find that outlining isn't appropriate for everything you read (for example, fiction), but it can assist you particularly well when you need to master a sizable amount of material. Two common methods of outlining are creating informal and formal outlines.

CREATING AN INFORMAL OUTLINE

An informal outline breaks down material into sections that correspond roughly to different parts of the material. Its purpose is to increase your awareness of the separate parts of what you've read. No strict format exists for informal outlines. Writers often use informal outlines to create their working plans, a way to lay out the major parts of an essay. Readers can imagine an informal outline when they read a selection. Here's an informal outline for an essay about weight lifting for women.

Informal Outline

<u>weights/how to use</u>

    safety is vital

    free weights

       don't bend at waist

       do align neck and back

       do look straight ahead

    weight machines—safety is easier

CREATING A FORMAL OUTLINE

A formal outline takes the concept of an informal outline a few steps further. It adheres to strict format requirements, using Roman numerals, letters, and numbers to show how ideas relate to others. Roman numerals identify main ideas. Letters identify major details. Numbers identify minor details if they're necessary to include. Here's a formal outline for an essay about weight lifting for women. Following it is a box that summarizes guidelines for creating formal outlines.

Formal Outline

  Title: Weight Lifting for Women

 I. Avoiding massive muscle development

   A. Role of women's biology

   B. Role of combining exercise types

     1. Anaerobic (weight lifting)

     2. Aerobic (swimming)

II. Using weights safely

   A. Free weights

   B. Weight machines (built-in safeguards)

Guidelines for a Formal Outline

FORMAT

  I. First main idea

    A. First major detail

    B. Second major detail

      1. First minor detail

      2. Second minor detail

        a. First smaller detail

        b. Second smaller detail

(continued)

II. Second main idea
  A. First major detail
  B. Second major detail

RULES

- *Groupings:* Numbers, letters, and indentations identify groupings and levels of importance. Roman numerals (I, II, III) signal major subdivisions of the topic. Indented capital letters (A, B) signal the next level of generality. Even more indented Arabic numbers (1, 2, 3) show the third level of generality. And, finally, if absolutely necessary, indented lowercase letters (a, b) show the fourth level. Remember, all subdivisions must be at the same level of generality. For example, a main idea can't be paired with a supporting detail.

- *Levels:* Each level *must* have more than one entry. Don't enter a *I* unless there's a *II*; don't enter an *A* unless there's a *B*; don't enter a *1* unless there's a *2*; don't enter an *a* unless there's a *b*. If only one entry is possible, that entry is part of the heading in the next higher level.

  NO A. Free weights
         1. Safe lifting technique
       B. Weight machines
  YES A. Free weights
       B. Weight machines
  YES A. Free weights
         1. Unsafe lifting techniques
         2. Safe lifting techniques
       B. Weight machines

- *Headings:* Headings don't overlap. For example, whatever is covered in subdivision 1 must be distinct from whatever is covered in subdivision 2.

  NO A. Free weights
         1. Unsafe lifting techniques
         2. Not aligning head and neck
  YES A. Free weights
         1. Unsafe lifting techniques
         2. Safe lifting techniques

- *Parallelism:* Entries are grammatically parallel (all items start with a verb, or with a noun, or with any other word form). For example, all start with the -*ing* forms of verbs (*Helping, Assisting, Guiding*).

  NO A. Free weights
       B. Using weight machines
  YES A. Using free weights
       B. Using weight machines

- *Capitalization and Punctuation:* The first word of each entry is capitalized, and proper nouns are always capitalized. The items in a sentence outline end with a period (or a question mark, if needed). The items in a topic outline don't end with punctuation.

- *Introductory and Concluding Paragraphs:* These aren't part of a formal outline.

Your outline form itself depends on the material you're reading, your purpose in reading it, and how much you want to recall. If you're reading for a class or a test, your outline should include all the important main points and their supporting details. If you're reading for general recall only, your outline requires less detail. Although you will not always outline everything you read, you might want to practice the technique so that it becomes an easy way for you to make notes when thorough recall is important.

USING VISUALS

Mapping and outlines are techniques you do yourself to improve your understanding of what you've read. **Visuals** are images, charts, and graphs that are provided by the author. Visuals, which can include words as in cartoons or a caption beneath a photograph, are actually alternate texts that both enhance the author's written text and stand alone to make their own statement. The good news is that reading visuals is not so different from reading texts.

READING IMAGES

Images are visual representations provided by the authors to enhance the message they want their material to deliver. Images may be photographs, posters, cartoons, drawings, film or video, and artwork, for example. Images are as open to being "read" as words are. You can begin to read any one of these images using the techniques you are developing to read written material. When you look at an image, you are *reading on the line*. You are observing what is clearly stated visually. Ask yourself, what is it that I'm viewing? Literally describe the image presented. What does the image communicate to you? Next, if there are words accompanying the visual, what do they say? Are the words in contrast to the image, or do they support and create further curiosity about the image? If the image is included with a piece of writing, how does it relate to that writing?

College students live in an increasingly visual world—video games, Internet sites, and print advertising, for example—and must adjust to this shift by becoming proficient readers of alternate texts. The skills and strategies you practice in this chapter are designed to support you in reading the more common types of alternate texts you will encounter in your personal and academic experiences. Use the reading strategies you've been developing throughout your use of this textbook as you read the following visuals and answer the questions that accompany them.

ACTIVITY Q   READING IMAGES

Review the image in Figure 7.1 and answer the following questions. (Answers on pages 98–99.)

Figure 7.1

1. What are the main images in the illustration?

   _____

   _____

2. What type of building are the figures walking into? What visual clue(s) let(s) you know this?

   _____

   _____

3. What is the primary message of the illustration? What visual clue(s) support(s) your response?

   _____

   _____

   _____

   _____

ACTIVITY R   READING IMAGES

Review the image in Figure 7.2 and answer the following questions. (Answers on page 99.)

1. What are the main images in the illustration?

   _____

   _____

2. What do the envelopes represent? What visual clue(s) let(s) you know this?

_____

_____

_____

3. What is the primary message of the illustration? What visual clue(s) support(s) your response?

_____

_____

_____

_____

Figure 7.2

ACTIVITY S   READING IMAGES

Review the image in Figure 7.3 and answer the following questions. (Answers on page 99.)

1. What are the main images in the illustration?

_____

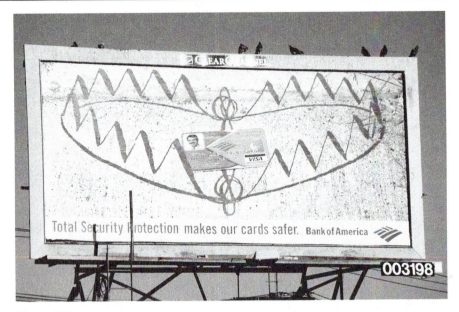

Figure 7.3

2. What do the words on the billboard add to the visual image?

_____

_____

_____

3. What is the primary message of the illustration? What visual clue(s) supports your response?

_____

_____

_____

READING CHARTS AND GRAPHS

Charts and graphs are visual representations that present large amounts of information clearly and quickly. The well-known quotation, "A picture is worth a thousand words," explains much about an author's choice to use charts and graphs. In your academic and personal reading, you may encounter a variety of types of graphs and charts. The most common types are bar graphs, line graphs, and pie charts. A **bar graph** compares values. A **line graph** indicates changes over a period of time. A **pie chart**, often called a pie graph, shows the relationship of parts to a whole.

Reading graphs and charts is not harder than reading text or images, but you need to be aware of certain characteristics. Bar and line graphs are presented on a *grid* that show the scale by which the graph is interpreted. They also have two *scales* that display what is being measured and how it is being measured. A pie chart, on the other hand, is presented as a circle and is usually represented in percentages. All three of the graphs/charts discussed may use a *key* to describe the elements being measured. The title of the graph/chart tells you what is being shown. The purpose of any one of these graphs/charts is to relate a large amount of information to the reader clearly and efficiently. When you use the basic elements just discussed along with your ability to understand what's stated, reading graphs and charts can be no more difficult than reading plain text.

ACTIVITY T   GRAPHS/CHARTS

Read the graphs/charts and answer the questions that follow. (Answers on page 99.)

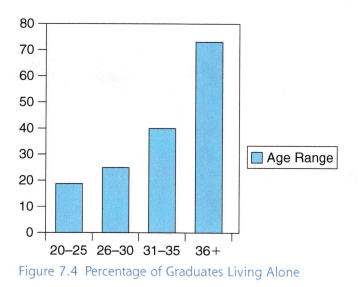

Figure 7.4 Percentage of Graduates Living Alone

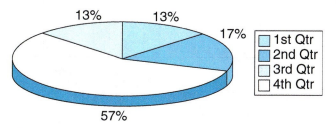

Figure 7.5 Percentage of Earnings per Quarter

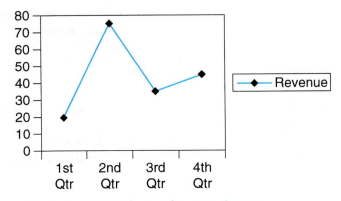

Figure 7.6 Increase in Earnings per Quarter

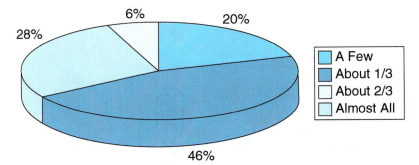

Figure 7.7 Business Leaders Say What Proportion of New Employees
Have the Writing Skills Desired

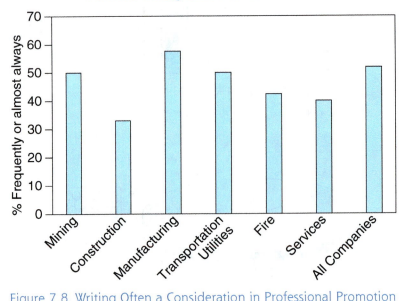

Figure 7.8 Writing Often a Consideration in Professional Promotion

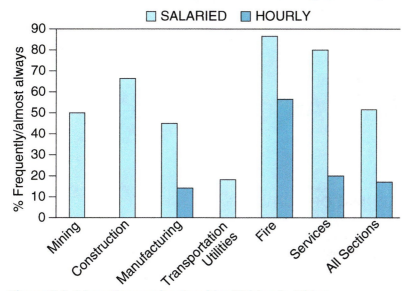

Figure 7.9 Many Companies Consider Writing in Hiring

_____ 1. According to Figure 7.4, which age range is most likely to live with other people?

_____ 2. In Figure 7.5, what is being measured by the pie chart?

_____ 3. According to Figure 7.6, which quarter had a decrease in earnings from the previous quarter?

4. According to Figure 7.7, what do the percentages represent?

_____

5. According to Figure 7.8, in what industries is writing considered in promotions at least 40% of the time?

_____

6. According to Figure 7.9, in which two sectors are hourly workers less likely to get hired if they have poor writing skills?

_____

MyReadingLab™ **How Can Maps, Outlines, and Visuals Help with Reading?**
For support in meeting this chapter's objectives, go to MyReadingLab and select *Outlining and Summarizing*.

Chapter 8

What Are "Inferences"?

LEARNING OBJECTIVES

- Define the term *inference*.
- Distinguish between valid and invalid inferences.

To make an **inference** in reading is to "read between the lines." Reading **between the lines** means understanding what's implied but not stated outright. When ideas are implied, you need to read between the lines to figure out what's not said directly, but is meant for the reader to realize, nevertheless. To make an inference, you arrive at a decision or opinion by drawing on what's said "on the lines," such as facts or evidence, to infer what isn't said but is nevertheless intended to be understood.

MAKING INFERENCES

In everyday life, everyone makes inferences. When we deal with people, ride in a car, or watch television, we make inferences. We use the five senses—sight, sound, touch, taste, and smell—to figure out what's going on. For example, when people smile sincerely, the look on their faces implies that they're happy or pleased. When you walk into a kitchen or restaurant filled with delicious smells, the scent implies that the person cooking is an excellent chef.

Here are more examples of your making inferences all the time:

- On your way to a classroom, you wave to a friend, but she does not wave back. You may infer that she is angry, that she is displeased with you, that her mind is on something else, or that she did not see you.
- As you're driving home, you come to a traffic light. On the side of the road sits an unshaven man wearing wrinkled, dirty clothes. He holds a sign that says, "Will work for food." You might infer that he is homeless, has no job, and is hungry. Or you might infer that this is

a rip-off. Rather than passersby offering him a job, the man expects people to give him a couple of dollars to buy food.

- You turn on the television to watch a program. The announcer mentions rolling blackouts, nuclear power, and conservation. You know that all the guests are environmentalists, so you infer that the program will be about an energy plan.

Making inferences is as natural for everyone as being human is. To use inference making in reading, however, isn't as automatic. In reading, you think about what the author says "on the lines" to lead you to make an inference about what the author doesn't say outright.

The ability to make inferences while you read is a learned skill. To make inferences, you take hints from what's stated and then fill in the gaps. You need to practice consciously so that you can easily understand more than what is said. Here are questions to keep in mind as you look for inferences:

- What does the author take for granted that I already know on the subject?
- What does the author take for granted about my attitudes toward the subject? Is the author's assumption accurate? Does the author give me room to have an open mind?
- What is the tone of the material? That is, how does the author say what's said? Are the words chosen to make the material clear or complicated? Honest or manipulative? Respectful or superior sounding? When humor is used, is the goal to help me understand the material or to distract me from thinking seriously about the subject?
- Does the author demonstrate a bias toward the material and try to make me accept the same bias?
- What unstated assumptions or conclusions does the author expect me to come to from reading the material?

To make correct inferences, a clear understanding of exactly what the author states is essential. You don't want to draw incorrect conclusions because you understood only part of the information given. Also, to make correct inferences, you are expected to draw on your prior knowledge. For example, if an author names a famous person without giving any details about him or her, the author is assuming that you know who the person is. Without that knowledge, you'll likely miss the message of the material. Therefore, you'll want to do research about the person so that the author's point is clear.

College-level readers dislike being manipulated by an author. For example, suppose an author seeks to convince readers that elderly parents should be put in nursing homes rather than cared for at home. You want to ask yourself whether the author is an expert on family life, on the elderly, or related areas. The answer should affect your reaction to the material. Perhaps the author is the owner of a nursing home, which means the author wants people to give him business by placing their elderly parents in his facility. This means that the author is biased and is trying to manipulate readers. Or, suppose that the author is a health-care professional, such as a doctor of internal medicine, a psychiatrist, or a rehabilitation specialist. You would want to see whether that professional provides only a medical view of the elderly without consideration of life in a nursing home from a resident's standpoint. Of course, sometimes information about the author is not revealed by what the writer says or implies. In such cases, especially if you're being influenced to change your mind on an issue, you want to do research about the author so that you'll be well informed.

OBSERVING INFERENCES IN ACTION

Often, the basic understanding of the main point of a piece depends on your ability to make good inferences. In "How to Stay Alive," Reading Selection 13 in this textbook, the author begins this way:

> Once upon a time, there was a man named Snadley Klabberhorn who was the healthiest man in the whole wide world. Snadley wasn't always the healthiest man in the whole wide world. When he was young, Snadley smoked what he wanted, drank what he wanted, ate what he wanted, and exercised only with young ladies in bed.

Much in the preceding paragraph implies that the author is using exaggeration and humor to drive home a point about some people's excessive concern with their health. The hints include the opening storybook phrase, "Once upon a time . . . "; the unusual, deliberately humorous name "Snadley Klabberhorn"; and the exaggerated statement that Snadley was the "healthiest man in the whole wide world." It takes reading inferentially to catch the message of the material. Also, if you happen to have prior knowledge about the author, Art Hoppe, you know that he usually writes humorous satire, poking fun at the problems and whims of human life. That's a further clue about the spirit of the essay.

Here are two examples of drawing inferences for you to observe. Both contain paragraphs from "Coretta Scott King: A Woman of Courage," by Paul Taylor. The message concerns Mrs. King's inner strength and courage in her devotion to her husband and the civil rights movement.

> Shortly before Dexter was born, Coretta again feared for her husband's life. He was arrested for leading a sit-in at a lunch counter in Atlanta. For this minor offense, the judge handed down a harsh sentence of 6 months hard labor at the State Penitentiary. Coretta was terribly upset. The penitentiary was 300 miles from the Kings' home in Atlanta. Pregnant and with two small children, she could rarely make the 8-hour trip to visit her husband.

She knew how black prisoners were treated in southern jails. Martin might be beaten—or worse.

Which of these statements can you infer from the preceding paragraph?

Coretta Scott King knew that black prisoners were poorly treated in southern jails because

    a. black prisoners complained more than white prisoners about poor food and health care in prison.
    b. the guards resented the civil rights movement and took out their anger on black prisoners.
    c. Coretta Scott King had been in jail and therefore knew that black prisoners were mistreated.
    d. The U.S. South had a long history of mistreatment of blacks both in and out of prison.

Answer: d

Here's another paragraph from the same source as the preceding paragraph.

Before lawyers had time to appeal the judge's decision, Martin was roughly dragged from his Atlanta jail cell. He was chained and handcuffed. In the middle of the night, he was taken to the penitentiary. When Coretta heard what had happened, she was distraught. Just as she was about to give up hope, the telephone rang. "Just a moment, Mrs. King," the long-distance operator said, "Senator John F. Kennedy wants to speak to you." "How are you, Mrs. King?" a warm voice inquired. After chatting a few minutes about her family and the new baby they were expecting, Senator Kennedy told Coretta he was concerned about Martin's arrest. "Let me know if there's anything I can do to help," he told her. The next day, Martin was released.

Which of these four statements can you infer from the preceding paragraph?

Coretta Scott King was about to give up hope because she felt that

    a. the lawyers were not very capable and therefore were unable to help her husband.
    b. the lawyers were secretly plotting with the judge to make sure that her husband was in jail.
    c. after the rough treatment given her husband in the Atlanta jail, there was almost no hope he could survive the even tougher world of the penitentiary.
    d. she would not be allowed to visit her husband while he was in the penitentiary.

Answer: c

PRACTICING WITH INFERENCES

Structured Reading offers much practice in the art of drawing inferences from reading. Following are four practices for you to try your skill at inference making. Then, every reading selection in the rest of this text-book includes a structured exercise to guide you into the patterns of thought that make someone a college-level reader.

ACTIVITY U INFERENCES 1

Read the following paragraph and answer the questions that follow it. (Answers on page 99.)

From "Travels with Lizbeth," by Lars Eighner

I find it hard to believe that anyone would have thought I had anything of much value. My clothes, besides being worn, would not fit many other people, and this should have been obvious to look at me. The little radio was of no appreciable value. Besides my papers, most of the bulk of what was taken was the remainder of Lizbeth's food and the bedding, which was warm enough, but could not have been sold. Other than a few dollars in postage, nothing could have been readily converted to cash. I was left with what I was wearing, a football practice jersey and my most ragged pair of jeans.

_____ 1. Read the paragraph again. What happened to the author's belongings?
   a. They were destroyed in a fire.
   b. They were borrowed but never returned.
   c. They were stolen.
   d. They were thrown out.

_____ 2. Read the paragraph again. Why does the author remark, "My clothes [. . .] would not fit many other people, and this should have been obvious to look at me"?
   a. The author wants people to look at him so he can show off his unusual appearance.
   b. By saying his size is unusual, the author implies he's hugely obese.
   c. Only a fool would be interested in the author's clothes.
   d. The author is happy to be rid of his ill-fitting, ragged clothes.

ACTIVITY V INFERENCES 2

Read the following paragraph and answer the questions that follow it. (Answers on page 99.)

From "Let's Get Well," by Adelle Davis

A study of the eating habits of individuals who could not reduce showed that they ate little throughout the day, obtained most of their food at dinner and during the evening, and had no appetite for breakfast. Anyone who has tried to reduce knows this pattern only too well. In the morning while the blood sugar is still high from food eaten the night before, will power is strong and resolutions firm. One vows he is going to stop feeling like the anchor on the *Queen Mary* and thinking of himself as a baby blimp; hence he forgoes or merely samples breakfast and lunch. As the bright star of success begins to glitter brilliantly before him, his blood sugar drops and he becomes exhausted, irritable, and starved. His undoing was not that he ate too much, but that he ate too little.

*Decide whether each statement below can be inferred (*Yes*) or cannot be inferred (*No*) from the reading selection.*

_____ 1. People need to eat three meals a day.
_____ 2. Fasting helps build moral character in people.
_____ 3. Lunch is the most important meal of the day.
_____ 4. Bad moods can be caused by low blood sugar.

ACTIVITY W   INFERENCES 3

Read the following paragraph and answer the questions that follow it. (Answers on page 99.)

From "Saint Valentine's Day" in *The New Yorker*

There are at least two saints after whom Saint Valentine's Day may have been named. One, known as "the lover's saint," was a third-century Italian bishop. In defiance of an edict of Claudius II, abolishing marriage, on the ground that it made restless soldiery, the good bishop secretly officiated at a number of wedding ceremonies, was pitched into jail, and died there. Or (there are a couple of other versions of his end) he was burned at the stake, at the behest of a Roman senator who objected to his marrying the senator's son to the daughter of an impoverished miller; or he choked to death on a fishbone. The other Saint Valentine was beheaded in 270 a.d., for refusing to renounce Christianity. While awaiting execution, he is supposed to have dashed off a farewell message to his jailer's blind daughter, signed "From Your Valentine." How he expected a blind girl to read the note the story doesn't say.

*Decide whether each statement below can be inferred (*Yes*) or cannot be inferred (*No*) from the reading selection.*

_____ 1. The saint who inspired Saint Valentine's Day might never be identified.

_____ 2. A Roman senator was held in greater respect than was a miller.

_____ 3. One requirement for sainthood is to have died by execution.

_____ 4. One Saint Valentine was in love with a jailer's daughter.

ACTIVITY X   INFERENCES 4

Read the following paragraph and answer the questions that follow it. (Answers on page 99.)

From "Computers," by Larry Long and Nancy Long

At the Skalny Basket Company, in Springfield, Ohio, Cheryl Hart insisted on daily backups of the small family-owned company's accounts receivables files [records of who owed money to the company]. The backups were inconvenient and took 30 minutes each day. Cheryl took the backup home each day in her briefcase, just in case. On December 23, she packed her briefcase and left for Christmas holidays. Five days later, Skalny Basket Company burned to the ground, wiping out all inventory and its computer system. The company was up in smoke, all except for a tape cassette that contained records of $600,000 accounts receivables. Cheryl said, "We thought we were out of business. Without the tape, we couldn't have rebuilt."

_____ 1. Read the paragraph again. What do the authors mean when they say, "Cheryl took the backup home each day in her briefcase, just in case"?

    a. Cheryl worried that someone would steal the information from the office.

    b. Cheryl wanted an extra copy of the files in case of disaster.

    c. Cheryl was considering stealing the company's files and escaping to Canada.

    d. Cheryl intended to work on the company's files while she was at home.

_____ 2. Read the paragraph again. Why did having the files of accounts receivables mean the company could rebuild?
   a. The accounts receivable had the original floor plans for the company's building.
   b. Cheryl Hart held all details of the company's inventory and operations in her head.
   c. The company had fire insurance, so there would be money to reconstruct its building.
   d. By knowing whom to bill for purchased baskets, the company's income wouldn't stop.

MyReadingLab™ **What Are "Inferences"?**
For support in meeting this chapter's objectives, go to MyReadingLab and select *Inference*.

Chapter 9

What Is "Critical Reading"?

Critical reading calls for "reading between the lines," a concept explained in Chapter 2 in Part 1. Here the concept has a different focus: the one needed for making inferences (explained in Chapter 8 in Part 1). Reading critically means analyzing how each author presents the ideas in each piece of writing. Critical reading is much like critical thinking. Both require you to *question*, *compare*, and *evaluate*. The three most important areas for critical reading are (1) being able to tell the difference between a fact and an opinion, so that the material doesn't manipulate you; (2) being able to determine the author's strategies, so as to understand the audience, purpose, and tone of a reading selection; and (3) being able to state in one or two sentences the primary message of a reading. This chapter and Chapters 10 and 11 will discuss the strategies that will support you in mastering these areas of critical reading.

CRITICAL READING: DECIDING BETWEEN FACT AND OPINION

As a reader, you're often called on to make judgments about whether the material is objective rather than subjective, or whether it's honest or distorted. Here are two statements, one a fact and the other an opinion, each followed by a critical analysis.

- Rebecca is the friendliest contestant in the pageant. [**"Friendliest" is an opinion. Being friendly means something different to each of us. Even if you happen to agree that Rebecca is the friendliest contestant, your assessment is still an opinion.**]

- Rebecca's peers elected her as the friendliest contestant in the pageant. [**"Friendliest" is not the issue here. Rather, it's the fact that Rebecca has been *voted* the friendliest contestant in the pageant. The vote is a fact.**]

Test for Facts: E R O

E = Experiment For example, "The Glaser study showed that elder residents of retirement homes in Ohio who learned progressive relaxation and guided imagery enhanced their immune function and reported better health than did the other residents."

R = Research For example, "According to the Americans' Use of Time Project, when we don't have to do anything else, most Americans mainly watch television."

O = Observation For example: "After a perfectly miserable, aggravating day, a teacher comes home and yells at her children for making too much noise. Another individual, after an equally stressful day, jokes about what went wrong during the all-time most miserable moment of the month. [. . .] The first is displacing anger onto someone else. The second uses humor to vent frustration."

Facts are statements that can be verified. You can "test" whether a statement is a fact or opinion by applying to it the three tests listed in the box. If the statement passes any one of the three tests, it's a fact. The examples in the box are from "A Personal Stress Survival Guide," which is Reading Selection 28 in this textbook.

Opinions are statements of personal beliefs. They contain ideas that can't be verified or confirmed. As such, opinions are open to debate. Opinions often contain abstract ideas, information that can't be proven, and/or emotionally charged words.

Sometimes an opinion is written so that it appears to be a fact. This is especially true when a quotation is involved. A quotation isn't automatically a fact. True, someone made the statement, but whether the content of the quotation expresses a fact or an opinion is what counts. For example, an author might quote a horse owner as follows: "Having a healthy horse to ride, work, show, or even keep as a pet is a rare privilege." The content of the quotation expresses an opinion, one certainly not shared by all. In contrast, the following quotation expresses a fact: A horse owner reports, "It costs me $600 a year to feed my horse."

OBSERVING FACT AND OPINION IN ACTION

Sometimes, even without doing any reading, you can decide whether a statement is a fact or an opinion.

Write F *or* O *in the blank.*

_____ 1. Health investigators have not found the cause of illness that affected two dozen workers at a hazardous waste processing plant.

_____ 2. Last year Jarred and Jossie missed school nine days.

_____ 3. Sometimes the best way to judge a truck is to look under one.

_____ 4. Nothing is better on a cold, winter day than a warm bowl of soup or stew—except maybe a loaf of homemade bread.

_____ 5. Bull sharks are common along beaches in the South.

_____ 6. "You have to love mushrooms to work here," says the owner of Oakhaven Mushroom Farm.

_____ 7. When I was a youngster, my grandfather used to bring me rusty bicycles, old rope, and broken toys he found in the junkyard.

_____ 8. In *Bon Appetit* magazine's fourth annual reader survey, cheesecake topped the list of dessert favorites.

_____ 9. Clark LaGrange, drama director at ECS, will be remembered for his enthusiasm, sense of humor, and patience under production pressure.

_____10. No healthy child is going to suffer because Shelby County Schools are turning the thermostat down to 68 degrees.

Answers: 1. F; 2. F; 3. O; 4. O; 5. F; 6. O; 7. F; 8. F; 9. O; 10. O

Now try reading a passage and then deciding whether the statements following are facts or opinions. These paragraphs, published in *The Washington Post*, speak about Wendell Arbuckle, who was an expert on ice cream, who wrote a major book on the topic, and who served as an ice cream consultant throughout the world.

(1) During the past four years, he has been doing this sort of tasting throughout the United States, but also in Germany, France, Switzerland, Britain, and Japan. He also has done consulting work by mail with firms in about 20 countries [. . .] all of which, he said, signals an "explosion of interest" around the world in American-style ice cream.

(2) He refused to say, though, which brand of ice cream he likes best. "It depends on what people want," he said. "They all can be good for you." His own favorite flavor, he said, is plain vanilla. "It's the basis of the industry and it goes with almost everything."

Decide if the content of each statement, whether or not it's a quotation, is a fact or an opinion. Write F *or* O *in the blank.*

_____ 1. *From paragraph 1:* During the past four years he has been doing this sort of tasting throughout the United States, but also in Germany, France, Switzerland, Britain, and Japan.

_____ 2. *From paragraph 2:* "He refused to say, though, which brand of ice cream he likes best."

_____ 3. *From paragraph 2:* All brands of ice cream "can be good for you," according to Arbuckle.

Answers: 1. F; 2. F; 3. O

PRACTICING WITH FACT OR OPINION

ACTIVITY Y CRITICAL READING: FACT OR OPINION 1

Read the following paragraph and answer the question that follows it. (Answers on page 99.)

From "Warriors Don't Cry," by Melba Pattillo Beals

I don't remember life without Grandmother India. Mother and Daddy had lived with her in North Little Rock even before I was born. When they purchased our Little Rock house, Grandma came with them. Unlike Mother, who was delicate and fair, Grandma was tall and copper-skinned. She had pronounced cheekbones and huge deep-set almond-shaped eyes that peered at me from behind wire-rimmed spectacles. She had a regal posture and a fearless attitude. My happiest evenings were spent listening to her read aloud from the Bible, from Archie comic books, or from Shakespeare. I sometimes gave up my favorite radio programs like the *Edgar Bergen and Charlie McCarthy Show, Our Miss Brooks,* and *The Aldrich Family* to hear her read to me.

Decide whether the content of each statement, even if it's a quotation, is a fact or an opinion. Write F or O in the blank.

_____ 1. "Mother and Daddy had lived with her in North Little Rock even before I was born."

_____ 2. "She had a regal posture and a fearless attitude."

_____ 3. Grandma wore wire-rimmed spectacles.

_____ 4. "My happiest evenings were spent listening to her read aloud."

ACTIVITY Z CRITICAL THINKING: FACT OR OPINION 2

Read the following paragraph and answer the questions following it. (Answers on page 99.)

From "Words Still Count with Me," by Herbert Mitgang

Octavio Paz, poet-diplomat, won the Nobel Prize in literature in 1990—the first Mexican writer to achieve the high honor.
Since many authors and civilians consider the Nobel political and
geographical, I thought it would not be impolite to ask him if the
prize was for him or for his country. He didn't seem surprised,
and his answer was philosophical: "To me, a poet represents not
only a region but the universe. Writers are the servants of language. Language is the common property of society, and writers
are the guardians of language. A writer has two loyalties. First, he
belongs to the special tribe of writers. Then he also belongs to a
culture, to his own country. Mine is Mexico."

Decide whether the content of each statement, even if it quotes someone, is a
fact or an opinion. Write F or O in the blank.

_____ 1. Octavio Paz was the first Mexican writer to win the Nobel
Prize in literature.
_____ 2. "A poet represents not only a region but the universe."
_____ 3. "Writers are the servants of language."
_____ 4. Writers should be loyal to the tribe of writers and to their
cultures.

ACTIVITY AA   CRITICAL READING: FACT OR OPINION 3

Read the following paragraph and answer the questions following it. (Answers
on page 99.)

From "Top Ten Cities for Hispanics," in *Hispanics,* by Diana A. Terry-Azios

Tampa, located on Florida's West Coast, just 84 miles from
Orlando, is an ideal location for outdoor activities. *Runner's*
World magazine named it one of the top ten cities for runners,
and more than 200 species of fish, including sport fish, inhabit
the bay. The climate is semi-tropical; temperatures average
62 degrees during the winter and 81 degrees in the summer.
The Meyers Group, of Irvine, California, ranked Tampa thir-
teenth of the nation's top twenty hottest real estate markets.
Although Tampa is one of the nation's oldest cities, its residents make it one of the youngest cities, with the median age
around 35. The crime rate is higher than average in Tampa, but
the cost-of-living is relatively low. And with jobs, transportation, recreation and climate receiving top-tenth percentile rat-
ings, Tampa offers the best in quality-of-life.

Decide if the content of each statement, whether or not it's a quotation, contains a fact or an opinion. Write F or O in the blank.

_____ 1. *Runner's World* magazine named Tampa one of the top ten cities for runners.

_____ 2. The median age of Tampa's residents is around 35.

_____ 3. "Tampa offers the best in quality-of-life."

_____ 4. For someone interested in outdoor activities, Tampa is ideal.

ACTIVITY BB   CRITICAL READING: FACT OR OPINION 4

Read the following paragraph and answer the questions that follow it. (Answers on page 99.)

From "Total Television," 4th edition, by Alex McNeil

Because of its impact on American audiences and on the style of television comedy, *All in the Family* is perhaps the single most influential program in the history of broadcasting. In terms of production techniques, the series added nothing new; in some ways, it represented a return to the old days of television: one basic set, a small cast, and little reliance on guest stars. *I Love Lucy*, TV's first smash hit sitcom, was the first to be filmed before a live audience; *All in the Family* was the first sitcom to be videotaped, and unlike the vast majority of sitcoms of the 1960s, it was performed before a live audience.

Decide if the content of each statement, whether or not it quotes someone, contains a fact or an opinion. Write F or O in the blank.

_____ 1. *All in the Family* is perhaps the single most influential program in the history of broadcasting.

_____ 2. *I Love Lucy* was the first sitcom to be filmed before a live audience.

_____ 3. *All in the Family* was the first sitcom to be videotaped and performed before a live audience.

MyReadingLab™ **What Is "Critical Thinking"?**
For support in meeting this chapter's objectives, go to MyReadingLab and select *Critical Thinking*.

Chapter 10

Critical Reading: What Are "The Author's Strategies"?

LEARNING OBJECTIVES

- Question the author's intent, craft, clarity, and organization of a passage.
- Identify a selection's intended audience, purpose, and tone.

The **author's strategies** refer to the approaches the author uses to relate information to the reader. There are three primary elements of an author's strategies that you will need in order to gain an accurate understanding of a piece of writing. The elements that you will focus on are audience, purpose, and tone.

THE AUTHOR'S STRATEGIES: AUDIENCE, PURPOSE, AND TONE

To begin, let's look at audience. When authors begin to write, they often have an intended audience in mind. The intended **audience** is the group of people who will most likely be interested in and read the material. Your task as the critical reader is to determine for what group of people the material seems to be written. To do this, you may look at certain choices the author has made, such as the way the material is presented (narrative or comparison and contrast, for example), the information the author has included and the information the author assumes the reader knows, the choice of language, and the purpose of the piece of writing. Examining these factors will lead you to determine who the intended audience of the material is. Here are a few examples of the types of audiences a writer may gear his or her writing toward:

- A general audience, intended to reach a wide population of readers
- A specific audience, from a particular historical era or cultural background, for example

- A skeptical or unsupportive audience, who are generally opposed to the author's points or beliefs
- A sympathetic audience, who are generally accepting of the author's points or beliefs
- A specific audience, such as an editor or politician
- A specific individual, such as a letter to X (and ask yourself who is X?)

Sometimes determining the audience can be quite easy. For example, if you are reading a magazine for car enthusiasts, you can assume the articles in the magazine are geared toward people who are interested in cars. At other times, determining the audience may be less obvious, and you will need to examine the level of the language, the author's presentation of information, and the point conveyed by the author.

AUDIENCE

Read the following paragraphs and answer the question that follows them.

From "Don't Sell Your Ambitions Short to 'Keep It Real'," by Leonard Pitts

An open letter to African-American kids. The other day, I used a big word in this column. The word was brobdingnagian; it's from a book called *Gulliver's Travels* by Jonathan Swift, a fantasy about a man whose adventures take him to a number of strange lands. One of those lands was Brobdingnag, where the people were all giants. Thus, "brobdingnagian" is a big word that means, well . . . *big*. (I like using it because it's odd and kind of ugly-sounding.)

Anyway, some guy e-mailed me about it. Here's what he said: "Uncle Tom: Stop trying to act like the white man and mastering his culture[. . .]." Whether it was meant as a joke or not, it made me laugh out loud.

You know the crazy part? When white people prejudge us, when they say blacks can't do this, that or the other, when they demand that we conform to their expectations of what black is, we have no problem calling them on it. But when black people do the same thing, we're more apt to soul-search about why we don't fit in. You have to wonder at that. Should it really matter whether it's a white person or a black one who presumes us to be less than we are? Doesn't the presumption stink either way?

People—black and white—will always have expectations and when you refuse to live by those expectations, they'll call you names; they'll shut you out. It's not easy, but I guarantee that if you stay with it, you'll find that it is worthwhile. I guess what I'm telling you is this: Please have the guts to be who you are. And to dream brobdingnagian dreams.

_____ 1. The main audience for this reading is.

    a. African Americans and others who enjoy reading *Gulliver's Travels*, by Jonathan Swift, especially because of its big words.

    b. African-American teenagers and young adults who drop out of school and turn to a life of crime.

    c. African Americans and others who might allow their friends and others to discourage them from being all that they can be.

    d. African Americans and others who use big words rather than common, everyday words understood by everyone.

Answer: c

Read the following paragraphs and answer the question that follows them.

From "Memoirs" by Liz Miller

When you picture a typical American classroom, what do you see? There is probably a certain degree of organized chaos in the room: scattered art supplies, posters on the wall, and students either working in groups or half-paying attention to the teacher. A similarly aged classroom in South Korea might not look so different at first glance but actually functions very differently.

One of the major differences between American and South Korean elementary school students is the amount of time they spend learning. In United States public schools, children typically attend school for six or seven hours a day, Monday through Friday. Once they finish class on a weekday, they either go home or participate in an extracurricular activity of some kind. In South Korea, it is not uncommon for a child as young as ten years old to attend a second, private "academy" every day after school. Some stay as late as 10:00 at night studying English, math, or whatever subject their parents believe will allow them to succeed academically. Most Korean schools are even in session every other Saturday to squeeze in some extra learning time.

_____ 1. The main audience for "Memoirs" is

    a. anyone who is planning to teach English as a second language to South Korean elementary students.

    b. anyone who is majoring in elementary education at an American college or university.

    c. anyone who is examining the differences in the time American and South Korean students spend studying.

    d. anyone who is drafting a curriculum guide for elementary school teachers in the United States.

Answer: c

To Narrate	Tells a story Uses chronological order Main idea is generally not stated Contains the who, what, and where of an event or incident
To Describe	Uses descriptive language Paints a verbal picture Main idea is generally not stated Describes using the five senses
To Inform/Expose	Explains and discusses ideas Presents information objectively Gives examples Gives definitions or characteristics Analyzes or questions ideas Shows both sides of an issue
To Entertain	Uses humor Amuses
To Persuade/Convince	Advocates the author's opinion Tries to alter or influence the reader's viewpoint or course of action Evaluates or judges Praises, admires, or gives honor to

Determining the intended audience is a practice that is often used in conjunction with determining the author's purpose. Once you have determined whom the author is speaking to, you can begin to consider what the author intends to say to that audience. Thus, the **author's purpose** is the reason he or she is presenting the material and what the author intends to accomplish in presenting it. There are five major purposes for writing, although authors may take differing approaches to accomplishing a purpose. The five major purposes are to narrate, to describe, to inform or expose, to entertain, and to persuade or argue.

Here is an overview of the five purposes of writing and the characteristics that can help you identify the purpose.

PURPOSE

Below are some paragraphs that illustrate the five purposes for writing.

The following paragraph is an example of narrative:

One time when my roommate and I were driving back to college after a long spring weekend, an icy rainstorm surprised us.

The weather had been unseasonably temperate, but while we were maneuvering our vehicle through the mountain passes, the unexpected winter squall occurred. We had just driven by an exit, and the sign told us that we had thirty-four miles to go before we hit the next one. The roads over the mountains are complicated to manipulate the car around during pleasant weather, but the glare ice made them treacherous. As we came around a curve, we saw a Cadillac hit the guardrails on one side of the highway then proceed across the next lane to hit the guardrails on the other side. It was distressing, but it seemed comical because the incidents were situations comic strip writers use each day. The car next to us started to creep into our lane so I turned the steering wheel slightly only to have my Volkswagen slide off the road. We lingered awhile, debating what to do, when a tow truck pulled in behind my automobile. When I conveyed to the driver that I would be unable to afford a tow, he expressed amusement and declared he would earn a sufficient amount that day. He and his partner hoisted my vehicle off the shoulder of the roadway, placed it on the parkway, smiled as we entered the car, and waved as we drove away.

(Hughes, Suzanne and Levine-Brown, Patti, *Florida Exit Test Study Guide for Reading*, p. 30, Saddle River, NJ: Prentice Hall, 2005.)

The following paragraph is an example of description:

Walking to the ranch house from the shed, we saw the Northern Lights. They looked like talcum powder fallen from a woman's face. Rouge and blue eye shadow streaked the spires of a white light which exploded, then pulsated, shaking the colors down—like lives—until they faded from sight.

(Troyka, Lynn Quitman, and Hesse, Douglas, *Handbook for Writers*, 7th ed., p. 101, Upper Saddle River, NJ: Prentice Hall, 2005.)

The following paragraph is an example of exposition (inform):

About 1600 A.D., William Gilbert, the same man who investigated the properties of amber, undertook the first serious study of magnets. He found, among other things, that the attractive property of the magnet was concentrated at its two opposite ends, called poles, with very little attractive force between the poles. He theorized that the earth is a huge magnet with its magnetic north pole near its geographic north pole and its magnetic south pole near its geographic south pole. It is the attraction between the north-seeking pole of the compass (which is, in reality, a south pole) and the north pole of the earth that causes the compass to act as it does.

(Troyka, Lynn Quitman, and Thweatt, Joseph, *Structured Reading*, 5th ed., p. 286, Upper Saddle River, NJ: Prentice Hall, 1999.)

The following paragraphs are an example of entertainment:

A vacationer at a summer resort, which was located near a state mental hospital, stopped during a walk to watch one of the inmates "painting" the fence with a dry brush and an empty bucket.

"I don't really belong here," the patient confided, "but my people say I believe anything anyone tells me and do crazy things. They say I took $10,000 out of my savings account when someone told me the banks aren't safe, and I don't know where I hid it."

"Really?" said the vacationer, his eyes brightening.

"Oh, I know all right," protested the patient. He pointed to a big sycamore in the woods adjacent to the institution. "I buried it under that tree until I get out of here."

Early the next morning the vacationer was back to see the inmate, who was again "painting" the fence. The vacationer looked exhausted and sleepy.

"Say," he asked resentfully, "are you sure it was under that big sycamore where you buried your $10,000?"

The patient gleefully looked him over from head to foot and then laughed heartily. "Get yourself a brush and bucket, pal," he said. "You're just like me."

(Braude, Jacob M., *Human Interest Stories*, p.77, Englewood Cliffs, NJ: Prentice Hall, 1981.)

The following paragraph is an example of argument:

Keeping wild animals as pets must be outlawed. Though exotic creatures may look like Simba or Tigger, they are still completely wild, and it is in the wild that they belong. As pointed out in *Wild Animals Are Not Pets*, "The only ones who benefit from the practice of sales of exotic animals as pets are the breeders and sellers. These people make an enormous amount of money by exploiting these animals once they are sold." Poachers also profit when they capture baby wild animals from their native habitats and sell them as pets to the highest bidder. The best way for humans to see and experience wild animals in safe environments is to visit and support zoos and wildlife parks that specialize in providing professionally constructed natural habitats for animals. In such settings, people can enjoy wild animals without putting humans and the animals at risk.

(Troyka, Lynn Quitman, and Hesse Douglas, *Handbook for Writers*, 7th ed., p. 163, Englewood Cliffs, NJ: Prentice Hall, 2005.)

Recognizing the characteristics of a piece of writing will aid you in determining an author's reason for writing. Sometimes, the purpose is easily identifiable. Take the case of an editorial in a daily newspaper where a writer states, "The use of cell phones on public transportation must be kept to a minimum." From this statement, you can determine that the writer's purpose is to convince readers to support his position. Other times, the purpose of the material must be inferred using the characteristics implicit in the material. Overall, you must keep in mind that determining the author's purpose will increase your understanding of the material being read.

Read the following paragraph and answer the question that follows it.

Before the days of television, people were entertained by exciting radio shows such as *Superman*, *Batman*, and "War of the Worlds." Of course, the listener was required to pay careful attention to the story if all details were to be comprehended. Better yet, while listening to the stories, listeners would form their own images of the actions taking place. When the broadcaster would give brief descriptions of the Martian space ships invading earth, for example, every member of the audience would imagine a different space ship. In contrast, television's version of "War of the Worlds" will not stir the imagination at all, for everyone can clearly see the actions taking place. All viewers see the same space ship with the same features. Each aspect is clearly defined, and, therefore, no one will imagine anything different from what is seen. Thus, television can't be considered an effective tool for stimulating the imagination.

(Tryoka, Lynn Quitman, and Hesse, Douglas, *Handbook for Writers*, 7th ed., p. 91, Englewood Cliffs, NJ: Prentice Hall, 2005.)

_____ 1. The author's main purpose in writing this reading is to

    a. entertain.

    b. describe.

    c. narrate.

    d. convince.

Answer: d

Read the following paragraph and answer the question that follows it.

Annie led me through two short hall-ways into their living room. "He's quite intelligent, really. . . . When he first sees you, he'll make an awful rumpus, but you mustn't let on that you're afraid. If you do, he'll never stop. . . . We crossed the room to a window set in the far end of a wall facing the rear of the house. Through the window I saw a large, wide room made of concrete with steel bars to the left. Severed tree trunks, a few boulders and hanging ropes filled the space. A tire swing on a hemp-style cable hung from the ceiling. At the far end, Hugo sat playing with a small object that I could not see. When Annie spoke too him, his great head swung around sharply, and for a moment he froze, cutting his eyes straight at me. He rose slowly and then charged toward the window at full speed, slamming into it with a thunderous sound. He bellowed with rage, pounded his chest and threw himself around the caged room, smashing into everything in his path. He attacked the window again to roar and beat the bars. . . . He leapt on the steel bars to the left and rocketed himself back and forth, screaming his displeasure. He jumped to the ledges on the right wall, up and down, over and over, beating the walls and floor with his fists, his arms, his whole body. . . . Then he stopped.

(Troyka, Lynn Quitman and Thweatt, Joseph, *Structured Reading*, 7th ed., p. 330, Upper Saddle River, NJ: Prentice Hall, 2009.)

_____ The author's main purpose in writing this reading is to

    a. describe.

    b. entertain.

    c. narrate.

    d. inform.

Answer: a

TONE

The third element of an author's strategies that you will need to pay attention to is the tone. The **tone** can be defined as the author's attitude and mood toward the subject being written about and the approach taken toward the audience. One way to consider tone is to think of how you hear people when they are speaking to you. Not only do you hear the words the people say, but you also hear the emotional impact of *how* they say it. Consequently, both elements, the words spoken and the way the words are spoken, contribute to the ultimate meaning you get from a person's statement. In the same way, authors use the words written and the attitude or mood implicit in the words to express tone to readers. Tone is described using the range of words used to explain human emotions. For example, the tone of a reading can be sarcastic, joyful, resigned, straightforward, angry, nostalgic, or admiring.

To determine the author's tone, examine the author's audience, purpose, and language. When examining the author's language, pay particular attention to a word's denotation, the dictionary definition of a word, and a word's connotation, which includes the emotional weight of a word. For example, if a writer says that someone is "unhappy," the statement seems mostly objective. On the other hand, if the writer describes the person as "pitiful," the statement carries a negative judgment. Thus, when determining tone, view both *what* the author says and *how* the author says it.

The tone of the following paragraph is matter-of-fact.

Indeed, when binge drinking came to the forefront last year with a rash of alcohol-related college deaths, the nation was stunned by the loss. There was Scott Krueger, the 18-year-old fraternity pledge at the Massachusetts Institute of Technology, who died of alcohol poisoning after downing the equivalent of 15 shots in an hour. There was Leslie Baltz, a University of Virginia senior, who died after she drank too much and fell down a flight of stairs. Lorraine Hanna, a freshman at Indiana University of Pennsylvania, was left alone to sleep off her night of New Year's Eve partying. Later that day her twin sister found her dead—with a blood-alcohol content (BAC) of 0.429 percent.

(Henry, D.J., *The Master Reader*, 3rd ed., p. 616, Upper Saddle River, NJ: Longman, 2011.)

The tone of the following paragraph is balanced.

As things stand, accountability between states is highly skewed. Poor and weak states are easily held to account, because they need foreign assistance. But large and powerful states, whose actions have the greatest impact on others, can be constrained only by their own people, working through their domestic institutions.

(Henry, D. J., *The Master Reader*, 3rd ed., p. 659, Englewood Cliffs, NJ: Longman, 2011.)

Read the following paragraph and answer the question that follows it.

Your dad checked on you before he left, and you were sleeping. The day before you guys had spent the afternoon washing and detailing your cars, the sun warm, listening to Earth, Wind and Fire. It was a good, good day. You told your friends how nice it was. Your dad said the same thing, that day and later. After he came home from church and called your name and found you in your bedroom with the shotgun, he called your mom, and she and McKenzie jumped in her truck and sped the four hours home, and soon the house was filled with people, while your dad kept saying how perfect Saturday afternoon had been, and how happy you had seemed, and how he didn't understand.

(Tryoka, Lynn Quitman and Thweatt, Joseph, *Structured Reading*, 7th ed., p. 197, Upper Saddle River, NJ: Prentice Hall, 2009.)

_____ 1. The author's tone in this reading is

    a. lively.

    b. bitter.

    c. disbelieving.

    d. impartial.

Answer: c

Read the paragraph below and answer the question that follows it.

I am 33 years old and I just called in sick. I'm not really sick. In fact, I'm not the least bit sick. I am totally faking it. And as I dance around my living room singing, "Sick day, sick day!" I think, "Ah, it's good to be nine!" The call was award-winning. A slightly raspy voice with a hint of fatigue combined with a slow, deliberate delivery. "I started throwing up around 3 A.M.," I told my boss. "I'm exhausted and I can't even keep water down. I must have caught that bug that's going around the office." I was told to stay home, rest, and feel better. Exactly what I had in mind.

(McWhorter Kathleen T., *Efficient and Flexible Reading*, 9th ed., p. 298, Upper Saddle River, NJ: Longman., 2011.)

_____ 1. The author's tone in this reading is

    a. objective.

    b. celebratory.

    c. indifferent.

    d. worried.

Answer: b

OBSERVING THE AUTHOR'S STRATEGIES IN ACTION

Questions about an author's strategies are best answered after you've finished your first pass at reading the material. To guide you in determining the audience, purpose, and tone of a reading, *Structured Reading* provides multiple-choice questions that ask you to select the correct answer from among four. Here's an example from "My World Now" by Anna Mae Halgrim Seaver.

This is my world now; it's all I have left. You see, I'm old. And, I'm not as healthy as I used to be. I'm not necessarily happy with it, but I accept it. Occasionally, a member of my family will stop in to see me. He or she will bring me some flowers or a little present, maybe a set of slippers—I've got eight pair. We'll visit for awhile and then they will return to the outside world and I'll be alone again. Oh, there are other people here in the nursing home. Residents, we're called. The majority are about my age. I'm 84. Many are in wheelchairs. The lucky ones are passing through—a broken hip, a diseased heart, something has brought them here for rehabilitation. When they're well, they'll be going home.

Most of us are aware of our plight—some are not. Varying stages of Alzheimer's have robbed several of their mental capacities. We listen to endlessly repeated stories and questions. We meet them anew daily, hourly, or more often. We smile and nod gracefully each time we hear a retelling. They seldom listen to my stories, so I've stopped trying.

_____ 1. The main audience for "My World Now" is

  a. nursing home employees being trained for their jobs.

  b. people who are interested in what life is like for a nursing home resident.

  c. people who are in nursing homes.

  d. people who have put someone in a nursing home.

_____ 2. The author's main purpose in this essay is to

  a. inform.

  b. entertain.

  c. frighten.

  d. persuade.

_____ 3. The author's tone in this reading is

  a. irrational.

  b. nostalgic.

  c. sad.

  d. objective.

Answers: 1. b; 2. a; 3. c

PRACTICING WITH THE AUTHOR'S STRATEGIES

ACTIVITY CC   CRITICAL READING: THE AUTHOR'S STRATEGIES 1

Read the following paragraphs and answer the questions that follow them. (Answers on page 99.)

From "You Are How You Eat," by Enid Nemy

The most irritating of all ice cream eaters are the elegant creatures who manage to devour a whole cone with delicate little nibbles and no dribble. The thermometer might soar, the pavement might melt, but their ice cream stays as firm and as rounded as it was in the scoop. No drips, no minor calamities—and it's absolutely not fair, but what can you do about it?

Some of the strangest ice cream fans can be seen devouring sundaes and banana splits. They are known as "layer by layer" types. First they eat the nuts and coconut and whatever else is sprinkled on top. Then they eat the sauce; then the banana, and finally the ice cream, flavor by flavor. Some might feel that they are eating ingredients and not a sundae or a split, but what do they care?

_____ 1. The main audience for "You Are How You Eat" is

    a. people who eat a lot of ice cream.

    b. the general reading public.

    c. anyone who likes watching other people eat.

    d. people who read magazines about ice cream.

_____ 2. The author's purpose in writing this reading is to

    a. inform.

    b. narrate.

    c. describe.

    d. entertain.

_____ 3. The author's tone in this reading is

    a. annoyed.

    b. nostalgic.

    c. humorous.

    d. frustrated.

ACTIVITY DD   CRITICAL READING: THE AUTHOR'S STRATEGIES 2

Read the following paragraph and answer the questions that follow it. (Answers on page 99.)

From "Home" in Steps in Composition, by Lynn Quitman Troyka and Jerrold Nudelman

These days Americans of all ages lead such hectic lives that home is often little more than a place to sleep and change clothes. Family members see each other in passing; they seldom share activities, let alone a daily meal. In the morning, Mom and Dad rush off to work at 7:30 and the children leave for school a half hour later. At 3:30, Betty goes directly from school to her part-time job at Burger King. After returning to an empty house, Jason goes out to play for a while and then eats dinner alone. When his parents arrive home at 6:30, he is in his bedroom doing his homework. When Betty comes in the door a few hours later, she yells a quick "hello" to her parents, grabs some leftovers from the refrigerator, and heads for her room to eat and relax. Because the family members have different schedules, they have little chance to spend time with each other.

_____ 1. The main audience for "Home" is

    a. people who miss their families.

    b. people who have never married.

    c. people who are interested in American families.

    d. people who have a busy family life.

_____ 2. The author's purpose in writing this reading is to

    a. inform.

    b. persuade.

    c. entertain.

    d. argue.

_____ 3. The author's tone in this reading is

    a. angry.

    b. humorous.

    c. annoyed.

    d. straightforward.

ACTIVITY EE   CRITICAL READING: THE AUTHOR'S STRATEGIES 3

Read the following paragraphs and answer the questions that follow them. (Answers on page 99.)

From "American Schools Should Take a Lesson from Japan" in Steps in Composition, by Lynn Quitman Troyka and Jerrold Nudelman

It is a widely accepted fact that many of America's schools are doing a poor job of educating the nation's young people. Research studies indicate that about 30 percent of American high school students drop out before graduating. In some high school systems, fewer than half of the students who enter ever graduate. We should not be surprised, then, that one in four Americans is illiterate—unable to read and write at the most basic level. What can be done? American schools should take a lesson from Japan, where strict rules of behavior, very demanding school schedules, and high academic standards have produced nearly 100 percent literacy.

_____ 1. The main audience for this reading is

    a. people who believe American schools should lower graduation standards.

    b. people who believe American schools are working.

    c. people who are interested in American schools.

    d. people who are interested in Japanese schools.

_____ 2. The author's purpose in writing this reading is to

    a. expose.

    b. narrate.

    c. entertain.

    d. describe.

_____ 3. The author's tone in this reading is

    a. concerned.

    b. naive.

    c. pessimistic.

    d. hopeless.

ACTIVITY FF CRITICAL READING: THE AUTHOR'S STRATEGIES 4

Read the following paragraphs and answer the questions that follow them. (Answers on page 99.)

From Baseball Anecdotes, by Daniel Okrent and Steve Wulff

A baseball reporter once asked a coach of long and varied experience what were his fondest memories of a lifetime in the game. The coach was removing his uniform after a spring training workout, an aging man whose shrunken chest and loose-fitting skin made him seem—to anyone but an experienced denizen of baseball clubhouses—incredibly out-of-place in that world of speed and muscle and skill. Yet, at the same time, the entire history of baseball seemed to reside in the gray stubble on his face, the wrinkles in his neck, the dry flesh on his arms and legs.

"Which stories do you want?" he asked the reporter. "The true ones or the other ones?"

_____ 1. The main audience for "Baseball Anecdotes" is

    a. people who are curious about baseball coaching.

    b. people who believe coaches should be athletic.

c. people who are interested in baseball.

d. people who read magazines about athletes and coaches.

_____ 2. The author's purpose in writing this reading is to

a. argue.

b. narrate.

c. inform.

d. describe.

_____ 3. The author's tone in this reading is

a. objective.

b. sentimental.

c. surprised.

d. admiring.

MyReadingLab™ **Critical Reading: What Are "The Author's Strategies"?**
For support in meeting this chapter's objectives, go to MyReadingLab and select *Purpose and Tone*.

Chapter 11

Critical Reading: What Is a "Summary"?

LEARNING OBJECTIVES

- Identify the main points of a reading selection.
- Capture the author's intended audience, purpose, and tone.

A **summary** is the process by which you compress and restate the author's central theme and main ideas using your own words. A summary is objective and meant to convey the gist of the author's message. It is not an evaluation, explanation, or response to what the author said. Being able to summarize effectively develops after you have successfully navigated the other stages of the reading process, including identifying the central theme and main ideas and making inferences. As a result, when you are able to write and identify appropriate summaries, you are well on your way to having mastered the reader's process to reading effectively.

WRITING A SUMMARY

Writing a summary is an important addition to your arsenal of reading strategies. Summary writing is especially important in the college classroom, as you will be required to read and understand numerous texts for writing and research projects. Summary writing reflects your ability to efficiently "sum up" the main message of a piece of writing—and in doing so, demonstrate your comprehension of the material. To compose effective summaries, ask yourself these questions:

- What is the central theme?
- What are the stated and implied main ideas?
- What details are necessary to include?
- What is the author's purpose?

Once you have answered these questions, you are ready to begin drafting your summary. To draft your summary, look at the responses you wrote down for the preceding questions. How can you bring together the central message as presented in your responses? Write several versions of your summary. Write as many versions as it takes to find the summary that most effectively captures the author's message. Keep in mind these tips:

- Summaries are brief.
- Restate the author's ideas, not your response to those ideas.
- Use your own words.
- Avoid unnecessary details.

There are some stumbling blocks on the way to writing effective summaries. For many students, summary writing is often mistaken for writing a synthesis. A **synthesis** is when you bring together the author's message and connect it with your own experience and other sources to produce an alternate view of the original topic. As noted earlier, a summary does not add anything to the author's point. Another stumbling block that you may encounter is writing a paraphrase rather than a summary. A **paraphrase** is a restatement of the author's ideas in your own words. However, a summary is a condensed restatement of the author's *central or main* ideas. So, although paraphrasing and summary both include restating the author's point in your own words, the type of information restated is the key difference.

OBSERVING SUMMARY IN ACTION

The type of summary exercise you will encounter after the reading selections in *Structured Reading* will ask you to identify the appropriate summary of a piece of writing. How do you know what is an appropriate summary? To start, reflect on the questions you would ask yourself if you were writing the summary. What are the author's main ideas? What details need to be included? Then, based on your answers to these questions, determine which of the suggested summaries most effectively conveys the author's message. Here is an excerpt from "Collegians Predisposed to Road Rage" by Andrew J. Pulskamp to practice identifying the best summary of a passage.

Age isn't the only factor in aggressive driving. A social psychologist at the University of Hawaii, Leon James did research which shows that being a road hog has a lot to do with gender and what kind of car a person drives. James says, in general, men are more aggressive drivers than women. And as far as cars go, if the highways were oceans then sports cars, trucks, and sports utility vehicles would be the sharks, whereas economy cars, family cars, and vans would be the angel fish. There are no hard-line explanations as to why different cars are driven more or less aggressively, but James thinks most likely there are multiple factors at play. It might have to do with the idea that more aggressive people are drawn to certain cars, and it could also mean that certain vehicles make drivers feel more aggressive. After all, it's easier to feel like the king of the road when one is cruising around in a Ford Explorer rather than a Dodge Neon.

_____ 1. What is the best summary of this passage?

   a. In general, women tend to be safer drivers than men, who are often considered aggressive drivers.

   b. Men who drive certain vehicles are more aggressive drivers than women, especially if they drive a sports car or an SUV.

   c. Aggressive drivers, for the most part, do not drive economy cars, family cars, and vans.

   d. A driver of a Ford Explorer is more aggressive than a driver of a Dodge Neon.

Answer: 1. b

PRACTICING WITH SUMMARY

ACTIVITY GG SUMMARY 1

Read the following excerpt from "Houses to Save the Earth" by Seth Shulman and select the summary that best conveys the author's message. (Answers on page 99.)

Despite the sound of it, the house doesn't look newfangled or avant-garde. In fact, without Loken's animated descriptions, a visitor would never guess the origins of the materials—a feature he says was important when he set out in 1990 to build his "recycled" house. "I wanted to show that you could use recycled building materials without making any compromises on the type of house most Americans want," says Loken, 45. "This meant that the place had to look like any other house if the ideas behind it were going to catch on." Since his house was completed in 1992, Loken's efforts have caught on in ways he never imagined, helping to spawn one of the country's hottest trends in house construction. In fact, over the past few years, Loken has become something of a guru to an alternative-materials movement among builders. He travels the country regularly giving lectures about his building techniques. So far, 12,000 people, including architects and builders from around the world, have made the pilgrimage to his Missoula home.

_____ 1. What is the best summary of this passage?

    a. Recycled materials can be used to build houses that most Americans like without compromising any of the features they want.

    b. Loken is an expert in the field of alternative materials and built a house in Missoula to showcase his knowledge.

    c. After Loken built his house of recycled materials, he now travels the country to share his ideas and techniques with others about using recycled materials.

    d. Using alternative building materials became a new option for builders and architects after Loken completed his "recycled house" in 1992.

ACTIVITY HH   SUMMARY 2

Read the following excerpt from "In Praise of the F Word" by Mary Sherry and select the summary that best conveys the author's message. (Answers on page 99.)

Tens of thousands of 18-year-olds will graduate this year and be handed meaningless diplomas. These diplomas will not look any different from those awarded their luckier classmates. Their validity will be questioned only when their employers discover that these graduates are semiliterate.

Eventually a fortunate few will find their way into education-repair shops—adult-literacy programs, such as the one where I teach basic grammar and writing. There, high school graduates and high school dropouts pursuing graduate-equivalency certificates will learn the skills they should have learned in school. They will also discover they have been cheated by our educational system.

_____ 1. What is the best summary of this passage?

    a. High schools are graduating many students who haven't done the work to learn the basic skills.

    b. Some high school dropouts are going to get their diplomas or equivalency certificates.

    c. Employers are discovering that high schools are not teaching students what they need to know.

    d. Students are graduating from high school with a diploma but lack the basic skills that high schools are meant to teach.

ACTIVITY II   SUMMARY 3

Read the following excerpt from "A Lady's Life in the Rocky Mountains" by Isabella L. Bird and select the summary that best conveys the author's message. (Answers on page 99.)

I had gone to sleep with six blankets on, and a heavy sheet over my face. Between two and three I was awakened by the cabin being shifted from underneath by the wind, and the sheet was frozen to my lips. I put out my hands, and the bed was thickly covered with fine snow. Getting up to investigate matters, I found the floor some inches deep in parts in fine snow, and a gust of fine, needlelike snow stung my face. The bucket of water was solid ice. I lay in bed freezing till sunrise, when some of the men came to see if I "was alive," and to dig me out. They brought a can of hot water, which turned to ice before I could use it. I dressed standing in snow, and my brushes, boots, and etceteras were covered with snow.

_____ 1. What is the best summary of this passage?

   a. A woman describes the conditions she went through while living in the Rocky Mountains.

   b. A woman complains about how she suffered during her stay in the Rocky Mountains.

   c. A woman describes how quickly water freezes in the Rocky Mountains.

   d. A woman gives examples of how cold the weather is in the Rocky Mountains.

ACTIVITY JJ   SUMMARY 4

Read the following excerpt from "Every Kid Needs Some Manual Arts" by William Raspberry and select the summary that best conveys the author's message. (Answers on page 99.)

Today's youngsters, except for those deemed slow enough to be consigned to shop class, are unlikely to be taught even how to make a shoeshine box or replace a frayed lamp cord. My prep school children are innocent of any such household skills and uninterested in acquiring them. But it isn't just prep school children who are deprived of the chance to learn rudimentary manual skills. Probably most academically gifted youngsters are hustled into "academic" tracks whose focus is almost entirely on courses that will help them to get into college. One result is that those who don't go on to college are likely to leave high school unable to earn a decent living. It's a mistake, and not just for the boys. A small part of the reason is cost. Shop classes large enough to accommodate all the children at a school take too much space and too much money. But a larger part is our either/or mentality with regard to academic and manual training. Smart kids do books; dumb kids do tools.

_____ 1. What is the best summary of this passage?

    a. Boys should be required to enroll in shop classes so that they can get good jobs after high school graduation.

    b. The author believes his prep school children could not make a shoebox or repair a frayed lamp cord.

    c. All students should have the opportunity to take shop classes and learn a manual skill whether they plan to attend college or not.

    d. If students are not given training in a manual skill, they will not be able to earn enough money when they graduate high school.

MyReadingLab™ **Critical Reading: What Is a "Summary"?**
For support in meeting this chapter's objectives, go to MyReadingLab and select *Outlining and Summarizing.*

Chapter 12

What Is "Reader's Response"?

LEARNING OBJECTIVES

• Explore the connection between the reading selection and your prior knowledge.
• Share a spoken or written response to a question concerning the reading selection.

Reader's response means that you are expected to express your own opinions by answering two open-ended questions. Based on what you've read, your previous experience, and your best reasoning, here's the opportunity for *your* response, *your* opinion, *your* thinking. This is the realm of questions with no right or wrong answers. They express *your* point of view. Of course, if your peers or instructor challenges your viewpoint, you want to be ready to explain your line of reasoning and defend your conclusion.

Whether you express your responses through discussion or writing, always start by restating the question. Doing this reminds your listeners or readers what has prompted your response. Follow immediately with a clear one- or two-sentence statement of your point of view (in writing, called a "topic sentence"). Next, support your opinion with specific details in the form of facts, examples, names, incidents, and other concrete material.

If you supply more than one supporting detail, tie your presentation together with transitional words so that your audience knows what's coming next. Just as a driver watches for traffic signals and road signs to anticipate what's ahead, listeners and readers need directional signals (in the form of transitional words) to know what's coming next. Here's a list of frequently used transitional words and phrases.

Transitional Expressions

Relationship	Expressions
ADDITION	also, in addition, too, moreover, and, besides, furthermore, equally important, then, finally
EXAMPLE	for example, for instance, thus, as an illustration, namely, specifically
CONTRAST	but, yet, however, nevertheless, nonetheless, conversely, in contrast, still, at the same time, on the one hand, on the other hand, whereas
COMPARISON	similarly, likewise, in the same way
CONCESSION	of course, to be sure, certainly, granted
RESULT	therefore, thus, as a result, so, accordingly
SUMMARY	hence, in short, in brief, in summary, in conclusion, finally
TIME ORDER	first, second, third, next, then, finally, afterwards, before, soon, later, meanwhile, subsequently, immediately, eventually, currently
PLACE	in the front, in the foreground, in the back, in the background, at the side, adjacent, nearby, in the distance, here, there

SUMMARY OF PART 1

The goal of *Structured Reading* is to give you structured strategies for upgrading your reading skills to a college level. Part 1 has two purposes. First, Chapters 1–4 explain how the reading process works. They offer you information about previewing a reading, predicting during reading, developing a college-level vocabulary, and the *SQ3R* method for reading and remembering textbook material.

Second, Chapters 5–11 get you working on the seven specific approaches to reading that research shows can greatly upgrade your reading ability. They are finding central themes and main ideas in reading; distinguishing between major and minor details; making inferences while reading; telling the difference between facts and opinions in reading; identifying the author's strategies; writing summaries; and bringing your personal, informed response to what you've read. There is also a chapter on making maps and/or outlines after reading to support you in comprehending and remembering what you read and using visuals while you read to enhance and expand the information provided to you by the author.

Throughout Part 1, *Structured Reading* provides many opportunities for you to apply what you're learning by practicing each separate skill. Then, in Parts 2–6, each of 30 whole—never abridged or excerpted—reading selections is followed by exercises that allow you to combine the separate skills. By using all your structured reading skills together, repeatedly, you'll have upgraded your ability to read successfully at a college level.

MyReadingLab™ **What Is "Reader's Response"?**
For support in meeting this chapter's objectives, go to MyReadingLab and select *Reading Skills Diagnostic Post-Test*.

Answers to Activities in Part 1

Activity A: No right or wrong answers here.

Activity B: 1. b; 2. b; 3. c; 4. c; 5. a; 6. b; 7. c; 8. a; 9. b; 10. c.

Activity C: 1. ambiguous; 2. monotone; 3. geriatrics; 4. malamute; 5. skeptical; 6. chagrin; 7. coherence; 8. sinuate; 9. phi, theta, kappa; 10. polyester.

Activity D: 1. a; 2. c; 3. b; 4. b; 5. c; 6. b; 7. a; 8. c; 9. b; 10. a.

Activity E: 1. a; 2. b; 3. b; 4. a; 5. a; 6. c; 7. c; 8. b; 9. a; 10. c.

Activity F: 1. c; 2. b; 3. a; 4. b; 5. c; 6. c; 7. c; 8. c; 9. b; 10. a.

Activity G: 1. c; 2. b; 3. a.

Activity H: 1. a; 2. Answers will vary; here's one possibility: Dell's secret of success is that all managers get personally involved in the details of the business; 3. d.

Activity I: 1. c; 2. b; 3. a.

Activity J: 1. Answers will vary; here's one possibility: Salmon is now available for year-round distribution; 2. b; 3. d.

Activity K: 1. calm; 2. noises; 3. happy.

Activity L: 1. T; 2. ND; 3. ND; 4. F.

Activity M: 1. Major; 2. Major; 3. Minor; 4. Major.

Activity N: 1. Internet; 2. Key words; 3. Labor.

Activity O: See page 100.

Activity P: See page 100.

Activity Q: 1. The people going in the building and coming out and falling off the edge, and the buildings in the background. 2. A schoolhouse. The people have books in their hands and walk out wearing graduation caps. 3. Answers may vary. The primary message is that graduates are falling into the gap between what their education has given them and what the business world needs. The clues are the gap, the conveyor belt sending them over the edge, and the high-rise buildings across the gap.

Activity R: 1. The cellular phone, the floating envelopes, the antennae in the background, and the snakes. 2. E-mail or text messages sent through the phone. The envelopes are coming from the phone and appear to be being transmitted by the antennae through space. 3. Answers may vary. The primary message is that sometimes dangerous or harmful communications are being sent through e-mail or text messages. The visual clue is the group of snakes traveling with the envelopes that are coming from the phone.

Activity S: 1. The billboard featuring a credit card with a jaw trap drawn around it. 2. The words "Total Security Protection makes our cards safer" indicate that the jaw trap is provided by the credit card company to protect the credit card owner. 3. Answers may vary. The primary message is that the owner of the credit card being featured can feel safe knowing his or her card is protected.

Activity T: 1. 20–25; 2. earnings; 3. 3rd quarter. 4. The proportion of new employees who have the writing skills desired. 5. Mining, Manufacturing, Transportation/Utilities, Fire, and Services. 6. Fire and Services.

Activity U: 1. c; 2. c.

Activity V: 1. Yes; 2. No; 3. No; 4. Yes.

Activity W: 1. Yes; 2. Yes; 3. No; 4. No.

Activity X: 1. b; 2. d.

Activity Y: 1. Fact; 2. Opinion; 3. Fact; 4. Fact.

Activity Z: 1. Fact; 2. Fact; 3. Opinion; 4. Opinion.

Activity AA: 1. Fact; 2. Fact; 3. Opinion; 4. Opinion.

Activity BB: 1. Opinion; 2. Fact; 3. Fact.

Activity CC: 1. b; 2. d; 3. c.

Activity DD: 1. c; 2. a; 3. d.

Activity EE: 1. c; 2. a; 3. a.

Activity FF: 1. c; 2. d; 3. d.

Activity GG: 1. c.

Activity HH: 1. d.

Activity II: 1. a.

Activity JJ: 1. c.

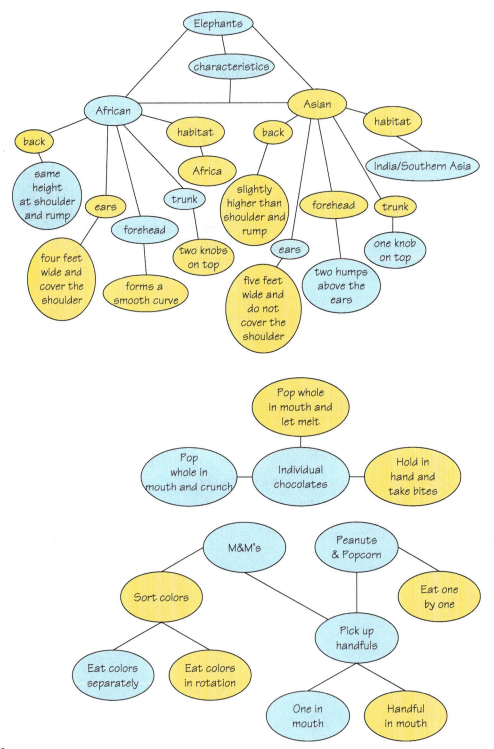

Part 2

Thinking: Getting Started

"There is always one moment in childhood when the door opens and lets the future in."

Graham Greene, *The Power and the Glory*

The selections in Part 2 concern people in various situations: from someone's misconstruing a man's actions to befriend a young girl to that of a family's adopting a mutilated pit bull puppy.

Before you read each selection, think about these questions:

"A Real Loss" (Selection 1)—How many different types of child abuse can you name?

"To Catch a Thief" (Selection 2)—What would you do if you saw someone stealing an item from a store?

"'Freegans' Salvage Food from the City's Bountiful Garbage" (Selection 3)—Would you be willing to eat a meal prepared with food from a Dumpster?

"Seoul Searching" (Selection 4)—What problems do you think a couple would encounter by adopting a child of a race different from theirs?

"Darkness at Noon" (Selection 5)—What accommodations have been made at your school for handicapped students?

"Ugly and Lovable" (Selection 6)—How would you react if you saw a pet being mistreated by its owner?

A Real Loss

Fern Kupfer

LEARNING OBJECTIVES
- Give examples of how people can be suspicious of good deeds.

THINKING: GETTING STARTED
- How many different types of child abuse can you name?

(1) I was sitting in back of a little girl flying as an unaccompanied minor, put on the plane by a mother who placed a Care Bear in her arms and told her to remind Daddy to call when she got to California. The girl adjusted her seat belt and sniffed back a tear, bravely setting her jaw.

(2) As we prepared for takeoff, the man next to the girl asked her the name of her bear and nodded in approval, saying Furry was a good name for a bear. When the little girl told him she was 6 years old, the man replied that he had a daughter who was 6 years old. His daughter was missing the same teeth, in fact. He asked how much money the tooth fairy was giving out in New York these days.

(3) By the time we were in the air, the man and the little girl were playing tic-tac-toe, and she revealed to him the names of her favorite friends. Somewhere over Ohio, I fell asleep, awakened by my mother instinct when I heard a child announce that she had to go to the bathroom.

(4) "It's in the back, right?" I heard the girl say to the man. She looked **tentative.** The flight attendants were busy collecting lunch trays.

(5) "Do you want me to take you there?" the man asked, standing.

(6) At once my **antennae** were up and, leaning into the aisle, I **craned** my neck, practically knocking heads with the woman in the seat across from me. For one moment our eyes locked. She had been listening, too, and both of us had the same idea. Would this man go into the bathroom with the child? I held my breath as he held open the bathroom door. Suddenly, he became **transformed** in my eyes—the dark business suit looked **sinister,** the friendly smile really a lure to something evil.

(7) Then the man showed the little girl how the lock worked and waited outside the door. The woman and I sighed in relief. She said, "Well, you can't be too careful these days."

(8) I've thought about that man on the plane since then, and the image of him and the little girl always leaves an empty sorrow. I know that a new **heightened** consciousness about child **molestation** is in itself a good thing.

I know that sexual abuse of children is awful, and that we must guard against it. But it saddened me that I looked at someone who understood a child's fear and saw a child molester.

(9) These are trying times for men. We women say how we want men to be sensitive and **nurturing,** to be caring and affectionate. But my sense is that now these qualities cannot be readily displayed without arousing suspicion. Perhaps there is some sort of **ironic retribution** for all those years of accepting the male stereotypes. But there is a real loss here for us all when we must always be **wary** of the kindness of strangers.

Thousands of children, unaccompanied minors, travel alone every day by air.

Here are some of the more difficult words in "A Real Loss."

antennae
(paragraph 6)

an·tenna (an ten′ə) *n.* ⟦L, earlier *antemna*, sail yard⟧ **1** *pl.* **··nae** (-ē) or **··nas** either of a pair of movable, jointed sense organs on the head of most arthropods, as insects, crabs, or lobsters; feeler: see INSECT, illus. **2** *pl.* **··nas** *Radio, TV* an arrangement of wires, metal rods, etc. used in sending and receiving electromagnetic waves; aerial

craned
(paragraph 6)

crane (krān) *n.* ⟦ME < OE *cran:* akin to Du *kraan*, Ger *kranich* < IE **gr-on* < base **ger-*: see CROW[1]⟧ **1** *pl.* **cranes** or **crane** *a)* any of a family (Gruidae) of usually large gruiform wading birds with very long legs and neck, and a long, straight bill *b)* popularly, any of various unrelated birds, as herons and storks **2** any of various machines for lifting or moving heavy weights by means of a movable projecting arm or a horizontal beam traveling on an overhead support **3** any device with a swinging arm fixed on a vertical axis ⟦a fireplace *crane* is used for holding a kettle⟧ —*vt., vi.* **craned, cran′·ing 1** to raise or move with a crane **2** to stretch (the neck) as a crane does, as in straining to see over something

heightened
(paragraph 8)

heighten (hīt′'n) *vt., vi.* ⟦< prec. + -EN⟧ **1** to bring or come to a high or higher position; raise or rise **2** to make or become larger, greater, stronger, brighter, etc.; increase; intensify —*SYN.* INTENSIFY —**height′·ener** *n.*

ironic
(paragraph 9)

ironic (ī rän′ik) *adj.* **1** meaning the contrary of what is expressed **2** using, or given to the use of, irony **3** having the quality of irony; directly opposite to what is or might be expected **4** marked by coincidence or by a curious or striking juxtaposition of events: regarded by many as a loose usage Also **iron′i·cal** —**iron′i·cally** *adv.*

irony[1] (ī′rə nē, ī′ər nē) *n., pl.* **··nies** ⟦Fr *ironie* < L *ironia* < Gr *eirōneia* < *eirōn*, dissembler in speech < *eirein*, to speak < IE base **wer-*, to speak > WORD⟧ **1** *a)* a method of humorous or subtly sarcastic expression in which the intended meaning of the words is the direct opposite of their usual sense ⟦the *irony* of calling a stupid plan "clever"⟧ *b)* an instance of this **2** the contrast, as in a play, between what a character thinks the truth is, as revealed in a speech or action, and what an audience or reader knows the truth to be: often **dramatic irony 3** a combination of circumstances or a result that is the opposite of what is or might be expected or considered appropriate ⟦an *irony* that the firehouse burned⟧ **4** *a)* a cool, detached attitude of mind, characterized by recognition of the incongruities and complexities of experience *b)* the expression of such an attitude in a literary work **5** the feigning of ignorance in argument: often called **Socratic irony** (after Socrates' use of this tactic in Plato's *Dialogues*) —*SYN.* WIT[1]

molestation
(paragraph 8)

mo·lest (mə lest′, mō-) *vt.* ⟦ME *molesten* < OFr *molester* < L *molestare* < *molestus*, troublesome < *moles*, a burden: see MOLE[3]⟧ **1** to annoy, interfere with, or meddle with so as to trouble or harm, or with intent to trouble or harm ☆**2** to make improper advances to, esp. of a sexual nature **3** to assault or attack (esp. a child) sexually —**mo·les·ta·tion** (mō′les tā′shən, mäl′əs-) *n.* —**mo·lest′er** *n.*

nurturing
(paragraph 9)

nur·ture (nur′chər) *n.* ⟦ME < OFr *norreture* < LL *nutritura*, pp. of L *nutrire*, to nourish: see NURSE⟧ **1** anything that nourishes; food; nutriment **2** the act or process of raising or promoting the development of; training, educating, fostering, etc.: also **nur′·tur·ance 3** all the environmental factors, collectively, to which one is subjected from conception onward, as distinguished from one's nature or heredity —*vt.* **··tured, ··tur·ing 1** to feed or nourish **2** *a)* to promote the development of *b)* to raise by educating, training, etc. —**nur′·tur·ant** *adj.* or **nur′·tural** —**nur′·turer** *n.*

retribution
(paragraph 9)

ret·ri·bu·tion (re′trə byoo′shən) *n.* ⟦ME *retribucioun* < OFr *retribution* < LL(Ec) *retributio* < L *retributus*, pp. of *retribuere*, to repay < *re-*, back + *tribuere*, to pay: see TRIBUTE⟧ punishment for evil done or reward for good done; requital —**re·tribu·tive** (ri trib′yoo tiv) *adj.* or **re·trib′u·to·ry** (-tôr′ē) —**re·trib′u·tively** *adv.*

sinister
(paragraph 6)

sin·is·ter (sin'is tər) *adj.* ⟦ME *sinistre* < L *sinister,* left-hand, or unlucky (side), orig. lucky (side) < IE base **sene-,* to prepare, achieve > Sans *sániyān,* more favorable: early Roman augurs faced south, with the east (lucky side) to the left, but the Greeks (followed by later Romans) faced north⟧ **1** *a)* [Archaic] on, to, or toward the left-hand side; left *b) Heraldry* on the left side of a shield (the right as seen by the viewer) (opposed to DEXTER) **2** threatening harm, evil, or misfortune; ominous; portentous *[sinister* storm clouds*]* **3** wicked, evil, or dishonest, esp. in some dark, mysterious way *[a sinister* plot*]* **4** most unfavorable or unfortunate; disastrous *[met a sinister* fate*]* —**sin'·is·terly** *adv.* —**sin'·is·ter·ness** *n.*

SYN.—**sinister**, in this connection, applies to that which can be interpreted as presaging imminent danger or evil *[a sinister* smile*]*; **baleful** refers to that which is inevitably deadly, destructive, pernicious, etc. *[a baleful* influence*]*; **malign** is applied to that which is regarded as having an inherent tendency toward evil or destruction *[a malign* doctrine*]*

tentative
(paragraph 4)

ten·ta·tive (ten'tə tiv) *adj.* ⟦LL *tentativus* < pp. of L *tentare,* to touch, try: see TENT²⟧ **1** made, done, proposed, etc. experimentally or provisionally; not definite or final *[tentative* plans, a *tentative* explanation*]* **2** indicating timidity, hesitancy, or uncertainty *[a tentative* caress*]* —**ten'·ta·tively** *adv.* —**ten'·ta·tive·ness** *n.*

transformed
(paragraph 6)

trans·form (trans fôrm'; *for n.* trans'fôrm') *vt.* ⟦ME *transformen* < L *transformare* < *trans-,* TRANS- + *formare,* to form < *forma,* FORM⟧ **1** to change the form or outward appearance of **2** to change the condition, nature, or function of; convert **3** to change the personality or character of **4** *Elec.* to change (a voltage or current value) by use of a transformer **5** *Linguis.* to change by means of a syntactic transformational rule **6** *Math.* to change (an algebraic expression or equation) to a different form having the same value **7** *Physics* to change (one form of energy) into another —*vi.* [Rare] to be or become transformed —*n. Math.* the process or result of a mathematical transformation —**trans·form'·able** *adj.* —**trans·form'a·tive** *adj.*

SYN.—**transform**, the broadest in scope of these terms, implies a change either in external form or in inner nature, in function, etc. *[she was transformed* into a happy girl*]*; **transmute**, from its earlier use in alchemy, suggests a change in basic nature that seems almost miraculous *[transmuted* from a shy youth into a sophisticated man about town*]*; **convert** implies a change in details so as to be suitable for a new use *[to convert* an attic into an apartment*]*; **metamorphose** suggests a startling change produced as if by magic *[a tadpole is metamorphosed* into a frog*]*; **transfigure** implies a change in outward appearance which seems to exalt or glorify *[his whole being was transfigured* by love*]* See also CHANGE

wary
(paragraph 9)

wary (wer'ē) *adj.* **war'i·er, war'i·est** ⟦< WARE² + -Y²⟧ **1** cautious; on one's guard **2** characterized by caution *[a wary* look*]* —*SYN.* CAREFUL —**wary of** careful of

1A   VOCABULARY

From the context of "A Real Loss," explain the meaning of each of the vocabulary words shown in boldface in the following sentences.

1. *From paragraph 4:* She looked **tentative**.

_____

_____

_____

Name   Date

2. *From paragraph 6:* At once my **antennae** were up and, leaning into the aisle, I **craned** my neck.

_____

_____

_____

3. *From paragraph 6:* Suddenly, he became **transformed** in my eyes—the dark business suit looked **sinister**.

_____

_____

_____

4. *From paragraph 8:* I know that a new **heightened** consciousness about child **molestation** is in itself a good thing.

_____

_____

_____

5. *From paragraph 9:* We women say how we want men to be sensitive and **nurturing**.

_____

_____

_____

6. *From paragraph 9:* Perhaps there is some sort of **ironic retribution** for all those years of accepting the male stereotypes.

_____

_____

_____

7. *From paragraph 9:* But there is a real loss here for us all when we must always be **wary** of the kindness of strangers.

_____

_____

_____

1B   CENTRAL THEME AND MAIN IDEAS

Choose the best answer.

_____ 1. What is the central theme of "A Real Loss"?

    a. These are trying times for men because all the media attention on child molestation has made even their simple kindnesses toward children appear to be evil.

    b. The author felt sorry for the little girl who had to fly from New York to California by herself, but at the same time the author admired the child's bravery.

    c. Child molesters can find victims everywhere, even on airplanes, so all travelers should be suspicious of anyone who is kind to children flying alone.

    d. Because of her increased awareness that some people are child molesters, the author now realizes that she has become suspicious of people who are kind to children they do not know.

_____ 2. What is the main idea of paragraph 6?

    a. Airplane passengers often listen to other people's conversations and exchange glances about what is said.

    b. Becoming suspicious, the author leaned far into the aisle and nearly bumped heads with another watchful woman.

    c. As she waited to see what the man would do, he suddenly changed in her eyes into an evil person.

    d. The man opened the bathroom door for the little girl as the author held her breath.

1C   MAJOR DETAILS

Decide whether each detail is Major *or* Minor *based on the context of the reading selection.*

_____ 1. The author was sitting in back of a little girl who was flying alone.

_____ 2. The little girl's mother placed a Care Bear in the girl's arms.

_____ 3. The little girl was going to California.

_____ 4. The little girl knew how to adjust her seat belt.

_____ 5. The bear's name was Furry.

_____ 6. Both the girl and the man's daughter were six years old.

_____ 7. The little girl announced that she had to go to the bathroom.

_____ 8. At that moment, the flight attendants were busy collecting lunch trays, so the man offered to take the girl to the bathroom.

Name   Date

_____ 9. The man showed the girl how the lock worked, and then he waited for her outside the door.

_____ 10. The other woman sighed in relief.

_____ 11. The author's image of the man and the little girl on the plane left her with a feeling of loss.

_____ 12. A new heightened consciousness about child molestation is in itself a good thing.

1D   INFERENCES

Choose the best answer.

_____ 1. _Read paragraph 1 again._ Why did the little girl's mother tell her to remind Daddy to call?
   a. The mother did not want to spend the money to call California herself.
   b. The mother wanted to know that the girl had arrived safely after the long trip.
   c. The father was not considerate of the woman's feelings, so he had to be reminded to call.
   d. The mother wanted to know that the girl's father was in good health.

_____ 2. _Read paragraph 2 again._ Why did the man say Furry was a good name?
   a. He had once had a bear named Furry.
   b. He wanted to make the little girl settle down so that she would not bother him and he could rest or read quietly.
   c. He wanted to make her feel comfortable and secure.
   d. The bear was very fluffy, and so Furry seemed an appropriate name.

_____ 3. _Read paragraph 3 again._ Why did the little girl's announcement that she had to go to the bathroom wake up the author?
   a. The child was speaking very loudly and moving around in her seat, indicating that she was very uncomfortable.
   b. The author was afraid the little girl might have an accident unless someone took her to the bathroom right away.
   c. As a mother, the author thought she should be the one asked to take the little girl to the bathroom if the flight attendants were busy.
   d. As a mother, the author was used to listening—even in her sleep—for children's calls for help.

_____ 4. *Read paragraph 7 again*. By saying "Well, you can't be too careful these days," the woman was communicating that she was

a. annoyed at the flight attendants for being too busy to take the little girl to the bathroom.

b. angry that the little girl had asked the man for help instead of turning to a nearby woman.

c. slightly embarrassed that she had worried about what the man might do to the little girl.

d. somewhat worried that the girl was too little to learn how to use the bathroom lock.

_____ 5. *Read paragraphs 8 and 9 again*. What does the author mean when she says, "there is a real loss here for us all when we must always be wary of the kindness of strangers"?

a. Constant suspicion is a poisonous feeling, preventing people from enjoying some of the pleasanter moments in life, such as watching a man being kind to a child.

b. Because there is rarely a way of telling who might be evil, people stop talking to strangers and miss chances to make friends.

c. Years ago fewer child molesters existed, so children's lives were safer, and their parents had peace of mind that now has been lost.

d. Because people today are constantly on the lookout for child molesters, nice people like the author are afraid to be kind to strangers' children for fear of being suspected of molestation.

_____ 6. The word *loss* used in the title refers to

a. the author's loss of trust of adults who are kind to children.

b. the little girl's having to leave her mother behind.

c. the negative effect on children when divorced parents live long distances apart.

d. the man's missing his own little girl who was also six years old.

1E CRITICAL READING: FACT OR OPINION

Decide whether each statement, even if it quotes someone, contains a Fact *or an* Opinion.

_____ 1. *From paragraph 1:* "The girl adjusted her seat belt and sniffed back a tear [. . .]."

_____ 2. *From paragraph 2:* "He asked her how much money the tooth fairy was giving out in New York these days."

Name   Date

_____ 3. *From paragraph 3:* "[. . .] she revealed to him the names of her favorite friends."

_____ 4. *From paragraph 4:* "She looked tentative."

_____ 5. *From paragraph 6:* "[. . .] he became transformed in my eyes [. . .]."

_____ 6. *From paragraph 6:* "[. . .] the dark business suit looked sinister."

_____ 7. *From paragraph 7:* "The woman and I sighed in relief."

_____ 8. *From paragraph 7:* "[. . .] you can't be too careful these days."

_____ 9. *From paragraph 8:* "[. . .] a new heightened consciousness about child molestation is in itself a good thing."

_____ 10. *From paragraph 9:* "These are trying times for men."

1F   CRITICAL READING: THE AUTHOR'S STRATEGIES

Choose the best answer.

_____ 1. The main audience for "A Real Loss" is
   a. anyone who lets young children travel alone.
   b. anyone who identifies with the loss of trust in our society.
   c. anyone who has a fear of child molesters.
   d. anyone who has been sexually abused.

_____ 2. The author's purpose in writing this reading is to
   a. persuade.
   b. argue.
   c. inform.
   d. entertain.

_____ 3. The author's tone in this reading is
   a. angry.
   b. unsure.
   c. bitter.
   d. sad.

1G   READER'S PROCESS: SUMMARIZING YOUR READING

_____ 1. What is the best summary of "A Real Loss"?
   a. A woman explains her feelings about a conversation she overheard on a cross-country flight to California.

b. A woman explains how our fears of child molesters affect the way we view innocent men when they are around children.

c. A woman explains her feelings about men who talk to children who are traveling alone.

d. A woman explains how she and other women feel about men who sexually abuse children.

1H   READER'S RESPONSE: TO DISCUSS OR WRITE ABOUT

1. Why do some people consider it "unmanly" when men are kind, considerate, and wholesomely affectionate toward children?

2. Traditionally, American society has not encouraged men to be especially affectionate, even toward their own children. But attitudes seem to be changing. Discuss the benefits for men, for women, and for children when men are free to express wholesome affection.

HOW DID YOU DO?
1   A Real Loss

SKILL (number of items)	Number Correct		Points for each		Score
Vocabulary (11)	_____	×	2	=	_____
Central Theme and Main Ideas (2)	_____	×	6	=	_____
Major Details (12)	_____	×	3	=	_____
Inferences (6)	_____	×	2	=	_____
Critical Reading: Fact or Opinion (10)	_____	×	1	=	_____
Critical Reading: The Author's Strategies (3)	_____	×	2	=	_____
Reader's Process: Summarizing Your Reading (1)	_____	×	2	=	_____
	(Possible Total: 100) Total				_____

To Catch a Thief

Stephen Holt

LEARNING OBJECTIVES

- **Summarize the steps a man takes to see that his neighbor is brought to justice for petit larceny.**

THINKING: GETTING STARTED

- **What would you do if you saw someone stealing an item from a store?**

(1) Several months ago, I began noticing the business section missing from my *New York Times*, which I have delivered to my home on Gramercy Park. I presumed the deliveryman was at fault and sent several **indignant** e-mails to customer service. I was repeatedly assured that the paper was being delivered intact. Gradually, it occurred to me that a neighbor might be stealing it.

(2) My wife suggested that I post a note in the lobby stating: "Please Stop Taking My Business Section." Although I agreed that this might deter the person, it would have done nothing to satisfy me. Since I am president of a company and an involved father of two boys, my morning train ride is one of few moments in the day that I have to read the paper, which is typically on top of a stack on a table in our lobby. I needed to confront the person depriving me of this simple pleasure. I needed justice. I decided to try a **stakeout.**

(3) On my third attempt, I hit pay dirt. The sanctity of my paper had been violated twice that week. From a back hallway, I watched a neighbor stop and **peruse** my paper before leaving. Ten minutes later he returned with dry cleaning in hand. Then, in a quick, snakelike motion, he grabbed my paper and jumped into the elevator. Prepared to confront someone exiting the building, I was not anticipating this turn of events. To catch him red-handed, I would have to race up many flights of stairs and beat the elevator to his floor. Harking back to my track years in boarding school, I took off like a rocket and reached his floor as the elevator door opened. Snatching the paper from his hands, I saw my name on the address label. Pumped with adrenaline from my sprint, I unleashed a **tirade** of **epithets.** I then produced a camera from my back pocket and snapped a picture of him. Disoriented by the sudden onslaught, he began to apologize. I said that I was going to have him evicted and that I would file charges with

the police. "Isn't there something we can do to keep this between us?" he asked. I told him he was a **sociopath,** that this was the biggest mistake of his life.

(4) Shortly thereafter, a note appeared under my door: "I want to formally apologize for taking your newspaper this morning. It was completely careless and based totally in laziness on my part.... I am absolutely prepared to do whatever it takes to make amends with you. I hope we can solve this between the two of us, without the involvement of the building and/or the authorities."

(5) I knew that he could afford to buy his own newspaper. I went to the police. The next morning I wrote this response: "Thank you for your note. I believe that you are sorry about what happened. I also believe that this feeling stems more from getting caught than from a genuine sense of **contrition** for your actions. You wrote that taking my paper was 'careless.' I believe it was carelessness that allowed me to catch you in the act of pilfering. I would use such words as *dishonest* and *insensitive* to describe your actions. Getting on the 6 train only to find that the business section is missing *again* is an incredible aggravation.

(6) "I have met with a detective from the 13th Precinct. He informed me that I could have you arrested for **misdemeanor** petit **larceny.** He said you would be put in handcuffs and brought to the police station. I agreed to a cooling-off period. . . . There is also the option of petitioning the co-op board to have you evicted. If this were an isolated occasion, I could accept

Shoplifters have no conscience. This allows them to steal, not feel guilty about stealing, and actually believe they are doing nothing wrong.

your apology at face value. That this has been a recurring problem, and the premeditated way in which I saw you take my paper, makes resolution more difficult. I welcome your suggestions."

(7) Two days later he replied: "Thank you for your note. Thank you for being open to a dialogue towards resolution to this thoughtless and utterly embarrassing incident. I want you to know that I love living in [our building]. With this exception, I have been a model tenant and solid citizen of the community. The last thing I would wish to do is foster a sense of ill will, deception or **animosity** in an otherwise idyllic environment. I am truly sorry. As far as resolution and **restitution** go . . . broken trust and loss of (potential) friendship are not easily repaired. . . . It is up to me to do everything in my power to rectify this issue. . . . I would like to purchase a new one-year subscription to *The New York Times* for you. Please accept the enclosed check for $384. I do not expect money to repair the loss of trust or respect. I hope you might view this as a good faith gesture on my part to make amends and move forward."

(8) Left with the question of how to proceed, I solicited the advice of friends. Those who had been victims of similar crimes felt I should make an example of him and pursue arrest. Others felt that the humiliation of being caught was enough and that I should cash the check and move on. I began this process, however, not for monetary gain, nor with the intention of ruining someone's life. For me, justice was found in catching the thief in the act. Restitution came in the profound humiliation he experienced. I decided to endorse his check to *The New York Times* to buy *him* a one-year subscription. He will now know that a few hundred dollars cannot erase past **transgressions.** His paper will be a daily reminder of his crime, and will serve as an insurance policy against future newspaper theft in our building (at least until his subscription runs out).

Here are some of the more difficult words in "To Catch a Thief."

animosity
(paragraph 7)

ani·mos·ity (an'ə mäs'ə tē) *n., pl.* -ties ⟦ME *animosite* < L *animositas*, boldness, spirit < *animosus*, spirited < *animus*: see fol.⟧ a feeling of strong dislike or hatred; ill will; hostility —*SYN.* ENMITY

contrition
(paragraph 5)

con·tri·tion (kən trish'ən) *n.* ⟦ME *contricioun* < OFr *contrition* < LL(Ec) *contritio*, grief: see prec.⟧ 1 remorse for having done wrong 2 *Theol.* sorrow for having offended God: **perfect contrition** is such sorrow arising out of pure love of God —*SYN.* PENITENCE

epithets
(paragraph 3)

epi·thet (ep'ə thet', -thət) *n.* ⟦L *epitheton* < Gr, lit., that which is added < *epitithenai*, to put on, add < *epi-*, on + *tithenai*, to put, DO[1]⟧ 1 an adjective, noun, or phrase, often specif. a disparaging one, used to characterize some person or thing (Ex.: "egghead" for an intellectual) 2 a descriptive name or title (Ex.: Philip the Fair; America the Beautiful) —**epi·thet'ic** *adj.* or **epi·thet'i·cal**

indignant
(paragraph 1)

in·dig·nant (in dig'nənt) *adj.* ⟦L *indignans*, prp. of *indignari*, to consider as unworthy or improper, be displeased at < *in-*, not + *dignari*, to deem worthy < *dignus*, worthy: see DIGNITY⟧ feeling or expressing anger or scorn, esp. at unjust, mean, or ungrateful action or treatment —**in·dig'·nantly** *adv.*

larceny
(paragraph 6)

lar·ceny (lär′sə nē) *n.*, *pl.* **-nies** 〖ME < Anglo-Fr *larcin* < OFr *larrecin* < L *latrocinium* < *latrocinari*, to rob, plunder < *latro*, mercenary soldier, robber < Gr *latrōn* < *latron*, wages, pay < IE *lēi-*, to possess, acquire > OE *læs*, landed property〗 *Law* the taking of personal property without consent and with the intention of permanently depriving the owner of it; theft: in some states of the U.S., and formerly in England, larceny in which the value of the property equals or exceeds a specified amount is *grand larceny*, and larceny involving lesser amounts is *petit* (or *petty*) *larceny* — **SYN.** THEFT —**lar′·cenist** *n.* or **lar′·cener** —**lar′·cenous** *adj.* —**lar′·cenous·ly** *adv.*

misdemeanor
(paragraph 6)

mis·de·meanor (mis′də mēn′ər) *n.* 〖MIS-¹ + DEMEANOR〗 **1** [Rare] the act of misbehaving **2** *Law* any minor offense, as the breaking of a municipal ordinance, for which statute provides a lesser punishment than for a felony: the penalty is usually a fine or imprisonment for a short time (usually less than one year) in a local jail, workhouse, etc.: Brit. sp. **mis′·de·mean′·our**

peruse
(paragraph 3)

pe·ruse (pə rōōz′) *vt.* **··rused′**, **··rus′·ing** 〖LME *perusen*, to use up, prob. < L *per-*, intens. + ME *usen*, to USE〗 **1** [Obs.] to examine in detail; scrutinize **2** to read carefully or thoroughly; study **3** to read in a casual or leisurely way —**pe·rus′er** *n.*

restitution
(paragraph 7)

res·ti·tu·tion (res′tə tōō′shən, -tyōō′-) *n.* 〖ME < MFr < L *restitutio* < *restitutus*, pp. of *restituere*, restore < *re-*, again + *statuere*, to set up: see STATUE〗 **1** a giving back to the rightful owner of something that has been lost or taken away; restoration **2** a making good for loss or damage; reimbursement **3** a return to a former condition or situation **4** *Physics* the recovery of its shape by an elastic body after pressure or strain is released —**SYN.** REPARATION —**res′·ti·tu′·tive** *adj.*

sociopath
(paragraph 3)

so·cio·path (sō′sē ə path′, -shē-) *n.* 〖SOCIO- + (PSYCHO)PATH〗 a person suffering from psychopathic personality, whose behavior is aggressively antisocial —**so′·cio·path′ic** *adj.*

stakeout
(paragraph 2)

stake·out (-out′) *n.* **1** the staking out of police, etc. in a surveillance of a location, suspected criminal, etc. **2** an area so staked out

tirade
(paragraph 3)

ti·rade (tī′rād′, tī rād′) *n.* 〖Fr < It *tirata*, a volley < pp. of *tirare*, to draw, fire < VL *tirare*〗 a long, vehement speech, esp. one of denunciation; harangue

transgressions
(paragraph 8)

trans·gres·sion (-gresh′ən) *n.* the act or an instance of transgressing; breach of a law, duty, etc.; sin

2A VOCABULARY

Using the vocabulary on pages 115–116, fill in this crossword puzzle.

Across

9. expressing anger
10. returning what has been stolen
11. keeping a close watch on an area
12. theft

Down

1. disrespectful remarks
2. a long speech
3. breaking laws
4. a minor offense
5. hatred or ill will
6. examine closely
7. person who exhibits ill will
8. remorse for having done wrong

2B CENTRAL THEME AND MAIN IDEAS

Choose the best answer.

_____ 1. What is the central theme of "To Catch a Thief"?
   a. A New Yorker steals the *New York Times* business section from the building's lobby.
   b. Stephen Holt decides not to prosecute the neighbor for stealing the *New York Times*.
   c. The thief offers Stephen Holt money to avoid prosecution for misdemeanor petit larceny.
   d. To get justice, Stephen Holt sets up a stakeout, confronts the thief, and gets revenge.

_____ 2. What is the main idea of paragraph 2?
   a. Stephen Holt's wife offers her husband a suggestion to deter newspaper theft.
   b. To see justice prevail, Stephen Holt devises a plan to catch the newspaper thief.
   c. The thief steals only the business section of the *New York Times*.
   d. Stephen Holt reads the *New York Times* on Train 6 every morning.

2C MAJOR DETAILS

Number the following details from the story according to the order in which they occurred. Number the events 1 to 11, with 1 next to the event that happened first.

_____ 1. Stephen Holt confronts a neighbor with the stolen newspaper at the elevator door.

_____ 2. Stephen Holt writes e-mails to customer service to complain about the missing newspaper.

_____ 3. Stephen Holt suspects the possibility of a neighbor stealing the newspaper.

_____ 4. Stephen Holt meets with a detective at the 13th Precinct.

_____ 5. The thief writes Stephen Holt a second note and includes a check for a one-year subscription to the *New York Times*.

_____ 6. Stephen Holt endorses the check and has a one-year subscription to the *New York Times* sent to the thief.

_____ 7. Stephen Holt writes a note to the thief and accuses the thief of carelessness, not remorse.

Name   Date

_____ 8. Stephen Holt receives a note of apology from the neighbor who offers to make amends.

_____ 9. After several attempts to catch the thief, Stephen Holt sees a neighbor steal his paper.

_____10. The *New York Times* assures Stephen Holt that the deliveryman is not at fault.

_____11. Stephen Holt notices the business section missing from the *New York Times*.

2D INFERENCES

Decide whether each statement can be inferred (Yes) or cannot be inferred (No) from the reading selection.

_____ 1. Stephen Holt's neighbor liked stealing newspapers.

_____ 2. Stephen Holt's neighbor stole only Holt's newspaper from the lobby.

_____ 3. Stephen Holt rode the train to his company because he did not own a car.

_____ 4. Stephen Holt felt great satisfaction in catching his neighbor with the stolen newspaper.

_____ 5. Until he was caught, the neighbor never realized the seriousness of stealing a newspaper.

_____ 6. The neighbor worried that Stephen Holt might convince the co-op board to have him evicted from the building.

_____ 7. The neighbor is unlikely to steal a newspaper from the building's lobby again.

_____ 8. Stephen Holt wrote a note of apology to customer service for mistakenly thinking the deliveryman was at fault for the missing newspaper section.

2E CRITICAL READING: FACT OR OPINION

Decide whether each statement, even if it quotes someone, contains a Fact or an Opinion.

_____ 1. *From paragraph 2:* "I needed justice."

_____ 2. *From paragraph 3:* "On my third attempt, I hit pay dirt."

_____ 3. *From paragraph 3:* [. . .] he was a sociopath [. . .].

_____ 4. *From paragraph 5:* "I believe it was carelessness that allowed me to catch you in the act of pilfering."

_____ 5. *From paragraph 6:* "I agreed to a cooling-off period."

_____ 6. *From paragraph 7:* "With this exception, I have been a model tenant and solid citizen of the community."

_____ 7. *From paragraph 7:* "[. . .] broken trust and loss of (potential) friendship are not easily repaired [. . .]."

_____ 8. *From paragraph 8:* "His paper [. . .] will serve as an insurance policy against future newspaper theft in our building [. . .]."

2F   CRITICAL READING: THE AUTHOR'S STRATEGIES

Choose the best answer.

_____ 1. Stephen Holt's main audience for "To Catch a Thief" is
   a. the complaint department of his newspaper delivery service.
   b. other residents in his apartment building whose newspapers are delivered.
   c. readers of a newspaper or magazine for general readers.
   d. his newspaper-stealing neighbor and, eventually, his family.

_____ 2. The author's purpose in writing this reading is to
   a. describe.
   b. narrate.
   c. expose.
   d. entertain.

_____ 3. The author's tone in this reading is
   a. confused.
   b. objective.
   c. unforgiving.
   d. amused.

2G   READER'S PROCESS: SUMMARIZING YOUR READING

_____ 1. What is the best summary of "To Catch a Thief"?
   a. A man tells how he uncovers the thief of the business section of his copy of the *New York Times*, which is delivered to him daily, and then decides to report him to the police.
   b. A man tells how angry and frustrated he became over not being able to discover the identity of the person who has been stealing daily the business section of his delivered copy of the *New York Times*.

Name   Date

    c. A man tells how he dealt with the person in the apartment building where he lives who was stealing daily the business section of his delivered copy of the *New York Times*.

    d. A man tells how he decided to write a letter to his neighbors to publicly embarrass the thief who steals the business section of his daily-delivered copy of the *New York Times*.

2H READER'S RESPONSE: TO DISCUSS OR WRITE ABOUT

1. Petit larceny is often defined as the theft of another's property or money under the value of $500. If convicted, the person could be imprisoned (not to exceed six months) or fined (not to exceed $1,000). If you had been Stephen Holt, would you have pursued prosecution of the neighbor for stealing the newspaper? If "yes," then what would be your reasons for doing so? If "no," then why would you not pursue action?

2. Until recently people could pump gasoline for their vehicles and then pay the cashier after they had filled up their tanks. Most stations today require a prepay at the pump with a credit card or a cash deposit held by the cashier. Pumping gas into a car and then driving off without paying for the gasoline is theft. Why do you think people would risk losing their driver's licenses and receiving a fine for a tank of gas?

HOW DID YOU DO?
2 To Catch a Thief

SKILL (number of items)	Number Correct		Points for each		Score
Vocabulary (12)	_____	×	2	=	_____
Central Theme and Main Ideas (2)	_____	×	7	=	_____
Major Details (11)	_____	×	2	=	_____
Inferences (8)	_____	×	2	=	_____
Critical Reading: Fact or Opinion (8)	_____	×	2	=	_____
Critical Reading: The Author's Strategies (3)	_____	×	2	=	_____
Reader Response: Summarizing Your Reading (1)	_____	×	2	=	_____
	(Possible Total: 100) *Total*				_____

Name   Date

"Freegans" Salvage Food from the City's Bountiful Garbage

Elizabeth Giegerich

LEARNING OBJECTIVES

- List the reasons freegans eat food from a Dumpster.

THINKING: GETTING STARTED

- Would you be willing to eat a meal prepared with food from a Dumpster?

(1) With his bare hands, Adam Weissman **vigilantly** digs through a trash bag filled with rotten fruits and vegetables, old cleaning products, and a few **salvageable** pieces of produce. Weissman tosses aside a rotten orange but quickly grabs an **edible** apple and some radishes. In about five minutes, he's taken more items from the trash than he's left behind. He and others like him give true meaning to the phrase "one man's trash is another's treasure."

(2) Weissman, 30, is a freegan, a member of a subculture that only eat food that is free and vegan (vegetarians whose diets consist of plant products exclusively), which requires frequent trips to the trash for weekly groceries. Freegans have been **scavenging** the streets for over a decade to find the best garbage sites to find good food. One New York City group has mastered the practice commonly known as Dumpster diving so well that they now hold trash tours to teach others how and where to find the best stuff available. "I became actively involved because it made sense to me that if there is food in the trash, like anything else that people throw out that is perfectly good, it makes more sense to take from there than to keep on consuming more," said Janet Kalish, 45, a volunteer for freegan .info, a Web site dedicated to information for and on freegans. Freegans say that between 9 p.m. and midnight, almost everything that can be found on the shelves of a supermarket can be found in a supermarket's trash and in Dumpsters—and in edible form.

(3) They reject **capitalism** and **globalization** on ethical grounds and believe that these systems are the cause of almost everything harmful in the world, from global warming to starving children in Third World countries. They profess to be disgusted by society's excessive wastefulness, and Dumpster diving is one way they "non-participate" in consumer culture. They salvage everything from sealed protein drinks, to Oreo cookies, to jarred garlic, to bagels. Few report knowing of anyone getting sick from

eating out of the trash. "We take common-sense precautions," when it comes to choosing safe food, said Weissman. With produce, "we take the same food precautions you'd take with things in your refrigerator, wash things appropriately, throw away things that look spoiled."

(4) On one recent trash tour held by Kalish, about 12 people followed her lead to the trash placed in front of D'Agostinos, Dunkin' Donuts, Gristedes, and several other food stores along Third Ave. in Manhattan. In front of a D'Agostinos, Kalish squeezed a salvaged loaf of bread to show it was still moist and fresh. "It is easy and clean," she said. "Because it has been double-wrapped and its expiration date is just today." Divers placed dozens of those loaves into reusable grocery bags and continued to sift through the trash. They made quick decisions about what looked best to take and what was better left.

(5) Most nights, freegans run into homeless persons hungrily digging through the trash. Because the trash is usually abundant and free, it's something everyone is willing to share. On the tour, Kalish first offered the others her best finds before bagging them, and when two people reached for the same piece of fruit, they were both quick to ask the other if he or she wanted it. "I have a goal every time to take more than I can eat and share it," said Kalish, "and on the way home I often fulfill that goal."

Dumpster diving is done by people who could afford to purchase items but choose to dive for treasures.

Here are some of the more difficult words in "'Freegans' Salvage Food from the City's Bountiful Garbage."

Vocabulary List

capitalism
(paragraph 3)

capi·tal·ism (kap′ət ′l iz′əm) *n.* **1** an economic system in which all or most of the means of production and distribution, as land, factories, communications, and transportation systems, are privately owned and operated in a relatively competitive environment through the investment of capital to produce profits: it has been characterized by a tendency toward the concentration of wealth, the growth of large corporations, etc. that has led to economic inequality, which has been dealt with usually by increased government action and control **2** the principles, methods, interests, power, influence, etc. of capitalists, especially of those with large holdings

edible
(paragraph 1)

ed·ible (ed′ə bəl) *adj.* [LL *edibilis* < L *edere*, EAT] fit to be eaten — *n.* anything fit to be eaten; food: *usually used in pl.* —**ed′·ibil′·ity** (-bil′ə tē) *n.* or **ed′·ible·ness**

globalization
(paragraph 3)

glob·al·ize (glō′bəl īz′) *vt.* -·ized′, -·iz′·ing to make global; esp., to organize or establish worldwide —**glob′·ali·za′·tion** *n.*

salvageable
(paragraph 1)

sal·vage (sal′vij) *n.* [Fr < MFr < *salver*, to SAVE[1]] **1** *a)* the voluntary rescue of a ship or its cargo at sea from peril such as fire, shipwreck, capture, etc. *b)* compensation paid for such a rescue *c)* the ship or cargo so rescued *d)* the recovery of a sunken or wrecked ship or its cargo as by divers **2** *a)* the saving or rescue of any goods, property, etc. from destruction, damage, or waste *b)* any material, goods, etc. thus saved and sold or put to use *c)* the value, or proceeds from the sale, of such goods, specif. of damaged goods, as involved in insurance claim settlements —*vt.* -·vaged, -·vag·ing to save or rescue from shipwreck, fire, flood, etc.; engage or succeed in the salvage of (ships, goods, etc.) —**sal′·vage·abil′·ity** *n.* —**sal′·vage·able** *adj.* —**sal′·vager** *n.*

scavenging
(paragraph 2)

scav·enge (skav′inj) *vt.* -·enged, -·eng·ing [back-form. < fol.] **1** to clean up (streets, alleys, etc.); remove rubbish, dirt, or garbage from **2** to salvage (usable goods) by rummaging through refuse or discards **3** to remove burned gases from (the cylinder of an internal-combustion engine) **4** *Metallurgy* to clean (molten metal) by using a substance that will combine chemically with the impurities present —*vi.* **1** to act as a scavenger **2** to look for food

vigilantly
(paragraph 1)

vigi·lant (vij′ə lənt) *adj.* [Fr < L *vigilans*, prp. of *vigilare*, to watch < *vigil*, awake: see VIGIL] staying watchful and alert to danger or trouble —*SYN.* WATCHFUL —**vig′i·lantly** *adv.*

3A   VOCABULARY

Using the dictionary entries on page 124, fill in the blanks.

1. Freegans reject the concept of _____, the integration of economics and societies all over the world.

2. The supermarket had a wide array of _____ fruits on display.

3. The characteristic feature of modern _____ is mass production of goods intended for consumption by the masses.

Name   Date

4. The dog _____ guarded the sleeping baby.

5. _____ in garbage cans is sometimes the food source for the homeless.

6. Freegans often find discards that they consider _____ in Dumpsters.

3B   CENTRAL THEME AND MAIN IDEAS

Choose the best answer.

_____ 1. What is the central theme of "'Freegans' Salvage Food from the City's Bountiful Garbage"?
   a. Dumpster diving involves rummaging through the garbage cans of retailers.
   b. Freegans believe in boycotting an economics system in which the profit motive has overshadowed ethical concerns.
   c. Freegans remove salvageable food from trash cans and Dumpsters to prepare edible food.
   d. Freegans dig through Dumpsters alone or in groups but share their discoveries openly with one another.

_____ 2. What is the main idea of paragraph 2?
   a. Rather than shopping for groceries at a supermarket, freegans prefer scavenging the streets to find a free source for food.
   b. Freegans are people who have mastered the practice of Dumpster diving.
   c. The practice of rummaging through the garbage of retailers is becoming more accepted now than a decade ago.
   d. Freegans are best identified as a subculture, a set of people with distinct behavior and beliefs.

_____ 3. What is the main idea of paragraph 3?
   a. Freegans consider Dumpster diving a practice to protest against the high prices of food in supermarkets.
   b. Disgusted with society's wastefulness and consumer emphasis, freegans support Dumpster diving.
   c. Freegans are very selective in the food they salvage from Dumpsters.
   d. Few report knowing of people getting sick from food salvaged from supermarket and restaurant Dumpsters.

3C   MAJOR DETAILS

Decide whether each detail is Major *or* Minor *based on the context of the reading selection.*

_____ 1. Freegan.info is a website devoted to information on and for freegans.

_____ 2. Freegans often scavenge for food between 9 p.m. and midnight.

_____ 3. Freegans reject capitalism and globalization on ethical grounds.

_____ 4. Freegans salvage everything from sealed protein drinks to bagels.

_____ 5. In front of a D'Agostinos, Janet Kalish salvaged a loaf of bread that was moist and fresh.

_____ 6. The trash in Dumpsters is usually abundant and free.

3D   INFERENCES

*Decide whether each of the following statements can be inferred (*Yes*) or cannot be inferred (*No*) from the reading selection.*

_____ 1. Dumpster diving is not for everyone.

_____ 2. Dumpster diving is considered a great resource by many people.

_____ 3. Dumpster divers enjoy the practice of Dumpster diving.

_____ 4. Dumpster divers use long poles to pull up items from the Dumpster in the evening.

_____ 5. Dumpster diving can be profitable.

_____ 6. In the evening, Dumpster divers run the risk of arrest because of trespassing.

3E   CRITICAL READING: THE AUTHOR'S STRATEGIES

Choose the best answer.

_____ 1. The main audience of "'Freegans' Salvage Food from the City's Bountiful Garbage" is
   a. persons interested in becoming a spokesperson for the support of Freeganism.
   b. consumers who are outraged at our country's wasting enormous resources, especially food.

Name   Date

      c. the unemployed who struggle to put food on the table for
        their families.

      d. readers who are unaware of a small group of people who
        uphold minimum consumer consumption and the recycling
        of food.

_____ 2. The author's purpose in writing this reading is to
      a. convince
      b. describe.
      c. inform.
      d. narrate.

_____ 3. The author's tone is this reading is
      a. sincere.
      b. sarcastic
      c. satiric.
      d. skeptical.

3F READER'S PROCESS: SUMMARIZING YOUR READING

_____ 1. What is the best summary of "'Freegans' Salvage Food from
      the City's Bountiful Garbage"?

      a. Rather than contributing to further waste, freegans practice
        salvaging edible food from garbage cans to protest society's
        emphasis on consumerism.

      b. To combat New York City's garbage crisis, freegans support
        the city's efforts of recycling, especially salvageable food
        from Dumpsters.

      c. Freegans and the homeless have joined forces to identify exces-
        sive waste sites in New York's restaurants and supermarkets.

      d. Freegans are concerned that our country's resources are
        being used up faster than they are being replaced, so they
        support the recycling of garbage.

3G READER'S RESPONSE: TO DISCUSS OR WRITE ABOUT

1. Each year the United States generates approximately 230 million tons
   of "trash." This is about 4.6 pounds per person per day. What, if anything, does your neighborhood or community do about solid waste?
   Has this effort been successful? Why or why not?

2. Traditionally, most people who resort to Dumpster diving are forced
   to do so out of economic necessity. Others practice Dumpster diving
   for personal reasons. Would you be willing to be taken on a trash tour
   in New York? Why or why not?

3. What could be the rewards and dangers of participating in Dumpster diving? What do you think your family's trash would tell about your lifestyle?

HOW DID YOU DO?

3   "Freegans" Salvage Food from the City's Bountiful Garbage

SKILL (number of items)	Number Correct		Points for each		Score
Vocabulary (6)	_____	×	3	=	_____
Central Theme and Main Ideas (3)	_____	×	8	=	_____
Major Details (6)	_____	×	4	=	_____
Inferences (6)	_____	×	3	=	_____
Critical Reading: The Author's Strategies (3)	_____	×	4	=	_____
Reader Response: Summarizing Your Reading (1)	_____	×	4	=	_____
	(Possible Total: 100) Total				_____

Name   Date

Seoul Searching

Rick Reilly

LEARNING OBJECTIVES

- Contrast the effects of adoption on the birth mother, adoptive parents, and adoptee.

THINKING: GETTING STARTED

- What problems do you think a couple would encounter when adopting a child of a race different from theirs?

(1) After 11 years and 6,000 miles, we still hadn't met our daughter's mother. We had come only this close: staked out in a van across from a tiny Seoul coffee shop, the mother inside with a Korean interpreter, afraid to come out, afraid of being discovered, afraid to meet her own flesh.

(2) Inside the van, Rae, our 11-year-old Korean adopted daughter, was trying to make sense of it. How could we have flown the entire family 6,000 miles from Denver to meet a woman who was afraid to walk 20 yards across the street to meet us? Why had we come this far if she was only going to reject Rae again? We were told we had an hour. There were 40 minutes left. The cell phone rang. "Drive the van to the alley behind the coffee shop," said the interpreter. "And wait."

(3) When a four-month-old Rae was hand-delivered to us at Gate B-7 at Denver's Stapleton Airport, we knew someday we would be in Korea trying to find her birth mother. We just never dreamed it would be this soon. Then again, since Rae was a toddler, we've told her she was adopted, and she has constantly asked about her birth mother. "Do you think my birth mother plays the piano like I do? "Do you think my birth mother is pretty?" And then, at 10, after a day of too many stares: a teary "I just want to meet someone I'm related to." "When they start asking that," the adoption therapist said, "you can start looking."

(4) We started looking. We asked the agency that had arranged the adoption, Friends of Children of Various Nations, to begin a search. Within six months our caseworker, Kim Matsunaga, told us they had found the birth mother but she was highly reluctant to meet us. She had never told anyone about Rae. In Korea, the shame of unwed pregnancy is huge. The mother is **disowned,** the baby **rootless.** Kim guessed she had told her parents she was moving to the city to work and had gone to a home for unwed mothers.

(5) Kim told us the agency was taking a group of Colorado and New Mexico families to Korea in the summer to meet birth relatives. She said if we went, Rae's would probably show up. "The birth mothers almost always show up," she said. Almost. We were unsure. And then we talked to a family who had gone the year before. They said it would be wonderful. At the very least, Rae would meet her foster mother, who had cared for her those four months. She would meet the doctor who delivered her. Hell, I had never met the doctor who delivered me. But meeting the birth mother was said to be the sweetest. A 16-year-old Korean-American girl told Rae, "I don't know, it just kinda fills a hole in your heart." We risked it. Five plane tickets to Seoul for our two redheaded birth boys—Kellen, 15, and Jake, 13—Rae, me and my wife Linda. We steeled Rae for the chance that her birth mother wouldn't show up. Come to think of it, we steeled ourselves.

(6) At first, it was wonderful. We met Rae's foster mother, who swooped in and rushed for Rae as if she were her long-lost daughter, which she almost was. She bear-hugged her. She stroked her hair. She touched every little nick and scar on her tan arms and legs. "What's this from?" she asked in Korean. She had fostered 31 babies, but it was as if she'd known only Rae. Rae was half **grossed** out, half purring. Somebody had just rushed in with the missing four months of her life. The **foster** mother wept. We wept.

(7) All of us, all six American families, sat in one room at a home for unwed mothers outside Seoul across from 25 unwed mothers, some who had just given up their babies, some soon to. They looked into unmet children's futures. We looked into our unmet birth mothers' pasts. A 17-year-old Korean-American girl—roughly the same age as the **distraught** girls in front of her—rose and choked out, "I know it's hard for you now, but I want you to know I love my American family." Another 17-year-old adoptee met not only her birth father but also her four elder birth sisters. They were still a family—had always been one—but they had given her up as one mouth too many to feed. Then they told her that her birth mother had died of an **aneurysm** two weeks earlier. So how was she supposed to feel now? Joy at finding her father and her sisters? Grief at 17 years without them? Anger at being given up? Gratitude for her American parents? Horror at coming so close to and then losing her birth mother? We heard her story that night on the tour bus, went to our hotel room and wept some more.

(8) All these kids—even the three who never found their birth relatives—were piecing together the puzzle of their lives at whiplash speed. This is where you were born. This is the woman who held you. This was the city, the food, the smells. For them, it was two parts home ("It's so nice," Rae said amid a throng of Koreans on a street. "For once, people are staring at Kel and Jake instead of me") and three parts I'm-never-coming-here-again

Approximately 120,000 children are adopted each year in the United States. In adolescence, the adopted child is likely to have an interest in his or her birth parents.

(a teenage boy ate dinner at his foster parents' home only to discover in mid-bite that they raise dogs for meat).

(9) When the day came for our visit with Rae's birth mother we were told, "It has to be handled very, very carefully." She had three children by a husband she had never told about Rae, and she was terribly afraid someone would see her. And that's how we found ourselves hiding in that van like Joe Friday, waiting for the woman of a lifetime to show up. It is a very odd feeling to be staring holes in every Korean woman walking down a Korean street, thinking that your daughter may have sprung from her womb. All we knew about her was that she 1) might have her newborn girl with her, 2) was tiny—the birth certificate said she was 4 ft. 10 in.—and 3) would look slightly more nervous than a cat burglar.

(10) First came a youngish, **chic** woman pushing a stroller. "That might be her!" yelled Rae—until she strolled by. Then a short, fat woman with a baby tied at her stomach. "There she is!" yelled Rae—until she got on a bus. Then a pretty, **petite** woman in yellow with an infant in a baby carrier. "I know that's her!" yelled Rae—and lo and behold, the woman quick-stepped into the coffee shop across the street. The only problem was, she didn't come out. She stayed in that coffee shop, talking to the interpreter for what seemed like six hours but was probably only 20 minutes. We

stared at the dark windows of the shop. We stared at the cell phone. We stared at one another. What was this, Panmunjom? Finally, the interpreter called Kim: Drive down the alley and wait. We drove down the alley and waited. Nothing.

(11) By this time, I could have been the centerfold for *Psychology Today*. Rae was still calm. I told her, "If she's not out here in five minutes, I want you to walk right in and introduce yourself." Rae swallowed. Suddenly, at the van window . . . and now, opening the van door . . . the woman in yellow with the baby. And just as suddenly, inside . . . sitting next to her daughter. Our daughter—all of ours. She was nervous. She wouldn't look at us, only at her baby and the interpreter. "We'll go somewhere," said the interpreter. Where do you go with your deepest, darkest secret? We went to a park. Old Korean men looked up from their chess games in astonishment to see a **gaggle** of whites and redheads and Koreans sit down at the table next to them with cameras, gifts and notebooks. Rae presented her birth mother with a book she had made about her life—full of childhood pictures and purple-penned poems—but the woman showed no emotion as she looked at it. Rae presented her with a silver locket—a picture of herself inside—but again, no eye contact, no hugs, no touches. The woman was either guarding her heart now the way she'd done 11 years ago, or she simply didn't care anymore, maybe had never cared.

(12) Months before, Rae had drawn up a list of 20 questions she wanted to ask at the big moment. Now, unruffled, she pulled it out of her little purse. Some of us forgot to breathe. "Why did you give me up?" Rae asked simply. All heads turned to the woman. The interpreted answer: Too young, only 19 then, no money, great shame. "Where is my birth dad?" The answer: No idea. Only knew him for two dates. Long gone. Still no emotion. I ached for Rae. How would she handle such iciness from the woman she had dreamed of, fantasized about, held on to? Finally, this one: "When I was born, did you get to hold me?" The woman's lips parted in a small gasp. She swallowed and stared at the grass. "No," she said slowly, "they took you from me." And that's when our caseworker, Kim, said, "Well, now you can." That did it. That broke her. She **lurched,** tears running down her cheeks, reached for Rae and pulled her close, holding her as if they might take her again. "I told myself I wouldn't cry," she said. The interpreter wept. Linda wept. I wept. Right then, right that minute, the heavens opened up, and it poured a **monsoon** starter kit on us, just an all-out Noah. Yeah, even the sky wept.

(13) Any sane group of people would have run for the van, but none of us wanted the moment to end. We had finally got her, and we would float to Pusan before we would give her up. We were all crying and laughing and trying to fit all of us under the birth mother's tiny pink umbrella. But the rain was so loud you couldn't talk. We ran for the van and sat in there, Rae holding her half sister and her birth mother holding the daughter she must have thought she would never see. Time was so short. Little sentences contained whole lifetimes. She thanked us for raising her baby.

"You are a very good family," she said, eyeing the giants around her. "Very strong and good." And how do you thank someone for giving you her daughter? Linda said, "Thank you for the gift you gave us." The birth mother smiled bittersweetly. She held Rae with one arm and the book and the locket tight with the other.

(14) Then it was over. She said she had to get back. She asked the driver to pull over so she could get out. We started pleading for more time. Meet us for dinner? No. Breakfast tomorrow? No. Send you pictures? Please, no. The van stopped at a red light. Somebody opened the door. She kissed Rae on the head, stroked her hair one last time, stepped out, finally let go of her hand and closed the door. The light turned green. We drove off and watched her shrink away from us, dropped off on the corner of Nowhere and Forever. I think I was still crying when I looked at Rae. She was beaming, of course, which must be how you feel when a hole in your heart finally gets filled.

Here are some of the more difficult words in "Seoul Searching."

aneurysm
(paragraph 7)

aneu·rysm or **aneu·rism** (an′yoo̅ riz′əm, -yə-) *n.* [ModL *aneur-isma* < Gr *aneurysma* < *ana-*, up + *eurys*, broad: see EURY-] a sac formed by local enlargement of the weakened wall of an artery, a vein, or the heart, caused by disease or injury —**an′eu·rys′·mal** *adj.* or **an′eu·ris′·mal** (-riz′məl)

chic
(paragraph 10)

chic (shēk) *n.* [Fr, orig., subtlety < MLowG *schick*, order, skill or MHG *schicken*, behavior, arrangement] smart elegance of style and manner: said esp. of women or their clothes —☆*adj.* stylish in a smart, pleasing way

disowned
(paragraph 4)

dis·own (dis ōn′) *vt.* to refuse to acknowledge as one's own; repudi-ate; cast off

distraught
(paragraph 7)

dis·traught (di strôt′) *adj.* [ME, var. of prec.] **1** extremely trou-bled; mentally confused; distracted; harassed **2** driven mad; crazed —*SYN.* ABSENT-MINDED

foster
(paragraph 6)

fos·ter (fôs′tər, fäs′-) *vt.* [ME *fostren* < OE *fostrian*, to nourish, bring up < *fostor*, food, nourishment < base of *foda*, FOOD] **1** to bring up with care; rear **2** to help to grow or develop; stimulate; promote [to *foster* discontent] **3** to cling to in one's mind; cherish [*foster* a hope] —*adj.* **1** having the standing of a specified member of the family, though not by birth or adoption, and giving, receiv-ing, or sharing the care appropriate to that standing [*foster* parent, *foster* brother] **2** designating or relating to such care —**fos′·terer** *n.*

gaggle
(paragraph 11)

gag·gle (gag′əl) *n.* [ME *gagel* < *gagelen*, to cackle: orig. echoic] **1** a flock of geese **2** any group or cluster

grossed
(paragraph 6)

gross (grōs) *adj.* [ME *grose* < OFr *gros*, big, thick, coarse < LL *grossus*, thick] **1** big or fat and coarse-looking; corpulent; burly **2** glaring; flagrant; very bad [a *gross* miscalculation] **3** dense; thick **4** *a*) lacking fineness, as in texture *b*) lacking fine distinctions or specific details **5** lacking in refinement or perception; insensitive; dull **6** vulgar; obscene; coarse [*gross* language] **7** [Slang] unpleas-ant, disgusting, offensive, etc. **8** with no deductions; total; entire [*gross* income]: opposed to NET² **9** [Archaic] evident; obvious —*n.* [ME *groos* < OFr *grosse*, orig. fem. of *gros*] **1** *pl.* **gross′es** overall total, as of income, before deductions are taken **2** *pl.* **gross** twelve dozen —*vt., vi.* to earn (a specified total amount) before expenses are deducted —*SYN.* COARSE —**gross out** [Slang] to disgust, shock, offend, etc. —**in the gross 1** in bulk; as a whole **2** wholesale: also **by the gross** —**gross′ly** *adv.* —**gross′·ness** *n.*

Vocabulary List

lurched
(paragraph 12)

lurch[1] (lurch) *vi.* [< ?] **1** to roll, pitch, or sway suddenly forward or to one side **2** to stagger —*n.* [earlier *lee-lurch* < ?] a lurching movement; sudden rolling, pitching, etc.
lurch[2] (lurch) *vi.* [ME *lorchen*, var. of LURK] [Obs.] to remain furtively near a place; lurk —*vt.* **1** [Archaic] to prevent (a person) from getting his fair share of something **2** [Obs.] to get by cheating, robbing, tricking, etc. —*n.* [Obs.] the act of lurching —**lie at (or on) the lurch** [Archaic] to lie in wait
lurch[3] (lurch) *n.* [Fr *lourche*, name of a 16th-c. game like backgammon, prob. < OFr, duped < MDu *lurz*, left (hand), hence unlucky, akin to MHG *lërz*, left, *lürzen*, to deceive] [Archaic] a situation in certain card games, in which the winner has more than double the score of the loser —**leave someone in the lurch** to leave someone in a difficult situation; leave someone in trouble and needing help

monsoon
(paragraph 12)

mon·soon (män so͞on′) *n.* [MDu *monssoen* < Port *monção* < Ar *mausim*, a time, a season] **1** a seasonal wind of the Indian Ocean and S Asia, blowing from the southwest from April to October, and from the northeast during the rest of the year **2** the season during which this wind blows from the southwest, characterized by heavy rains **3** any wind that reverses its direction seasonally or blows constantly between land and adjacent water —**mon·soon′al** *adj.*

petite
(paragraph 10)

pe·tite (pə tēt′) *adj.* [Fr, fem. of *petit*] small and trim in figure: said of a woman —*SYN.* SMALL —**pe·tite′·ness** *n.*

rootless
(paragraph 4)

root·less (-lis) *adj.* having no roots or no stabilizing ties, as to society —**root′·less·ly** *adv.* —**root′·less·ness** *n.*

4A VOCABULARY

Using the dictionary entries on pages 133–134, fill in the blanks.

1. The model wore a _____ gown designed by the late American designer Patrick Kelly.

2. The father _____ his wayward son so that he would not receive any of the family inheritance.

3. Because he did not know his birth parents, the child felt _____.

4. Many people are _____ out by horror movies that show blood and guts.

5. _____ from grief, the young widow flung herself overboard.

6. If left untreated, an _____ generally results in death.

7. The Balinese dancers are very slight and _____.

8. A _____ generally includes strong winds and heavy rains.

9. Before children are adopted, they often live with a _____ parent.

Name   Date

10. A _____ of eager shoppers crowded outside the store, waiting for the doors to open.

11. The bicyclist _____ forward when he hit a deep hole in the street.

4B CENTRAL THEME AND MAIN IDEAS

Choose the best answer.

_____ 1. What is the central theme of "Seoul Searching"?
   a. The Reillys adopted a four-month-old baby girl from Korea.
   b. In Korea, having a child out of wedlock is considered a disgrace.
   c. An adoption agency arranged for a group of adopted children to meet their birth parents.
   d. At the age of eleven, Rae's constant desire to meet her birth mother came true.

_____ 2. What is the main idea of paragraph 3?
   a. The Reillys picked up four-month-old Rae at Denver's Stapleton Airport.
   b. Rae's constant desire to know about her birth mother sent the Reillys back to Korea sooner than they expected.
   c. The Reillys could not answer Rae's unending questions she asked about her birth mother.
   d. From the time she was a toddler, the Reillys told Rae she was adopted.

_____ 3. What is the main idea of paragraph 11?
   a. As the family waited in an alley, Rick Reilly was nervous, but Rae was calm.
   b. Holding a baby, a woman dressed in yellow appeared at the van window.
   c. The interpreter finally convinced the birth mother to meet the daughter she had never seen.
   d. Because she was nervous, the birth mother looked only at her baby and the interpreter.

4C MAJOR DETAILS

Decide whether each detail is Major *or* Minor *based on the context of the reading selection.*

_____ 1. The Reillys flew 6,000 miles from Colorado to Korea for Rae to meet her birth mother.

_____ 2. Friends of Children of Various Nations began a search to find Rae's birth mother.

_____ 3. Kim Matsanaga was the caseworker assigned to locate Rae's birth mother.

_____ 4. The birth mother was very reluctant to meet Rae and her adoptive parents.

_____ 5. Rae's foster mother had looked after thirty-one babies at the home.

_____ 6. Rae's birth mother had three other children.

_____ 7. The interpreter was to meet the birth mother in a coffee shop.

_____ 8. Rae's birth mother showed no emotion when Rae began asking her questions.

_____ 9. Rae had a list of twenty questions to ask her birth mother.

_____ 10. A heavy rain drenched the Reillys, the birth mother, caseworker, and the interpreter as they visited in the park.

4D   INFERENCES

Decide whether each statement can be inferred (Yes) or cannot be inferred (No) from the reading selection.

_____ 1. The Reillys would have preferred to adopt an American baby rather than a Korean baby.

_____ 2. After eleven years, the foster mother still cared for Rae.

_____ 3. Upon returning to Korea, Rae felt comfortable because she looked like most of the people around her.

_____ 4. The birth mother took a great risk to meet Rae and her adopted family.

_____ 5. The Reillys could see a resemblance between Rae and her birth mother.

_____ 6. The birth mother's answers were not truthful.

_____ 7. The birth mother regretted she was not allowed to hold her daughter at birth.

_____ 8. The birth mother could never show Rae's gifts to her husband and children.

_____ 9. The birth mother was glad that she met with Rae and the Reillys.

_____ 10. Rae would have preferred to have been adopted by a Korean, not an American, couple.

Name   Date

4E CRITICAL READING: THE AUTHOR'S STRATEGIES

Choose the best answer.

_____ 1. Rick Reilly's main audience for "Seoul Searching" is
     a. Korean children adopted by American families who need the courage to ask to look for either or both of their birth parents.
     b. Americans thinking of adopting Korean children who fear the children will grow up and desert their American families.
     c. Adopted people interested in the stories of how others like them found either or both of their birth parents.
     d. Families and others interested in what happens when adopted children meet either or both of their birth parents.

_____ 2. The author's purpose in writing this reading is to
     a. narrate.
     b. describe.
     c. argue.
     d. entertain.

_____ 3. The overall tone of this reading is
     a. pessimistic.
     b. joyful.
     c. heartfelt.
     d. resentful.

4F READER'S PROCESS: SUMMARIZING YOUR READING

_____ 1. What is the best summary of "Seoul Searching"?
     a. An American family travels with their adopted Korean daughter to Korea to help her find her birth mother.
     b. Birth mothers of adopted Korean children rarely want to be located later by those children because the mothers want to keep the adoptions secret.
     c. Instructions for arrangements need to be made in advance to hold secret meetings in Korea between adopted Korean children and their birth mothers.
     d. Families with adopted children from countries other than the United States are torn apart when the adopted children decide they want to return to their birth mothers.

4G   READER'S RESPONSE: TO DISCUSS OR WRITE ABOUT

1. Rae's birth mother gave up her daughter because in Korea an unwed mother is disowned. Do you think the birth mother made the right choice? Why or why not? How do you suppose the birth mother felt after meeting the daughter she had never seen? Explain your response.

2. Adoption results in the birth parent's giving up parenting rights and responsibilities to another set of parents, permanently. Adoption costs can range from $2,000 for an adoption through a public agency to $30,000 for an international adoption. How much would you be willing to spend to adopt a child? If you were considering adoption, would you have conditions or requirements with regard to the child's age, race, and ethnicity; mental and physical ability; and parental background? Be specific with your answers.

HOW DID YOU DO?
4   Seoul Searching

SKILL (number of items)	Number Correct		Points for each		Score
Vocabulary (11)	_____	×	2	=	_____
Central Theme and Main Ideas (3)	_____	×	9	=	_____
Major Details (10)	_____	×	2	=	_____
Inferences (10)	_____	×	2	=	_____
Critical Reading: The Author's Strategies (3)	_____	×	3	=	_____
Reader's Process: Summarizing Your Reading (1)	_____	×	2	=	_____
	(Possible Total: 100) *Total*				_____

Darkness at Noon

Harold Krents

LEARNING OBJECTIVES

• **Explain how handicaps do not prevent a person from achieving one's goal.**

THINKING: GETTING STARTED

• **What accommodations have been made at your school for handicapped students?**

(1) Blind from birth, I have never had the opportunity to see myself and have been completely dependent on the image I create in the eye of the observer. To date it has not been **narcissistic.**

(2) There are those who assume that since I can't see, I obviously also cannot hear. Very often people will converse with me at the top of their lungs, **enunciating** each word very carefully. Conversely, people will also often whisper, assuming that since my eyes don't work, my ears don't either. For example, when I go to the airport and ask the ticket agent for assistance to the plane, he or she will **invariably** pick up the phone, call a ground hostess and whisper, "Hi, Jane, we've got a 76 here." I have concluded that the word "blind" is not used for one of two reasons: Either they fear that if the dread word is spoken, the ticket agent's **retina** will immediately detach, or they are reluctant to inform me of my condition of which I may not have been previously aware.

(3) On the other hand, others know that of course I can hear, but believe that I can't talk. Often, therefore, when my wife and I go out to dinner, a waiter or waitress will ask Kit if "*he* would like a drink" to which I respond that "indeed *he* would." This point was graphically driven home to me while we were in England. I had been given a year's leave of absence from my Washington law firm to study for a diploma-in-law degree at Oxford University. During the year I became ill and was hospitalized. Immediately after admission, I was wheeled down to the X-ray room. Just at the door sat an elderly woman—elderly I would judge from the sound of her voice. "What is his name?" the woman asked the orderly who had been wheeling me.

"What's your name?" the orderly repeated to me.

"Harold Krents," I replied.

"Harold Krents," he repeated.

"When was he born?"

"When were you born?"

"November 5, 1944," I responded.

"November 5, 1944," the orderly **intoned.**

(4) This procedure continued for approximately five minutes at which point even my saint-like disposition deserted me. "Look," I finally blurted out, "this is absolutely ridiculous. Okay, granted I can't see, but it's got to have become pretty clear to both of you that I don't need an interpreter."

"He says he doesn't need an interpreter," the orderly reported to the woman.

(5) The toughest **misconception** of all is the view that because I can't see, I can't work. I was turned down by over forty law firms because of my blindness, even though my qualifications included a cum laude degree from Harvard College and a good ranking in my Harvard Law School class. The attempt to find employment, the continuous frustration of being told that it was impossible for a blind person to practice law, the rejection letters, not based on my lack of ability but rather on my disability, will always remain one of the most **disillusioning** experiences of my life.

(6) Fortunately, this view of limitation and **exclusion** is beginning to change. On April 16, 1976, the Department of Labor issued regulations that **mandate** equal-employment opportunities for the handicapped. By and large, the business community's response to offering employment to the disabled has been enthusiastic.

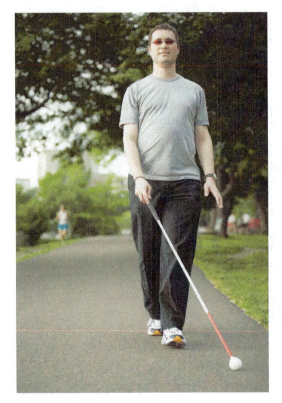

The long, white cane is an indication of ability as opposed to disability and serves as a symbol of independence for its users.

(7) I therefore look forward to the day, with the expectation that it is certain to come, when employers will view their handicapped workers as a little child did me years ago when my family still lived in Scarsdale. I was playing basketball with my father in our backyard according to procedures we had developed. My father would stand beneath the hoop, shout, and I would shoot over his head at the basket attached to the garage. Our next-door neighbor, aged five, wandered over into our yard with a playmate. "He's blind," our neighbor whispered to her friend in a voice that could be heard distinctly by Dad and me. Dad shot and missed; I did the same. Dad hit the rim: I missed entirely; Dad shot and missed the garage entirely. "Which one is blind?" whispered back the little friend.

(8) I would hope that in the near future when a plant manager is touring the factory with the foreman and comes upon a handicapped and non-handicapped person working together, his comment after watching them work will be, "Which one is disabled?"

Here are some of the more difficult words in "Darkness at Noon."

Vocabulary List

disillusioning
(paragraph 5)

dis·il·lu·sion (dis'i lōō'zhən) *vt.* **1** to free from illusion or false ideas; disenchant **2** to take away the ideals or idealism of and make disappointed, bitter, etc. —*n.* DISILLUSIONMENT

enunciating
(paragraph 2)

enun·ci·ate (ē nun'sē āt', i-; *also*, -shē-) *vt.* **··at′ed, ··at′ing** [< L *enuntiatus*, pp. of *enuntiare* < *e-*, out + *nuntiare*, to announce < *nuntius*, a messenger] **1** to state definitely; express in a systematic way [to *enunciate* a theory] **2** to announce; proclaim **3** to pronounce (words), esp. clearly and distinctly —*vi.* to pronounce words, esp. clearly and distinctly; articulate —*SYN.* UTTER[2] — **enun′·cia′·tion** (-sē ā′-) *n.* —**enun′·cia′·tive** (-āt′iv, -ə tiv) *adj.* — **enun′·cia′·tor** *n.*

exclusion
(paragraph 6)

ex·clude (eks klōōd', iks-) *vt.* **··clud′ed, ··clud′·ing** [ME *excluden* < L *excludere* < *ex-*, out + *claudere*, CLOSE[3]] **1** to refuse to admit, consider, include, etc.; shut out; keep from entering, happening, or being; reject; bar **2** to put out; force out; expel —**ex·clud′·able** *adj.* —**ex·clud′er** *n.*

SYN.—**exclude** implies a keeping out or prohibiting of that which is not yet in [to *exclude* someone from membership]; **debar** connotes the existence of some barrier, as legal authority or force, which excludes someone from a privilege, right, etc. [to *debar* certain groups from voting]; **disbar** refers only to the expulsion of a lawyer from the group of those who are permitted to practice law; **eliminate** implies the removal of that which is already in, usually connoting its undesirability or irrelevance [to *eliminate* waste products]; **suspend** refers to the removal, usually temporary, of someone from some organization, institution, etc., as for the infraction of some rule [to *suspend* a student from school] — *ANT.* admit, include

ex·clu·sion (eks klōō'zhən, iks-) *n.* [ME *exclusioun* < L *exclusio* < pp. of *excludere*] **1** an excluding or being excluded **2** a thing excluded —**to the exclusion of** so as to keep out, bar, etc. —**ex·clu′·sion·ar′y** *adj.*

intoned
(paragraph 3)

in·tone (in tōn') *vt.* **··toned′, ··ton′·ing** [ME *entonen* < OFr *entoner* < ML *intonare*: IN-[1] & TONE] **1** to utter or recite in a singing tone or in prolonged monotones; chant **2** to give a particular intonation to **3** to sing or recite the opening phrase of (a chant, canticle, etc.) —*vi.* to speak or recite in a singing tone or in prolonged monotones; chant —**in·ton′er** *n.*

invariably
(paragraph 2)

in·vari·able (in ver′ē ə bəl) *adj.* [ML *invariabilis*] not variable; not changing; constant; uniform —*n.* an invariable quantity; constant —**in·var′i·abil′·ity** *n.* or **in·var′i·able·ness** —**in·var′i·ably** *adv.*

mandate
(paragraph 6)

man·date (man′dāt′) *n.* ⟦L *mandatum*, neut. pp. of *mandare*, lit., to put into one's hand, command, entrust < *manus*, a hand + pp. of *dare*, to give: see MANUAL & DATE[1]⟧ **1** an authoritative order or command, esp. a written one **2** [Historical] *a*) a commission from the League of Nations to a country to administer some region, colony, etc. (cf. TRUSTEESHIP, sense 2) *b*) the area so administered (cf. TRUST TERRITORY) **3** the wishes of constituents expressed to a representative, legislature, etc., as through an election and regarded as an order **4** *Law a*) an order from a higher court or official to a lower one: a **mandate on remission** is a mandate from an appellate court to the lower court, communicating its decision in a case appealed *b*) in English law, a bailment of personal property with no consideration *c*) in Roman law, a commission or contract by which a person undertakes to do something for another, without recompense but with indemnity against loss *d*) any contract of agency —*vt.* **··dat′ed, ··dat′·ing 1** to assign (a region, etc.) as a mandate **2** to require as by law; make mandatory —**man·da′·tor** *n.*

misconception
(paragraph 5)

mis·con·ceive (mis′kən sēv′) *vt., vi.* **··ceived′, ··ceiv′·ing** to conceive wrongly; interpret incorrectly; misunderstand —**mis′·con·cep′·tion** (-sep′shən) *n.*

narcissistic
(paragraph 1)

nar·cis·sism (när′sə siz′əm; *chiefly Brit,* när sis′iz′əm) *n.* ⟦Ger *Narzissismus* (< *Narziss,* NARCISSUS) + *-ismus,* -ISM⟧ **1** self-love; interest, often excessive interest, in one's own appearance, comfort, importance, abilities, etc. **2** *Psychoanalysis* arrest at or regression to the first stage of libidinal development, in which the self is an object of erotic pleasure Also **nar′·cism′** —**nar′·cis·sist** *n., adj.* —**nar′·cis·sis′·tic** *adj.*

retina
(paragraph 2)

reti·na (ret″n ə) *n., pl.* **··nas** or **··nae** (-ē′) ⟦ML, prob. < L *rete* (gen. *retis*), net < IE base *ere-, loose, separate > Gr *erēmos,* solitary, Lith *rētis,* sieve & (prob.) L *rarus,* rare⟧ the innermost coat lining the interior of the eyeball, containing various layers of photoreceptive cells that are directly connected to the brain by means of the optic nerve: see EYE, illus.

5A VOCABULARY

Using the dictionary entries on pages 141–142, fill in the blanks.

1. The rear part of the eyeball that is sensitive to light is called the
   _____

2. In the United States the _____ of any person from employment because of his race, color, or sex is both illegal and immoral.

3. It is _____ when we discover that a public official has used his or her office to force people to pay bribes.

4. The diplomat spoke precisely, carefully _____ each word clearly for his audience.

5. Some people are so self-centered and convinced of their own importance that they can easily be labeled "_____."

6. The restaurant owners decided to _____ all smokers from the main dining room.

Name   Date

7. The higher court issued a _____ that reversed the lower court's ruling concerning discrimination.

8. A person with employable skills will _____ have better job opportunities than will a person without such skills.

9. An adult can _____ a child very quickly if that adult sets a bad example by breaking the law or by being cruel to people.

10. At the funeral the minister _____ special passages from the Bible.

11. The tenant was acting under the serious _____ that he could continue to occupy his apartment without paying rent.

5B   CENTRAL THEME AND MAIN IDEAS

Choose the best answer.

_____ 1. What is the central theme of "Darkness at Noon"?
  a. The author leads a very fulfilling life as a lawyer and husband.
  b. Blind people often have difficulty finding jobs because employers prefer to hire sighted people.
  c. Handicapped people need to organize and campaign for better laws to protect them.
  d. People often assume that because blind people cannot see, they cannot hear, learn, or work.

_____ 2. What is the main idea of paragraph 2?
  a. It is generally assumed that people who cannot see cannot hear.
  b. The way that many people behave in the presence of the blind can be described as downright "silly."
  c. Some people think that it is improper to use the word "blind" in the presence of blind people.
  d. Airline personnel use the number "76" to refer to blind people.

_____ 3. What is the main idea of paragraph 5?
  a. The worst frustration for the author was when 40 or more law firms refused to hire him because he was blind.
  b. Many employers think that if a lawyer cannot see, he or she cannot work.
  c. The author got his undergraduate degree from Harvard College and his law degree from Harvard Law School.
  d. The rejection letters sent to the author were disillusioning.

5C   MAJOR DETAILS

Decide whether each detail is Major *or* Minor *based on the context of the reading selection.*

_____ 1. The author has been blind from birth.

_____ 2. People often shout at blind people and pronounce every word with great care.

_____ 3. Airline personnel use a code to refer to blind people.

_____ 4. The author goes out to dinner with his wife, Kit.

_____ 5. If a blind person and a sighted person are together, other people will usually communicate with them by talking with the sighted person.

_____ 6. The author was given a year's leave of absence from his Washington law firm to study for a diploma-in-law degree at Oxford University.

_____ 7. The author had to be hospitalized while he was studying in England.

_____ 8. In 1976 the Department of Labor issued regulations that require equal employment opportunities for the handicapped.

_____ 9. On the whole, the business community's response to offering employment to the handicapped has been enthusiastic.

_____ 10. The author and his father played basketball in the backyard using a special system they had worked out.

_____ 11. The author's father shot for the basket and missed completely.

_____ 12. The neighbor's friend was not sure if the author or his father was blind.

5D   INFERENCES

Decide whether each statement can be inferred (Yes) *or cannot be inferred* (No) *from the reading selection.*

_____ 1. The title of the essay suggests that it is sighted people, not blind people, who cannot "see."

_____ 2. The author feels that he is greatly admired by people who meet him.

_____ 3. The author feels that he can make his point more effectively with humor than with a stern lecture.

Name   Date

_____ 4. The author often eats in restaurants with his wife, Kit.

_____ 5. The author was highly entertained by the conversation in the hospital between the elderly lady and the orderly.

_____ 6. The author got good grades at Harvard Law School because he was given special privileges reserved for blind students.

_____ 7. The April 10, 1976, Department of Labor regulations were enacted because the author had complained publicly about the discrimination he experienced while looking for a job.

_____ 8. The author's father was a much better basketball player than was the author.

5E CRITICAL READING: FACT OR OPINION

Decide whether each statement contains a Fact *or an* Opinion.

_____ 1. *From paragraph 1:* "Blind from birth, I have never had the opportunity to see myself [. . .]."

_____ 2. *From paragraph 2:* "[. . .] they fear that if the dread word is spoken, the ticket agent's retina will immediately detach [. . .]."

_____ 3. *From paragraph 3:* "I had been given a year's leave of absence from my Washington law firm to study for a diploma-in-law degree at Oxford University."

_____ 4. *From paragraph 5:* "I was turned down by over forty law firms because of my blindness [. . .]."

_____ 5. *From paragraph 6:* "By and large, the business community's response to offering employment to the disabled has been enthusiastic."

_____ 6. *From paragraph 7:* "Dad shot [the basketball] and missed the garage entirely."

5F CRITICAL READING: THE AUTHOR'S STRATEGIES

Choose the best answer.

_____ 1. The main audience for "Darkness at Noon" is
a. people who have been discriminated against.
b. people who do not trust blind people.
c. people who enjoy stories of achievement.
d. people who have treated the disabled badly.

_____ 2. The author's purpose in writing this essay is to
   a. narrate.
   b. entertain.
   c. expose.
   d. describe.

_____ 3. The author's tone in this reading is
   a. objective.
   b. happy.
   c. arrogant.
   d. emotional.

5G   READER'S PROCESS: SUMMARIZING YOUR READING

_____ 1. What is the best summary of "Darkness at Noon"?
   a. Harold Krents tells how his life is frustrating because of his blindness and how the government is changing the laws to make his life better.
   b. Harold Krents tells how people discriminated against him in his everyday life and in his employment search due to his blindness and how attitudes and perceptions of the disabled are slowly changing for the better.
   c. Harold Krents tells how employers refused to hire him because of his blindness even though he graduated from Harvard.
   d. Harold Krents tells how annoying people were to him because of his blindness and how federal regulations are making his life and the lives of other disabled people much easier.

5H   READER'S RESPONSE: TO DISCUSS OR WRITE ABOUT

1. How do you think physically handicapped people feel when they have to be with people who "can't see the person behind the handicap"? Using specific examples, explain your ideas fully.

2. In recent years our society has started to pay more attention to the needs of people who are physically handicapped. Do you think that society is doing enough? Using specific examples, explain your point of view.

HOW DID YOU DO?

5 Darkness at Noon

SKILL (number of items)	Number Correct		Points for each		Score
Vocabulary (11)	_____	×	3	=	_____
Central Theme and Main Ideas (3)	_____	×	4	=	_____
Major Details (12)	_____	×	2	=	_____
Inferences (8)	_____	×	2	=	_____
Critical Reading: Fact or Opinion (6)	_____	×	1	=	_____
Critical Reading: The Author's Strategies (3)	_____	×	2	=	_____
Reader's Process: Summarizing Your Reading (1)	_____	×	3	=	_____

(Possible Total: 100) *Total* _____

Ugly and Lovable

Larry Levin

LEARNING OBJECTIVES

- Explain how handicaps do not prevent people from achieving their goals.

THINKING: GETTING STARTED

- How would you react if you saw a pet being mistreated by its owner?

(1) Two months after our twin sons, Dan and Noah, turned 12, we had a family crisis. Buzzy, our black-and-white cat, began dying. We had rescued Buzz when he was 5 weeks old and he'd been a loving friend—a **boon** companion. But now he was 14 and the end was near.

(2) When I came home from work one Friday, he was lying beneath the dining-room table, unable to move. The next day the boys and I—heartbroken—took him to the hospital. We stroked him on the ride over, and then one of the technicians gently took Buzz from the carrier and into the treatment room. We all knew it was good-bye. I was both surprised and moved by my sons' willingness to confront sickness and death: it showed remarkable maturity and strength. It was also a testament to their deep connection with Buzz.

(3) Just as we were getting ready to leave, a staff member emerged from a back room with a pure-white pup on a leash. The dog was a visual **oxymoron.** The right side of him was adorable, but the left side of his face looked as if it had melted—it was all flamingo-pink scar tissue. His head appeared swollen, distorted. His right ear was flopped over itself. His left ear was a jagged stump of flesh a thumb's width high. The back of his lower left lip drooped below his jawline.

(4) As soon as this dog saw us, he started this strange little dance and strained toward us. Noah went down on one knee. With a sudden explosive force, the pup tore the leash out of the technician's grasp and rocketed into Noah, knocking him over. Noah fell backward and lay stretched out as the dog stood on his chest, licking his face without pause. The boys started laughing as Dan reached over and began to pet the dog, which **wriggled** over to him and lapped at his face. I went to join the excitement and cradled the dog in my arms as he licked my face and neck. When I touched the pup I felt that I had never met an animal with such soft fur. He was a **plush** toy come to life, as smooth as butter. The boys crowded

around and the pup covered us with kisses. We fell instantly and completely in love.

(5) I asked our vet, "What happened to him?" It seemed rather obvious to me that the dog had been badly burned in a fire.

(6) "He was a 'bait dog,'" the doctor answered matter-of-factly.

(7) "What?" I asked.

(8) "He was used as bait for a fighting dog. That's how they teach them to fight. They'll use anything they can get. Poodles, cats, you name it."

(9) "Where do they get them?"

(10) "Strays. Pet napping." He raised the first two fingers of each hand to form air quotes. "'Free to Good Home' ads. Wherever and however they can."

(11) "Where did this guy come from?" Dan asked.

(12) "He was brought into the ER several weeks ago right after a police raid. They found him bleeding to death in a cage. The SPCA told them to bring him here. We didn't expect him to survive."

(13) "Who does he belong to?" I asked, certain that an animal with such charm and personality and with so much affection—who had been at the hospital for several weeks—would by now have found an owner. When the vet told me, "No one," I felt amazingly fortunate.

(14) Then I said to the boys, grinning, "Guys? How about it? Should we adopt him?" They both agreed without the slightest moment's hesitation.

(15) The vet told us that the volunteer who was fostering him would continue his training—Oogy was only 4 months old—and then deliver him

People are attracted to dog fighting mainly because of greed. It is not unusual for $20,000 to $30,000 to change hands in a single fight.

to us in about a week. I felt giddy. After leaving the hospital I considered the uniqueness of the weekend's lessons. While facing the loss of a loved companion, we had begun Saturday morning consumed by sadness, without any indication that anything other than **bleakness** would be our lot for the day. Instead, we had encountered a totally opposite experience. I knew the boys would appreciate the way in which events had unfolded. It represented a lesson one rarely had the opportunity to illustrate with such **immediacy:** life going out one door and in another.

(16) And then I started thinking about a name. I laughed out loud. There was no way to deny it: This was one ugly dog. If his face had been a mask, no one would have wanted to wear it. Of course, I knew we could not call him that. We could not name a dog Ugly. And then my thoughts jumped to a term I had used when I was a teenager: "oogly," as in, "Man, that is one *oogly* sweater." And suddenly, just like that, I said Oogy out loud and knew without a doubt that that was it.

(17) We mourned Buzzy for weeks and to this day we remember him and the love he shared with tremendous fondness. But the gap in our lives was about to be filled in a sudden and decisive way. Ten days later the hospital volunteer's station wagon pulled up in our driveway a little after 9 A.M. Oogy placed his front paws on the top of the backseat, stared at me, his tail wagging furiously, and began to bark. When I opened the car door he rushed forward like air escaping a vacuum seal, and I scooped him up while he wiggled and licked me unrelentingly. "Hello, Oogy," I said. "From now on, that's you. You're Oogy. Oogy, Oogy, Oogy. Oogy for the rest of your days. You're in our family now."

(18) Oogy's first day with us went quickly, and soon enough it was bath time. I placed the puppy between my legs so I could massage his wounds with lotion as the vet had directed. I began with small, circular strokes to rub the dampened gauze pad over the raw pink flesh that was the left side of Oogy's head. It was as though I were trying to wipe away all that had happened to him. The blue liquid turned soapy-looking as I massaged the leathery skin. I talked quietly to him the entire time. "Yes," I told him, just as I would tell him every day for those first six months, "you're a *good* boy. This didn't happen because of you. This does not mean you're a bad doggy, an undeserving dog. We love you very much. You didn't deserve this. Nobody does. You're a lovely doggy. You'll never have to be scared again. No one and nothing will ever hurt you again." Oogy never moved or **fidgeted** or tried to pull away.

(19) After the wound cleaning, we were ready for the next phase of Oogy's introduction into our lives. Ever since the boys were born, we had read to them after bath time. Now that they were 12 and had their own bedrooms, we alternated rooms. Depending on how tired they were, the boys frequently fell asleep in the same bed. The first night Oogy was with us I read to them in Noah's room. I put a pillow against the wall and

stretched out across the foot of the bed. The boys climbed in and got under the covers. Oogy jumped onto the bed and curled up at their feet. I read for 20 minutes and by then Noah was asleep, as was Oogy. I asked Dan if he wanted to go back to his own room." Stay here," he mumbled, his eyes unable to open. Then he turned over onto his side and he, too, drifted off.

(20) The original plan had called for Oogy to spend his nights in the sheltering confines of his crate. But when the time came I simply could not bring myself to remove him from Noah's bed. Instead, I reached over and switched off the lamp. The picture of the three of them sleeping together that first night, illuminated by light outside the window, where a wind rustled the trees, imprinted itself **indelibly** in my memory. Two young boys, backs to each other, curling hair against pillows, and a little white one-eared dog between them. Then, exhausted by the whirlwind events of the day, the book on my lap, I drifted off, and we slept until my wife, Jennifer, came home and woke me.

(21) "Hello, Oogy," she whispered. "Welcome to our house." His tail thumped the bed, but other than that Oogy did not move. The little guy was surrounded by love for the first time in his life, and he wasn't about to give that up for anything.

Here are some of the more difficult words in "Ugly and Lovable."

bleakness
(paragraph 15)

bleak[1] (blēk) *adj.* ⟦ME *bleik* < ON *bleikr*, pale: see BLEACH⟧ **1** exposed to wind and cold; unsheltered; treeless; bare **2** cold and cutting; harsh **3** not cheerful; gloomy; dreary **4** not promising or hopeful *[a bleak future]* **5** [Obs.] pale; wan —**bleak'ly** *adv.* — **bleak'·ness** *n.*

boon
(paragraph 1)

boon[2] (bōōn) *adj.* ⟦ME & OFr *bon* < L *bonus*, good⟧ **1** [Archaic] kind, generous, pleasant, etc. **2** merry; convivial: now only in **boon companion**, a close friend

fidgeted
(paragraph 18)

fidget (fij'it) *n.* ⟦< obs. *fidge*, to fidget < ME *fichen* < ? or akin to ON *fikja*, to fidget⟧ **1** the state of being restless, nervous, or uneasy **2** a fidgety person —*vi.* to move about in a restless, nervous, or uneasy way —*vt.* to make restless or uneasy —**the fidgets** restless, uneasy feelings or movements

immediacy
(paragraph 15)

im·me·di·a·cy (i mē'dē ə sē) *n.* the quality or condition of being immediate; esp., direct pertinence or relevance to the present time, place, purpose, etc.

indelibly
(paragraph 20)

in·del·i·ble (in del'ə bəl) *adj.* ⟦L *indelibilis* < *in-*, not + *delibilis*, perishable < *delere*, to destroy: see DELETE⟧ **1** that cannot be erased, blotted out, eliminated, etc.; permanent; lasting **2** leaving an indelible mark *[indelible ink]* —**in·del'·ibil'·ity** *n.* —**in·del'·ibly** *adv.*

oxymoron
(paragraph 3)

oxy·mo·ron (äk'si môr'än') *n.,* pl. ··**mo'ra** (-rə) ⟦LGr *oxymōron* < neut. of *oxymōros*, acutely silly: see OXY-[2] & MORON⟧ a figure of speech in which opposite or contradictory ideas or terms are combined (Ex.: thunderous silence, sweet sorrow) —**ox'y·mo·ron'ic** *adj.*

plush
(paragraph 4)

plush (plush) *n.* 〔Fr *pluche* < *peluche* < OFr *peluchier*, to pluck < VL **piluccare:* see PLUCK〕 a fabric with a soft, thick, deep pile — *adj.* **1** of or made of plush **2** [Informal] luxurious, as in furnishings

wriggled
(paragraph 4)

wrig·gle (rig′əl) *vi.* --gled, --gling 〔MLowG *wriggeln,* akin to OFris *wrigia:* see WRY〕 **1** to move to and fro with a twisting, writhing motion; twist and turn; squirm **2** to move along with a wriggling motion **3** to make one's way by subtle or shifty means; dodge; equivocate /to *wriggle* out of a difficulty/ —*vt.* **1** to cause to wriggle **2** to bring into a specified condition, form, etc. by wriggling —*n.* a wriggling movement or action —**wrig′·gly** *ad* --**alier,** --**gli·est**

6A   VOCABULARY

Choose the best answer.

_____   1. If children **wriggled** when they were restless, they
      a. yawned.
      b. groaned.
      c. twisted.
      d. complained.

_____   2. Ideas that are **indelibly** written in a person's mind are
      a. indescribable.
      b. short-lived.
      c. deliberate.
      d. permanent.

_____   3. Two good friends who were **boon** companions would be
      a. boastful.
      b. overwhelmed.
      c. devastated.
      d. close.

_____   4. Carpet that is **plush** would feel
      a. soft.
      b. stiff.
      c. rough.
      d. damp.

_____   5. Showing **bleakness** in one's facial expressions is to display
      a. gloom.
      b. energy.
      c. cheerfulness.
      d. enthusiasm.

Name   Date

_____ 6. An example of an **oxymoron** is
   a. light as a feather.
   b. wise fool.
   c. he's as strong as an ox.
   d. "Peter Piper picked a peck of pickled peppers."

_____ 7. If making the arrangements for the anniversary celebration required **immediacy**, then the reply should be
   a. impressive.
   b. delayed.
   c. canceled.
   d. prompt.

_____ 8. If Micah **fidgeted** throughout the lecture, then he
   a. coughed.
   b. slept.
   c. moved.
   d. talked.

6B   CENTRAL THEME AND MAIN IDEAS

Choose the best answer.

_____ 1. What is the central theme of "Ugly and Lovable"?
   a. As a puppy, Oogy was a "bait dog" used to train other dogs to fight.
   b. From his very first night, Oogy was a beloved part of the family.
   c. Although abused and mutilated, Oogy brought the Levin family more love than they could ever have imagined.
   d. Oogy, covered with scars, missing an ear, and near death, was saved when the police brought him to the veterinarian's hospital.

_____ 2. What is the main idea of paragraph 2?
   a. The Levin boys' cat, Buzz, unable to move, was very sick.
   b. The Levin boys and their father took Buzz to the hospital.
   c. The technician at the hospital handled Buzz carefully.
   d. Knowing that their cat was very sick, the Levin boys accepted that it was time to have Buzz put down.

_____ 3. What is the main idea of paragraph 17?
   a. After being hospitalized for several weeks, Oogy was glad to be at the Levins' home.
   b. The sadness the Levins felt with the loss of Buzz was replaced with happiness when Oogy arrived.

c. The Levins grieved over the death of Buzz as they reflected on the happiness he had brought them.

d. A volunteer from the hospital delivered a happy Oogy to the waiting arms of Mr. Levin.

6C MAJOR DETAILS

Decide whether each detail listed here is Major *or* Minor *based on the context of the reading selection.*

_____ 1. The Levins had rescued Buzzy, the family cat, when he was five weeks old.

_____ 2. A staff member at the hospital emerged from the back room with a pure-white puppy on a leash.

_____ 3. Oogy's soft fur was as smooth as butter.

_____ 4. Oogy had been used as a bait dog.

_____ 5. The SPCA told the police to bring Oogy to the veterinarian's hospital.

_____ 6. Even after Oogy arrived at the Levins' home, Mr. Levin continued to treat his wounds.

_____ 7. Ever since Dan and Noah had been born, the parents read to them after their baths.

_____ 8. Rather than spending his first night in his crate, Oogy slept in Noah's bed.

6D INFERENCES

Choose the best answer.

_____ 1. *Read paragraph 4 again.* Oogy broke free from the technician's grasp because Oogy's

a. eyesight was poor, and he wanted to be able to see the Levins better.

b. keen sense of smell would tell him whether he could trust the Levinses.

c. leash on his neck was too tight, and he took the opportunity to break free.

d. need for a pat and assuring, loving, human touch was tremendous.

_____ 2. *Read paragraph 14 again.* Without hesitation, Dan and Noah agreed to adopt Oogy because
   a. they thought he would become a good guard dog.
   b. they saw an opportunity to take a pet no on else wanted.
   c. they realized he had the potential to both give and receive love.
   d. they felt that their father wanted them to adopt the dog.

_____ 3. *Read paragraph 20 again.* Mr. Levin let Oogy sleep in Noah's bed because
   a. Mr. Levin was too tired to take Oogy to his crate.
   b. Mr. Levin did not want to separate Oogy from the love and acceptance that Oogy and the boys shared.
   c. Mr. Levin did not want to run the risk of awakening the boys when he picked up Oogy.
   d. Mr. Levin believed Oogy would cry and whimper if he put him in his crate.

6E   CRITICAL READING: FACT AND OPINION

Decide whether each statement contains a Fact *or* Opinion.

_____ 1. *From paragraph 1:* "Two months after our twin sons, Dan and Noah, turned 12, we had a family crisis."

_____ 2. *From paragraph 4:* "He was a plush toy come to life, as smooth as butter."

_____ 3. *From paragraph 5:* "It seemed rather obvious to me that the dog had been badly burned in a fire."

_____ 4. *From paragraph 8:* "He was used as a bait dog for fighting."

_____ 5. *From paragraph 20:* "The picture of the three of them sleeping together that first night, illuminated by lights outside the window, where a wind rustled, imprinted itself indelibly in my memory."

_____ 6. *From paragraph 21:* "The little guy was surrounded by love for the first time in his life, and he wasn't about to give that up for anything."

6F   CRITICAL READING: THE AUTHOR'S STRATEGIES

Choose the best answer.

_____ 1. The main audience for "Ugly and Lovable" would be
   a. anyone who is considering pet adoption.
   b. anyone who is in need of inspiration.
   c. anyone who is interested in animal rescue.
   d. anyone who is involved with dog-fighting operations.

_____ 2. The author's purpose in writing this reading is to
   a. narrate.
   b. entertain.
   c. inform.
   d. convince.

_____ 3. The author's tone in this reading is
   a. playful.
   b. serious.
   c. arrogant.
   d. convincing.

6G   READER'S PROCESS: SUMMARIZING YOUR READING

_____ 1. What is the best summary of "Ugly and Lovable"?
   a. A bait dog was brought to the hospital of a veterinarian. A volunteer at the hospital continued to foster Oogy until he was well enough to be taken to the home of the Levins, who adopted him.
   b. Oogy, a bait dog, was recovering from wounds at a veterinarian's hospital. While the Levins were at the hospital, a technician walked out with Oogy. When the eyes of Oogy met those of the Levinses, they fell instantly in love with Oogy.
   c. Oogy was a bait dog found by police during a dog-fighting raid. Brought to the veterinarian's hospital, Oogy wasn't expected to survive but did. Unable to resist Oogy's charms, the Levinses decided to adopt him to replace their dying cat.
   d. Police rescued Oogy, who had been left to die in a cage by dog fighters. After several weeks of treatment and loving care by a veterinarian, Oogy recovered sufficiently to be offered for adoption.

6H   READER'S RESPONSE: TO DISCUSS OR WRITE ABOUT

1. Did you know that approximately 4 million adoptable dogs and cats are killed each year due to overpopulation? In animal shelters, 25–30 percent of those dogs for adoption are purebred. The other 70–75 percent, of course, are lovable, wonderful mixed-breed pets, just waiting for a chance to be someone's perfect new friend. Have you ever adopted a pet rather than buying one from a dog breeder or pet store? If so, what was your experience? If not, why would you choose to buy rather than adopt?

2. In a survey conducted by PetPlace.com, 76 percent of the dog owners called frequently or occasionally to leave a message on their

answering machine so that their dogs could hear their voices. When you are away from your pet, have you ever done this? Why or why not? If you don't have a pet, do you think this is a strange or acceptable practice? Explain.

HOW DID YOU DO?
6   Ugly and Lovable

SKILL (number of items)	Number Correct		Points for each		Score
Vocabulary (8)	_____	×	2	=	_____
Central Theme and Main Ideas (3)	_____	×	8	=	_____
Major Details (8)	_____	×	3	=	_____
Inferences (3)	_____	×	4	=	_____
Critical Reading: Fact or Opinion (6)	_____	×	2	=	_____
Critical Reading: The Author's Strategies (3)	_____	×	3	=	_____
Reader Response: Summarizing Your Reading (1)	_____	×	3	=	_____

(Possible Total: 100) *Total*   _____

Part 3

Thinking: Getting Started

"It is better to lose one minute in life . . . than to lose life in a minute."

Author Unknown

The selections in Part 3 concern people's actions, ranging from a young boy on a bicycle who is distracted by a friend's shout to a man hiding his inability to read from his employers, friends, and children.

Before you read each selection, think about these questions:

"Summer" (Selection 7)—Can you recall an incident from childhood when your actions caused a friend's injury?

"Brains the Ultimate Sex Appeal" (Selection 8)—Do you think "being educated" is as important as "being sexy"?

"Genes and Behavior" (Selection 9)—Which do you believe has a greater influence on human behavior—genes or environment?

"Divorcing Couples Seek Solace in Ring-Smashing Ceremonies" (Selection 10)—Would you want to commemorate the end of a marriage with a ceremony?

159

"Flour Children" (Selection 11)—Would you recommend high school students be required to take a course in sex education and parenting?

"The Magic Words Are 'Will You Help Me?'" (Selection 12)—Have you ever been in a situation in which you were too self-conscious to ask for help?

Summer

Jonathan Schwartz

LEARNING OBJECTIVES
- **Name the consequences of not being situationally aware.**

THINKING: GETTING STARTED
- **Can you recall an incident from childhood when your actions caused a friend's injury?**

(1) I am running down an alley with a stolen **avocado,** having climbed over a white brick fence and into the forbidden back yard of a carefully **manicured estate** at the corner of El Dorado and Crescent Drive in Beverly Hills, California. I have snatched a rock-hard Fuerte avocado from one of the three avocado trees near the fence. I have been told that many **ferocious** dogs patrol the grounds; they are killers, these dogs. I am **defying** them. They are nowhere to be found, except in my mind, and I'm out and gone and in the alley with their growls directing my imagination. I am running with fear and **exhilaration,** beginning a period of summer.

(2) Emerging from the shield of the alley I cut out into the open. Summer is about running, and I am running, protected by distance from the dogs. At the corner of Crescent Drive and Lomitas I spot Bobby Tornitzer on a bike. I shout *"Tornitzer!"* He turns his head. His bike wobbles. An automobile moving rapidly catches Tornitzer's back wheel. Tornitzer is thrown high into the air and onto the concrete sidewalk of Crescent Drive. The driver, a woman with gray hair, swirls from the car **hysterically** and **hovers** noisily over Tornitzer, who will not survive the accident. I hold the avocado to my chest and stand, frozen, across the street. I am shivering in the heat, and sink to my knees. It is approximately 3:30 in the afternoon. It is June 21, 1946. In seven days I will be 8 years old.

Although bike riding is a lot of fun, it can be hazardous. Wearing a helmet reduces injuries and death.

Here are some of the more difficult words in "Summer."

Vocabulary List

avocado
(paragraph 1)

☆**avo·cado** (av′ə kä′dō, ä′və-) *n., pl.* --**dos** ⟦altered (infl. by earlier Sp *avocado*, now *abogado*, advocate) < MexSp *aguacate* < Nahuatl *a:wakaλ*, avocado, lit., testicle; so named from its shape⟧ **1** a widespread, thick-skinned, pear-shaped tropical fruit, yellowish green to purplish black, with a single large seed and yellow, buttery flesh, used in salads; alligator pear **2** the tree (*Persea americana*) of the laurel family on which it grows **3** a yellowish-green color

AVOCADO

defying
(paragraph 1)

defy (dē fī′, di-; *also, for n.*, dē′fī) *vt.* --**fied′**, --**fy′·ing** ⟦ME *defien* < OFr *defier*, to distrust, repudiate, defy < LL *disfidare* < *dis*-, from + *fidare*, to trust < *fidus*, faithful: see FAITH⟧ **1** to resist or oppose boldly or openly **2** to resist completely in a baffling way [the puzzle *defied* solution] **3** to dare (someone) to do or prove something **4** [Archaic] to challenge (someone) to fight —*n., pl.* --**fies** a defiance or challenge

estate
(paragraph 1)

es·tate (ə stāt′, i-) *n.* ⟦ME & OFr *estat*, STATE⟧ **1** *a*) state or condition [to restore the theater to its former *estate*] *b*) a condition or stage of life [to come to man's *estate*] *c*) status or rank **2** [Historical] esp. in feudal times, any of the three social classes having specific political powers: the first estate was the Lords Spiritual (clergy), the second estate the Lords Temporal (nobility), and the third estate the Commons (bourgeoisie): see also FOURTH ESTATE **3** property; possessions; capital; fortune **4** the assets and liabilities of a dead or bankrupt person **5** landed property; individually owned piece of land containing a residence, esp. one that is large and maintained by great wealth **6** [Brit.] DEVELOPMENT (sense 4) **7** [Archaic] display of wealth; pomp **8** *Law a*) the degree, nature, extent, and quality of interest or ownership that one has in land or other property *b*) all the property, real or personal, owned by one

exhilaration
(paragraph 1)

ex·hila·rate (eg zil'ə rāt', ig-) *vt.* ··rat'ed, ··rat'·ing ⟦< L *exhilaratus*, pp. of *exhilarare*, to gladden < *ex-*, intens. + *hilarare*, to gladden < *hilaris*, glad: see HILARIOUS⟧ **1** to make cheerful, merry, or lively **2** to invigorate or stimulate —*SYN.* ANIMATE —**ex·hil'a·ra'tive** *adj.*
ex·hila·ra·tion (eg zil'ə rā'shən, ig-) *n.* ⟦LL *exhilaratio*⟧ **1** the act of exhilarating **2** an exhilarated condition or feeling; liveliness; high spirits; stimulation

ferocious
(paragraph 1)

fe·ro·cious (fə rō'shəs) *adj.* ⟦< L *ferox* (gen. *ferocis*), wild, untamed < *ferus*, FIERCE + base akin to *oculus*, EYE + -OUS⟧ **1** fierce; savage; violently cruel **2** [Informal] very great [a *ferocious* appetite] —**fe·ro'·ciously** *adv.* —**fe·ro'·cious·ness** *n.*

hovers
(paragraph 2)

hover (huv'ər, häv'-) *vi.* ⟦ME *hoveren*, freq. of *hoven*, to stay (suspended)⟧ **1** to stay suspended or flutter in the air near one place **2** to linger or wait close by, esp. in an overprotective, insistent, or anxious way **3** to be in an uncertain condition; waver (*between*) — *n.* the act of hovering —**hov'er·er** *n.*

hysterically
(paragraph 2)

hys·teri·cal (hi ster'i kəl) *adj.* ⟦prec. + -AL⟧ **1** of or characteristic of hysteria **2** *a)* like or suggestive of hysteria; emotionally uncontrolled and wild *b)* extremely comical **3** having or subject to hysteria —**hys·ter'i·cally** *adv.*

manicured
(paragraph 1)

mani·cure (man'i kyoor') *n.* ⟦Fr < L *manus*, a hand + *cura*, care: see CURE⟧ a trimming, cleaning, and sometimes polishing of the fingernails, esp. when done by a manicurist —*vt.* ··cured', ··cur'ing **1** *a)* to trim, polish, etc. (the fingernails) *b)* to give a manicure to **2** [Informal] to trim, clip, etc. meticulously [to *manicure* a lawn]

Vocabulary List

7A VOCABULARY

Match eight of the imaginary quotations with a vocabulary word listed on pages 162–163.

1. "If you walk too near that savage animal, it will attack you."

   _____

2. "Look at those neatly trimmed bushes and that beautifully edged lawn." _____

3. "Mr. Lloyd Dexter lives in a huge house surrounded by acres of woods." _____

4. "Sometimes my doctor prescribes pain killers for my headaches."

   _____

5. "The young parents ran to the lifeguard in a panic when they thought their child might be drowning." _____

6. "While the eggs are beginning to hatch, the bird is fluttering protectively over its nest." _____

7. "I think skydivers sometimes think they can ignore the laws of gravity." _____

8. "Wow! That ice cold shower certainly gives me a feeling of high spirits." _____

9. "What do you call that pear-shaped, yellowish-green fruit on the table?" _____

10. "No person should drive while under the influence of alcohol or drugs." _____

7B   MAIN IDEA AND IMAGES

Choose the best answer.

_____ 1. Another title for this story could be
    a. June 21, 1946.
    b. Killer Dogs.
    c. My Eighth Birthday.
    d. The Alley.

_____ 2. The main image in paragraph 1 is of a young boy
    a. climbing a white brick fence.
    b. snatching avocados.
    c. running with fear and exhilaration.
    d. defying ferocious dogs.

_____ 3. The main image in paragraph 2 is of
    a. Tornitzer riding his bike.
    b. the playful, then horrified boy.
    c. the seven-year-old emerging from the alley.
    d. the hysteria of the woman driver.

7C   MAJOR DETAILS

Decide whether each detail is Major *or* Minor *based on the context of the reading selection.*

_____ 1. The seven-year-old was running from imagined ferocious dogs.

_____ 2. The stolen avocado was still hard.

_____ 3. The avocado tree was on an estate.

_____ 4. The seven-year-old froze in horror when he saw the accident.

_____ 5. Bobby Tornitzer was riding his bike.

_____ 6. A car hit Tornitzer's bike.

_____ 7. Tornitzer was going to die.

_____ 8. A woman was driving the car.

_____ 9. The street was called Crescent Drive.

7D   INFERENCES

Decide whether each statement below can be inferred (Yes) or cannot be inferred (No) from the story.

_____ 1. Climbing over other people's fences is against the law.

_____ 2. This experience probably left a deep emotional scar on the seven-year-old.

_____ 3. The seven-year-old was being punished for stealing an avocado.

_____ 4. Seven-year-old children are destructive.

_____ 5. A single moment can drastically alter lives.

_____ 6. The seven-year-old hated Tornitzer.

_____ 7. Women are poor drivers.

_____ 8. The driver was drunk.

_____ 9. Tornitzer had recently arrived in America, and so he did not understand English very well.

_____10. Tornitzer was also seven years old.

7E   CRITICAL READING: THE AUTHOR'S STRATEGIES

Choose the best answer.

____ 1. The main audience for "Summer" is
    a. young readers.
    b. readers of fiction.
    c. readers of nonfiction.
    d. readers of all ages.

_____ 2. The author's purpose in writing this reading is to
   a. expose.
   b. persuade.
   c. narrate.
   d. describe.

_____ 3. The author's tone in this reading is
   a. upset.
   b. hard-hearted.
   c. gentle.
   d. pessimistic.

7F   READER'S PROCESS: SUMMARIZING YOUR READING

_____ 1. What is the best summary of "Summer"?
   a. A man tells how, at the age of seven years old, he shouted at a friend after stealing an avocado and caused the friend to be hit by a car.
   b. A man tells how, at the age of seven years old, he was responsible for the tragic death of a friend.
   c. A man tells how, at the age of seven years old, he stole an avocado and ran down the street in a state of excitement.
   d. A man tells how, at the age of seven years old, his childish act led to the tragic death of a friend who was run over by a car.

7G   READER'S RESPONSE: TO DISCUSS OR WRITE ABOUT

1. Was there a dramatic event, good or bad, in your childhood that you will never forget? Describe and discuss its effect on you.

2. What are your feelings about children who use the street rather than the sidewalk to jog, skate, or ride a bicycle? If they are hit by a car, should the driver be held responsible? Explain your point of view.

HOW DID YOU DO?
7 Summer

SKILL (number of items)	Number Correct		Points for each		Score
Vocabulary (10)	_____	×	3	=	_____
Main Ideas and Images (3)	_____	×	5	=	_____
Major Details (9)	_____	×	3	=	_____
Inferences (10)	_____	×	2	=	_____
Critical Reading: The Author's Strategies (3)	_____	×	2	=	_____
Reader's Process: Summarizing Your Reading (1)	_____	×	2	=	_____
	(Possible Total: 100) *Total*				_____

Brains the Ultimate Sex Appeal

Wendi C. Thomas

LEARNING OBJECTIVES

- Evaluate the value of intelligence as it relates to sex appeal.

THINKING: GETTING STARTED

- Do you think "being educated" is as important as "being sexy"?

(1) It's a question I've been asked more than once, most recently Saturday at a dinner party. "What will it take to get kids excited about learning?" It's a good question for which there is no one answer.

(2) It will take a combination of creative and committed teachers, adequate and well-spent funding, a focused school board and administration, involved parents, disciplined students, and a supportive faith and business community. And maybe, one more thing. "We need to make being educated sexy," said Reynaldo Glover, chairman of the board at Nashville's Fisk University. His comments came last month at a gathering of black opinion writers.

(3) Learning has to become sexy. Not jump-in-bed sexy. Just "he's a hottie" sexy. Desirable, attractive, **alluring.** Like Glover says, "If a guy can't read, he gets nothing." Unfortunately, that's not always the way it works. Too often, young men and women are **idolized** for their expensive jewelry, not their extensive vocabulary. We hold high those things that are **temporal** and fleeting, and look with **disdain** on those things, like a good education, that last.

(4) So just for the record, here's what's hot: Spending more on your car than your home. Buying more clothes than books. **Mangling** the English language. Dropping out of high school. Bragging about getting shot, committing crimes, or being uneducated.

(5) What is sexy? A bachelor's, master's or doctorate degree. Perfect **diction.** Familiarity with, if not command of, another language (Ebonics and slang don't count). Being able to have an intelligent conversation about current affairs. Having favorite authors, not just favorite albums.

(6) By these **criteria,** Waldon Hagan, who earned his PhD at the University of Memphis, is hot. Know what brought him to Memphis from a

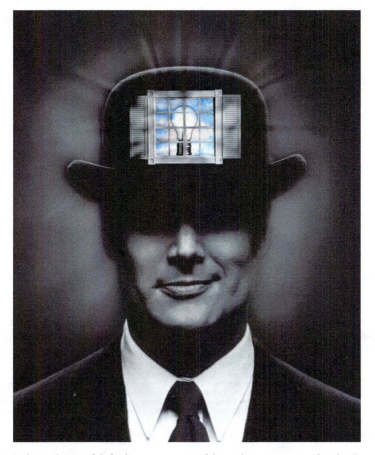

Is it sexist to think that sex appeal is as important as brains?

teaching job in Florida? A book, specifically James Baldwin's *If Beale Street Could Talk*. How hot is that? It's not that Hagan, now an administrator in Fisk University's education department, came from a **privileged** background. He grew up in the projects and only went to college after being rejected by the Marines.

(7) But somewhere along the way, learning changed him. Wednesday at the Memphis Cook Convention Center, the city and county will host the Learning for Success education **summit.** It's already a sellout, which is a good sign. The goal is to find solutions to the challenges facing public schools. The sessions scheduled are what you'd expect: on the No Child Left Behind Act, leadership development, and academic standards. Just maybe, they'll address what may be a missing link: how to make education sexy.

Here are some of the more difficult words in "Brains the Ultimate Sex Appeal."

Vocabulary List

alluring
(paragraph 3)

al·lur·ing (ə loor'iŋ, a-) *adj.* tempting strongly; highly attractive; charming —**al·lur'·ingly** *adv.*

criteria
(paragraph 6)

cri·te·ri·on (krī tir'ē ən) *n., pl.* **-ria** (-ē ə) or **-ri·ons** [< Gr *kritērion*, means of judging < *kritēs*, judge; akin to *kritikos*: see fol.] a standard, rule, or test by which something can be judged; measure of value —*SYN.* STANDARD

diction
(paragraph 5)

dic·tion (dik'shən) *n.* [L *dictio*, a speaking (in LL, word) < pp. of *dicere*, to say, orig., point out in words < IE base **deik-*, to point out > Gr *deiknynai*, to prove, Ger *zeigen*, to show, OE *teon*, to accuse, *tæcan*, TEACH] 1 manner of expression in words; choice of words; wording 2 manner of speaking or singing; enunciation

disdain
(paragraph 3)

dis·dain (dis dān') *vt.* [ME *disdeinen* < OFr *desdaignier* < VL **disdignare*, for LL *dedignare* < L *dedignari* < *dis-*, DIS- + *dignari*: see DEIGN] to regard or treat as unworthy or beneath one's dignity; specif., to refuse or reject with aloof contempt or scorn —*n.* the feeling, attitude, or expression of disdaining; aloof contempt or scorn —*SYN.* DESPISE

idolized
(paragraph 3)

idol·ize (īd''l īz') *vt.* **··ized', ··iz'ing** 1 to make an idol of 2 to love or admire excessively; adore —*vi.* to worship idols —**i'doli·za'·tion** *n.*

mangling
(paragraph 4)

man·gle[1] (maŋ'gəl) *vt.* **··gled, ··gling** [ME *manglen* < Anglo-Fr *mangler*, prob. freq. of OFr *mehaigner*, MAIM] 1 to mutilate or disfigure by repeatedly and roughly cutting, tearing, hacking, or crushing; lacerate and bruise badly 2 to spoil; botch; mar; garble [to *mangle* a text] —*SYN.* MAIM —**man'·gler** *n.*
man·gle[2] (maŋ'gəl) *n.* [Du *mangel* < Ger < MHG, dim. of *mange*, a mangle < L *manganum* < Gr *manganon*, war machine, orig. deceptive device < IE base **meng-*, to embellish deceptively > MIr *meng*, deceit, L *mango*, falsifying dealer] a machine for pressing and smoothing cloth, esp. sheets and other flat pieces, between heated rollers —*vt.* **··gled, ··gling** to press in a mangle —**man'·gler** *n.*

privileged
(paragraph 6)

privi·leged (-lijd) *adj.* 1 having one or more privileges 2 like or having the status of privileged communication; confidential 3 having special favored status 4 *Naut.* designating the vessel that has the right of way: see BURDENED

summit
(paragraph 7)

sum·mit (sum'it) *n.* [ME *sommete* < OFr, dim. of *som*, summit < L *summum*, highest part < *summus*, highest: see SUM] 1 the highest point, part, or elevation; top or apex 2 the highest degree or state; acme ☆3 a) the highest level of officials; specif., in connection with diplomatic negotiations, the level restricted to heads of government [a meeting at the *summit*] b) a conference at the summit —*adj.* ☆of the heads of government [a *summit* parley]

temporal
(paragraph 3)

tem·po·ral[1] (tem'pə rəl, -prəl) *adj.* [ME < L *temporalis* < *tempus*, time: see TEMPER] 1 lasting only for a time; transitory; temporary, not eternal 2 of this world; worldly, not spiritual 3 civil or secular rather than ecclesiastical 4 of or limited by time 5 *Gram.* expressing distinctions in time; pertaining to tense —*n.* a temporal thing, power, etc. —**tem'·po·rally** *adv.*
tem·po·ral[2] (tem'pə rəl, -prəl) *adj.* [LL *temporalis* < L *tempora*: see TEMPLE[2]] of or near the temple or temples (of the head)

8A VOCABULARY

Choose the best answer.

_____ 1. A **summit** refers to a meeting held
   a. at a satisfactory level for contestants.
   b. at the most appropriate time for participants.
   c. at an unusual location for tourists.
   d. with the highest level of officials.

_____ 2. A **privileged** background suggests growing up with
   a. regulations.
   b. advantages.
   c. relationships.
   d. hardships.

_____ 3. **Criteria** are standards used in making a
   a. judgment.
   b. paragraph.
   c. greeting.
   d. send-off.

_____ 4. An **alluring** advertisement is
   a. disappointing.
   b. attractive.
   c. colorless.
   d. unpleasant.

_____ 5. A radio announcer with good **diction** uses words that are
   a. sometimes controversial.
   b. easily understood.
   c. frequently inspirational.
   d. always convincing.

_____ 6. **Mangling** a language is
   a. shortening the vowel sounds.
   b. speaking distinctly.
   c. using three-syllable words.
   d. tearing it apart.

_____ 7. **Idolized** people are
   a. disliked.
   b. considerate.
   c. adored.
   d. ridiculed.

_____ 8. Things that are **temporal**
   a. hold up forever.
   b. last only a short time.
   c. retain their monetary value.
   d. appear in the night sky.

_____ 9. To show **disdain** is to
   a. exhibit preferred treatment.
   b. deny a privilege or right.
   c. show affection openly.
   d. look down on a person or thing.

8B   CENTRAL THEME AND MAIN IDEAS

Choose the best answer.

_____ 1. What is the central theme of "Brains the Ultimate Sex Appeal"?
   a. To solve the challenges facing public schools, Memphis hosted an education summit.
   b. High school dropouts are more likely to be interested in material possessions than in an education.
   c. One possible answer to getting students interested in learning is to make it desirable.
   d. A popular topic at dinner parties is "What will it take to get kids excited about learning?"

_____ 2. What is the main idea of paragraph 6?
   a. Waldon Hagan worked as a teacher in Florida.
   b. A book influenced Waldon Hagan to leave Florida for Memphis.
   c. Waldon Hagan grew up in the projects.
   d. James Baldwin is the author of _If Beale Street Could Talk._

8C   MAJOR DETAILS

Decide whether each detail is Major _or_ Minor _based on the context of the reading selection._

_____ 1. No one specific answer exists for getting students excited about learning.

_____ 2. According to Reynaldo Glover, making education sexy is a possible solution to get students interested in learning.

_____ 3. Reynaldo Glover made his comments about learning at Fisk University in Nashville.

Name   Date

_no___ 4. Somewhere along the way, learning changed Waldon Hagan.

_yi___ 5. Waldon Hagan earned his PhD at the University of Memphis.

_nd___ 6. Students often put more value on temporary, not lasting, things.

8D INFERENCES

Decide whether each statement can be inferred (Yes) or cannot be inferred (No) from the reading selection.

_No__ 1. The author, Wendi C. Thomas, is a public school teacher in Memphis.

_y___ 2. Reynaldo Glover's suggestion to make learning sexy is the best solution to resolve educational problems.

_y___ 3. Many black opinion writers agree with Reynaldo Glover's proposal—to get students excited about learning, make being educated sexy.

_NO__ 4. Students generally do not consider a college degree as "hot."

_NO__ 5. Waldon Hagan would have attended college even if he had not been rejected by the Marines.

_NO__ 6. Home ownership is not considered "hot" in some communities.

_No__ 7. One of the topics at the Learning for Success education summit was about the effect of drugs on young minds.

_y___ 8. Changing students' attitudes about learning begins with the parents.

8E CRITICAL READING: FACT OR OPINION

Decide whether each statement contains a Fact *or* Opinion.

_____ 1. *From paragraph 1:* "It's a question I've been asked more than once [. . .]."

_O___ 2. *From paragraph 3:* "If a guy can't read, he gets nothing."

_O___ 3. *From paragraph 3:* "Learning has to become sexy."

_F___ 4. *From paragraph 3:* "Too often, young men and women are idolized for their expensive jewelry, not their extensive vocabulary."

_____ 5. *From paragraph 7:* "The goal of the Learning for Success summit is to find solutions to the challenges facing public schools."

_____ 6. *From paragraph 6:* "He grew up in the projects."

8F   CRITICAL READING: THE AUTHOR'S STRATEGIES

Choose the best answer.

_____ 1. Wendi Thomas's main audience for "Brains the Ultimate Sex Appeal" is
   a. people who frequently attend dinner parties.
   b. general reading public, including students.
   c. teenage students and their young siblings.
   d. teachers, school board members, and school administrators.

_____ 2. The author's purpose in writing this reading is to
   a. inform.
   b. narrate.
   c. describe.
   d. entertain.

_____ 3. The author's tone in this reading is
   a. irrational.
   b. nostalgic.
   c. concerned.
   d. frustrated.

8G   READER'S PROCESS: SUMMARIZING YOUR READING

_____ 1. What is the best summary of "Brains the Ultimate Sex Appeal"?

   a. Young people care only about what's "hot," in cars, clothes, and street slang, which is why so many of them drop out of school and never achieve success in life.

   b. Being educated with an advanced degree and a well-developed vocabulary is not possible for many young people because they are not intelligent.

   c. Taking the trouble to finish high school and get a higher education is a waste of time for young people today because impressing peers is more important.

   d. Teachers, administrators, board members, parents, and the local community need to work together to show students that being educated is "sexy."

Name

Date

8H   READER'S RESPONSE: TO DISCUSS OR WRITE ABOUT

1. Motivation is probably the most significant issue educators can target to improve learning. If you had an opportunity to share your ideas with a panel of educators, what suggestions would you offer to motivate students to learn in elementary school? Middle school? High school?

2. Wendi Thomas listed a number of things considered "hot." Do you agree or disagree with the list? Why? What item(s) would you drop or add to the "hot" list?

HOW DID YOU DO?
8   Brains the Ultimate Sex Appeal

SKILL *(number of items)*	Number Correct		Points for each		Score
Vocabulary (9)	_____	×	2	=	_____
Central Theme and Main Ideas (2)	_____	×	8	=	_____
Major Details (6)	_____	×	3	=	_____
Inferences (8)	_____	×	3	=	_____
Critical Reading: Fact or Opinion (6)	_____	×	2	=	_____
Critical Reading: The Author's Strategies (3)	_____	×	3	=	_____
Reader's Process: Summarizing Your Reading (1)	_____	×	3	=	_____

(Possible Total: 100) *Total*   _____

Genes and Behavior: A Twin Legacy

Constance Holden

LEARNING OBJECTIVES

• Summarize the importance genes play in twins' traits.

THINKING: GETTING STARTED

• Which do you believe has a greater influence on human behavior—genes or environment?

(1) Biology may not be **destiny,** but **genes** apparently have a far greater influence on human behavior than is commonly thought. Similarities ranging from **phobias** to hobbies to bodily gestures are being found in pairs of twins separated at birth. Many of these behaviors are "things you would never think of looking at if you were going to study the **genetics** of behavior," says psychologist Thomas J. Bouchard, Jr., director of the Minnesota Center for Twin and Adoption Research at the University of Minnesota.

(2) Bouchard reports that so far, exhaustive psychological tests and questionnaires have been completed with approximately 50 pairs of **identical twins** reared apart, 25 pairs of **fraternal twins** reared apart and comparison groups of twins reared together. "We were amazed at the similarity in posture and expressive style," says Bouchard. "It's probably the feature of the study that's grabbed us the most." Twins tend to have similar mannerisms, gestures, speed and tempo in talking, habits, and jokes.

(3) Many of the twins dressed in similar fashion—one male pair who had never previously met arrived in England sporting identical beards, haircuts, wire-rimmed glasses and shirts. (Their photo shows them both with thumbs hooked into their pants tops.) One pair had practically the same items in their toilet cases, including the same brand of cologne and a Swedish brand of toothpaste.

(4) Although many of the separated pairs had differing types of jobs and educational levels, the investigators are finding repeated similarities in hobbies and interests—one pair were both volunteer firefighters, one pair were deputy sheriffs, a male pair had similar workshops in their basements and a female pair had strikingly similar kitchen arrangements. In one case, two women from different social classes, one of whom was a pharmacological technician and the other a bookkeeper and a high school dropout, had results on their **vocational**-interest tests that were "remarkably similar."

(5) Bouchard doesn't have enough information on abnormal behavior or **psychopathology** to make generalizations, but he has found repeated similarities. One pair of women were both very superstitious; another pair would burst into tears at the drop of a hat, and questioning revealed that both had done so since childhood. "They were on a talk show together and both started crying in response to one of the questions," says Bouchard. A third pair had the same fears and phobias. Both were afraid of water and had adopted the same coping strategy: backing into the ocean up to their knees. Bouchard took them to a shopping center one day, driving up a long, winding parking ramp to let them off. He later learned that they were both so frightened by the drive they sat on a bench for two hours to collect themselves.

(6) The most striking example of common psychopathology, however, came from a pair of fraternal twins reared apart. One had been reared by his own (poor) family; the other had been adopted into a "good solid upper-middle-class family." Both are now considered to be antisocial personalities, suffering from lack of impulse control, and both have criminal histories. Although fraternal twins share, on average, 50 percent of their genes, Bouchard suggests that the overlap is probably considerably more with this pair.

(7) Another eerie **congruence** that occurred in the absence of identical genes was observed in the case of two identical-twin women reared apart. Each has a son who has won a statewide mathematics contest, one in Wyoming, one in Texas.

The likelihood of having identical twins is about one in 250.

(8) Personality similarities between the identical twins reared apart are almost as **pervasive** as they are with identical twins reared together, according to the results of a test developed by University of Minnesota psychologist Auke Tellegen. His personality questionnaire contains scales such as "social closeness," "harm avoidance" and "well-being." The researchers were especially surprised to find that "traditionalism"—a trait implying **conservatism** and respect for authority—can be inherited. In fact, says Bouchard, his and other studies have found about 11 personality traits that appear to have significant genetic input.

(9) Overall, the emerging findings of the Minnesota study constitute a powerful **rebuttal** to those who maintain that environmental influences are the primary shaping forces of personality. The textbooks are going to have to be rewritten, Bouchard predicts.

Here are some of the more difficult words in "Genes and Behavior: A Twin Legacy."

Vocabulary List

congruence
(paragraph 7)

con·gru·ence (käŋ′grōō əns, kän′-; kən grōō′əns) *n.* ⟦ME < L *congruentia*: see fol.⟧ **1** the state or quality of being in agreement; correspondence; harmony **2** *Geom.* the property of a plane or solid figure whereby it coincides with another plane or solid figure after it is moved, rotated, or flipped over **3** *Math.* the relation between two integers each of which, when divided by a third (called the *modulus*), leaves the same remainder Also **con′·gru·ency**

conservatism
(paragraph 8)

con·serva·tism (kən sur′və tiz′əm) *n.* the principles and practices of a conservative person or party; tendency to oppose change in institutions and methods
con·serva·tive (kən sur′və tiv) *adj.* ⟦OFr *conservatif* < LL *conservativus*⟧ **1** conserving or tending to conserve; preservative **2** tending to preserve established traditions or institutions and to resist or oppose any changes in these [*conservative* politics, *conservative* art] **3** of or characteristic of a conservative **4** [C-] designating or of the major political party of Great Britain or the similar one in Canada that is characterized by conservative positions on social and economic issues ✩**5** moderate; cautious; safe [a *conservative* estimate] **6** [C-] *Judaism* designating or of a movement that accepts traditional forms and religious ritual that have been adapted to modern life with moderation and flexibility —*n.* **1** [Archaic] a preservative **2** a conservative person **3** [C-] a member of the Conservative Party of Great Britain or of the Progressive Conservative Party of Canada —**con·serv′a·tively** *adv.* —**con·serv′·a·tive·ness** *n.*

destiny
(paragraph 1)

des·tiny (des′tə nē) *n., pl.* ··nies ⟦ME *destine* < OFr *destinee*, fem. pp. of *destiner*: see prec.⟧ **1** the seemingly inevitable or necessary succession of events **2** what will necessarily happen to any person or thing; (one's) fate **3** that which determines events: said of either a supernatural agency or necessity —*SYN.* FATE

fraternal twins
(paragraph 2)

fra·ter·nal (frə tur′nəl) *adj.* ⟦ME < ML *fraternalis* < L *fraternus*, brotherly < *frater*, BROTHER⟧ **1** of or characteristic of a brother or brothers; brotherly **2** of or like a fraternal order or a fraternity **3** designating twins, of either the same or different sexes, developed from separately fertilized ova and thus having hereditary characteristics not necessarily the same: cf. IDENTICAL (sense 3) —**fra·ter′·nal·ism′** *n.* —**fra·ter′·nally** *adv.*

genes
(paragraph 1)

☆**gene** (jēn) *n.* ⟦< Ger *gen,* short for *pangen* (< *pan-,* PAN- + *-gen,* -GEN, after PANGENESIS)⟧ *Genetics* any of the units occurring at specific points on the chromosomes, by which hereditary characters are transmitted and determined: each is regarded as a particular state of organization of the chromatin in the chromosome, consisting primarily of DNA and protein: see DOMINANT, RECESSIVE, MENDEL'S LAWS

genetics
(paragraph 1)

ge·net·ics (jə net'iks) *n.* ⟦GENET(IC) + -ICS⟧ **1** the branch of biology that deals with heredity and variation in similar or related animals and plants **2** the genetic features or constitution of an individual, group, or kind

identical twins
(paragraph 2)

iden·ti·cal (ī den'ti kəl) *adj.* ⟦prec. + -AL⟧ **1** the very same **2** exactly alike or equal: often followed by *with* or *to* **3** designating twins, always of the same sex, developed from a single fertilized ovum and very much alike in physical appearance: cf. FRATERNAL (sense 3) —*SYN.* SAME —**iden'·ti·cally** *adv.*

pervasive
(paragraph 8)

per·va·sive (pər vā'siv) *adj.* tending to pervade or spread throughout —**per·va'·sively** *adv.* —**per·va'·sive·ness** *n.*

phobias
(paragraph 1)

pho·bia (fō'bē ə, fō'byə) *n.* ⟦ModL < Gr *phobos,* fear: see prec.⟧ an irrational, excessive, and persistent fear of some particular thing or situation

psychopathology
(paragraph 5)

psycho·pa·thol·ogy (sī'kō pə thäl'ə jē) *n.* ⟦PSYCHO- + PATHOLOGY⟧ **1** the science dealing with the causes and development of mental disorders **2** psychological malfunctioning, as in a mental disorder —**psy'cho·path'o·log'i·cal** (-path'ə läj'i kəl) *adj.* —**psy'cho·pa·thol'o·gist** *n.*

rebuttal
(paragraph 9)

re·but (ri but') *vt.* --**but'·ted,** --**but'·ting** ⟦ME *rebuten* < Anglo-Fr *reboter* < OFr *rebuter* < *re-,* back + *buter,* to thrust, push: see BUTT²⟧ **1** to contradict, refute, or oppose, esp. in a formal manner by argument, proof, etc., as in a debate **2** [Obs.] to force back; repel —*vi.* to provide opposing arguments —*SYN.* DISPROVE —**re·but'·table** *adj.*
re·but·tal (-but''l) *n.* a rebutting, esp. in law

vocational
(paragraph 4)

vo·ca·tional (-shə nəl) *adj.* **1** of a vocation, trade, occupation, etc. ☆**2** designating or of education, training, a school, etc. intended to prepare one for an occupation, sometimes specif. in a trade —**vo·ca'·tion·al·ism'** *n.* —**vo·ca'·tion·ally** *adv.*

9A   VOCABULARY

Using the vocabulary words listed on pages 178–179, fill in the blanks.

1. Police statistics show that there is _____ between the amount of drug use and the number of burglaries in any neighborhood.

2. Specific areas of the brain control specific behaviors, and as scientists' knowledge of such connections improves, methods may be developed to repair damaged or misformed parts of the brain and cure some kinds of _____.

3. Although some people believe that fate controls their lives, polls indicate that on the average, Americans believe that they control their own _____.

4. _____ is the study of heredity in animals and plants, including how _____ transmit various characteristics.

5. Students who plan to learn a trade choose to attend a _____ school.

6. People with excessive and persistent fears ought to seek professional counseling before _____ destroy their lives.

7. Expressions based on sports are _____ in our society; even people who have never seen a basketball game may speak of being "fouled" by an unfair competitor.

8. Most people think of twins as looking absolutely alike; actually, such complete resemblance is typical only of _____, and _____ often look very different from one another.

9. _____ of candidates who call for a return to the "good old days" is appealing to voters who are uncomfortable with rapid change.

10. The band members compiled a list of songs with social messages as a _____ to charges that rock music encourages irresponsible behavior.

9B   CENTRAL THEME AND MAIN IDEAS

Choose the best answer.

_____ 1. What is the central theme of "Genes and Behavior: A Twin Legacy"?
a. Extensive psychological tests and questionnaires have been completed by numbers of identical and fraternal twins.
b. Carefully controlled studies show that many identical as well as fraternal twins, even when they are reared apart, tend to dress in similar fashion.
c. Studies of twins, both identical and fraternal, provide evidence for the theory that genes have a greater influence on human behavior than is commonly thought.
d. Thorough research about both identical and fraternal twins reveals that even if they are raised apart, they generally share the same phobias, hobbies, and gestures.

_____ 2. What is the main idea of paragraph 2?
    a. Bouchard has studied fraternal and identical twins, some reared apart and some reared together.
    b. Bouchard has studied only identical twins, some reared apart and some together.
    c. Bouchard has studied only fraternal twins, some reared apart and some together.
    d. Bouchard has studied fraternal and identical twins, all of whom were raised apart.

_____ 3. What is the main idea of paragraph 5?
    a. Research shows that abnormal behavior in separated identical twins is rare.
    b. Studies reveal that female identical twins are more likely than male identical twins to develop fears and phobias.
    c. Fear of long, winding ramps seems to be genetically determined, according to the research of Dr. Bouchard.
    d. Researchers have not found enough examples of abnormal behavior in separated identical twins to be certain that a pattern exists.

9C   MAJOR DETAILS

Decide whether each detail is true (T), false (F), or not discussed (ND).

_____ 1. Thomas J. Bouchard is the director of the Minnesota Center for Twin and Adoption Research.

_____ 2. The behavior of separated twins is being compared with the behavior of a group of 25 pairs of twins raised together.

_____ 3. Even though many of the separated twins have different jobs, they often share the same hobbies and interests.

_____ 4. One pair of identical twins, who burst into tears easily, both cried when asked to appear on a talk show.

_____ 5. Twins who are afraid of water are usually also afraid of the dark and of animals.

_____ 6. One set of separated fraternal twins both had antisocial personalities and grew up to be criminals.

_____ 7. A woman's twin sons won mathematics competitions in Wyoming and Texas.

_____ 8. Social closeness is essential for happiness in humans.

_____ 9. Environmental influences are the most important shapers of personality.

_____ 10. Genes determine almost all personality traits.

9D   INFERENCES

Choose the best answer.

_____ 1. *Read paragraph 1 again.* What does the author mean by "Biology may not be destiny"?
   a. Most psychologists believe that biology controls people's destinies.
   b. Most psychologists believe that biology does not control people's destinies.
   c. The debate over whether biology or environment controls people's destinies has been going on for a long time.
   d. The author is not sure whether biology is destiny, so she is showing that she does not support the conclusions of Bouchard's study.

_____ 2. *Read paragraph 1 again.* Why does Bouchard say these behaviors are "things you would never think of looking at if you were going to study the genetics of behavior"?
   a. These behaviors seemed too unimportant for scientists to observe.
   b. These behaviors seemed too intimate to allow scientists to observe them.
   c. Psychologists assumed these relatively external characteristics could not be biologically based.
   d. Psychologists assumed that the causes of these behaviors were too complicated for current methods of observation.

_____ 3. *Read paragraph 5 again.* Why does Bouchard need more information before he can make generalizations?
   a. He has not yet found a strong pattern of particular kinds of abnormal behavior among separated identical twins.
   b. The government says researchers must have ten examples before they can make a generalization about a psychological issue.
   c. He is afraid of being sued if he makes a statement that might later be shown to be inaccurate.
   d. He does not want to embarrass the people in the small group he has studied, and so he is looking for additional, anonymous twins to study.

9E CRITICAL READING: THE AUTHOR'S STRATEGIES

Choose the best answer.

_____ 1. The main audience for "Genes and Behavior: A Twin Legacy" is
   a. people who are interested in the behavior of twins.
   b. people who are interested in the influence of genetics on human behavior.
   c. people who are interested in similarities of identical twins.
   d. people who are parents of twins.

_____ 2. The author's purpose in writing this reading is to
   a. persuade.
   b. entertain.
   c. inform.
   d. narrate.

_____ 3. The author's tone in this reading is
   a. grim.
   b. objective.
   c. sensational.
   d. sincere.

9F READER'S PROCESS: SUMMARIZING YOUR READING

_____ 1. What is the best summary of "Genes and Behavior: A Twin Legacy"?
   a. The writer reports on a study that showed that identical and fraternal twins have similar inherited traits.
   b. The writer reports on a study that showed striking similarities in the personalities, behavior, and interests of twins who were reared apart.
   c. The writer reports on a study that showed that genetics is an important factor in predicting human behavior.
   d. The writer reports on a study that showed that twins share many traits.

9G   READER'S RESPONSE: TO DISCUSS OR WRITE ABOUT

1. Should parents of twins encourage them to dress and act differently or alike? Using specific examples, explain your point of view.

2. Sometimes fertility drugs are used by women to increase the possibility of pregnancy. Women who use these drugs sometimes have multiple births of four or more children. How do you feel about this? Are these women violating the Law of Nature? Give specific reasons to support your point of view.

HOW DID YOU DO?
14   Genes and Behavior: A Twin Legacy

SKILL (number of items)	Number Correct		Points for each		Score
Vocabulary* (12)	_____	×	3	=	_____
Central Theme and Main Ideas (3)	_____	×	4	=	_____
Major Details (10)	_____	×	3	=	_____
Inferences (3)	_____	×	3	=	_____
Critical Reading: The Author's Strategies (3)	_____	×	3	=	_____
Reader's Process: Summarizing Your Reading (1)	_____	×	4	=	_____
			(Possible Total: 100) *Total*		_____

*Questions 4 and 8 in this exercise call for two separate answers each. In computing your score, count each separate answer toward your number correct.

Name   Date

Divorcing Couples Seek Solace in Ring-Smashing Ceremonies

Sandra Barron

LEARNING OBJECTIVES

- Describe a divorce ceremony unique to the Japanese culture.

THINKING: GETTING STARTED

- Would you want to commemorate the end of a marriage with a ceremony?

(1) When Hiroki Terai was a child, he once asked his parents why there was no such thing as a divorce ceremony; and they laughed at him. Now, as Japan's first professional "**charisma** divorce planner," he watches with satisfaction as soon-to-be-former couples join hands on a **mallet** and smash rings, beginning new, separate lives.

(2) Last March, a friend of Terai's from college, on the verge of his own divorce, echoed that life-long question. "Japanese culture celebrates both beginnings and endings," he said. "Why is only the beginning of a marriage marked?" A month later, Terai held his first divorce ceremony for that friend at a restaurant in Shinjuku. Word got out, and it struck a chord. Requests started coming in. After performing a few more on his own, he teamed up with day-trip specialists Friendly Travel to run the ceremonies as a half-day package tour for ¥3,000 per person.

(3) The parting couple meets near Sensoji Temple in Asakusa and rides in separate **rickshaws** with friends and relatives following on foot to a "Divorce Mansion," a **doppelganger** of Japan's **ubiquitous** wedding halls. There, they stand before their guests and listen as Terai recounts the circumstances leading up to the decision to separate (they've briefed him in individual meetings beforehand). He says that although one side, usually the wife, will often demand a blunt statement about exactly what went wrong, he opts for tact. "I won't just come out and say 'he cheated,'" Terai says. "I'll say something indirect that gets the message across. And I always add that 'there are surely circumstances known only to the two people involved.'"

(4) The guests of honor each make speeches; and then, as at a Japanese wedding party, one person is chosen to speak on behalf of the assembled friends, preferably someone who has been divorced. This speech almost always starts with *"Rikon omedeto gozaimasu"* (congratulations on your

divorce). The friend emphasizes that divorce is another kind of beginning, and that friends will continue to be there. Up until this point, there's "a strange sort of vibe," Terai says. "People don't know how to respond, whether they should clap or stay quiet."

(5) Then comes the key moment: the smashing of the rings. "I based it on the image of the cake cutting." In their "final joint act," the two each put one hand on a mallet. In a light-hearted stroke of symbolism, the mallet has a frog on it to represent the couple "changing" into singles. (The words for "frog" and "change" are homonyms in Japanese.) After the smashing of the rings, Terai says the mood changes as well. The audience applauds spontaneously, and looks of relief and happiness come over the couple.

(6) Staying with the *kaeru* theme, the Divorce Mansion's **mascot** is a friendly looking pink frog statue Terai had made to order. The battered rings are dropped into the frog's mouth and left there. Although the statue seems to be giving the peace sign, it's actually flashing a warning of sorts: Terai said the **gesture** reflects the fact that, with the most recent stats at 250,000 divorces a year, "two out of six couples in Japan get divorced." The frog may be cartoonish, but the ceremonies are absolutely no joke.

(7) "Once a couple has decided to break up, I'd like to see them make a clean, clear break that lets them both move forward," Terai says. "The

A Japanese couple uses a hammer to smash one of their wedding rings to symbolize the end of their 13-year marriage during their "divorce ceremony."

message is really powerful." The reaction has been serious, too. Terai says he's gotten about a hundred inquiries from people across Japan who say they would like to start similar services. And although he's ushered only 23 couples to singledom, he says he's gotten hundreds more requests for ceremonies that didn't reach the final stages of planning because— surprise—the couples wouldn't work on it together.

(8) Although the divorce rate in Japan has been on a gentle decline since peaking in 2002, you wouldn't know it from its appearance lately in the news and pop culture. Attention has been drawn to divorce both by high-profile international child custody cases and **lurid** stories of *wakaresaseya*, the shady business of hiring an actor who serves as both temptation and private eye to (among other things) break up marriages.

(9) NHK (Japanese Broadcasting Corporation), following up last year's comedy-drama "Konkatsu Rikatsu" (Marriage Seeking, Divorce Seeking), is now running a five-part drama called "Rikon Dokyo" (Divorce Cohabitation) based on a popular manga of the same name by Cocco Kashiwaya. The story is about a divorced couple with a young daughter who split up after eight years of marriage and then move back in together for financial reasons.

(10) Smell the potential for a happy ending? So does Terai, at least once in a while. Two of his ceremonies have ended up with the couples deciding to stay together. One man and woman, both in their fifties, reached the end of the ceremony and then decided to reconsider after they missed the rings with three blows in a row. Not so fast with the hearts and doves, though. Since he started being profiled in the Japanese and Korean media in the last year, Terai has had over 800 total inquiries. With bookings well into the future, we don't think he'll be out of work any time soon.

Here are some of the more difficult words in "Divorcing Couples Seek Solace in Ring-Smashing Ceremonies."

charisma
(paragraph 1)

cha·ris·ma (kə rɪz'mə) *n., pl.*
--mata (-mə tə) [[Gr(Ec), gift of God's grace < Gr, favor, grace < *charizesthai*, to show favor to < *charis*, grace, beauty, kindness < *chairein*, to rejoice at < IE base *ĝher-, to desire, like > YEARN]] **1** *Christian Theol.* a divinely inspired gift, grace, or talent, as for prophesying, healing, etc.: also **char·ism** (kar'iz'əm) **2** a special quality of leadership that captures the popular imagination and inspires allegiance and devotion **3** a special charm or allure that inspires fascination or devotion [the film star's *charisma*]

doppelganger
(paragraph 3)

doppel·gäng·er (däp'əl geŋ'ər) *n.* [[Ger < *doppel*, double + *gänger*, goer: see GANG²]] the supposed ghostly double or wraith of a living person

gesture
(paragraph 6)

ges·ture (jes'chər) *n.* [[ME < ML *gestura*, mode of action < L *gestus*, pp. of *gerere*, to bear, carry]] **1** a movement, or movements collectively, of the body, or of part of the body, to express or emphasize ideas, emotions, etc. **2** anything said or done to convey a state of mind, intention, etc.; often, something said or done merely for effect or as a formality [a *gesture* of sympathy] —*vi.* **·tured, ·tur·ing** to make or use a gesture or gestures —*vt.* to express with a gesture or gestures —**ges'·tural** *adj.* —**ges'·turer** *n.*

Vocabulary List

187

lurid
(paragraph 8)

lu·rid (loor′id) *adj.* 〚L *luridus*, pale yellow, ghastly〛 **1** [Rare] deathly pale; wan **2** glowing through a haze, as flames enveloped by smoke **3** *a)* vivid in a harsh or shocking way; startling; sensational *b)* characterized by violent passion or crime *[a lurid* tale*]* —**lu′·rid·ly** *adv.* —**lu′·rid·ness** *n.*

mallet
(paragraph 1)

mal·let (mal′ət) *n.* 〚ME *malyet* < MFr *maillet,* dim. of *mail* < OFr *maile:* see MAUL〛 **1** a kind of hammer, usually with a heavy wooden head and a short handle, for driving a chisel, etc.: see HAMMER, illus. **2** *a)* a long-handled hammer with a cylindrical wooden head, used in playing croquet *b)* a similar instrument, but with a longer, flexible handle, used in playing polo **3** a small, light hammer, usually with a felt-covered head, used for playing a vibraphone, xylophone, etc.

mascot
(paragraph 6)

mas·cot (mas′kät′, -kət) *n.* 〚Fr *mascotte* < Prov *mascot,* dim. of *masco,* sorcerer (< ?): in pop. use, after *La Mascotte* (1880), operetta by E. *Audran* (1840-1901), Fr composer〛 **1** any person, animal, or thing supposed to bring good luck **2** any person, animal, or thing adopted by a group, esp. a sports team as a symbol or for good luck *[the team's mascot* is a bear*]*

rickshaws
(paragraph 3)

rick·shaw or **rick·sha** (rik′shô′) *n.* JINRIKISHA

ubiquitous
(paragraph 3)

ubiqui·tous (yōō bik′wə təs) *adj.* 〚see fol. & -OUS〛 present, or seeming to be present, everywhere at the same time; omnipresent —**ubiq′ui·tously** *adv.* —**ubiq′ui·tous·ness** *n.*

10A   VOCABULARY

Choose the best answer.

_____ 1. **Charisma** is best defined as
   a. arrogance.
   b. talkativeness.
   c. charm.
   d. professionalism.

_____ 2. A **doppelganger** would be a
   a. symbol.
   b. decorated entry.
   c. radar device.
   d. ghost.

_____ 3. **Gesture** can best be understood as
   a. agreement.
   b. movement.
   c. penalty.
   d. ceremony.

Name   Date

_____ 4. A **lurid** story would be
   a. untrue.
   b. amusing.
   c. bland.
   d. shocking.

_____ 5. A **mallet** is a type of
   a. hammer.
   b. tablet.
   c. mat.
   d. glove.

_____ 6. A **mascot** is supposed to bring
   a. intelligence.
   b. protection.
   c. good luck.
   d. wealth.

_____ 7. **Rickshaws** are used for
   a. conversation.
   b. entertainment.
   c. warmth.
   d. transportation.

_____ 8. If something is **ubiquitous,** it is
   a. weather resistant.
   b. present everywhere.
   c. often hidden.
   d. badly maintained.

10B   CENTRAL THEME AND MAIN IDEAS

Choose the best answer.

_____ 1. What is the central theme of "Divorcing Couples Seek Solace in Ring-Smashing Ceremonies"?
   a. The divorce rate is on the decline in Japan.
   b. The divorce ceremony in Japan makes divorcing inexpensive.
   c. Divorce ceremonies are a thriving business in Japan.
   d. A divorce ceremony often provides an acceptable way out for couples who are divorcing.

_____ 2. What is the main idea of paragraph 6?
   a. The Divorce Mansion's mascot is a pink frog statue.
   b. Fewer than 50 percent of Japanese marriages end in divorce.
   c. The divorce ceremony recognizes the seriousness of divorce through a light-hearted ritual.
   d. The Divorce Mansion's mascot appears to give the peace sign.

10C MAJOR DETAILS

Decide whether each detail is true (T), false (F), or not discussed (ND).

_____ 1. Hiroki Terai is Japan's first professional divorce planner.

_____ 2. Terai's first divorce ceremony was held for a childhood friend of his in a restaurant.

_____ 3. The so-called Divorce Mansion was converted from a garage in Tokyo's Asakusa area.

_____ 4. The parting couple, relatives, and friends meet near Sensoji Temple and then walk to the Divorce Mansion.

_____ 5. The word "frog" sounds the same as the word "change" in Japanese.

_____ 6. The divorce rate in Japan is on the increase.

_____ 7. Friends and relatives bring congratulatory money in envelopes to give the parting couple at the ceremony.

_____ 8. As part of the divorce ceremony, one person speaks on behalf of the assembled friends.

10D INFERENCES

Decide whether each statement that follows can be inferred (Yes) or cannot be inferred (No) from the reading selection.

_____ 1. Divorce ceremonies are gaining popularity in Japan.

_____ 2. The parting couple dresses in formal attire at the divorce ceremony.

_____ 3. The holding of the hammer symbolizes the couple's last cooperative act before they smash their wedding rings.

_____ 4. In Japan, women often give up on divorce for the sake of their children.

_____ 5. Parting couples must fill out and sign a formal application at a government office before the divorce ceremony.

Name   Date

10E   CRITICAL READING: THE AUTHOR'S STRATEGIES

Choose the best answer.

_____ 1. The main audience for "Divorcing Couples Seek Solace in Ring-Smashing Ceremonies" is
a. people who are considering a divorce.
b. people who are interested in Japanese traditions and ceremonies.
c. people who are thinking about opening a divorce ceremony business.
d. people who are planning to take a vacation in Japan.

_____ 2. The author's purpose in writing this reading is to
a. convince.
b. describe.
c. inform.
d. narrate.

_____ 3. The author's tone in this reading is
a. comical.
b. resentful.
c. reflective.
d. pessimistic.

10F   READER'S PROCESS: SUMMARIZING YOUR READING

_____ 1. What is the best summary of "Divorcing Couples Seek Solace in Ring-Smashing Ceremonies"?
a. The divorce ceremony gives Japanese women an opportunity to speak out publicly about their dissatisfaction and unhappiness during their marriage.
b. Rather than end on a sad note, the divorce ceremony provides the Japanese a social occasion to untie the knot before friends and family.
c. Hiroki Terai, Japan's first divorce ceremony planner, came up with the idea for a money-making business, which has the possibility of spreading through Asia.
d. The divorce ceremony, which is held in a Divorce Mansion, ends in a ring-smashing with a giant frog-shaped hammer.

10G　READER'S RESPONSE: TO DISCUSS OR WRITE ABOUT

1. Many people get married with big, elaborate, expensive ceremonies. Given that half the marriages in the United States end in divorce, would you be willing to spend an additional $600 (in American money) for a divorce ceremony? Explain. What advantages or disadvantages do you see in such a ceremony? Do we have anything comparable to the divorce ceremony in the United States?

2. In the United States, divorce has become an increasing reality in the past century. Marriage is no longer considered a permanent institution. Why is divorce no longer the taboo it once was? What are the major reasons for divorce? How does divorce affect the children of divorced parents? Explain.

HOW DID YOU DO?
10　Divorcing Couples Seek Solace in Ring-Smashing Ceremonies

SKILL (number of items)	Number Correct		Points for each		Score
Vocabulary (8)	_____	×	3	=	_____
Central Theme and Main Ideas (2)	_____	×	6	=	_____
Major Details (8)	_____	×	3	=	_____
Inferences (5)	_____	×	5	=	_____
Critical Reading: The Author's Strategies (3)	_____	×	4	=	_____
Reader's Process: Summarizing Your Reading (1)	_____	×	3	=	_____
(Possible Total: 100) Total					_____

Flour Children

Lexine Alpert

LEARNING OBJECTIVES

- Enumerate responsibilities associated with a teen pregnancy.

THINKING: GETTING STARTED

- Would you recommend that high school students be required to take a course in sex education and parenting?

(1) "Hey, Mister V., what are you doing dressed like that?" says a student as he enters the classroom at San Francisco's Mission High School. "I'm getting ready to deliver your baby," replies the sex education teacher, in surgical greens from cap to booties. "Do you have to take this thing so seriously?" asks another, laughing nervously as she watches her teacher bring out rubber gloves. "Yes, babies are a serious matter," he answers. As the students settle into their seats, Robert Valverde, who has been teaching sex education for four years—and "delivering babies" for three—raises his voice to **convene** the class.

(2) "Welcome to the nursery," he announces. "Please don't breathe on the babies. I just brought them from the hospital." The students' giggles quickly change to moans as Valverde delivers a "baby"—a five-pound sack of flour—to each student. "You must treat your baby as if it were real twenty-four hours a day for the next three weeks," he says. "It must be brought to every class. You cannot put the baby in your locker or your backpack. It must be carried like a baby, lovingly, and carefully in your arms. Students with jobs or other activities must find babysitters." To make sure the baby is being cared for at night and on weekends, Valverde calls his students at random. "If the baby is lost or broken, you must call a funeral parlor and find what it would cost to have a funeral," he says. The **consequence** is a new, heavier baby—a ten-pound flour sack.

(3) Valverde came up with the flour baby idea after hearing that some sex education classes assign students the care of an egg; he decided to try something more realistic. "A flour sack is heavier and more **cumbersome**—more like a real baby," Valverde says. To heighten the realism, he has the students dress their five-pound sacks in babies' clothes, complete with diaper, blanket, and bottle.

(4) "The primary goal is to teach responsibility," says Valverde. "I want those who can't do it to see that they can't, and to acknowledge that the

In "Baby Think It Over," a program designed to deter teen pregnancy, students learn parenting responsibility. Carrie takes a history test while she holds a key in the baby's back to keep it from crying.

students who can are doing something that is very difficult and embarrassing." After 36 classes and more than a thousand students, Valverde's project seems to be having the effect he wants. "I look at all the **circumstantial** evidence—the kids are talking to their parents in ways they never have before, and for the first time in their lives, they are forced to respond to an external environment. They have to fill out forms every day saying where they'll be that night and who's taking care of the baby. If their plans change I make them call me and say who's with the baby. They're forced to **confront** people's comments about their babies."

(5) Lupe Tiernan, vice-principal of the **predominantly** Hispanic and Asian inner-city high school, believes Valverde's class has helped to maintain the low number of teenage pregnancies at her school. "His students learn that having a baby is a **novelty** that wears off very quickly, and by three weeks, they no longer want any part of it," she says.

(6) At the beginning of the assignment, some students' parental **instincts** emerge right away. During the first week, sophomore Cylenna Terry took the rules so seriously that she was kicked out of her English class for refusing to take the baby off her lap and place it on the floor as instructed. "I

said, 'No way am I putting my baby on the floor.'" Others, especially the boys, learn early that they can't cope with their new role. "I just couldn't carry the baby around," says Enrique Alday, 15. "At my age it was too embarrassing so I just threw it in my locker." He failed the class.

(7) By the second week, much of the novelty has worn off and the students begin to feel the babies are **intruding** on their lives. "Why does it have to be so heavy?" Cylenna Terry grumbles. "It's raining out—how am I supposed to carry this baby and open up my umbrella at the same time?" She has noticed other changes as well. "There's no way a boy is even going to look at me when I have this in my arms. No guys want to be involved with a girl who has a baby—they just stay clear."

(8) Rommel Perez misses baseball practice because he can't find a babysitter. Duane Broussard, who has helped care for his one-year-old nephew who lives in his household, learns new respect for how hard his mother and sister work at childcare. "At least this baby doesn't wake me in the middle of the night," he says. Maria Salinis says, "My boyfriend was always complaining about the sack and was feeling embarrassed about having it around. I told him, 'Imagine if it was a real baby.' It made us ask important questions of one another that we had never before considered."

(9) On the last day of the assignment, the temporary parents come to class dragging their feet. Valverde calls the students one by one to the front of the room to turn in their babies. Most, their paper skin now fragile from wear, are returned neatly **swaddled** in a clean blanket. But others have ended up broken and lying in the bottom of a trash bin; a half-dozen students wound up with ten-pound babies. The students' **consensus** is that babies have no place in their young lives. "I know that if I had a baby it would mess up my future and hold me down. After this class, I don't want to have a baby. I couldn't handle it," says 15-year-old Erla Garcia. "It was only a sack of flour that didn't cry or scream, didn't need to be fed or put to sleep, and I still couldn't wait to get rid of it."

Here are some of the more difficult words in "Flour Children."

circumstantial (paragraph 4)	**cir·cum·stan·tial** (sur'kəm stan'shəl) *adj.* **1** having to do with, or depending on, circumstances **2** not of primary importance; incidental **3** full or complete in detail **4** full of pomp or display; ceremonial —**cir'·cum·stan'·tially** *adv.*
confront (paragraph 4)	**con·front** (kən frunt') *vt.* [Fr *confronter* < ML *confrontare* < L *com-*, together + *frons*, forehead: see FRONT¹] **1** to face; stand or meet face to face **2** to face or oppose boldly, defiantly, or antagonistically **3** to bring face to face (*with*) [to *confront* someone with the facts] **4** to set side by side to compare —**con·fron·ta·tion** (kän' frən tā'shən) *n.* or **con·front'al** —**con'·fron·ta'·tion·al** *adj.* —**con'·fron·ta'·tion·ist** *n., adj.*

Vocabulary List

consensus
(paragraph 9)

con·sen·sus (kən sen′səs) *n.* ⟦L < pp. of *consentire:* see fol.⟧ **1** an opinion held by all or most **2** general agreement, esp. in opinion

consequence
(paragraph 2)

con·se·quence (kän′si kwens′, -kwəns) *n.* ⟦OFr < L *consequentia* < *consequens,* prp. of *consequi,* to follow after < *com-,* with + *sequi,* to follow: see SEQUENT⟧ **1** a result of an action, process, etc.; outcome; effect **2** a logical result or conclusion; inference **3** the relation of effect to cause **4** importance as a cause or influence *[a matter of slight consequence]* **5** importance in rank; influence *[a person of consequence]* —*SYN.* EFFECT, IMPORTANCE —**in consequence (of)** as a result (of) —**take the consequences** to accept the results of one's actions

convene
(paragraph 1)

con·vene (kən vēn′) *vi.* ··vened′, ··ven′ing ⟦ME *convenen* < OFr *convenir* < L *convenire* < *com-,* together + *venire,* to COME⟧ to meet together; assemble, esp. for a common purpose —*vt.* **1** to cause to assemble, or meet together **2** to summon before a court of law — *SYN.* CALL —**con·ven′er** *n.*

cumbersome
(paragraph 3)

cum·ber·some (kum′bər səm) *adj.* hard to handle or deal with as because of size, weight, or many parts; burdensome; unwieldy; clumsy —*SYN.* HEAVY —**cum′·ber·somely** *adv.* —**cum′·ber·some·ness** *n.*

instincts
(paragraph 6)

in·stinct (in′stiŋkt′; *for adj.* in stiŋkt′, in′stiŋkt′) *n.* ⟦< L *instinctus,* pp. of *instinguere,* to impel, instigate < *in-,* in + **stinguere,* to prick: for IE base see STICK⟧ **1** (an) inborn tendency to behave in a way characteristic of a species; natural, unlearned, predictable response to stimuli *[suckling is an instinct in mammals]* **2** a natural or acquired tendency, aptitude, or talent; bent; knack; gift *[an instinct for doing the right thing]* **3** *Psychoanalysis* a primal psychic force or drive, as fear, love, or anger; specif., in Freudian analysis, either the life instinct (Eros) or the death instinct (Thanatos) —*adj.* filled or charged *(with) [a look instinct with pity]* —**in·stinc·tual** (in stiŋk′chōō əl) *adj.*

intruding
(paragraph 7)

in·trude (in trōōd′) *vt.* ··trud′ed, ··trud′ing ⟦L *intrudere* < *in-,* in + *trudere,* to thrust, push: see THREAT⟧ **1** to push or force (something in or upon) **2** to force (oneself or one's thoughts) upon others without being asked or welcomed **3** *Geol.* to force (liquid magma, etc.) into or between solid rocks —*vi.* to intrude oneself —**in·trud′er** *n.*

novelty
(paragraph 5)

nov·el·ty (näv′əl tē) *n., pl.* ··ties ⟦ME *novelte* < OFr *noveleté* < LL *novellitas*⟧ **1** the quality of being novel; newness; freshness **2** something new, fresh, or unusual; change; innovation **3** a small, often cheap, cleverly made article, usually for play or adornment: *usually used in pl.* —*adj.* having characteristics that are new, unusual, atypical, etc. *[a novelty tune]*

predominantly
(paragraph 5)

pre·domi·nant (prē däm′ə nənt, pri-) *adj.* ⟦Fr *prédominant* < ML *predominans,* prp. of *predominari:* see PRE- & DOMINANT⟧ **1** having ascendancy, authority, or dominating influence over others; superior **2** most frequent, noticeable, etc.; prevailing; preponderant —*SYN.* DOMINANT —**pre·dom′i·nance** *n.* or **pre·dom′i·nancy,** *pl.* ··cies —**pre·dom′i·nantly** *adv.*

swaddled
(paragraph 9)

swad·dle (swäd′'l) *vt.* ··dled, ··dling ⟦ME *swathlen,* prob. altered (infl. by *swathen,* to SWATHE[1]) < *swethlen* < OE *swethel,* swaddling band, akin to *swathian,* to SWATHE[1]⟧ **1** to wrap (a newborn baby) in swaddling clothes, a blanket, etc. **2** to bind in or as in bandages; swathe —*n.* ⟦ME *swathil* < OE *swethel:* see the *vt.*⟧ a cloth, bandage, etc. used for swaddling

11A VOCABULARY

Using the vocabulary words on pages 195–196 fill in this crossword puzzle.

Across

1. forcing oneself on others
3. the logical result of an action
4. to call together
7. difficult to handle; heavy
9. to face or meet face to face
10. wrapped in long pieces of cloth

Down

2. something unusual
3. full or complete in detail
5. inborn tendencies
6. opinion held by most people
8. most noticeably

11B   CENTRAL THEME AND MAIN IDEAS

Choose the best answer.

_____ 1. What is the central theme of "Flour Children"?
   a. Mr. Valverde hopes to teach students the responsibility involved in having children.
   b. Students learn that taking care of a baby is a 24-hour-a-day job.
   c. Students learn that babies may cause them to miss out on planned events in their lives.
   d. High school girls learn that boys are not interested in girls who have babies.

_____ 2. What is the main idea of paragraph 2?
   a. Mr. Valverde intends to check up on his students to make sure they take the project seriously.
   b. Failure to take good care of the baby will result in a new, heavier baby.
   c. The flour babies must be treated as if they were real babies.
   d. Students do not take their flour babies seriously.

_____ 3. What is the main idea of paragraph 8?
   a. Students often missed after-school activities to care for their babies.
   b. Students learn that they probably don't want to have babies.
   c. Many students were embarrassed at having to care for a flour baby.
   d. The flour babies affected students' lives in different ways.

11C   MAJOR DETAILS

Decide whether each detail is true (T), false (F), or not discussed (ND).

_____ 1. Mr. Valverde takes his job teaching sex education very seriously.

_____ 2. For the first time students are not forced to respond to an external environment.

_____ 3. Flour sacks instead of eggs are used because they more nearly resemble caring for an infant.

_____ 4. San Francisco's Mission High School Board requires this course of all students.

_____ 5. The students' parents have agreed to participate in the flour babies' care.

_____ 6. Students were concerned about the embarrassment of carrying a flour baby.

Name   Date

_____ 7. To make the babies seem more real, students must equip them with clothes, diapers, and bottles.

_____ 8. Students who communicate with their parents do well as flour baby parents.

11D INFERENCES

Choose the best answer.

_____ 1. *Read paragraph 6 again.* By refusing to put her flour sack on the floor during English, Cylenna Terry is showing that
a. she is afraid any damage would result in getting a larger baby.
b. she has accepted the responsibility of a baby.
c. she knows someone would tell Mr. Valverde.
d. she is too embarrassed to let anyone see it on the floor.

_____ 2. *Read paragraph 9 again.* "The temporary parents came to class dragging their feet" indicates that they were
a. tired of playing this game.
b. anxious to find out if they had passed.
c. certain they did not want to have real babies.
d. hesitant to part with their babies after all.

11E CRITICAL READING: FACT OR OPINION

Decide whether each statement, even if it quotes someone, contains a Fact *or an* Opinion.

_____ 1. *From paragraph 1:* "Yes, babies are a serious matter [. . .] ."

_____ 2. *From paragraph 4:* "The primary goal is to teach responsibility [. . .] ."

_____ 3. *From paragraph 5:* " [. . .] [the] class has helped to maintain the low number of teen pregnancies at her school."

_____ 4. *From paragraph 6:* "At my age, it was too embarrassing [. . .] ."

_____ 5. *From paragraph 7:* "No guys wanted to be involved with a girl who has a baby [. . .] ."

_____ 6. *From paragraph 9:* " [. . .] babies have no place in their young lives."

11F   CRITICAL READING: THE AUTHOR'S STRATEGIES

Choose the best answer.

_____ 1. The main audience for "Flour Children" is
a. sex education teachers.
b. teenage parents.
c. high school students.
d. anyone interested in sex education for teens.

_____ 2. The author's purpose in writing this reading is to
a. describe.
b. persuade.
c. inform.
d. narrate.

_____ 3. The author's tone in this reading is
a. hopeful.
b. objective.
c. bitter.
d. judgmental.

11G   READER'S PROCESS: SUMMARIZING YOUR READING

_____ 1. What is the best summary of "Flour Children"?
a. A journalist reports on how several teenagers felt about caring for a baby after a sex education class assignment that lasts three weeks.
b. A journalist reports on a sex education program that teaches high school students about how hard it really is to take care of a baby for three weeks.
c. A journalist reports on a sex education program that teaches students responsibility by having them care for a sack of flour as their newborn baby for three weeks.
d. A journalist reports on a high school sex education teacher whose students are assigned the task of caring for a five-pound "baby" for three weeks.

11H   READER'S RESPONSE: TO DISCUSS OR WRITE ABOUT

1. If you were a high school student and had the option to register for a sex education class that required students to care for flour sack babies, would you enroll? Give specific reasons for your decision.

2. From a parent's point of view, do you think sex education and parenthood classes should be taught in the public schools? Explain your point of view.

HOW DID YOU DO?
11 Flour Children

SKILL (number of items)	Number Correct		Points for each		Score
Vocabulary (11)	_____	×	2	=	_____
Central Theme and Main Ideas (3)	_____	×	4	=	_____
Major Details (8)	_____	×	4	=	_____
Inferences (2)	_____	×	4	=	_____
Critical Reading: Fact or Opinion (6)	_____	×	3	=	_____
Critical Reading: The Author's Strategies (3)	_____	×	2	=	_____
Reader's Process: Summarizing Your Reading (1)	_____	×	2	=	_____

(Possible Total: 100) *Total* _____

The Magic Words Are "Will You Help Me?"

Michael Ryan

LEARNING OBJECTIVES

• Explain the barriers resulting from illiteracy. ·

THINKING: GETTING STARTED

• Have you ever been in a situation in which you were too self-conscious to ask for help?

(1) I had been listening to Tom Harken's life story for almost an hour when the question that had formed in my mind suddenly emerged from his lips: "How did I get from there to here?" he said in a tone of real amazement. "How did that happen?" We all have been taught that America is a land where anyone can go from rags to riches, despite whatever **obstacles** fate may throw at us. But as I listened to Harken, 59, I understood for the first time just how many obstacles one human being can overcome—and just how far determination and courage can carry any one of us.

(2) The man across from me was a millionaire, the owner of eight **franchises** of the Casa Olé restaurant chain in Texas. His office is filled with mementos of his friendships with the great and famous, from members of Congress to Supreme Court Justices, from Henry Kissinger to Norman Vincent Peale. Yet, 48 years ago, this **robust** man was a sickly child. And, more than that, he had a secret he was too ashamed to tell anyone.

(3) "I grew up in Lakeview, Mich.," Harken told me. "I was a sick kid. I had tuberculosis. I developed polio. One day I was riding a bicycle; the next day I was in a hospital, in an iron lung." Just a few decades ago, polio was a terrifying disease that struck tens of thousands of children and adults. Many died or were paralyzed; some lived for months in iron lungs—huge, barrel-like machines that compressed and released lungs too weak to breathe for themselves. "I was in a room the size of a gymnasium, with 35 or 40 iron lungs," Harken recalled. "Imagine being in a hospital. It looks like you're never going to get out of the darned thing, and everybody's crying all around you. I was 11."

(4) It took more than a year of therapy for Tom to recover enough to go home. "I have one leg that's shorter than the other—that's the only evidence of the illness," he said. "The day I got out of that hospital was a great day. I still remember coming home with my mom and dad." But

Just because a child's parents are illiterate does not mean the child will be unsuccessful learning to read. Illiterate parents often make good motivators in getting their children to read.

the great day soon turned sour, because Tom also had tuberculosis, and officials worried that he might still be contagious. "The next thing I knew, I was **quarantined** to one room in the house for a year," he said.

(5) Harken used to tell people his life went back to normal when this second nightmare ended. He went back to school, joined the Air Force and built up his successful business career. All that is true; but, until four years ago, the story Tom Harken told people was not his whole story. And sharing it would be the most difficult act of his life. "In 1992, I won the Horatio Alger Award," he told me. The award, given to men and women who have overcome **adversity** to achieve greatness, has been awarded to such luminaries as Gen. Colin Powell, Maya Angelou and Bob Hope. Harken was thrilled—and humbled—to be chosen to receive it. "I got really emotional while I was dictating my acceptance speech, and I started wondering whether I should talk about it," he recalled. "I'd never talked about it. Melba knew, but nobody else." "It" was Tom Harken's long-held secret: For most of his life, he had been **illiterate,** unable to read even the simplest sentences, to order from printed menus or to fill out a form.

(6) The origin of the problems is easy to understand: After missing years of school, Tom returned to a classroom run by a teacher who ridiculed him. "He took me up to the board and said, 'Can you spell cat?'" Harken said, "I was nervous and shy, and he said again, 'Spell cat!' He was hollering at me. Then he made me sit down." That humiliation turned

Tom off to reading—and school. With his parents' **reluctant** permission, he dropped out. Later, he enlisted in the Air Force, where he filled in multiple-choice tests at random, unable to read the questions. While he was serving in Oklahoma, Harken had two strokes of luck: He took an after-duty job in sales and learned that he had an **aptitude** for business. And he met the woman he still calls "Miss Melba," now his wife of 38 years. "I had to tell her that I couldn't read or write, because I needed her to fill out the marriage license," he recalled, emotion flooding his voice. But Melba saw something in this bright young man. "He was ambitious," she said. "And he was so smart. He was so exciting to talk to that I was never afraid he wouldn't succeed."

(7) Succeed he did—with help from Melba. When he moved to Beaumont, Tex., and developed a door-to-door vacuum-cleaner sales business, she would help him write up his order each night. "I have a good memory," he said. "I would memorize names and addresses, employers and credit information, and then Melba would write them down." Working together, they expanded into a recreational vehicle dealership and then into restaurant franchises. But the small humiliations were always there. "Whenever we went to a restaurant, I would order a cheeseburger," Harken said. "Everybody sells cheeseburgers. But one day I ordered a cheeseburger, and the waitress looked at me and said, 'What's the matter, can't you read? We don't make cheeseburgers.'"

(8) The Harkens had two sons, Tommy and Mark, both now grown and working in the family business. But Tom felt the sting of his illiteracy constantly as the boys were growing up. "They would crawl into my lap and ask me to read them something, like the Sunday comics," he said. "Melba would rescue me. She'd come over and say, 'Daddy's busy. I'll read that to you.'" A regular churchgoer, Harken recalled one occasion when he was attending Sunday school: "They passed the Scripture along, and everybody read a verse. I could feel my stomach tying itself in knots as it came closer to me, and I finally said, 'I have to go to the bathroom,' and I just left there and went home." He realized that he had to do something. He went to Melba for help. "She taught me word by word, over a course of years," Harken told me. "I was hard to teach. I got very angry sometimes." Harken worked his way through simple sentences to the point where he could read parts of the Bible aloud—as he did at the weddings of two of his employees. "That's still hard for me," he said, but Melba immediately cut him off. "You did it very well," she told him.

(9) When he was selected for the Horatio Alger Award, Harken thought about standing up in front of some of America's most important people and telling them that, until recently, he had been illiterate. Then he decided to do it. "I got teary-eyed," he told me. "Melba said I should do it and I should tell our two kids first." His sons were amazed by their father's story. "They were absolutely stunned," Harken recalled. But their reaction was nothing compared to the response of those attending the Horatio Alger awards ceremony in May 1992. They gave Harken a

standing ovation. Colin Powell, the Rev. Robert Schuller and other dignitaries rushed to shake his hand.

(10) For many people, that triumphant evening would have been the end of a lifelong journey. For Harken, though, it was just a beginning. Since that night, he has given more than 300 speeches around the country, telling children and adults about the importance of **literacy.** After one speech, an 87-year-old woman approached him to say that she had just learned to read. "I couldn't read to my children or my grandchildren, but now I can read to my great-grandchildren," she told him. After another speech, an African-American man who was starting reading lessons told Harken that he had **dispelled** an **onerous** racist image: "He said that, before he heard me, he thought that only black people could be illiterate," Harken said. "He didn't know that illiteracy happens in every color."

(11) Harken's message is one he wants to get out to anyone who will listen: "I want people to know that they can go into any library and just say the magic words, 'Will you help me?' Just say those words, and someone will help you learn how to read. The Literacy Volunteers of America are everywhere, and they're ready to help. Everybody should know that." It occurred to me that Tom Harken's whole life might have been changed if that one teacher had not ridiculed him. "Sure, it probably would have altered a lot of my life," Harken said. "But I'm not sure I'd want it altered. You never know your own strength until you've paid the price—and Miss Melba and I have paid the price."

Here are some of the more difficult words in "The Magic Words Are 'Will You Help Me?'"

adversity
(paragraph 5)

ad·ver·sity (ad vur′sə tē, əd-) *n.* ⟦ME < OFr *adversité, aversite* < L *adversitas* < *adversus,* prec.⟧ **1** a state of wretchedness or misfortune; poverty and trouble **2** *pl.* **-ties** an instance of misfortune; calamity

aptitude
(paragraph 6)

ap·ti·tude (ap′tə tōōd′, -tyōōd′) *n.* ⟦ME < LL *aptitudo* < L *aptus:* see APT[1]⟧ **1** the quality of being apt or appropriate; fitness **2** a natural tendency or inclination **3** a natural ability or talent **4** quickness to learn or understand —*SYN.* TALENT

dispelled
(paragraph 10)

dis·pel (di spel′) *vt.* **··pelled′, ··pel′·ling** ⟦ME *dispellen* < L *dispellere* < *dis-,* apart + *pellere,* to drive: see FELT⟧ to scatter and drive away; cause to vanish; disperse —*SYN.* SCATTER

franchises
(paragraph 2)

fran·chise (fran′chīz′) *n.* ⟦ME < OFr < *franc,* free: see FRANK[1]⟧ **1** [Archaic] freedom from some restriction, servitude, etc. **2** any special right, privilege, or exemption granted by the government, as to be a corporation, operate a public utility, etc. **3** the right to vote; suffrage: usually preceded by *the* **4** *a)* the right to market a product or provide a service, often exclusive for a specified area, as granted by a manufacturer or company *b)* a business granted such a right *☆5 a)* the right to own a member team as granted by a league in certain professional sports *b)* such a member team —*vt.* **··chised′, ··chis′·ing** to grant a franchise to —*adj.* designating a player on a professional team who is regarded as being essential to that team's success

illiterate
(paragraph 5)

il·lit·er·ate (i lit′ər it) **adj.** ⟦L *illiteratus*, unlettered: see IN-² & LITERATE⟧ **1** ignorant; uneducated; esp., not knowing how to read or write **2** having or showing limited knowledge, experience, or culture, esp. in some particular field *[musically illiterate]* **3** violating accepted usage in language *[an illiterate sentence]* —**n.** an illiterate person; esp., a person who does not know how to read or write —**SYN.** IGNORANT —**il·lit′er·ate·ly adv.**

literacy
(paragraph 10)

lit·era·cy (lit′ər ə sē) **n.** the state or quality of being literate; specif., *a)* ability to read and write *b)* knowledgeability or capability *[computer literacy]*

obstacles
(paragraph 1)

ob·sta·cle (äb′stə kəl) **n.** ⟦OFr < L *obstaculum*, obstacle < *obstare*, to withstand < *ob-* (see OB-) + *stare*, to STAND⟧ anything that gets in the way or hinders; impediment; obstruction; hindrance

SYN.—**obstacle** is used of anything which literally or figuratively stands in the way of one's progress *[her father's opposition remained their only obstacle]*; **impediment** applies to anything that delays or retards progress by interfering with the normal action *[a speech impediment]*; **obstruction** refers to anything that blocks progress or some activity as if by stopping up a passage *[your interference is an obstruction of justice]*; **hindrance** applies to anything that thwarts progress by holding back or delaying *[lack of supplies is the greatest hindrance to my experiment]*; **barrier** applies to any apparently insurmountable obstacle that prevents progress or keeps separate and apart *[language differences are often a barrier to understanding]*

onerous
(paragraph 10)

on·er·ous (än′ər əs, ōn′-) **adj.** ⟦ME < MFr *onereus* < L *onerosus* < *onus*, a load: see ONUS⟧ **1** burdensome; laborious **2** *Law* involving a legal obligation that equals or exceeds the benefits *[onerous lease]* —**on′·er·ous·ly adv.** —**on′·er·ous·ness n.**

SYN.—**onerous** applies to that which is laborious or troublesome, often because of its annoying or tedious character *[the onerous task of taking inventory]*; **burdensome** applies to that which is wearisome or oppressive to the mind or spirit as well as to the body *[burdensome responsibilities]*; **oppressive** stresses the overbearing cruelty of the person or thing that inflicts hardship, or emphasizes the severity of the hardship itself *[oppressive weather, an oppressive king]*; **exacting** suggests the making of great demands on the attention, skill, care, etc. *[an exacting supervisor, exacting work]*

quarantined
(paragraph 4)

quar·an·tine (kwôr′ən tēn, kwär′-) **n.** ⟦It *quarantina*, lit., space of forty days < *quaranta*, forty < L *quadraginta* < base of *quattuor*, FOUR⟧ **1** *a)* the period, orig. 40 days, during which an arriving vessel suspected of carrying contagious disease is detained in port in strict isolation *b)* the place where such a vessel is stationed **2** any isolation or restriction on travel or passage imposed to keep contagious diseases, insect pests, etc. from spreading **3** the state of being quarantined **4** a place where persons, animals, or plants having contagious diseases, insect pests, etc. are kept in isolation, or beyond which they may not travel **5** any period of seclusion, social ostracism, etc. —**vt.** **·tined′, ·tin′·ing 1** to place under quarantine **2** to isolate politically, commercially, socially, etc. —**quar′·an·tin′·able adj.**

reluctant
(paragraph 6)

re·luc·tant (-tənt) **adj.** ⟦L *reluctans*, prp. of *reluctari*, to resist < *re-*, against + *luctari*, to struggle: see LOCK¹⟧ **1** opposed in mind *(to do something)*; unwilling; disinclined **2** marked by unwillingness *[a reluctant answer]* **3** [Rare] struggling against; resisting; opposing —**re·luc′·tantly adv.**

robust
(paragraph 2)

ro·bust (rō bust′, rō′bust′) **adj.** ⟦L *robustus*, oaken, hard, strong < *robur*, hard variety of oak, hardness, strength, earlier *robus*, prob. akin to *ruber*, RED⟧ **1** *a)* strong and healthy; full of vigor; hardy *b)* strongly built or based; muscular or sturdy **2** suited to or requiring physical strength or stamina *[robust work]* **3** rough; coarse; boisterous **4** full and rich, as in flavor *[a robust port wine]* —**ro·bust′·ly adv.** —**ro·bust′·ness n.**

12A VOCABULARY

Using the vocabulary words listed on pages 205–206, fill in the blanks.

1. At the age of four, Tamika showed an _____ for playing the drums.

2. Mom was _____ to let Quassim play ice hockey because his temperature was 100 degrees.

3. When my sister and I received an inheritance from our grandmother, we invested the money in a pizza _____.

4. The _____ appearance of that 70-year-old woman results from years of serious exercise.

5. The greatest _____ Dat Pham had to overcome as a college student was his deafness.

6. When I returned from overseas with my dog Hershey, she was _____ to make sure she had not picked up a contagious disease.

7. The cadets had to overcome many _____ in their outdoor survival training.

8. The Dallas _____ Council uses volunteers to help people of all ages learn to read.

9. Standing up and speaking in front of a class can be an _____ burden for some students.

10. The Queen's appearance at the balcony window _____ the rumor that she was hospitalized.

11. People who have almost never gone to school are often _____.

12B   CENTRAL THEME AND MAIN IDEAS

Choose the best answer.

_____ 1. What is the central theme of "The Magic Words Are 'Will You Help Me?'"
   a. Tom Harken's being belittled by a teacher drove him to drop out of school.
   b. Tom Harken's story shows that being able to read is not essential to becoming a successful businessperson.
   c. Tom Harken spent years covering up a secret shame until he finally asked for help.
   d. Tom Harken's success in business is the result of his wife's support and hard work.

_____ 2. What is the main idea of paragraph 5?
   a. Tom Harken's life returned to normal when he was well enough to attend school.
   b. The Horatio Alger Award recognized that Tom Harken overcame adversity to become successful.
   c. Only Melba Harken knew that her husband could neither read nor write.
   d. In his acceptance speech at the awards ceremony, Tom Harken planned to reveal the incredible adversity he had endured all his life.

_____ 3. What is the main idea of paragraph 11?
   a. Help in learning to read is available to anyone who asks.
   b. Tom Harken's life would have been different if a teacher had not embarrassed him.
   c. The Literacy Volunteers of America helps people learn to read.
   d. Tom Harken and his wife suffered embarrassment because he could not read.

12C   MAJOR DETAILS

Decide whether each detail listed here is Major *or* Minor *based on the context of the reading selection.*

_____ 1. Tom Harken grew up in Lakeview, Michigan.

_____ 2. As a child, Tom Harken had polio.

_____ 3. Tom Harken has one leg that is shorter than the other.

_____ 4. Tom Harken ordered a cheeseburger every time he went to a restaurant.

_____ 5. Tom Harken felt humiliated at not being able to spell "cat."

Name   Date

_____ 6. Tom and Melba Harken have been married 38 years.

_____ 7. Tom Harken served in the U.S. Air Force.

_____ 8. Tom Harken had a good memory.

_____ 9. Tom Harken's sons, Tommy and Mark, work in the family business.

_____ 10. Tom Harken asked his wife, Melba, to teach him to read.

12D INFERENCES

Choose the best answer.

_____ 1. *Reread paragraph 5*. Tom Harken dictated his acceptance speech because
   a. it gave his secretary something to do.
   b. it took less time than writing one.
   c. he liked to hear himself talk.
   d. he found writing a difficult activity.

_____ 2. *Reread paragraph 6*. The teacher embarrassed Tom Harken because the teacher
   a. hoped embarrassment would force the boy to answer a question.
   b. thought embarrassment would make the boy a better speller.
   c. felt embarrassment would help the boy overcome his shyness.
   d. used embarrassment to discipline unruly students.

_____ 3. *Reread paragraph 8*. Tom Harken felt he was "difficult to teach" because
   a. he did not study.
   b. his wife was not a trained teacher.
   c. he was impatient with his progress.
   d. he could not concentrate on anything for long.

12E CRITICAL READING: FACT OR OPINION

Decide whether each statement contains a Fact *or an* Opinion.

_____ 1. *From paragraph 1:* "America is a land where anyone can go from rags to riches [. . .]."

_____ 2. *From paragraph 3:* Many people either died or were paralyzed from polio.

_____ 3. *From paragraph 5:* Before learning to read, Tom Harken spoke to no one but his wife about his illiteracy.

_____ 4. *From paragraph 6:* Tom Harken learned that he had an aptitude for business.

_____ 5. *From paragraph 8:* Reading the Bible aloud at the wedding of
some of his employees was difficult for Tom Harken.

_____ 6. *From paragraph 10:* Since his acceptance speech for the Alger
Award, Tom Harken has spoken many times on the topic of
illiteracy.

_____ 7. *From paragraph 11:* The words "will you help me" are magic.

_____ 8. *From paragraph 11:* Anyone can get help learning to read by
contacting the Literacy Volunteers of America.

12F   CRITICAL READING: THE AUTHOR'S STRATEGIES

Choose the best answer.

_____ 1. The main audience for "The Magic Words 'Are Will You Help
Me?'" is
a. anyone needing encouragement to overcome a disability.
b. anyone who has experienced not being able to read.
c. anyone who works with adults who can't read.
d. anyone seeking help in learning to read.

_____ 2. The author's purpose in writing this reading is to
a. emphasize.
b. inform.
c. describe.
d. entertain.

_____ 3. The author's tone in this reading is
a. amused.
b. concerned.
c. objective.
d. admiring.

12G READER'S PROCESS: SUMMARIZING YOUR READING

_____ 1. What is the best summary of "The Magic Words Are 'Will You Help Me?'"?
   a. A journalist tells how Tom Harken built a successful business even though he couldn't read.
   b. A journalist tells how businessman Tom Harken learned to read with the help of his wife.
   c. A journalist tells how businessman Tom Harken coped with being illiterate while building a successful business.
   d. A journalist tells how businessman Tom Harken hid the fact that he was illiterate and finally decided to reveal his shameful secret.

12H READER'S RESPONSE: TO DISCUSS OR WRITE ABOUT

1. Have you or someone you know or have heard about ever felt humiliated privately or publicly by an incident in college, at work, or in a social setting? Being as specific as you can, explain what happened.

2. Melba Harken thought her husband, Tom, "was so smart" even though he could not read or write. Do you think someone can be smart without those skills? Using a specific experience you know about, explain why you think this is so.

HOW DID YOU DO?
12 The Magic Words Are "Will You Help Me?"

SKILL (number of items)	Number Correct		Points for each		Score
Vocabulary (11)	_____	×	2	=	_____
Central Theme and Main Ideas (3)	_____	×	5	=	_____
Major Details (10)	_____	×	4	=	_____
Inferences (3)	_____	×	1	=	_____
Critical Reading: Fact or Opinion (8)	_____	×	1	=	_____
Critical Reading: The Author's Strategies (3)	_____	×	3	=	_____
Reader's Process: Summarizing Your Reading (1)	_____	×	3	=	_____
(Possible Total: 100) *Total*					_____

Part 4

Thinking: Getting Started

"Someone once defined humor as a way to keep from killing yourself. I keep my sense of humor to stay alive."

Abe Burrows

The selections in Part 4 concern events, ranging from a satirical selection about a man who changed his habits just to stay alive to a mother and sons risking their lives to cross the Mexico-United States border to find a missing relative.

"How to Stay Alive" (Selection 13)—What changes are you willing to make in your lifestyle to stay healthy?

"Waging War on Wrinkles" (Selection 14)—How important is a youthful appearance to you?

"The Danger of Hoarding" (Selection 15)—Is there anything you own that you would find difficult to throw away?

"Forty Acres and a Holiday" (Selection 16)—What is the Emancipation Proclamation?

"My Mother's Blue Bowl" (Selection 17)—Is there any material object of your mother or your grandmother to which you have a sentimental attachment?

"In Search of Bernabé" (Selection 18)—What risks would you be willing to take to find a missing family member?

How to Stay Alive

Art Hoppe

LEARNING OBJECTIVES
- Contrast health warnings as valid and invalid.

THINKING: GETTING STARTED
- What changes are you willing to make in your lifestyle to stay healthy?

(1) Once upon a time there was a man named Snadley Klabberhorn, who was the healthiest man in the whole wide world.

(2) Snadley wasn't always the healthiest man in the whole wide world. When he was young, Snadley smoked what he wanted, drank what he wanted, ate what he wanted, and exercised only with young ladies in bed.

(3) He thought he was happy. "Life is absolutely peachy," he was fond of saying. "Nothing beats being alive."

(4) Then along came the Surgeon General's Report linking smoking to lung cancer, heart disease, **emphysema,** and tertiary coreopsis.

(5) Snadley read about The Great Tobacco Scare with a frown. "Life is so peachy," he said, "that there's no sense taking any risks." So he gave up smoking.

(6) Like most people who went through the hell of giving up smoking, Snadley became more interested in his own health. In fact, he became fascinated. And when he read a WCTU tract which pointed out that alcohol caused liver damage, brain damage, and acute **weltanschauung,** he gave up alcohol and drank dietary colas instead.

(7) At least he did until The Great Cyclamate Scare.

(8) "There's no sense in taking any risks," he said. And he switched to sugar-sweetened colas, which made him fat and caused dental caries. On realizing this he renounced colas in favor of milk and took up jogging, which was an awful bore.

(9) That was about the time of The Great Cholesterol Scare.

(10) Snadley gave up milk. To avoid cholesterol, which caused atherosclerosis, **coronary** infarcts, and **chronic** chryselephantinism, he also gave up meat, fats, and dairy products, subsisting on a diet of raw fish.

(11) Then came the Great **DDT** Scare.

(12) "The presence of large amounts of DDT in fish . . . " Snadley read with anguish. But fortunately that's when he met Ernestine. They were

made for each other. Ernestine introduced him to home-ground wheat germ, **macrobiotic** yogurt, and organic succotash.

(13) They were very happy eating this dish twice daily, watching six hours of color television together, and spending the rest of their time in bed.

(14) They were, that is, until The Great Color Television Scare.

(15) "If color tee-vee does give off radiations," said Snadley, "there's no sense taking risks. After all, we still have each other."

(16) And that's about all they had. Until The Great Pill Scare.

(17) On hearing that The Pill might cause **carcinoma,** thromboses, and lingering stichometry, Ernestine promptly gave up The Pill—and Snadley. "There's no sense taking any risks," she said.

(18) Snadley was left with jogging. He was, that is, until he read somewhere that 1.3 percent of joggers are eventually run over by a truck or bitten by rabid dogs.

(19) He then retired to a bomb shelter in his back yard (to avoid being hit by a meteor), installed an air purifier (after The Great Smog Scare) and spent the next 63 years doing Royal Canadian Air Force exercises and poring over back issues of *The Reader's Digest*.

(20) "Nothing's more important than being alive," he said proudly on reaching 102. But he never did say anymore that life was absolutely peachy.

(21) CAUTION: Being alive may be hazardous to your health.

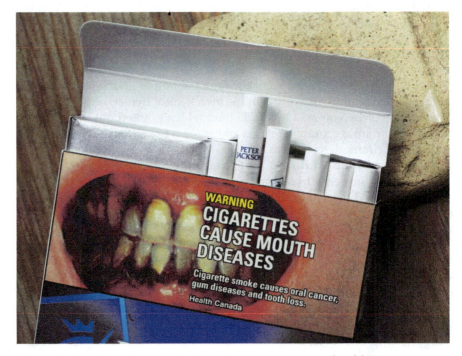

What else besides cigarettes is hazardous to a person's health?

Here are some of the more difficult words in "How to Stay Alive."

carcinoma
(paragraph 17)

car·ci·no·ma (kär′sə nō′mə) *n., pl.* ·**mas** or ·**mata** (-mə tə) ⟦L < Gr *karkinōma,* cancer < *karkinoun,* affect with a cancer < *karkinos,* crab: see CANCER⟧ any of several kinds of cancerous growths deriving from epithelial cells: see SARCOMA —**car′·ci·nom′a·tous** (-näm′ə təs, -nō′mə-) *adj.*

chronic
(paragraph 10)

chronic (krän′ik) *adj.* ⟦Fr *cronique* < L *chronicus* < Gr *chronikos,* of time < *chronos,* time⟧ **1** lasting a long time or recurring often: said of a disease, and distinguished from ACUTE **2** having had an ailment for a long time [a *chronic* patient] **3** continuing indefinitely; perpetual; constant [a *chronic* worry] **4** by habit, custom, etc.; habitual; inveterate [a *chronic* complainer] —*n.* a chronic patient —**chron′i·cally** *adv.* —**chro·nic·ity** (krə nis′ə tē) *n.*

SYN.—**chronic** suggests long duration or frequent recurrence and is used especially of diseases or habits that resist all efforts to eradicate them [*chronic* sinusitis]; **inveterate** implies firm establishment as a result of continued indulgence over a long period of time [an *inveterate* liar]; **confirmed** suggests fixedness in some condition or practice, often from a deep-seated aversion to change [a *confirmed* bachelor]; **hardened** implies fixed tendencies and a callous indifference to emotional or moral considerations [a *hardened* criminal]

coronary
(paragraph 10)

coro·nary (kôr′ə ner′ē, kär′-) *adj.* ⟦L *coronarius:* see CROWN⟧ **1** of, or in the form of, a crown **2** *Anat. a)* like a crown; encircling *b)* designating or relating to either of two arteries, or their branches, coming from the aorta and supplying blood directly to the heart muscle —☆*n., pl.* ·**nar′·ies** CORONARY THROMBOSIS

DDT
(paragraph 11)

DDT (dē′dē′tē′) *n.* ⟦d(ichloro)d(iphenyl)t(richloroethane)⟧ a powerful insecticide (ClC₆H₄)₂CHCCl₃, effective upon contact: its use is restricted by law due to damaging environmental effects

emphysema
(paragraph 4)

em·phy·se·ma (em′fə sē′mə; -zē′-) *n.* ⟦ModL < Gr *emphysēma,* inflation < *emphysaein,* to inflate, blow in < *en-,* in + *physaein,* to blow < IE *phus-* < base *pu-, *phu-,* echoic of blowing with puffed cheeks⟧ **1** an abnormal swelling of body tissues caused by the accumulation of air; esp., such a swelling of the lung tissue, due to the permanent loss of elasticity, or the destruction, of the alveoli, which seriously impairs respiration **2** HEAVES —**em′·phy·se′ma·tous** (-sē′mə təs, -sem′-) *adj.* —**em′·phy·se′mic** *adj., n.*

macrobiotic
(paragraph 12)

macro·bi·ot·ics (mak′rō bī ät′iks) *pl.n.* ⟦see prec. & -BIOTIC⟧ [*with sing. v.*] the study of prolonging life, as by special diets, etc. — **mac′ro·bi·ot′ic** *adj.*

weltanschauung
(paragraph 6)

Welt·an·schau·ung (velt′än shou′ooŋ) *n.* ⟦Ger, world view⟧ a comprehensive, esp. personal, philosophy or conception of the universe and of human life

"How to Stay Alive" has many unusual words in it. To help you read the essay easily, here are some quick definitions.

tertiary	(paragraph 4)	third
coreopsis	(paragraph 4)	tickseed plant
WCTU	(paragraph 6)	Women's Christian Temperance Union
cholesterol	(paragraph 9)	fatty substances in the blood
atherosclerosis	(paragraph 10)	hardening of the arteries

Name   Date   **217**

Vocabulary List

infarcts	(paragraph 10)	obstruction of blood vessels
chryselephantinism	(paragraph 10)	being overlaid with gold and ivory
yogurt	(paragraph 12)	a fermented milk food
succotash	(paragraph 12)	lima beans and corn cooked together
thromboses	(paragraph 17)	blood clots
stichometry	(paragraph 17)	practice of writing prose

13A   VOCABULARY

Choose the best answer.

_____ 1. If you had **emphysema**, you would
   a. be breaking the law.
   b. have trouble breathing.
   c. get frequent headaches.
   d. be unable to digest food.

_____ 2. The word **weltanschauung** is closest in meaning to
   a. peptic ulcers.
   b. a passion for German opera.
   c. cruelty to children.
   d. a personal philosophy of life.

_____ 3. The word **coronary** refers to
   a. the arteries leading to the heart.
   b. a medical examiner.
   c. kidney disease.
   d. the arteries leading to the brain.

_____ 4. A **chronic** illness is best described as
   a. painful.
   b. extremely expensive to treat.
   c. continuing indefinitely.
   d. likely to result in death.

_____ 5. **DDT** is best known as
   a. the FBI's list of "most wanted" criminals.
   b. a deadly insecticide.
   c. the cause of high blood pressure.
   d. a foreign sports car.

_____ 6. Anything that is **macrobiotic** is
   a. believed to prolong life.
   b. hazardous to your health.
   c. very delicious.
   d. pornographic.

_____ 7. **Carcinoma** is a medical term for
   a. tuberculosis.
   b. cancer.
   c. heart disease.
   d. measles.

13B CENTRAL THEME

Choose the best answer.

_____ 1. What is the central theme of "How to Stay Alive"?
   a. The secret of living to a ripe old age is avoiding indulgences that are hazardous to your health.
   b. Snadley Klabberhorn enjoyed life until he changed his habits in reaction to every health scare.
   c. Snadley Klabberhorn's main goal was to live to 102 without giving up smoking, drinking, sweets, and color television.
   d. Everyone should disregard health scares and live life to its fullest.

13C MAJOR DETAILS

Decide whether each detail is true (T), false (F), or not discussed (ND).

_____ 1. Snadley liked to say, "Nothing beats being alive."

_____ 2. With each new health scare, Snadley altered his life to avoid the danger.

_____ 3. The Great Noise Scare led Snadley to wear earplugs all the time.

_____ 4. Snadley's wife, Ernestine, refused to give up The Pill even after hearing about its health hazards.

_____ 5. Snadley liked to say, "Nothing beats being healthy."

_____ 6. Snadley finally retired to his bomb shelter to avoid all hazards.

_____ 7. By the time Snadley reached the age of 102, he no longer said that life was absolutely peachy.

13D INFERENCES

Choose the best answer.

_____ 1. "How to Stay Alive" implies that people
   a. should avoid anything that might cause disease.
   b. should live recklessly.
   c. cannot expect to avoid all health hazards.
   d. cannot live long in today's world.

_____ 2. *Read paragraphs 4, 10, and 17 again.* The author uses the words "tertiary coreopsis," "chronic chryselephantinism," and "stichometry," which are not medical terms. Why does he use them?
   a. He thinks big words will impress the reader.
   b. He likes to teach his readers difficult words.
   c. He thinks that they are connected with good health and staying alive.
   d. He is poking fun at the use of big technical words to name well-known diseases.

13E CRITICAL READING: THE AUTHOR'S STRATEGIES

Choose the best answer.

_____ 1. The main audience for "How to Stay Alive" is
   a. people who are trying to adopt a healthier lifestyle.
   b. people who have given up worrying about their health.
   c. people who worry about medical research reports.
   d. people who haven't had a medical checkup in a long time.

_____ 2. The author's purpose in writing this reading is to
   a. expose.
   b. describe.
   c. emphasize.
   d. entertain.

_____ 3. The author's tone in this reading is
   a. serious.
   b. humorous.
   c. concerned.
   d. angry.

Name   Date

13F   READER'S PROCESS: SUMMARIZING YOUR READING

_____ 1. What is the best summary of "How to Stay Alive"?
   a. The author suggests that we can't take medical research too seriously.
   b. The author suggests that perfect health isn't everything.
   c. The author suggests a list of foods and habits that should be avoided if one is to stay healthy.
   d. The author suggests that enjoying life is more important than living to a very old age.

13G   READER'S RESPONSE: TO DISCUSS OR WRITE ABOUT

1. Have you ever changed your habits because of health warnings? Using a specific example of a health warning, explain why you did or did not change your habits.

2. If the statement is true that you are what you eat, what are you? From your own experience, explain how who you are is a reflection of what you eat on a daily basis.

HOW DID YOU DO?
13   How to Stay Alive

SKILL (number of items)	Number Correct		Points for each		Score
Vocabulary (7)	_____	×	5	=	_____
Central Theme (1)	_____	×	7	=	_____
Major Details (7)	_____	×	6	=	_____
Inferences (2)	_____	×	4	=	_____
Critical Reading: The Author's Strategies (3)	_____	×	2	=	_____
Reader's Process: Summarizing Your Reading (1)	_____	×	2	=	_____

(Possible Total: 100) *Total*   _____

Waging War on Wrinkles

Jessica Dye

LEARNING OBJECTIVES

• List the best ways to prevent inevitable wrinkles.

THINKING: GETTING STARTED

• How important is a youthful appearance to you?

(1) It's an inescapable fact of life: wrinkles happen. Aging does not **discriminate;** it inevitably strikes us all, and our faces show it. Although there's no miracle cure for the effects of time on our skin, medical advances continue to bring new, effective ways to hold on to our youthful appearance. Stop at any cosmetics counter and you will see an array of beauty products claiming to reverse the signs of aging. The challenge is to separate the fact from fiction to find what really works.

(2) As in any battle, the key is understanding the opponent. Contrary to popular belief, a "one-size-fits-all" approach doesn't work when it comes to wrinkles. There are three different types of wrinkles: those caused by sun, by facial contractions, and by genetics and aging. Each requires a different type of treatment.

(3) Wrinkles caused by sun damage, or photoaging, are the easiest to combat because they are the easiest to prevent. Experts agree that the best line of defense is to use a good sunblock every day. "Look for a product with SPF 30," says Debra Jaliman, MD, a spokesperson for the American Academy of Dermatology. "Products with zinc and titanium are especially effective, as they block both UVA (Ultraviolet A) and UVB (Ultraviolet B) rays." Sun exposure causes **collagen** in the skin to break down, which causes fine lines and wrinkling. Products with **antioxidants** such as vitamin A, also known as retinoids, and vitamin C prompt skin to produce more collagen and diminish the effects of sun damage. **Exfoliants** such as alpha-hydroxy acids, which are derived mostly from milk and fruit products, also stimulate collagen production and smooth wrinkles by removing dead skin. Christine Poblete-Lopez, MD, assistant program director of the Cleveland Clinic **dermatology** department, recommends a skin care regimen involving the use of alpha-hydroxy acids and retinoids. "They improve a variety of skin problems, including fine wrinkles, and delay the aging process. Cosmeceutical products with these active ingredients can be dispensed at a physician's office and contain higher concentrations than you would get over the counter," she says.

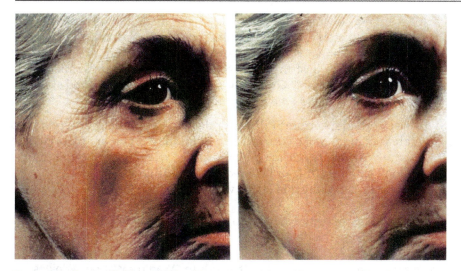

Reducing face wrinkles and looking younger can have a positive impact on how you are treated by others and on how you feel about yourself.

(4) The way we move our faces every day causes wrinkles that are more difficult to prevent and treat. These include "crow's feet" and lines around the mouth. You may have heard that there are facial exercises you can do to prevent such wrinkles from forming, but don't believe it. Repetitive movement causes the wrinkling, so these exercises will actually do more harm than good. "Facial contractions cause the skin to bend, wearing away its own natural collagen and **hyaluronic acid,**" says Karyn Grossman, MD, of Grossman Dermatology in Santa Monica, California. "Traditionally these types of wrinkles have best been treated with Botox." Botox is a nerve-paralyzing agent injected into the skin that prevents the muscle contractions that cause wrinkles. A treatment lasts between four and six months and then slowly wears off. Although popular, Botox injections are a very detailed procedure that should only be done in a doctor's office by a trained professional. Beware of creams that profess to contain similar ingredients; even if the claims are true, such substances must be carefully inserted into just the right muscles, and rubbing a **toxin** on your face could have disastrous results.

(5) Wrinkles that no one can escape are those caused by genetics and aging. These include smile lines, which extend from the nose to the mouth. New skin-tightening procedures such as Thermage, which uses radio-frequency technology to heat and tighten the skin from within, are now used to diminish wrinkles caused by aging. "The use of soft tissue fillers, such as Restylane, Perlane, or Radiesse, is also very effective in treating these types of wrinkles," says Poblete-Lopez. This process, known as soft tissue **augmentation,** involves the injection of a fatlike substance into the skin to elevate deep wrinkles. These procedures are very effective, but like Botox, should be performed only by a skilled professional.

(6) All these advances in technology have made the war on wrinkles increasingly winnable. What cosmetics companies don't want you to know, however, is that your most powerful weapon in this battle doesn't come in a jar. "The best thing anyone can do to prevent wrinkles is to adopt a healthy lifestyle," Grossman says. In addition to a good skin care routine, she recommends the following:

- Use a broad spectrum SPF (Sun Protection Factor) daily on all exposed areas of skin. Make sure to reapply midday if you are working and hourly if you are outside playing sports, relaxing, or shopping.
- Don't smoke, drink, or take recreational drugs.
- Maintain a healthy and stable weight, avoiding large multiple weight swings.
- Get plenty of rest each night to allow your body to repair the damage done during the day.

Here are some of the more difficult words in "Waging War on Wrinkles."

Vocabulary List

antioxidants
(paragraph 3)

anti·oxi·dant (an'tī äks'i dənt, an'tē-) *n.* a substance that slows down the oxidation of hydrocarbons, oils, fats, etc. and thus helps to check deterioration: antioxidants are added to many products, esp. foods and soaps —*adj.* serving to check oxidation

augmentation
(paragraph 5)

aug·men·ta·tion (ôg'men tā'shən, -mən-) *n.* 1 an augmenting or being augmented 2 a thing that augments; addition; increase 3 *Music* variation of a theme by lengthening, usually doubling, the time value of the notes: cf. DIMINUTION

collagen
(paragraph 3)

col·la·gen (käl'ə jən) *n.* 〖< Gr *kolla*, glue + -GEN〗 a fibrous protein found in connective tissue, bone, and cartilage —**col'·la·gen'ic** (-jən' ik) *adj.* —**col·lag·enous** (kə laj'ə nəs) *adj.*

dermatology
(paragraph 3)

der·ma·tol·ogy (dʉr'mə täl'ə jē) *n.* 〖DERMATO- + -LOGY〗 the branch of medicine dealing with the skin and its diseases —**der'·ma·to·log'ic** (-tə läj'ik) *adj.* or **der'·ma·to·log'i·cal** (-läj'i kəl) —**der'·ma·tol'o·gist** *n.*

discriminate
(paragraph 1)

dis·crimi·nate (di skrim'i nāt'; *for adj.,* -nit) *vt.* ··nat'ed, ··nat'·ing 〖< L *discriminatus*, pp. of *discriminare*, to divide, distinguish < *discrimen*, division, distinction < *discernere*: see DISCERN〗 1 to constitute a difference between; differentiate 2 to recognize the difference between; distinguish —*vi.* 1 to see the difference (*between* things); distinguish 2 to be discerning 3 to make distinctions in treatment; show partiality (*in favor of*) or prejudice (*against*) —*adj.* involving discrimination; distinguishing carefully —*SYN.* DISTINGUISH

exfoliants
(paragraph 3)

ex·fo·li·ate (eks fō'lē āt') *vt., vi.* ··at'ed, ··at'·ing 〖< LL *exfoliatus*, pp. of *exfoliare*, to strip of leaves < L *ex-*, out + *folium*, a leaf: see FOIL²〗 to cast or come off in flakes, scales, or layers, as skin, bark, rock. etc. —**ex·fo'·lia'·tion** *n.* —**ex·fo'·lia'·tive** *adj.*

hyaluronic acid
(paragraph 4)

hya·lu·ronic acid (hī'ə lōō rän'ik) 〖< HYAL(O)- + Gr *ouron*, URINE + -IC〗 a highly viscous mucopolysaccharide that holds cells together, lubricates body tissue, and blocks the spread of microorganisms: it is found in the skin, the vitreous humor of the eye, and the synovial fluid of the joints

toxin
(paragraph 4)

toxin (täk'sin) *n.* 〖TOX(IC) + -IN¹〗 1 any of various poisonous compounds produced by some microorganisms and causing certain diseases: see ENDOTOXIN, EXOTOXIN 2 any of various similar poisons, related to proteins, formed in certain plants, as ricin, or secreted by certain animals, as snake venom: toxins, when injected into animals or humans, typically initiate the formation of antitoxins

14A VOCABULARY

Choose the best answer.

_____ 1. A **toxin** is a compound that is
   a. safe.
   b. sticky.
   c. poisonous.
   d. tasteless.

_____ 2. To **discriminate** is to show
   a. disgust.
   b. interest.
   c. division.
   d. favor.

_____ 3. **Dermatology** is the study of the
   a. hair.
   b. skin.
   c. bones.
   d. stomach.

_____ 4. **Antioxidants** are substances added to products to check
   a. growth.
   b. paleness.
   c. deterioration.
   d. absorption.

_____ 5. **Augmentation,** a facial procedure used to treat wrinkles, requires
   a. eliminating tissue.
   b. decreasing tissue.
   c. flattening tissue.
   d. increasing tissue.

_____ 6. **Hyaluronic acid,** present in every tissue of the body, serves to
   a. separate certain cells.
   b. reduce certain cells.
   c. hold certain cells together.
   d. destroy certain cells.

_____ 7. **Collagen** is
   a. a fibrous protein.
   b. a porous cell.
   c. dead skin.
   d. an amino acid.

_____ 8. **Exfoliants** are substances used to
   a. remove dead cells.
   b. slow down skin growth.
   c. moisturize the skin.
   d. remove hair follicles.

14B   CENTRAL THEME AND MAIN IDEAS

Choose the best answer.

_____ 1. What is the central theme of "Waging War on Wrinkles"?
   a. Wrinkles are an inevitable part of the aging process.
   b. Too much sunlight is harmful for the skin.
   c. Cosmetics help reduce the signs of aging.
   d. Botox injections are an effective procedure to treat facial wrinkles.

_____ 2. What is the main idea of paragraph 3?
   a. A good sunblock and products with antioxidants and exfoliants help combat wrinkles caused by the sun.
   b. A skin care regimen using alpha-hydroxy acids and retinoids can reduce the appearance of wrinkles.
   c. Since cosmeceutical products contain a higher percentage of antioxidants and exfoliants, they are dispensed by physicians' offices.
   d. Wrinkles caused by the sun are the easiest to treat and to prevent.

14C   MAJOR DETAILS

Decide whether each detail is true (T), false (F), or not discussed (ND).

_____ 1. The best line of defense to prevent wrinkles caused by the sun is to use a good sunblock daily.

_____ 2. Wrinkles caused by sun damage are the hardest to prevent.

_____ 3. Sunlight is the only source of natural Vitamin D.

_____ 4. Exfoliants stimulate collagen production and smooth wrinkles.

_____ 5. Usually wrinkles tend to first appear between the eyes in the form of frown lines.

_____ 6. Facial exercises can prevent wrinkles from forming.

_____ 7. Botox is a therapy used to prevent muscle contractions that cause wrinkles.

Name   Date

_____ 8. The use of soft tissue fillers, known as augmentation, treats wrinkles caused by aging.

14D   INFERENCES

Decide whether each statement can be inferred (Yes) or cannot be inferred (No) from the reading selection.

_____ 1. Adopting a healthy lifestyle is much less expensive than buying cosmeceuticals to prevent wrinkles.

_____ 2. Not everyone can use Botox.

_____ 3. People cannot get rid of eye wrinkles until they know where they are coming from.

_____ 4. Cosmetic companies benefit greatly from the war against wrinkles.

_____ 5. Technology continues to look for products and techniques to combat wrinkles.

_____ 6. Drinking two to three glasses of water on an empty stomach helps to hydrate the skin.

14E   CRITICAL READING: THE AUTHOR'S STRATEGIES

Choose the best answer.

_____ 1. Jessica Dye's main audience for "Waging War on Wrinkles" is
   a. wealthy people who want to maintain a youthful appearance by reducing wrinkles.
   b. readers who want to know the benefits and risks involved in the use of Botox injections.
   c. women who are seeking an alternative to plastic surgery.
   d. men and women who are seeking information on the different types and treatment of wrinkles.

_____ 2. The author's purpose in writing this is to
   a. entertain.
   b. narrate.
   c. inform.
   d. persuade.

_____ 3. The overall tone of this reading is
   a. sensational.
   b. objective.
   c. depressing.
   d. gentle.

14F   READER'S PROCESS: SUMMARIZING YOUR READING

Choose the best answer.

_____ 1. What is the best summary of "Waging War on Wrinkles"?
  a. The writer describes the three types of wrinkles and possible treatments to delay the inevitable.
  b. The writer recommends using over-the-counter cosmetics compared to using Botox injections.
  c. The writer suggests that advances in technology will eventually win the war against wrinkles.
  d. The writer suggests that wrinkles can be reduced with a good skin care regimen and a healthy lifestyle.

14G   READER'S RESPONSE: TO DISCUSS OR WRITE ABOUT

1. Wrinkles are delicate creases caused by thin, sagging skin. Wrinkles are typically the result of aging and are especially visible on the face, neck, and hands. The cost of a Botox treatment varies from $300 to $1,000, depending on the geographical area, the surgeon's qualifications, the time of year, and the number of injections the patient will receive. If wrinkles are inevitable, why do people spend so much money to slow the process as well as to treat wrinkles?

2. Genetics are a part of wrinkle development, but some wrinkles can be prevented. Although millions of women—and men—spend millions of dollars on antiwrinkle treatments in department stores and at health spas, many users have started incorporating home remedies into their daily routines. Have you heard of any remedy to combat wrinkles using coconut, olive, or castor oil; fruits or other produce; or egg whites? If so, what is the procedure? How effective is it?

HOW DID YOU DO?
14 Waging War on Wrinkles

SKILL (number of items)	Number Correct		Points for each		Score
Vocabulary (8)	_____	×	2	=	_____
Central Theme and Main Ideas (2)	_____	×	8	=	_____
Major Details (8)	_____	×	4	=	_____
Inferences (6)	_____	×	4	=	_____
Critical Reading: The Author's Strategies (3)	_____	×	3	=	_____
Reader's Process: Summarizing Your Reading (1)	_____	×	3	=	_____

(Possible Total: 100) *Total* _____

The Danger of Hoarding

Joyce Cohen

LEARNING OBJECTIVES

• List the problems associated with hoarding.

THINKING: GETTING STARTED

• Is there anything you own that you would find difficult to throw away?

(1) For 25 years, a difficult-neighbor problem plagued Curtis and Elaine Colvin of Seattle. The neighbor's home and lawn resembled a junkyard. Finally, last spring, the elderly man was taken out of state by relatives. Konstantinos Apostolou bought the house—and sent in five men to clear the floor-to-ceiling junk.

(2) "It was the most disgusting thing I've ever seen in my life," says his son, George Apostolou. There was nowhere to walk, except for a narrow "goat path" connecting the rooms. The men hauled out seven Dumpsters' worth of clothes, books, magazines, spoiled food, firewood, car parts, tires, bank statements and 50-year-old tax records. "I feel bad for the guy," says Apostolou. "I'm sure he was ill." Just how ill is still little understood. The man was a classic hoarder—a condition usually considered freakish and laughable, or dismissed with cutesy terms like "pack rat" and "junkaholic."

(3) Only now is hoarding garnering serious attention. Within the past six years, about 10 **municipalities** have formed task forces so that public services can **collaborate** in cleaning up the property and helping the hoarder. And researchers are studying how hoarding differs from seemingly related conditions. **Hoarding** is currently considered one of the symptoms of obsessive–compulsive disorder (OCD).

(4) Hoarders don't just save stuff, but constantly acquire new stuff—to such a remarkable degree that it interferes with functioning and safety. It's unclear how widespread hoarding is, since the problem often surfaces only after a neighbor's complaint or a medical emergency. Randy Frost, a psychology professor at Smith College in Northampton, Mass., estimates that 2% to 3% of the population has OCD, and up to a third of those exhibit hoarding behavior.

(5) Real danger can lurk in homes overflowing with stuff. Floors buckle from the weight. People get buried under piles. Insects and rodents feast on rotting food. **Combustibles** ignite, endangering both occupants and

This hoarder's groceries and trash fill the floors and counters of a kitchen in Fairfax County, Virginia.

firefighters. Fairfax County, Va., formed one of the first task forces in 1998 after **squatters** settled in a house vacated by a hoarder, lit a fire in the fireplace and died in the ensuing blaze.

(6) Behavioral peculiarities among hoarders come as no surprise to researchers. For example, "They have rambling or overinclusive speech, where you ask them a question and they tell you a whole story with every possible detail before they get to the answer," says Sanjaya Saxena, a professor at UCLA's School of Medicine. They have high levels of anxiety, depression, and perfectionism. They are greatly indecisive—over what to eat, what to wear. They prepare for all **contingencies,** keeping items "just in case." But the true hallmark: "They apply emotions to a range of things that others would consider worthless," says Frost. Where most people see an empty roll of toilet paper, they see art supplies. At the same time, they tend to be **articulate** and well-educated, with sophisticated reasons for their saving and acquiring. What if they forgo a newspaper and with it the bit of knowledge that will change their life for the better?

(7) Though people with OCD—those who endlessly wash their hands or check the stove—acknowledge their behavior and are distressed by it, hoarders deny they have a problem. Brain scans show a difference in brain **abnormalities** between people with non-hoarding OCD and hoarding OCD, says Saxena of UCLA, who is studying the neurobiology of hoarding. Whereas non-hoarders show elevated brain activity in certain areas,

hoarders show decreased activity in the anterior cingulate gyrus, which deals with focus, attention and decision-making.

(8) Frost is developing cognitive behavioral treatments, but progress is slow. Almost always, if a place is cleaned out, the hoarding behavior returns immediately.

(9) In Pittsfield, Mass., fire chief Stephen Duffy tells of one elderly widow whose house had "debris piled higher than the bed, with one spot where she curled up on the mattress to sleep."

Here are some of the more difficult words in "The Danger of Hoarding."

Vocabulary List

abnormalities
(paragraph 7)

ab·nor·mal·ity (ab′nôr mal′ə tē) *n.* **1** the quality or condition of being abnormal **2** *pl.* **-ties** an abnormal thing; malformation

articulate
(paragraph 6)

ar·tic·u·late (är tik′yo̅o̅ lit, -yə-; *for v.*, -lāt′) *adj.* [L *articulatus*, pp. of *articulare*, to separate into joints, utter distinctly < *articulus*: see ARTICLE] **1** having parts connected by joints; jointed: usually **ar·tic′u·lat′ed 2** made up of distinct syllables or words that have meaning, as human speech **3** able to speak **4** expressing oneself easily and clearly **5** well formulated; clearly presented /an *articulate* argument/ —*vt.* **·lat′ed, ·lat′ing 1** to put together by joints; joint **2** to arrange in connected sequence; fit together; correlate /to *articulate* a science program for all grades/ **3** to utter distinctly; pronounce carefully; enunciate **4** to express clearly **5** *Phonet.* to produce (a speech sound) by moving an articulator —*vi.* **1** to speak distinctly; pronounce clearly **2** to be jointed or connected **3** *Phonet.* to produce a speech sound —**ar·tic′u·late·ly** *adv.* —**ar·tic′u·late·ness** *n.* or **ar·tic′u·lacy** (-lə sē) —**ar·tic′u·la′tive** (-lāt′iv) *adj.*

collaborate
(paragraph 3)

col·labo·rate (kə lab′ə rāt′) *vi.* **·rat·ed, ·rat′ing** [< LL(Ec) *collaboratus*, pp. of *collaborare*, to work together < L *com-*, with + *laborare*, to work: see LABOR] **1** to work together, esp. in some literary, artistic, or scientific undertaking **2** to cooperate with an enemy invader —**col·lab′o·ra′tion** *n.* —**col·lab′o·ra′tive** (-rāt′iv, -rə tiv) *adj.* —**col·lab′o·ra′tor** *n.*

combustibles
(paragraph 5)

com·bus·tible (kəm bus′tə bəl) *adj.* [Fr < ML *combustibilis*: see fol.] **1** that catches fire and burns easily; flammable **2** easily aroused; excitable; fiery —*n.* a flammable substance —**com·bus′·tibil′·ity** *n.* —**com·bus′·tibly** *adv.*

contingencies
(paragraph 6)

con·tin·gency (-jən sē) *n., pl.* **·cies** [see prec.] **1** the quality or condition of being contingent; esp., dependence on chance or uncertain conditions **2** something whose occurrence depends on chance or uncertain conditions; a possible, unforeseen, or accidental occurrence /be prepared for any *contingency*/ **3** some thing or event which depends on or is incidental to another /the *contingencies* of war/ —*SYN.* EMERGENCY

hoarding
(paragraph 3)

hoard (hôrd) *n.* [ME *hord* < OE, akin to Ger *hort*, Goth *huzd* < IE *keus-* < base *(s)keu-*, to cover, conceal > HIDE[1], Gr *skylos*, animal's skin] a supply stored up and hidden or kept in reserve —*vi.* to get and store away money, goods, etc. —*vt.* to accumulate and hide or keep in reserve —**hoard′er** *n.* —**hoard′·ing** *n.*

municipalities
(paragraph 3)

mu·nici·pal·ity (myo̅o̅ nis′ə pal′ə tē) *n., pl.* **-ties** [Fr *municipalité* < *municipal* < L *municipalis*, MUNICIPAL] **1** a city, town, etc. having its own incorporated government for local affairs **2** its governing officials

squatters
(paragraph 5)

squat·ter (skwät′ər) *n.* **1** a person or animal that squats, or crouches ☆**2** a person who settles on public or unoccupied land: see SQUAT (*vi.* 3 & 4) **3** a person who occupies illegally a vacant house, building, etc.

15A   VOCABULARY

Using the dictionary entries on page 232, fill in the blanks.

1. People who settle on unoccupied land or occupy vacant buildings are

   _____.

2. Wood and coal are _____.

3. _____ can best be identified as being different from ordinary conditions or the standard.

4. Squirrels can often be seen _____ nuts in the ground or in a tree for the winter.

5. The speaker was careful to _____ her words so that she could be understood by everyone.

6. The two students plan to _____ on the research assignment in sociology.

7. Highland Park is one of many small Texas _____ that have local self-government.

8. Scheduling an outdoor wedding in the spring or fall requires a couple to prepare for several _____.

15B   CENTRAL THEME AND MAIN IDEAS

Choose the best answer.

_____ 1. What is the central theme of "The Danger of Hoarding"?
   a. Hoarding is the accumulation of things that are of no value or have no real meaning.
   b. Compulsive hoarding is a variant of OCD and may be the result of some other underlying psychological problems.
   c. Neighbors and the community at large are often concerned about the private compulsive behavior of one person.
   d. The pollution of a home or its environs and the unwillingness or inability of the person to clean up represents a health hazard.

2. In your own words, give the main idea of paragraph 5.

   _____

   _____

3. In your own words, give the main idea of paragraph 6.

   _____

   _____

15C MAJOR DETAILS

Decide whether each detail is Major *or* Minor *based on the context of the reading selection.*

_____ 1. For 25 years, a difficult-neighbor problem plagued Curtis and Elaine Colvin of Seattle.

_____ 2. Once the elderly man was taken out of state by relatives, Konstantinos Apostolou bought the vacant house.

_____ 3. Only now is hoarding garnering serious attention.

_____ 4. Randy Frost, a psychology professor at Smith College, estimates that 2–3 percent of the population has OCD.

_____ 5. Fairfax County, Virginia, formed one of the first task forces in 1998 to clean up the property and help hoarders.

_____ 6. Brain scans show a difference in brain abnormalities between people with non-hoarding OCD and hoarding OCD.

_____ 7. Sanjaya Saxena, a professor at UCLA's School of Medicine, is studying the neurobiology of hoarding.

_____ 8. One elderly widow in Pittsfield, Massachusetts, had "debris piled higher than the bed. . . ."

15D INFERENCES

Decide whether each statement can be inferred (Yes) or cannot be inferred (No) from the reading selection.

_____ 1. Hoarding is far different from amassing possessions.

_____ 2. Hoarders can be undesirable neighbors.

_____ 3. Hoarding is more prevalent among men than women.

_____ 4. There is no single, simple, or straightforward explanation for compulsive hoarding.

_____ 5. The only way to deal effectively with hoarding is through cognitive therapy.

15E CRITICAL READING: FACT OR OPINION

Decide whether each statement contains a Fact *or* Opinion.

_____ 1. *From paragraph 2:* "It was the most disgusting thing I've ever seen in my life [. . .]."

Name   Date

_____ 2. *From paragraph 2:* "There was nowhere to walk, except for a narrow 'goat path' connecting the rooms."

_____ 3. *From paragraph 3:* "Hoarding is currently considered one of the symptoms of OCD."

_____ 4. *From paragraph 5:* "Real danger can lurk in homes overflowing with stuff."

_____ 5. *From paragraph 6:* "Hoarders have high levels of anxiety, depression, and perfectionism."

15F CRITICAL READING: THE AUTHOR'S STRATEGIES

Choose the best answer.

_____ 1. The main audience for "The Danger of Hoarding" is
   a. anyone who has a neighbor or relative who is a hoarder.
   b. anyone who has a form of obsessive–compulsive disorder.
   c. anyone who has the responsibility of heading a task force dealing with hoarding.
   d. anyone who wants a better understanding of the causes and dangers of hoarding.

_____ 2. The author's main purpose in writing this reading is to
   a. entertain.
   b. describe.
   c. inform.
   d. convince.

_____ 3. The author's tone in this reading is
   a. humorous.
   b. candid.
   c. sentimental.
   d. tragic.

15G READER'S PROCESS: SUMMARIZING YOUR READING

_____ 1. What is the best summary of "The Danger of Hoarding"?
   a. The author recounts the story of an elderly man in Seattle whose hoarding impacted his neighbors Curtis and Elaine Colvin.
   b. The author traces the hoarding behavior in a number of people whose actions suggest a symptom of OCD.
   c. The author looks at the widespread problem of hoarding, including the symptoms, dangers, and treatment.
   d. The author cites the actions taken by some municipalities to protect not only the hoarder but also the hoarder's neighbors and environs.

15H   READER'S RESPONSE: TO DISCUSS OR WRITE ABOUT

1. Most of us know someone we would define as a "pack rat," a person who lives by the rules of "one man's trash is another man's treasure." Do you know of or have you read about someone who hoards? If yes, what types of things does the person hoard? How has it affected the person's living space? Is the living space a hazard to the person's health or safety? Explain.

2. Animal hoarders may be male or female, wealthy or poor, young or old. Many hoarders begin with just a few animals and then let their "hobby" get out of control. Generally animal hoarders are individuals who have substituted pets for people in their lives. How do you think animal hoarding affects them physically, emotionally, and financially? Explain.

HOW DID YOU DO?
15   The Danger of Hoarding

SKILL (number of items)	Number Correct		Points for each		Score
Vocabulary (8)	_____	×	2	=	_____
Central Theme and Main Ideas (3)	_____	×	6	=	_____
Major Details (8)	_____	×	3	=	_____
Inferences (5)	_____	×	4	=	_____
Critical Reading: Fact or Opinion (5)	_____	×	2	=	_____
Critical Reading: The Author's Strategies (3)	_____	×	3	=	_____
Reader's Process: Summarizing Your Reading (1)	_____	×	3	=	_____

(Possible Total: 100) *Total*   _____

Name   Date

Forty Acres and a Holiday

Lisa Jones

LEARNING OBJECTIVES
- Explain the significance of Juneteenth.

THINKING: GETTING STARTED
- What is the Emancipation Proclamation?

(1) There are three legends told of how enslaved Africans in the Texas territory came to know of their freedom, and why the word didn't get to them until two months after the Civil War ended, which was a good two and a half years after Lincoln's **Emancipation** Proclamation. Or, to make it plain, rather late. One legend says the messenger, a black Union soldier, was murdered. Another says he arrived, but had been delayed by mule travel. (A variation on this is that he had stopped to get married.) The third and favored is that the news was withheld by white landowners so they could bleed one last crop from slave labor. What is held as fact is that June nineteenth—the day that federal troops rode into Galveston with orders to release those kept as slaves—has been celebrated for 127 years, in Texas and beyond, as Emancipation Day, as Jubilation day, as Juneteenth. The day the last ones heard.

(2) Juneteenth, the name, is one of those fab African-Americanisms, functional, rhythmic, at once concise and not too concise. It fuses the month of June with the number nineteen, and alludes to the fact that the holiday was held in adjoining states on different days of the month as folks got the word. Early emancipation **rituals** were not exclusive to Texas (South Carolina and Mississippi's fall in May)—or to the South. What may have been the first emancipation ceremony was held in New York as early as 1808 to mark the legal **cessation** of the slave trade.

(3) No state comes close to Juneteenth in Texas, the black folks' Fourth of July, with its parades, feasting, pageants, and preachifying. Emancipation day organizations in Texas date back to the turn of the century. The most powerful image from the early days must have been former slaves themselves, who, according to tradition, marched together at the end of parade lines. By the 1950s Juneteenth Day came to be linked with, not freedom from slavery, but segregation. On Juneteenth, Texas's **Jim Crow** cities would allow blacks to be citizens for twelve hours a year by granting them entry into whites-only parks and zoos. With the passage of civil rights legislation in the sixties,

refined black Texans abandoned Juneteenth to their country cousins and took to celebrating Independence Day in July along with their white brethren.

(4) A Juneteenth **renaissance** has been gathering steam since the mid-eighties, spurred by the Afrocentricity crusade. Beyond being a **hootenanny** for black Texas (the condescending folksy portrait favored by the local press), it's become a holiday eagerly adopted nationwide by African Americans in search of cultural signposts. Not to mention one that offers, as is required these days, a dramatic tube-and-T-shirt-friendly sound bite of black history. The J-Day momentum is due in large part to the efforts of a man you might call Daddy Juneteenth, state representative Al Edwards from Houston. Edwards sponsored the bill that made Juneteenth an official Texas holiday thirteen years ago, a feat in a state that still closes banks for Confederate Heroes Day. Juneteenth U.S.A., Edwards's organization, tracks J-Day rites across the county and is fundraising for a national educational headquarters. To Edwards the holiday has tremendous **secular** and sacred promise. He sees it as an economic vehicle for African Americans, as well as a day that should be observed with almost holy remembrance: "The Jews say if they ever forget their history, may their tongues cleave to the roof of their mouth. . . . Let the same happen to us."

(5) You can find Juneteenth rituals in all regions of the country now. States like California, where Texans migrated en masse, have held Juneteenth festivities for decades. The New York area's largest is in Buffalo, tapping into upstate's rich history of antislavery activity. Wisconsin counts at least five, including Milwaukee's, where Juneteenth has been celebrated since 1971 and is the best attended single-day cultural event in the state. Far from being family picnics, these festivals sometimes last for days, made possible by the legwork of community groups, city cooperation, and private sector donations. Juneteenth in Minneapolis, now in its seventh year, is building a rep as one of the most progressive and trend setting J-Day celebrations in the Texas **diaspora.** What began as a poetry reading in a church basement is now two weeks of programming, including a film festival and an Underground Railroad reenactment. At these celebrations old world often knocks against new world, when Miss Juneteenth pageants (inherited from towns like Brenham, Texas, which crowns a "Goddess of Liberty") share the stage with Afro-chic street fairs ablaze in faux kente.

(6) There are those who think Juneteenth is an embarrassment. That the holiday tells more of our ignorance and **subjugation** than of an inheritance that predates slavery in the Americas. Or that it's "too black" because it promotes a separate but not equal Fourth of July, or "not black enough" as it's often funded by white purses. And of course that it's far too symbolic and doesn't solve anything. What does a Juneteenth celebration mean anyway when the Freedman's Bureau never gave us our forty acres and a mule? (Not thrilled about news of the state holiday, one former Texas legislator had this to say: "Dancing up and down the streets, drinking red soda water, eating watermelons . . . I grew out of that.") But Juneteenth critics haven't put a dent in the holiday's grass-roots popularity.

Former state representative Al Edwards gives the closing comments during the 32nd Annual Honorable Al Edwards Juneteenth Emancipation Proclamation Reading and Prayer Breakfast on Saturday morning June 18, 2011, at Ashton Villa in Galveston, Texas, The annual event commemorates Union General Gordon Granger's arrival in Galveston and his reading of "General Order No. 3" from the balcony of Ashton Villa freeing all slaves in Texas on June 19, 1865. (AP Photo/the Galveston Country Daily News, Kevin M. Cox)

(7) Folks are hungrier than ever for rituals that enshrine our identity as hyphen Americans. Kwanzaa's **metamorphosis** in the last few years speaks to this need. And merchandising opportunities are never far behind: Evolving in two short decades from cultural nationalist position paper to mainstream ethnic festival profiled in the *Times*'s Living Section, Kwanzaa has spawned its own designer cookbook and Santa surrogate, Father Kwanzaa. Now Juneteenth spreads like spring fever. Also gaining steam are rites of passage ceremonies for young men and women that are based on ancient African models and seek to address modern urban ills. (The National Rites of Passage Organization held its fifth annual conference this year.) And spotted last year in *Sage: A Scholarly Journal on Black Women:* plans for a Middle Passage memorial holiday that would fall near Thanksgiving.

(8) Buried in their shopping **ethos,** we tend to forget holidays were once holy days that once defined us in more profound ways than what Nintendo jumbo pack we got for Christmas. Michael Chaney, an arts activist in Minneapolis, believes that Juneteenth rituals could be more than acts of racial communion; they could have a role in redefining America:

"We have to realize our own role as historians. We need to ascribe our treasures and offer them to the world. Juneteenth should be a day for all Americans to get in touch with the Africanism within."

(9) Juneteenth does have great possibilities as a new American holiday. Along with reuniting blood relatives, the families that emancipated slaves made embraced family beyond kin, family as community. In this tradition, modern Juneteenth doesn't circumscribe any Dick-and-Jane **paean** to the nuclear family. You can be a single parent, gay, from D.C. or Ann Arbor; it's a history that includes you. You can read the Emancipation Proclamation out loud or drink some red soda water if you damn please. Or just take a moment out of your day to think about all the folks that laid down nothing less than their lives so that you could see the twentieth century.

Here are some of the more difficult words in "Forty Acres and a Holiday."

Vocabulary List

cessation
(paragraph 2)

ces·sa·tion (se sā′shən) *n.* ⟦L *cessatio* < pp. of *cessare*, CEASE⟧ a ceasing, or stopping, either forever or for some time

diaspora
(paragraph 5)

Di·as·po·ra (dī as′pə rə) *n.* ⟦Gr *diaspora*, a scattering < *diasperein*, to scatter < *dia-*, across + *speirein*, to sow: see SPORE⟧ **1** *a)* the dispersion of the Jews after the Babylonian Exile *b)* the Jews thus dispersed *c)* the places where they settled **2** [d-] any scattering of people with a common origin, background, beliefs, etc.

emancipation
(paragraph 1)

eman·ci·pate (ē man′sə pāt′, i-) *vt.* **-·pat′ed, -·pat′ing** ⟦< L *emancipatus*, pp. of *emancipare* < *e-*, out + *mancipare*, to deliver up or make over as property < *manceps*, purchaser < *manus*, the hand (see MANUAL) + *capere*, to take (see HAVE)⟧ **1** to set free (a slave, etc.); release from bondage, servitude, or serfdom **2** to free from restraint or control, as of social convention **3** *Law* to release (a child) from parental control and supervision —*SYN.* FREE —**eman′·ci·pa′·tion** *n.* —**eman′·ci·pa′·tive** *adj.* or **eman′·ci·pa·to′ry** (-pe tôr′ē) —**eman′·ci·pa′·tor** *n.*

ethos
(paragraph 8)

ethos (ē′thäs′) *n.* ⟦Gr *ēthos*, disposition, character: see ETHICAL⟧ the characteristic and distinguishing attitudes, habits, beliefs, etc. of an individual or of a group

hootenanny
(paragraph 4)

☆**hooten·anny** (hōōt′'n an′ē) *n.*, *pl.* **-·nies** ⟦orig. in sense of "dingus," "thingamajig"; a fanciful coinage⟧ a meeting of folk singers, as for public entertainment

Jim Crow
(paragraph 3)

☆**Jim Crow** ⟦name of an early black minstrel song⟧ [*also* **j- c-**] [Informal] traditional discrimination against or segregation of blacks, esp. in the U.S. —**Jim′-Crow′** *vt.*, *adj.* —**Jim Crow′·ism′**

metamorphosis
(paragraph 7)

meta·mor·pho·sis (-môr′fə sis, -môr fō′sis) *n.*, *pl.* **-·ses′** (-sēz′) ⟦L < Gr *metamorphōsis* < *metamorphoun*, to transform, transfigure < *meta*, over (see META-) + *morphē*, form, shape⟧ **1** *a)* change of form, shape, structure, or substance; transformation, as, in myths, by magic or sorcery *b)* the form resulting from such change **2** a marked or complete change of character, appearance, condition, etc. **3** *Biol.* a change in form, structure, or function as a result of development; specif., the physical transformation, more or less sudden, undergone by various animals during development after the embryonic state, as of the larva of an insect to the pupa and the pupa to the adult, or of the tadpole to the frog **4** *Med.* a pathological change of form of some tissues

paean
(paragraph 9)

paean (pē′ən) *n.* ⟦L < Gr *paian*, hymn < *Paian*, the healing one, epithet of Apollo < *paiein*, to strike, touch < ? IE base **pēu-* > PAVE⟧ **1** in ancient Greece, a hymn of thanksgiving to the gods, esp. to Apollo **2** a song of joy, triumph, praise, etc.

renaissance
(paragraph 4)

ren·ais·sance (ren′ə säns′, -zäns′; ren′ə säns′, -zäns′; *chiefly Brit* ri nä′səns) *n.* ⟦Fr < *renaître*, to be born anew < OFr *renestre* < *re-* + VL **nascere*, for L *nasci*, to be born: see GENUS⟧ **1** a new birth; rebirth; renascence **2** *a*) [R-] the style and forms of art, literature, architecture, etc. of the Renaissance *b*) [*often* R-] any revival of art, literature, or learning similar to the Renaissance —*adj.* [R-] **1** of, characteristic of, or in the style of the Renaissance **2** designating or of a style of architecture developed in Italy and western Europe between 1400 and 1600, characterized by the revival and adaptation of classical orders and design —**the Renaissance 1** the great revival of art, literature, and learning in Europe in the 14th, 15th, and 16th cent., based on classical sources: it began in Italy and spread gradually to other countries and marked the transition from the medieval world to the modern **2** the period of this revival

rituals
(paragraph 2)

ritu·al (rich′o͞o əl) *adj.* ⟦L *ritualis*⟧ of, having the nature of, or done as a rite or rites [*ritual* dances] —*n.* **1** a set form or system of rites, religious or otherwise **2** the observance of set forms or rites, as in public worship **3** a book containing rites or ceremonial forms **4** a practice, service, or procedure done as a rite, especially at regular intervals **5** ritual acts or procedures collectively —*SYN.* CEREMONY —rit′u·ally *adv.*

secular
(paragraph 4)

secu·lar (sek′yə lər) *adj.* ⟦ME *seculer* < OFr < LL(Ec) *saecularis*, worldly, profane, heathen < L, of an age < *saeculum*, an age, generation < IE **seitlo-* < base **sei-*, to scatter, SOW²⟧ **1** *a*) of or relating to worldly things as distinguished from things relating to church and religion; not sacred or religious; temporal; worldly [*secular* music, *secular* schools] *b*) of or marked by secularism; secularistic **2** ordained for a diocese **3** *a*) coming or happening only once in an age or century *b*) lasting for an age or ages; continuing for a long time or from age to age —*n.* **1** a cleric ordained for a diocese **2** a person not a cleric; layman —sec′u·larly *adv.*

subjugation
(paragraph 6)

sub·ju·gate (sub′jə gāt′) *vt.* ·-gat′ed, ·-gat′ing ⟦ME *subiugaten* < L *subjugatus*, pp. of *subjugare*, to bring under the yoke < *sub-*, under + *jugum*, YOKE⟧ **1** to bring under control or subjection; conquer **2** to cause to become subservient; subdue —*SYN.* CONQUER —sub′ju·ga′tion *n.* —sub′ju·ga′tor *n.*

16A   VOCABULARY

Choose the best answer.

_____ 1. The **cessation** of the slave trade meant it was
   a. discussed.
   b. celebrated.
   c. approved.
   d. stopped.

_____ 2. Lincoln's **Emancipation** Proclamation concerned the slaves'
   a. capture.
   b. disobedience.
   c. freedom.
   d. duties.

_____ 3. A **hootenanny** involves a gathering of
   a. marchers.
   b. singers.
   c. dancers.
   d. demonstrators.

_____ 4. **Subjugation** of a people indicates that the group has been
    a. conquered.
    b. honored.
    c. released.
    d. subdivided.

_____ 5. A **paean** is a song of
    a. love.
    b. hate.
    c. joy.
    d. sadness.

_____ 6. **Secular** refers to things that are
    a. religious.
    b. secretive.
    c. expensive.
    d. worldly.

_____ 7. **Diaspora** is a word used to refer to people who have
    a. rebelled.
    b. scattered.
    c. assembled.
    d. disappeared.

_____ 8. **Rituals** are ceremonies that involve
    a. a set form.
    b. a debate.
    c. a rehearsal.
    d. candlesticks.

_____ 9. **Ethos** as used in this essay means
    a. habit.
    b. purpose.
    c. bargain.
    d. celebration.

_____ 10. **Jim Crow** is a term used to refer to the policy of
    a. integration.
    b. migration.
    c. segregation.
    d. compensation.

_____ 11. **Renaissance** as used in this essay means
    a. festival.
    b. revival.
    c. holiday.
    d. revolt.

Name   Date

_____ 12. A **metamorphosis** occurs when something undergoes a noticeable
   a. destruction.
   b. control.
   c. restoration.
   d. change.

16B   CENTRAL THEME AND MAIN IDEAS

Choose the best answer.

_____ 1. What is the central theme of "Forty Acres and a Holiday"?
   a. Lincoln's Emancipation Proclamation freed the slaves in territories still at war with the Union.
   b. Juneteenth gets its name from a combination of June and the number nineteen.
   c. Celebrated for over one hundred years, Juneteenth has increased in popularity as an American holiday to acknowledge the freeing of the slaves.
   d. Juneteenth is the oldest known celebration of the ending of slavery.

_____ 2. What is the main idea of paragraph 1?
   a. Texas, as well as other states, has celebrated June nineteenth for over 127 years in recognition of the Emancipation Proclamation.
   b. President Abraham Lincoln issued the Emancipation Proclamation during the Civil War to free the slaves.
   c. Federal troops arrived in Galveston, Texas, on June 19 to free those slaves still in bondage.
   d. Three legends have been passed down to explain why Lincoln's Emancipation Proclamation failed to reach Texas until two and a half years after its issue.

_____ 3. What is the main idea of paragraph 6?
   a. The Freedmen's Bureau did not give forty acres and a mule to the freed slaves.
   b. There are those who think Juneteenth is an embarrassment.
   c. Juneteenth is a state holiday in Texas.
   d. One of the most vocal critics of the Juneteenth holiday is a former Texas state legislator.

16C MAJOR DETAILS

Decide whether each detail is Major *or* Minor *based on the context of the reading selection.*

_____ 1. The black Union soldier was late bringing news of the Emancipation Proclamation to Texas because he stopped en route to marry.

_____ 2. Federal troops arrived in Galveston on June 19 with the news that the slaves were freed.

_____ 3. South Carolina and Mississippi celebrate the freeing of the slaves in May.

_____ 4. In the 1950s, Juneteenth Day came to be linked with segregation, not slavery.

_____ 5. One way African Americans in Texas celebrate Juneteenth is with a hootenanny.

_____ 6. Texas state representative Al Edwards sponsored a bill that made Juneteenth an official state holiday in 1980.

_____ 7. A Miss Juneteenth pageant is part of the Juneteenth celebration in Texas.

16D INFERENCES

Choose the best answer.

_____ 1. *Read paragraph 3 again.* In the early parade, the former slaves marched at the end of parade lines because
a. they were too weak to keep the fast pace of the younger participants.
b. the spectators wanted to see the dancers, musicians, floats, and honored guests first.
c. their presence served as a lasting reminder to the onlookers of the significance of the celebration.
d. they could not afford to buy showier clothes expected to be worn by parade participants.

_____ 2. *Read paragraph 5 again.* Why are two of the largest celebrations now in Milwaukee and Minneapolis?
a. These cities now have a black majority population.
b. Attendees prefer to celebrate in the cooler climate of Wisconsin and Minnesota.
c. Employers, both state and private, give employees the day off.
d. These cities have sound financial backing and support to offer a wide range of activities.

Name   Date

_____ 3. In paragraph 5, the "faux kente" seen at the Afro-chic street fairs is popular for all of these reasons *except*
   a. it is traditional African dress.
   b. it reminds African Americans of their ancestry.
   c. it is brightly colored material.
   d. it is inexpensive and comfortable.

_____ 4. In paragraph 7, the word *hyphen* in the phrase "hyphen Americans" suggests any people who seek to
   a. hide their ethnic identity.
   b. emphasize their ethnic identity.
   c. recognize their ethnic language.
   d. promote their ethnic holidays.

16E   CRITICAL READING: FACT OR OPINION

Decide whether each statement, even if it quotes someone, contains a Fact *or an* Opinion.

_____ 1. *From paragraph 2:* "Juneteenth, the name, is one of those fab African-Americanisms, functional, rhythmic, at once concise and not too concise."

_____ 2. *From paragraph 3:* "No state comes close to Juneteenth in Texas, the black folks' Fourth of July, with its parades, feasting, pageants, and preachifying."

_____ 3. *From paragraph 4:* "To Edwards the holiday has tremendous secular and sacred promise."

_____ 4. *From paragraph 5:* "What began as a poetry reading in a church basement is now two weeks of programming, including a film festival and an Underground Railroad reenactment."

_____ 5. *From paragraph 6:* "Dancing up and down the streets, drinking red soda water, eating watermelons [. . .] I grew out of that."

_____ 6. *From paragraph 7:* "Kwanzaa has spawned its own designer cookbook and Santa surrogate, Father Kwanzaa."

16F CRITICAL READING: THE AUTHOR'S STRATEGIES

Choose the best answer.

_____ 1. The main audience for "Forty Acres and a Holiday" is
   a. anyone who wants to organize or participate in a Juneteenth celebration.
   b. anyone who is interested in how African Americans feel about slavery.
   c. anyone who is interested in Juneteenth and other African-American holidays.
   d. anyone who is critical of Juneteenth or other African-American holidays.

_____ 2. The author's purpose in writing this reading is to
   a. entertain.
   b. describe.
   c. inform.
   d. convince.

_____ 3. The author's tone in this reading is
   a. defensive.
   b. sad.
   c. negative.
   d. reflective.

16G READER'S PROCESS: SUMMARIZING YOUR READING

_____ 1. What is the best summary of "Forty Acres and a Holiday"?
   a. The writer explains the origins of the Juneteenth holiday and how it has spread from Texas to all parts of the country.
   b. The writer explains the origins of Juneteenth celebrations and why such holidays are important to African Americans.
   c. The writer explains why some African Americans wish to celebrate holidays that emphasize their own cultural traditions.
   d. The writer explains that many activities make up Juneteenth celebrations in different parts of the country.

16H READER'S RESPONSE: TO DISCUSS OR WRITE ABOUT

1. On June 19, 1865, Major General Gordon Granger arrived in Galveston, Texas, with the news that the Civil War had ended and that the slaves were free. Describe what you think may have been the reactions to this news from the standpoint of either the former masters or the former slaves. Was it shock? Jubilation? Why did many of the

Name   Date

free men and women leave Texas and head north? What social, educational, and/or economic challenges would they have faced?

2. Every ethnic group has certain traditions or celebrations that it recognizes and observes. Describe one that either you or your family participates in. Does it relate to a specific event in history? Is it participated in by people of other races? Does it involve special outdoor activities, food, ceremonies, contests, parades, speeches, or gifts? Be specific as to how you observe this tradition or celebration.

HOW DID YOU DO?
16 Forty Acres and a Holiday

SKILL (number of items)	Number Correct		Points for each		Score
Vocabulary (12)	_____	×	2	×	_____
Central Theme and Main Ideas (3)	_____	×	5	×	_____
Major Details (7)	_____	×	2	×	_____
Inferences (4)	_____	×	4	×	_____
Critical Reading: Fact or Opinion (6)	_____	×	3	×	_____
Critical Reading: The Author's Strategies (3)	_____	×	3	×	_____
Reader's Process: Summarizing Your Reading (1)	_____	×	4	×	_____

(Possible Total: 100) *Total* _____

My Mother's Blue Bowl

Alice Walker

LEARNING OBJECTIVES
- Critique the sentiments a grown woman attaches to a blue bowl from her childhood.

THINKING: GETTING STARTED
- Is there any material object of your mother or your grandmother to which you have a sentimental attachment?

(1) Visitors to my house are often served food—soup, potatoes, rice—in a large blue stoneware bowl, noticeably chipped at the rim. It is perhaps the most precious thing I own. It was given to me by my mother in her last healthy days. The days before a massive stroke laid her low and left her almost speechless. Those days when to visit her was to be drawn into a **serene** cocoon of memories and present-day **musings** and to rest there, in temporary retreat from the rest of the world, as if still an infant, nodding and secure at her breast.

(2) For much of her life my mother longed, passionately longed, for a decent house. One with a yard that did not have to be cleared with an ax. One with a roof that kept out the rain. One with a floor that you could not fall through. She longed for a beautiful house of wood or stone. Or of red brick, like the houses her many sisters and their husbands had. When I was thirteen she found such a house. Green-shuttered, white-walled. Breezy. With a lawn and a hedge and giant pecan trees. A porch swing. There her gardens **flourished** in spite of the shade, as did her youngest daughter, for whom she sacrificed her life doing hard labor in someone else's house, in order to afford peace and prettiness for her child, to whose grateful embrace she returned each night.

(3) But, curiously, the minute I left home, at seventeen, to attend college, she abandoned the dream house and moved into the projects. Into a small, tight apartment of few breezes, in which I was never to feel comfortable, but that she declared suited her "to a T." I took **solace** in the fact that it was at least hugged by spacious lawn on one side, and by forest, out the back door, and that its isolated position at the end of the street meant she would have a measure of privacy. Her move into the projects—the best housing poor black people in the South ever had, she would occasionally declare, even as my father struggled to adjust to the cramped rooms and hard, unforgiving qualities of brick—was, I now understand, a step

in the direction of **divestiture,** lightening her load, permitting her worldly possessions to dwindle in significance and, well before she herself would turn to spirit, roll away from her.

(4) She owned little, in fact. A bed, a dresser, some chairs. A set of living-room furniture. A set of kitchen furniture. A bed and wardrobe (given to her years before, when I was a teenager, by one of her prosperous sisters). Her flowers: everywhere, inside the house and outside. Planted in anything she managed to get her green hands on, including old suitcases and abandoned shoes. She recycled everything, effortlessly. And gradually she had only a small amount of stuff—mostly stuff her children gave her: nightgowns, perfume, a microwave—to recycle or to use.

(5) Each time I visited her I **marveled** at the modesty of her desires. She appeared to have hardly any, beyond a thirst for a Pepsi-Cola or a hunger for a piece of fried chicken or fish. On every visit I noticed that more and more of what I remembered of her possessions seemed to be missing. One day I commented on this. Taking a deep breath, sighing and following both with a beaming big smile, which lit up her face, the room, and my heart, she said: "Yes, it's all going. I don't need it anymore. If there's anything you want, take it when you leave; it might not be here when you come back."

Familiar objects from childhood can often have endearing significance later in a person's life.

(6) The dishes my mother and father used daily had come from my house; I had sent them years before, when I moved from Mississippi to New York. Neither the plates nor the silver matched entirely, but it was all beautiful in her eyes. There were numerous cups, used by the scores of children from the neighborhood who continued throughout her life to come and go. But there was nothing there for me to want.

(7) One day, however, looking for a jar into which to pour leftover iced tea, I found myself probing deep into the wilderness of the overstuffed, airless pantry. Into the land of the old-fashioned, the outmoded, the outdated. The humble and the obsolete. There was a smoothing iron, a churn. A butter press. And two large bowls. One was cream and rose with a blue stripe. The other was a deep, vivid blue. "May I have this bowl, Mama?" I asked, looking at her and at the blue bowl with delight. "You can have both of them," she said, barely acknowledging them, and continuing to put leftover food away.

(8) I held the bowls on my lap for the rest of the evening, while she watched a TV program about cops and criminals that I found too horrifying to follow. Before leaving the room I kissed her on the forehead and asked if I could get anything for her from the kitchen; then I went off to bed. The striped bowl I placed on a chair beside the door, so I could look at it from where I lay. The blue bowl I placed in the bed with me. In giving me these gifts, my mother had done a number of astonishing things, in her typically offhand way. She had taught me a lesson about letting go of possessions—easily, without emphasis or regret—and she had given me a symbol of what she herself represented in my life.

(9) For the blue bowl especially was a **cauldron** of memories. Of cold, harsh, wintry days, when my brothers and sister and I trudged home from school burdened down by the silence and **frigidity** of our long trek from the main road, down the hill to our shabby-looking house. More rundown than any of our classmates' houses. In winter my mother's riotous flowers would be absent, and the shack stood revealed for what it was. A gray, decaying, too small **barrack** meant to house the **itinerant** tenant workers on a prosperous white man's farm.

(10) Slogging through sleet and wind to the sagging front door, thankful that our house was too far from the road to be seen clearly from the school bus, I always felt a wave of embarrassment and misery. But then I would open the door. And there inside would be my mother's winter flowers: a glowing fire in the fireplace, colorful handmade quilts on all our beds, paintings and drawings of flowers and fruits and, yes, of Jesus, given to her by who knows whom—and most of all, there in the center of the rough-hewn table, which in the tiny kitchen almost touched the rusty woodburning stove, stood the big blue bowl, full of whatever was the most tasty thing on earth.

(11) There was my mother herself. Glowing. Her teeth sparkling. Her eyes twinkling. As if she lived in a castle and her favorite princes and princesses had just dropped by to visit.

(12) The blue bowl stood there, seemingly full forever, no matter how deeply or **rapaciously** we dipped, as if it had no bottom. And she dipped up soup. Dipped up lima beans. Dipped up stew. Forked out potatoes. Spooned out rice and peas and corn. And in the light and warmth that was her, we dined. Thank you, Mama.

Here are some of the more difficult words in "My Mother's Blue Bowl."

Vocabulary List

barrack
(paragraph 9)

bar·rack[1] (bar′ək, ber′-) *n.* ⟦Fr *baraque* < Sp *barraca*, cabin, mud hut < *barro*, clay, mud < VL **barrum*, clay⟧ **1** [Rare] an improvised hut **2** [*pl., often with sing. v.*] *a*) a building or group of buildings for housing soldiers *b*) a large, plain, often temporary building for housing workmen, police, etc. —*vt., vi.* to house in barracks

cauldron
(paragraph 9)

cal·dron (kôl′drən) *n.* ⟦ME & Anglo-Fr *caudron* < OFr *chauderon* < L *calderia*: see CALDARIUM⟧ **1** a large kettle or boiler **2** a violently agitated condition like the boiling contents of a caldron

divestiture
(paragraph 3)

di·vest (də vest′, dī-) *vt.* ⟦altered < DEVEST⟧ **1** to strip *of* clothing, equipment, etc. **2** to deprive or dispossess *of* rank, rights, etc. **3** to disencumber or rid *of* something unwanted **4** *Law* DEVEST —*SYN.* STRIP[1]
di·vesti·ture (-ə chər) *n.* a divesting or being divested: also **di·vest′·ment** or **di·ves′·ture**

flourished
(paragraph 2)

flour·ish (flur′ish) *vi.* ⟦ME *florishen* < extended stem of OFr *florir*, to blossom < LL **florire* < L *florere* < *flos*, FLOWER⟧ **1** [Obs.] to blossom **2** to grow vigorously; succeed; thrive; prosper **3** to be at the peak of development, activity, influence, production, etc.; be in one's prime **4** to make showy, wavy motions, as of the arms **5** [Now Rare] *a*) to write in an ornamental style *b*) to perform a fanfare, as of trumpets —*vt.* **1** to ornament with something flowery or fanciful **2** ⟦first so used by John WYCLIFFE⟧ to wave (a sword, arm, hat, etc.) in the air; brandish —*n.* **1** [Rare] a thriving state; success; prosperity **2** anything done in a showy way, as a sweeping movement of the limbs or body **3** a waving in the air; brandishing **4** a decorative or curved line or lines in handwriting **5** an ornate musical passage; fanfare **6** [Obs.] a blooming or a bloom —**flour′·isher** *n.* —**flour′·ish·ing** *adj.*

frigidity
(paragraph 9)

frigid (frij′id) *adj.* ⟦ME < L *frigidus* < *frigere*, to be cold < *frigus*, coldness, frost < IE base **srig-*, coldness > Gr *rhigos*, frost⟧ **1** extremely cold; without heat or warmth **2** without warmth of feeling or manner; stiff and formal **3** habitually failing to become sexually aroused, or abnormally repelled by sexual activity: said of a woman —**fri·gidi·ty** (fri jid′ə tē) *n.* or **frig′id·ness** —**frig′id·ly** *adv.*

itinerant
(paragraph 9)

itin·er·ant (-ənt) *adj.* ⟦LL *itinerans*, prp. of *itinerari*, to travel < L *iter* (gen. *itineris*), a walk, journey < base of *ire*, to go: see YEAR⟧ traveling from place to place or on a circuit —*n.* a person who travels from place to place —**itin′·er·antly** *adv.*

marveled
(paragraph 5)

mar·vel (mär′vəl) *n.* ⟦ME *mervaile* < OFr *merveille*, a wonder < VL *mirabilia*, wonderful things, orig. neut. pl. of L *mirabilis*, wonderful < *mirari*, to wonder at < *mirus*, wonderful: see SMILE⟧ **1** a wonderful or astonishing thing; prodigy or miracle **2** [Archaic] astonishment —*vi.* **··veled** or **··velled**, **··vel·ing** or **··vel·ling** to be filled with admiring surprise; be amazed; wonder —*vt.* to wonder at or about: followed by a clause

musings
(paragraph 1)

mus·ing (myōō′ziŋ) *adj.* that muses; meditative —*n.* meditation; reflection —**mus′·ingly** *adv.*

rapaciously
(paragraph 12)

ra·pa·cious (rə pā′shəs) *adj.* ⟦< L *rapax* (gen. *rapacis*) < *rapere*, to seize (see RAPE[1]) + -OUS⟧ **1** taking by force; plundering **2** greedy or grasping; voracious **3** living on captured prey; predatory —**ra·pa′·ciously** *adv.* —**ra·pac·ity** (rə pas′ə tē) *n.* or **ra·pa′·cious·ness**

Vocabulary List

serene
(paragraph 1)

se·rene (sə rēn′) *adj.* ⟦L *serenus* < IE **ksero-*, dry (> Gr *xēros*, dry, OHG *serawēn*, to dry out) < base **ksā-*, to burn⟧ **1** clear; bright; unclouded *[a serene sky]* **2** not disturbed or troubled; calm, peaceful, tranquil, etc. **3** [S-] exalted; high-ranking: used in certain royal titles *[his Serene Highness]* —*n.* [Old Poet.] a serene expanse, as of sky or water —*SYN.* CALM —**se·rene′ly** *adv.* —**se·rene′·ness** *n.*

solace
(paragraph 3)

sol·ace (säl′is) *n.* ⟦ME < OFr *solaz* < L *solacium* < *solari*, to comfort < IE base **sel-*, favorable, in good spirits > SILLY⟧ **1** an easing of grief, loneliness, discomfort, etc. **2** something that eases or relieves; comfort; consolation; relief Also **sol′·ace·ment** (-mənt) —*vt.* **-·aced**, **-·ac·ing** **1** to give solace to; comfort; console **2** to lessen or allay (grief, sorrow, etc.) —*SYN.* COMFORT —**sol′·ac·er** *n.*

17A   VOCABULARY

Match 11 of the imaginary quotations with a vocabulary word listed on pages 251–252. Write "None" for the one extra quotation.

1. "In the early 1900s, many families washed their clothes by boiling them in a kettle over an open fire."

   1. _____

2. "Farm laborers who move from place to place to harvest seasonal crops are not paid well."

   2. _____

3. "After being lost in the mountains for two days, the hungry hikers ate the beef stew greedily."

   3. _____

4. "As Nikita lay in front of the cozy fire, her dreamy thoughts about a summer vacation brought a smile to her face."

   4. _____

5. "Enid Lake was calm again after the thunderstorm had passed."

   5. _____

6. "In his closing arguments, attorney Lance Minor made an intense plea for his client's acquittal."

   6. _____

7. "The commander housed the soldiers in temporary buildings until their permanent quarters were completed."

   7. _____

8. "Stephen's parents never visit him in Minnesota in the winter because of the extremely cold weather."

   8. _____

Name   Date

9. "The magician amazed us with his performance at the Orpheum Theater."

9. _____

10. "Getting rid of unwanted items can be done through a yard or garage sale."

10. _____

11. "To ease the pain of his father's death, Paul ate junk food for comfort."

11. _____

12. "Because of the moisture, the termites thrived in the wooden columns on my front porch.

12. _____

17B   CENTRAL THEME AND MAIN IDEAS

Choose the best answer.

_____ 1. What is the central theme of "My Mother's Blue Bowl"?
   a. Alice Walker's mother gave away most of her possessions except several items that her children had given her.
   b. The blue bowl filled Alice Walker with fond memories of her childhood with her mother.
   c. Alice Walker often serves food in the blue bowl her mother gave her.
   d. Alice Walker was embarrassed by the poverty she grew up in and her lack of new, pretty possessions.

_____ 2. What is the main idea of paragraph 3?
   a. Alice Walker left home at the age of 17.
   b. When Alice Walker went to college, her parents moved into the projects.
   c. The projects were the best housing many poor black families in the South could afford.
   d. As she aged, Alice Walker's mother wanted to own fewer and fewer possessions.

_____ 3. What is the main idea of paragraph 4?
   a. Alice Walker's mother owned few worldly possessions.
   b. Alice Walker's mother liked flowers inside and outside her house.
   c. Alice Walker's mother had a wealthy sister.
   d. Alice Walker's mother believed in recycling.

17C   MAJOR DETAILS

Decide whether each detail is true (T), false (F), or not discussed (ND).

_____ 1. Alice Walker's mother longed for a house of wood, stone, or brick.

_____ 2. The dream house of Alice Walker's mother was in Mississippi.

_____ 3. Alice Walker was an only child.

_____ 4. Alice Walker was a college graduate.

_____ 5. Alice Walker's mother had a fondness for Pepsi-Cola and fried chicken and fish.

_____ 6. Alice Walker's mother had few items in her kitchen pantry.

_____ 7. Alice Walker's mother did not own a television.

_____ 8. Alice Walker's mother had a talent for growing flowers.

_____ 9. Alice Walker's mother worked as a cleaning lady.

_____10. Alice Walker would sometimes walk to school rather than ride the school bus.

17D   INFERENCES

Choose the best answer.

_____ 1. *Read paragraph 6 again.* When Alice Walker left Mississippi for New York, she gave her old dishes to her mother because
    a. Alice Walker did not have enough money to buy a new set of dishes for her mother.
    b. Alice Walker knew her mother would prefer dishes that had a "history" in the family.
    c. Alice Walker feared the visiting neighborhood children would break or chip new dishes.
    d. Alice Walker did not want to pay for shipping her old dishes to her new home.

_____ 2. *Read paragraph 8 again.* Why did Alice Walker hold the bowls on her lap for the rest of the evening and then take the blue bowl to bed with her? Alice Walker
    a. was afraid her mother might change her mind.
    b. treasured the bowls and enjoyed holding them.
    c. thought her mother might break them.
    d. wanted to throw them away the first thing the next morning.

_____ 3. *Read paragraph 12 again.* What did Alice Walker imply when she wrote "And in the light and warmth that was her, we dined"?
   a. Her mother hugged them as they dined in the poorly insulated house that was cold in the winter.
   b. The family dined by candlelight because they had no electricity.
   c. Her mother entertained the family with stories that made them laugh.
   d. The children loved their mother so much that they did not notice their poor surroundings when with her.

17E CRITICAL READING: THE AUTHOR'S STRATEGIES

Choose the best answer.

_____ 1. The main audience for "My Mother's Blue Bowl" is
   a. anyone who places too much importance on material possessions.
   b. anyone who appreciates the sentimental value of worthless objects.
   c. anyone who identifies with the love and sacrifices parents make for their children.
   d. anyone who has lost a mother with whom they had a close relationship.

_____ 2. The author's purpose in writing this reading is to
   a. persuade.
   b. entertain.
   c. describe.
   d. narrate.

_____ 3. The author's tone in this reading is
   a. objective.
   b. nostalgic.
   c. depressing.
   d. scornful.

17F   READER'S PROCESS: SUMMARIZING YOUR READING

_____ 1. What is the best summary of "My Mother's Blue Bowl"?
   a. The writer tells about her sentimental attachment to a chipped blue bowl that belongs to her mother.
   b. The writer tells about how she received a chipped blue bowl from her mother shortly before her mother's death.
   c. The writer tells how she treasures a chipped blue bowl that reminds her of her mother's way of living her life and caring for her family.
   d. The writer tells how her mother rejected material things and had very few possessions to leave to her children.

17G   READER'S RESPONSE: TO DISCUSS OR WRITE ABOUT

1. Describe a woman in your family (or one whom you have read about or studied) who succeeded despite setbacks or obstacles. Describe her fully, but focus especially on the one outstanding quality that you think helped her succeed.

2. Think of a significant possession of your parent(s) that you would like to have. What memories do you associate with this object? Is there a significant object from your childhood that you think your child(ren) would want? Why?

How Did You Do?
17 My Mother's Blue Bowl

SKILL (number of items)	Number Correct		Points for each		Score
Vocabulary (12)	_____	×	2	=	_____
Central Theme and Main Ideas (3)	_____	×	6	=	_____
Major Details (10)	_____	×	4	=	_____
Inferences (3)	_____	×	2	=	_____
Critical Reading: The Author's Strategies (3)	_____	×	3	=	_____
Reader's Process: Summarizing Your Reading (1)	_____	×	3	=	_____

(Possible Total: 100) *Total*   _____

Name   Date

From In Search of Bernabé

Graciela Limón

LEARNING OBJECTIVES

- Identify the risks illegal aliens take to cross the border into the United States.

THINKING: GETTING STARTED

- What risks would you be willing to take to find a missing family member?

(1) Luz and Arturo arrived at the Tijuana bus terminal forty hours later, exhausted and bloated from sitting in their cramped seats. As soon as they stepped out of the bus, they were approached by a woman who asked them if they wanted to cross the border that night. Without waiting for an answer, she told them she could be their guide. The price was five hundred American dollars apiece.

(2) Luz stared at the woman for a few moments, caught off guard by the suddenness of what was happening. More than her words, it was the woman's appearance that held Luz's attention. She was about thirty-five. Old enough, Luz figured, to have experience in her business. The woman was tall and slender, yet her body conveyed muscular strength that gave Luz the impression that she would be able to lead them across the border. The *coyota* returned Luz's gaze, evidently allowing time for the older woman to make up her mind. She took a step closer to Luz, who squinted as she concentrated on the woman's face. Luz regarded her dark skin and high forehead, and the deeply set eyes that steadily returned her questioning stare. With a glance, she took in the *coyota*'s faded Levi's and plaid shirt under a shabby sweatshirt, and her eyes widened when she saw the woman's scratched, muddy cowboy boots. She had seen only men wear such shoes.

(3) Luz again looked into the woman's eyes. She was tough, and Luz knew that she had to drive a hard bargain. She began to cry. "*!Señora, por favor!*" Have a heart! How can you charge so much? We're poor people who have come a long way. Where do you think we can find so many *dólares*? All we have is one hundred dollars to cover the two of us. Please! For the love of your mamacita!" The woman crossed her arms over her chest and laughed out loud as she looked into Luz's eyes. She spoke firmly. "Señora, I'm not in the habit of eating fairy tales for dinner. You've been in Mexico City for a long time. I have eyes, don't I? I can tell that you're not

starving. Both of you have eaten a lot of enchiladas and tacos. Just look at those *nalgas!*" She gave Luz a quick, hard smack on her behind. Then, ignoring the older woman's look of outrage, the *coyota* continued to speak rapidly. "Look, Señora. Just to show you that I have feelings, I'll consider guiding the both of you at the reduced rate of seven hundred dollars. Half now; the rest when I get you to Los Angeles. Take it or leave it!" Luz knew that she was facing her match. She answered with one word, "*Bueno.*"

(4) The *coyota* led them to a man who was standing nearby. He was wearing a long overcoat, inappropriate for the **sultry** weather in Tijuana. The coat had a purpose, though, for it concealed deep inner pockets which were filled with money. The *coyota* pulled Luz nearer to the man, then whispered into her ear. "This man will change your **pesos** into American dollars. A good rate, I guarantee." When Arturo began to move closer, the *coyota* turned on him. "You stay over there!" Arturo obeyed.

(5) Even though she felt distrust, Luz decided that she and Arturo had no alternative. However, she needed to speak with him, so she pulled him to the side. "Hijo, we're taking a big chance. We can be robbed, even killed. Remember the stories we've been hearing since we left home. But what can we do? We need someone to help us get across, so what does it matter if it's this one, or someone else? What do you say?" Arturo agreed

A sign near the United States/Mexico border warns illegal immigrants of the dangers in crossing the Yuha desert. The sign reads, "Careful! Don't risk your life to the elements. It's not worth the hardship!" Symbols represent, clockwise from left, sunstroke, mountains, rattlesnakes, canals, lack of water, and desert habitat.

with her. "Let's try to make it to the other side. The sooner the better. I think you made a good bargain. We have the money, don't we?" "With a little left over when we get to Los Angeles."

(6) Before they returned to where the others were waiting, she turned to a wall. She didn't want anyone to see what she was doing. Luz withdrew the amount of pesos she estimated she could exchange for a little more than seven hundred American dollars. She walked over to the money **vendor,** and no sooner had the man placed the green bills on her palm than she heard the *coyota*'s sharp voice. "Three hundred and fifty dollars, *por favor!*" She signaled Luz and Arturo to follow her to a waiting car. They went as far as Mesa Otay, the last stretch of land between Mexico and California. There, the *coyota* instructed them to wait until it got dark. Finally, when Luz could barely see her hand in front of her, the woman gave the signal. "*!Vámonos!*"

(7) They walked together under the cover of darkness. As Luz and Arturo **trekked** behind the woman, they sensed that they were not alone, that other people were also following. Suddenly someone issued a warning, "*!La Migra! !Cuidado!*" The *coyota* turned with unexpected speed, and murmured one word, "*!Abajo!*" All three fell to the ground, clinging to it, melting into it, hoping that it would split open so that they could crawl into its safety. Unexpectedly a light flashed on. Like a giant eye, it seemed to be coming from somewhere in the sky, slowly scanning the **terrain.** No one moved. All that could be heard were the crickets and the dry grass rasping in the mild breeze. The light had not detected the bodies crouched behind bushes and rocks. It flashed out as suddenly as it had gone on.

(8) "*!Vámonos!*" The *coyota* was again on her feet and moving. They continued in the dark for hours over rough, rocky terrain. The *coyota* was sure-footed but Luz and Arturo bumped into rocks and tripped over gopher holes. Luz had not rested or eaten since she had gotten off the bus. She was fatigued but she pushed herself fearing she would be left behind if she stopped. Arturo was exhausted too, but he knew that he still had reserves of energy, enough for himself and for Luz.

(9) Dawn was breaking as they ascended a hill. Upon reaching the summit, they were struck with awe at the sight that spread beneath their feet. Their heavy breathing stopped abruptly as their eyes glowed in disbelief. Below, even though **diffused** by dawn's advancing light, was an illuminated sea of streets and buildings. A blur of neon formed a mass of light and color, edged by a highway that was a ribbon of liquid silver. Luz and Arturo wondered if fatigue had caused their eyes to trick them because as far as they could see there was brilliance, limited only in the distance by a vast ocean. To their left, they saw the lights of San Diego unfolding beneath them, and their heart stopped when they realized that farther north, where their eyes could not see, was their destination. Without thinking, Luz and Arturo threw their arms around one another and wept.

(10) The lights of San Diego receded behind them. The *coyota* had guided Luz and Arturo over an inland trail, taking them past the U.S.

Immigration Station at San Onofre, and then down to connect with the highway. A man in a car was waiting for them a few yards beyond Las Pulgas Road on California Interstate 5. The driver got out of the car as they approached, extending a rough hand first to Luz, and then to Arturo. "*Me llamo Ordaz.*" Ordaz turned to the *coyota* and spoke in English. His words were casual, as if he had seen her only hours before. "You're late. I was beginning to worry."

(11) "The old bag slowed me down." The *coyota* spoke to the man in English, knowing that her **clients** were unable to understand her. Then, she switched to Spanish to introduce herself to Luz and Arturo. "*Me llamo Petra Traslaviña.* I was born back in San Ysidro on a dairy farm. I speak English and Spanish." There was little talk among them beyond this first encounter. The four piled into a battered Pontiac station wagon, and with Ordaz at the wheel, they headed north. The woman pulled out a pack of Mexican cigarettes, smoking one after the other, until Ordaz started to cough. He opened the window complaining, "*Por favor*, Petra, you wanna choke us to death?" "Shut up!" she retorted rapidly, slurring the English *sh*. The phrase engraved itself in Luz's memory. She liked the sound of it. She liked its effect even more, since she noticed that Ordaz was silenced by the magical phrase. Inwardly, Luz practiced her first English words, repeating them over and again under her breath.

(12) Luz and Arturo were quiet during the trip mainly because they were frightened by the speed at which Ordaz was driving. As she looked out over the *coyota*'s shoulder, Luz knew that she didn't like what she was feeling and hearing. She even disliked the smell of the air, and she felt especially threatened by the early morning fog. When the headlights of oncoming cars broke the grayness, her eyes squinted with pain. The hours seemed endless, and they were relieved when Ordaz finally steered the Pontiac off the freeway and onto the streets of Los Angeles. Like children, Luz and Arturo looked around craning their necks, curiously peering through the windows and seeing that people waited for their turn to step onto the street. Luz thought it was silly the way those people moved in groups. No one ran out onto the street, leaping, jumping, dodging cars as happened in Mexico City and back home. Right away, she missed the vendors peddling **wares,** and the stands with food and drink.

(13) Suddenly, Luz was struck by the thought that she didn't know where the *coyota* was taking them. As if reading Luz's mind, the woman asked, "Do you have a place you want me to take you to?" Rattled by the question, Luz responded timidly. "No. We didn't have time to think." "I thought so. It's the same with all of you."

(14) The *coyota* was quiet for a while before she whispered to Ordaz, who shook his head in response. They engaged in a heated exchange of words in English, the driver obviously disagreeing with what the *coyota* was proposing. Finally, seeming to have nothing more to say, Ordaz shrugged his shoulders, apparently accepting defeat. The *coyota* turned to her passengers. "*Vieja*, I know of a place where you two can find a roof and a meal until you

find work. But . . . " She was hesitating. "!*Mierda!* . . . just don't tell them I brought you. They don't like me because I charge you people money."

(15) What she said next was muttered and garbled. Luz and Arturo did not understand her so they kept quiet, feeling slightly uneasy and confused. By this time Ordaz was on Cahuenga Boulevard in Hollywood. He turned up a short street, and pulled into the parking lot of Saint Turibius Church, where the battered wagon spurted, then came to a stand-still. "*Hasta aquí.* You've arrived."

(16) The *coyota* was looking directly at Luz, who thought she detected a warning sign in the woman's eyes. "It was easy this time, Señora. Remember, don't get caught by *la Migra*, because it might not be so good next time around. But if that happens, you know that you can find me at the station in Tijuana." Again, the *coyota* seemed to be fumbling for words. Then she said, "Just don't get any funny ideas hanging around these people. I mean, they love to call themselves *voluntarios*, and they'll do anything for nothing. *Yo no soy así.* I'll charge you money all over again, believe me!" The *coyota* seemed embarrassed. Stiffly, she shifted in her seat, pointing at a two-story, Spanish-style house next to the church. "See that house?" Luz nodded. "*Bueno.* Just walk up to the front door, knock, and tell them who you are, and where you're from. They'll be good to you. But, as I already told you, don't mention me."

(17) She turned to Arturo. "Take care of yourself, *muchacho*. I've known a few like you who have gotten themselves killed out there." With her chin, she pointed toward the street. When Arturo opened his mouth to speak, the *coyota* cut him off curtly. "My three hundred and fifty dollars, *por favor*." She stretched out her hand in Luz's direction without realizing that her words about other young men who resembled Arturo had had an impact on Luz. "Petra, have you by any chance met my son? His name is Bernabé and he looks like this young man?"

(18) The *coyota* looked into Luz's eyes. When she spoke her voice was almost soft. "They all look like Arturo, Madre. They all have the same fever in their eyes. How could I possibly know your son from all the rest?" Luz's heart shuddered when the *coyota* called her madre. Something told her that the woman did know Bernabé. This thought filled her with new hope, and she gladly reached into her purse. She put the money into the *coyota*'s hand, saying, "*Hasta pronto.* I hope, Petra, that our paths will cross again sooner or later."

(19) Luz and Arturo were handed the small bundles they had brought with them from Mexico City. As they stepped out of the car, the engine cranked on, backfiring loudly. When it disappeared into the flow of traffic, both realized that even though only three days had passed since they had left Mexico, they had crossed over into a world unknown to them. They were aware that they were facing days and months, perhaps even years, filled with dangers neither of them could imagine.

(20) Feeling **apprehensive,** they were silent as they approached the large house that their guide had pointed out. They didn't know that the

building had been a **convent** and that it was now a refuge run by priests and other volunteers. Neither realized that they were entering a sanctuary for the displaced and for those without documents or jobs. When they were shown in, Luz and Arturo were surprised at how warmly they were received. No one asked any questions. Afterwards, they were given food to eat and a place to sleep.

Here are some of the more difficult words in "In Search of Bernabé."

Vocabulary List

apprehensive
(paragraph 20)

ap·pre·hen·sive (-hen′siv) *adj.* ⟦ME < ML *apprehensivus* < pp. of L *apprehendere*, APPREHEND⟧ **1** able or quick to apprehend or understand **2** having to do with perceiving or understanding **3** anxious or fearful about the future; uneasy —**ap′·pre·hen′·sively** *adv.* —**ap′·pre·hen′·sive·ness** *n.*

clients
(paragraph 11)

cli·ent (klī′ənt) *n.* ⟦OFr < L *cliens,* follower, retainer < IE base **klei-,* to lean, as in L *clinare* (see INCLINE); basic sense, "one leaning on another (for protection)"⟧ **1** [Archaic] a person dependent on another, as for protection or patronage **2** a person or company for whom a lawyer, accountant, advertising agency, etc. is acting **3** a customer **4** a person served by a social agency **5** a nation, state, etc. dependent on another politically, economically, etc.: also **client state** **6** *Comput.* a terminal or personal computer that is connected to a SERVER (sense 3) —**cli·en·tal** (klī′ən təl, klī en′təl) *adj.*

convent
(paragraph 20)

con·vent (kän′vənt, -vent′) *n.* ⟦OFr < L *conventus,* assembly (in ML(Ec), religious house, convent), orig. pp. of *convenire,* CONVENE⟧ **1** a community of nuns or, sometimes, monks, living under strict religious vows **2** the building or buildings occupied by such a community —**SYN.** CLOISTER

diffused
(paragraph 9)

dif·fuse (di fyo͞os′; *for v.,* -fyo͞oz′) *adj.* ⟦ME < L *diffusus,* pp. of *diffundere,* to pour in different directions < *dis-,* apart + *fundere,* to pour: see FOUND²⟧ **1** spread out or dispersed; not concentrated **2** using more words than are needed; long-winded; wordy —*vt., vi.* **-·fused′, -·fus′·ing 1** to pour, spread out, or disperse in every direction; spread or scatter widely **2** *Physics* to mix by diffusion, as gases, liquids, etc. —**SYN.** WORDY —**dif·fuse′·ly** *adv.* —**dif·fuse′·ness** *n.*

pesos
(paragraph 4)

peso (pā′sō; *Sp* pe′sð) *n., pl.* **-·sos′** (-sōz′; *Sp,* -sðs) ⟦Sp, lit., a weight < L *pensum,* something weighed < neut. pp. of *pendere:* see PENSION⟧ the basic monetary unit of: *a)* Argentina *b)* Chile *c)* Colombia *d)* Cuba *e)* the Dominican Republic *f)* Mexico *g)* the Philippines *h)* Uruguay: see the table of monetary units in the Reference Supplement

sultry
(paragraph 4)

sul·try (sul′trē) *adj.* **-·trier, -·tri·est** ⟦var. of SWELTRY⟧ **1** oppressively hot and moist; close; sweltering **2** extremely hot; fiery **3** *a)* hot or inflamed, as with passion or lust *b)* suggesting or expressing smoldering passion —**sul′·trily** *adv.* —**sul′·tri·ness** *n.*

terrain
(paragraph 7)

ter·rain (tə rān′) *n.* ⟦Fr < L *terrenum* < *terrenus,* of earth, earthen < *terra,* TERRA⟧ **1** ground or a tract of ground, esp. with regard to its natural or topographical features or fitness for some use **2** *Geol.* TERRANE (sense 1)

trekked
(paragraph 7)

trek (trek) *vi.* **trekked, trek′·king** ⟦Afrik < Du *trekken,* to draw; akin to MHG *trecken*⟧ **1** [South Afr.] to travel by ox wagon **2** to travel slowly or laboriously **3** [Informal] to go, esp. on foot —*vt.* [South Afr.] to draw (a wagon): said of an ox —*n.* **1** [South Afr.] a journey made by ox wagon, or one leg of such a journey **2** any journey or leg of a journey **3** a migration **4** [Informal] a short trip, esp. on foot —**trek′·ker** *n.*

vendor
(paragraph 6)

wares
(paragraph 12)

ven·dor (ven′dər, ven dôr′) *n.* ⟦Anglo-Fr < Fr *vendre*⟧ **1** one who vends, or sells; seller **2** VENDING MACHINE

ware[1] (wer) *n.* ⟦ME < OE *waru*, merchandise, specialized use of *waru*, watchful care, in the sense "what is kept safe": for IE base see GUARD⟧ **1** any piece or kind of goods that a store, merchant, peddler, etc. has to sell; also, any skill or service that one seeks to sell: *usually used in pl.* **2** things, usually of the same general kind, that are for sale; a (specified) kind of merchandise, collectively: generally in compounds *[hardware, earthenware, glassware]* **3** dishes made of baked and glazed clay; pottery, or a specified kind or make of pottery

18A   VOCABULARY

Using the vocabulary words listed on pages 262–263, fill in this crossword puzzle.

Across

2. extremely hot
6. fearful
7. home for religious persons
8. tract of ground
10. unit of money in Latin America

Down

1. customers
3. things for sale
4. traveled slowly
5. seller
9. spread out

18B   CENTRAL THEME AND MAIN IDEAS

Choose the best answer.

_____ 1. What is the central theme of "In Search of Bernabé"?
   a. Luz bargained with a *coyota* to take her and Arturo across the Mexican border to the United States.
   b. Petra Traslaviña was a *coyota* who made her living by serving as a border guide.
   c. Luz and Arturo had over a 40-hour bus ride from their home to the Tijuana terminal.
   d. Luz and Arturo crossed the United States–Mexican border illegally with the help of a *coyota* to find a missing relative.

_____ 2. What is the main idea of paragraph 2?
   a. Luz was afraid of the woman who approached her at the Tijuana bus terminal.
   b. Luz carefully inspected the woman's appearance to determine her skill as a guide.
   c. The *coyota* was a tall, slim, and muscular woman who wore Levi's and a plaid shirt under a sweatshirt.
   d. Luz was surprised to see a woman wearing scratched, muddy cowboy boots generally worn by a male.

_____ 3. What is the main idea of paragraph 7?
   a. Luz, Arturo, and the *coyota* walked cautiously across the Mexican–United States border at night to avoid detection by the border patrol.
   b. Besides Luz and Arturo, there were others who crossed the border on foot.
   c. The immigration authorities used bright lights to search for illegal immigrants.
   d. The immigrants clung to the ground when someone issued a warning about the presence of the immigration authorities.

18C   MAJOR DETAILS

Decide whether each detail is true (T), false (F), or not discussed (ND).

_____ 1. Luz and Arturo's home was in Mexico City.

_____ 2. Luz brought the equivalent of only 700 American dollars to pay for a border guide.

_____ 3. The *coyota*, Luz, and Arturo trekked on foot across the border from Tijuana to Los Angeles.

_____ 4. Luz and Arturo spoke only Spanish.

_____ 5. The first English words Luz practiced were *shut up*.

_____ 6. Ordaz and Petra argued about the location where he was to take Luz and Arturo.

_____ 7. Luz and Artuo brought a lot of clothes with them.

_____ 8. The *coyota* gave Ordaz half of the $700 guide fee.

18D   INFERENCES

Decide whether each statement below can be inferred (Yes) or cannot be inferred (No) from the reading selection.

_____ 1. *Coyota* is a word used to refer to a smuggler of illegal aliens.

_____ 2. A *coyota* generally expects to bargain with the illegal aliens for the guide fee.

_____ 3. Because the *coyota* was a United States citizen, she wanted to be paid in American dollars.

_____ 4. Luz and Arturo would not have been able to cross the border successfully without the *coyota*'s help.

_____ 5. As a border guide, the *coyota* had never been caught by immigration authorities.

_____ 6. The *coyota* used a fictitious name when she identified herself to Luz and Arturo.

_____ 7. Ordaz was a nonsmoker.

_____ 8. Although Ordaz drove fast on the freeway, he observed the speed limit once he arrived in Los Angeles.

_____ 9. Bernabé was Arturo's brother.

_____ 10. The *coyota* had been Bernabé's guide when he crossed the Mexican–United States border.

_____ 11. The *coyota* always took her clients to the convent in Los Angeles if they had no destination.

_____ 12. The people at the refuge center assisted illegal aliens in getting United States visas.

18E   CRITICAL READING: FACT OR OPINION

Decide whether each statement, even if it quotes someone, contains a Fact *or an* Opinion.

_____ 1. *From paragraph 3:* From looking into the eyes of the *coyota*, Luz knew she had to drive a hard bargain.

_____ 2. *From paragraph 4:* "The coat had a purpose, though, for it concealed deep inner pockets which were filled with money."

_____ 3. *From paragraph 8:* "The *coyota* was sure-footed but Luz and Arturo bumped into rocks and tripped over gopher holes."

_____ 4. *From paragraph 9:* "Upon reaching the summit, they were struck with awe at the sight that spread beneath their feet."

_____ 5. *From paragraph 11:* "The old bag slowed me down."

_____ 6. *From paragraph 14:* "They don't like me because I charge you people money."

_____ 7. *From paragraph 16:* "I mean, they love to call themselves *voluntarios*, and they'll do anything for nothing."

_____ 8. *From paragraph 17:* "I've known a few like you who have gotten themselves killed out there."

18F   CRITICAL READING: THE AUTHOR'S STRATEGIES

Choose the best answer.

_____ 1. The main audience for *In Search of Bernabé* is
   a. anyone who is interested in illegal immigration.
   b. anyone who is curious about how Mexicans cross the border into California.
   c. anyone who works with immigrants who have just arrived in America.
   d. anyone who is interested in border patrol.

_____ 2. The author's purpose in writing this reading is to
   a. entertain.
   b. argue.
   c. inform.
   d. describe.

Name   Date

_____ 3. The author's tone in this reading is
   a. playful.
   b. sympathetic.
   c. pleasant.
   d. uncaring.

18G   READER'S PROCESS: SUMMARIZING YOUR READING

_____ 1. What is the best summary of *In Search of Bernabé?*
   a. The author tells how Arturo and Luz sneak across the Mexican border into Los Angeles in the middle of the night.
   b. The author tells how Arturo and Luz illegally cross the Mexican border in search of Bernabé in Los Angeles.
   c. The author tells how Arturo and Luz pay a professional smuggler to help them across the Mexican border into California.
   d. The author tells how Arturo and Luz leave Mexico and go to Los Angeles to find Luz's son.

18H   READER'S RESPONSE: TO DISCUSS OR WRITE ABOUT

1. Approximately 3.5–4 million Mexicans live and work illegally in the United States. In California, these migrants often work at low-paying jobs: restaurants, car washes, and construction and landscape companies. Many managers say that Americans will not take these jobs. Have you ever turned down a job because of the low wage? What was the job? The duties? The pay? If you have not turned down a low-paying job, then what is your opinion of someone who needs work but declines such a job offer?

2. In recent years the Border Patrol has used personnel, equipment, technology, and tactics across the United States' most vulnerable cross points to reduce the number of illegal migrants. This has forced migrants to seek routes that are dangerous—across deserts and rivers. As a result, many migrants hire *coyotes* or *polleros*, names given the smugglers who sometimes charge as much as $1,200 for their services. In some cases, the *coyotes* have abandoned their clients in the desert without food or water when they could not keep up the pace. If you were a Mexican without the proper papers and identification to enter the United States, would you consider hiring a *coyote?* Why? Luz looked directly into the eyes of the *coyote* to determine Petra's skill as a guide. How would you go about choosing a guide? How would you prepare yourself for the trip, which can take several days across the desert? What would you take with you? Be specific.

HOW DID YOU DO?
18 From In Search of Bernabé

SKILL *(number of items)*	Number Correct		Points for each		Score
Vocabulary (10)	_____	×	2	=	_____
Central Theme and Main Ideas (3)	_____	×	4	×	_____
Major Details (8)	_____	×	2	=	_____
Inferences (12)	_____	×	2	=	_____
Critical Reading: Fact or Opinion (8)	_____	×	2	=	_____
Critical Reading: The Author's Strategies (3)	_____	×	3	=	_____
Reader's Process: Summarizing Your Reading (1)	_____	×	3	×	_____

(Possible Total: 100) *Total*   _____

Part 5

Thinking: Getting Started

"The dog has been esteemed and loved by all the people on earth, and he has deserved this affection, for he renders services that have made him man's best friend."

Alfred Barbou

The selections in Part 5 concern choices, beginning with a selection about training a dog to detect explosives in airport luggage to a shopkeeper who chooses to humiliate a customer who speaks little English.

"They Sniff Out Trouble" (Selection 19)—Do you think dogs are the key to bomb detection at airports?

"Death Penalty Victims" (Selection 20)—What reasons can you give *for* or *against* the death penalty?

"Should a Wife Keep Her Name" (Selection 21)—Do you think a woman loses her identity when she takes her husband's name?

"I Became Her Target" (Selection 22)—How would you react if a teacher picked on you in class?

"Guns in Kids' Bedrooms? Ohio Hunting Town Approves" (Selection 23) —Do you think we live in a gun-culture society that supports romantic notions of families' learning to shoot and hunt together?

"Mute in an English-Only World" (Selection 24)—Should immigrants who apply for United States citizenship be required to learn English?

They Sniff Out Trouble

Gail Buchalter

LEARNING OBJECTIVES
- Explain the importance of bomb-sniffing dogs for security purposes.

GETTING STARTED
- Do you think dogs are the key to bomb detection at airports?

(1) Sgt. Mark McMurray slides his hands quickly across the cars in the parking lot, instructing his partner, Brandy, a Labrador mix, to sniff "high" or "low" for possible explosives. **Inhaling voraciously,** Brandy follows McMurray's orders. Suddenly, she stops and sits down—her signal that she has found a bomb. But no bomb squad was called in on this day. Mark McMurray and Brandy were one of the 94 regional championship teams from police departments, the Central Intelligence Agency, airports, and military facilities competing at the sixth annual National **Detector** Dog Trials, last April in Huntsville, Alabama. The "bomb" Brandy found was actually a nonworking explosive.

(2) Today, there are close to 15,000 **patrol** dogs in the US, 80% of which are crossed-trained in work that includes detecting narcotics, **cadavers,** and bombs. The annual Dog Trials—sponsored by the US Police **Canine** Association, one of several certifying organizations—helps establish a national standard for detector dogs. More important, it gives teams a chance to test skills that someday could save lives. "Protecting the public is what we are all about," says McMurray, 41, the K-9 Unit supervisor in Huntsville, which earned top honors in the bomb-detection category at the trials.

(3) As national security has tightened, bomb-sniffing dogs have become increasingly visible. "Since Sept. 11, our calls have at least doubled," says McMurray. "Whenever there's a breach of security at Huntsville International Airport, Brandy and I are called to rescreen the airplanes, luggage and people." McMurray has noticed a change in the public's attitude toward these dogs. "People used to feel that their rights were being violated when we searched them," he says. "Now they enjoy seeing our dogs and feel more secure."

(4) How are bomb dogs trained? To teach Brandy to recognize the six basic odors of explosives, McMurray says, he used a method called "odor imprintation." He placed 20 different odor combinations in Brandy's toys and played fetch. Eventually, he hid the bomb odors in small cans. As

About 700 bomb-sniffing dogs currently work at United States airports to detect up to a dozen different explosive compounds.

methods of concealing explosives **evolve**—including using shoes, as Richard Reid is accused of doing on a flight last December—so does the training. "We began putting small cans with odors in volunteers' socks," says McMurray. "Now I say 'shoe,' and Brandy searches low."

(5) Detector dogs—which typically include German shepherds, retrievers and Belgian Malinois—also rely on their highly developed **prey** drive, the instinctual need to hunt to survive. Brandy's drive was so strong that, as a puppy, all she wanted to do was chase balls. She was so unaffectionate that her owners decided to donate her to the Huntsville Police. (Most police departments buy their dogs from breeders.) McMurray gave her a reason to hunt and, in return, got a partner and a pet. "Brandy's a member of our family," says McMurray, who takes her home at the end of their workday, as do most handlers. Then it's back to work for these top bomb-detectors. "We've never found a real bomb," says Murray. "I'll be happy if we never do."

Here are some of the more difficult words in "They Sniff Out Trouble."

cadavers
(paragraph 2)

ca·daver (kə dav′ər) *n.* [L, prob. < *cadere*, to fall: see CASE[1]] a dead body, esp. of a person; corpse, as for dissection —*SYN.* BODY —**ca·dav′·eric** *adj.*

canine
(paragraph 2)

ca·nine (kā′nīn′) *adj.* [L *caninus* < *canis*, dog: see HOUND[1]] **1** of or like a dog **2** of the family (Canidae) of carnivores that includes dogs, wolves, jackals, and foxes —*n.* **1** a dog or other canine animal **2** a sharp-pointed tooth on either side of the upper jaw and lower jaw, between the incisors and the bicuspids, having a long single root; a cuspid or (in the upper jaw) eyetooth: see TEETH, illus.: in full **canine tooth**

detector
(paragraph 1)

de·tec·tor (dē tek′tər, di-; *also, esp. for 2 & 3,* dē′tek′-) *n.* **1** a person or thing that detects **2** an apparatus or device for indicating the presence of something, as electric waves **3** DEMODULATOR

evolve
(paragraph 4)

evolve (ē välv′, -vôlv′; i-) *vt.* **evolved′, evolv′·ing** [L *evolvere*, to roll out or forth < *e-*, out + *volvere*, to roll: see WALK] **1** to develop by gradual changes; unfold **2** to set free or give off (gas, heat, etc.) **3** to produce or change by evolution —*vi.* **1** to develop gradually by a process of growth and change ☆**2** to become disclosed; unfold —

inhaling
(paragraph 1)

in·hale (in hāl′, in′hāl′) *vt.* **··haled′, ··hal′·ing** [L *inhalare* < *in-*, in + *halare*, to breathe: see EXHALE] **1** to draw (air, vapor, etc.) into the lungs; breathe in **2** [Informal] to consume rapidly or voraciously [to *inhale* one's dinner] —*vi.* **1** to draw air, vapor, etc. into the lungs **2** to draw tobacco smoke into the lungs when smoking

patrol
(paragraph 2)

pa·trol (pə trōl′) *vt., vi.* **··trolled′, ··trol′·ling** [Fr *patrouiller*, altered < OFr *patouiller*, to paddle, puddle, patrol < *pate*, paw: see PATOIS] to make a regular and repeated circuit of (an area, town, camp, etc.) in guarding or inspecting —*n.* [Fr *patrouille* < the *v.*] **1** the act of patrolling **2** a person or persons patrolling **3** *a)* a small group of soldiers sent on a mission, as for reconnaissance *b)* a group of ships, airplanes, etc. used in guarding **4** a subdivision of a troop of Boy Scouts or Girl Scouts —**pa·trol′·ler** *n.*

prey
(paragraph 5)

prey (prā) *n.* [ME *preye* < OFr *preie* < L *praeda* < base of *prehendere*, to seize: see PREHENSILE] **1** [Archaic] plunder; booty **2** an animal hunted or killed for food by another animal **3** a person or thing that falls victim to someone or something **4** the mode of living by preying on other animals [a bird of *prey*] —*vi.* **1** to plunder; rob **2** to hunt or kill other animals for food **3** to make profit from a victim as by swindling **4** to have a wearing or harmful influence; weigh heavily Generally used with *on* or *upon* —**prey′er** *n.*

voraciously
(paragraph 1)

vo·ra·cious (vô rā′shəs, və-) *adj.* [L *vorax* (gen. *voracis*), greedy to devour < *vorare*, to devour < IE base **gwer-*, to devour, GORGE > Gr *bora*, food (of carnivorous beasts), L *gurges*, gorge] **1** greedy in eating; devouring or eager to devour large quantities of food; ravenous; gluttonous **2** very greedy or eager in some desire or pursuit; insatiable [a *voracious* reader] —**vo·ra′·ciously** *adv.* —**vo·rac′·ity** (-ras′ə tē) *n.* or **vo·ra′·cious·ness**

19A   VOCABULARY

Using the dictionary entries on page 273, fill in the blanks.

1. _____ the strong fumes, Erika began to cough.

2. Policemen use bicycles, not _____ cars, at the pedestrian mall.

3. The hungry lion _____ the food.

4. Buds _____ into flowers.

5. Birds and mice are the _____ of cats.

6. The medical examiner is often asked to perform an autopsy on _____.

7. A smoke _____ can prevent loss of life.

8. A _____ belongs to a group of meat-eating animals, including wolves and foxes.

19B   CENTRAL THEME AND MAIN IDEAS

Choose the best answer.

_____ 1. What is the central theme of "They Sniff Out Trouble"?
    a. U.S. Police Canine Association sponsors annual Dog Trials.
    b. Alabama policeman trains bomb-sniffing dogs.
    c. Police use detector dogs to protect people from bombs.
    d. Trainer uses hand signals to instruct bomb-sniffing dog.

_____ 2. What is the main idea of paragraph 4?
    a. Richard Reid is accused of hiding a bomb in his shoes.
    b. Trainers use "odor imprintation" to train dogs.
    c. Brandy can detect as many as 20 odors.
    d. Brandy searches "low" when she hears the word *shoe*.

19C   MAJOR DETAILS

Fill in the word or words that correctly complete each statement.

1. Sgt. Mark McMurray sometimes uses _____ signals for Brandy to sniff for possible explosives.

2. To signal she has found a bomb, Brandy _____ and _____ down.

3. Today there are nearly 15,000 _____ dogs in the United States.

4. The annual Dog Trials help establish a _____ _____ for detector dogs.

5. Since _____, the request for bomb-sniffing dogs has at least _____.

6. In hunting for explosives, detector dogs also rely on the highly developed _____ _____.

    Name   Date

7. Brandy's drive was so strong as a _____ that all she wanted to do was chase _____.

8. Sgt. McMurray gave her a _____ to _____ and, in return, got a _____ and a _____.

19D   INFERENCES

Decide whether each statement below can be inferred (Yes) or cannot be inferred (No) from the reading selection.

_____ 1. A Labrador is the best breed of dog to train for detecting explosives.

_____ 2. Before Brandy became a part of the K-9 Unit, she underwent militaristic obedience training.

_____ 3. In case of a violation in security at an airport, most travelers would understand the need to delay a flight for rescreening.

_____ 4. Brandy's owners considered having her put down before they donated her to the Huntsville Police Department.

_____ 5. Brandy is happy working as a bomb-detector dog.

19E   CRITICAL READING: THE AUTHOR'S STRATEGIES

Choose the best answer.

_____ 1. Gail Buchalter's main audience for "They Sniff Out Trouble" is people who
a. want to know how patrol dogs are trained.
b. are afraid of all dogs, including patrol dogs.
c. want to learn how to trick sniffing patrol dogs.
d. want to raise and train patrol dogs.

_____ 2. The author's primary purpose in this reading is to
a. argue.
b. describe.
c. inform.
d. persuade.

_____ 3. The author's tone in this reading is
a. sincere.
b. sensational.
c. sympathetic.
d. straightforward.

19F   READER'S PROCESS: SUMMARIZING YOUR READING

_____ 1. What is the best summary of "They Sniff Out Trouble"?

   a. Patrol dogs, sometimes called bomb dogs or detector dogs, are trained to recognize the scent of six different kinds of explosives. Brandy, trained by Sgt. Mark McMurray, is a regional champion in official Dog Trials, and she excels on the job at airports.

   b. Brandy, a dog trained by Sgt. McMurray to recognize the scent of six different explosives, won a regional championship and is now entered in the U.S. Police Canine Association's annual National Detector Dog Trials.

   c. About 15,000 dogs have been trained in the United States to recognize the scent of explosives. Sgt. McMurray trained bomb-dog Brandy, who was donated to the police department and is now his pet.

   d. The sixth-annual National Detector Dog Trials has attracted competing teams of trainers and dogs from police departments, the Central Intelligence Agency (CIA), and the military. Brandy, a bomb dog trained by Sgt. McMurray, has won a championship.

19G   READER'S RESPONSE: TO DISCUSS OR WRITE ABOUT

1. Because of the increase in international terrorism, the security measures at airports have increased significantly. Do you think the changes, such as those involving baggage, personal identification, and screening, have made flying safer than before? If you have flown recently, what was your experience with the new security measures, such as the full body scan?

2. Bomb-sniffing dogs are chosen because of their hunting skills as well as their sense of smell. A dog's smell is 50 times more sensitive than a human's. With this gift, dogs are employed to track missing persons, locate illegal drugs, detect firearms or explosives, and find the point of origin when arson has been committed. If you were involved in a situation where a dog was used to assist, would you trust the findings of the dog? Do you think animals should be given so much responsibility? Explain your response.

HOW DID YOU DO?
19 They Sniff Out Trouble

SKILL (number of items)	Number Correct		Points for each		Score
Vocabulary (8)	_____	×	2	=	_____
Central Theme and Main Ideas (2)	_____	×	9	=	_____
Major Details* (14)	_____	×	2	=	_____
Inferences (5)	_____	×	4	=	_____
Critical Reading: The Author's Strategies (3)	_____	×	5	=	_____
Reader's Process: Summarizing Your Reading (1)	_____	×	3	=	_____

(Possible Total: 100) *Total*   _____

*Questions 2 and 8 in this exercise call for separate answers. In computing your score, count each separate answer toward your number correct.

Selection 20
Death Penalty Victims

Bob Herbert

LEARNING OBJECTIVES

- Point out the effects that capital punishment has on both the participants and the observers.

THINKING: GETTING STARTED

- What reasons can you give *for* or *against* the death penalty?

(1) Leighanne Gideon was twenty-six when she witnessed an **execution** for the first time. Ms. Gideon is a reporter for *The Huntsville Item* in Texas, and part of her job has been to cover executions. Nowhere in the Western world is the death penalty applied as frequently as in Texas. Ms. Gideon has watched as fifty-two prisoners were put to death.

(2) In a **documentary** to be broadcast today on National Public Radio's *All Things Considered*, Ms. Gideon says: "I've walked out of the death chamber numb and my legs feeling like rubber sometimes, my head not really feeling like it's attached to my shoulders. I've been told it's perfectly normal—everyone feels it—and after awhile that numb feeling goes away. And indeed it does." But other things linger. "You will never hear another sound," Ms. Gideon says, "like a mother wailing whenever she is watching her son be executed. There's no other sound like it. It is just this **horrendous** wail and you can't get away from it. . . . That wail surrounds the room. It's definitely something you won't ever forget."

(3) Not much attention has been given to the emotional price paid by the men and women who participate in—or witness—the fearful business of executing their fellow beings. The documentary, titled "Witness to an Execution," is narrated by Jim Willett, the warden at the unit that houses the execution chamber in Huntsville, where all of the Texas executions take place. "Sometimes I wonder," Mr. Willett says, "whether people really understand what goes on down here, and the effect it has on us."

(4) Fred Allen was a guard whose job was to help strap prisoners on the **gurneys** on which they would be killed. He participated in 130 executions and then had a breakdown, which he describes in the documentary. I called him at his home in Texas. He is still shaken. "There were so many," he said, his voice halting and at times trembling. "A lot of this stuff I just want to try to forget. But my main concern is the individuals who are still in the process. I want people to understand what they're going through. Because I don't want what happened to me to happen to them."

The state of Texas executes prisoners by lethal injection inside the Huntsville, Texas, unit.

(5) Everyone understands that the **condemned** prisoners have been convicted of murder. No one wants to free them. But this **relentless bombardment** of state-**sanctioned homicide** is another matter entirely. It is almost impossible for staff members and others in the death chamber to ignore the reality of the prisoners as physically healthy human beings—men and (infrequently) women who walk, talk, laugh, cry and sometimes pray. Killing them is not easy. "It's kind of hard to explain what you actually feel when you talk to a man, and you kind of get to know that person," says Kenneth Dean, a major in the Huntsville corrections unit. "And then you walk him out of a cell and you take him in there to the chamber and tie him down and then a few minutes later he's gone." Jim Brazzil, a **chaplain** in the unit, recalls a prisoner who began to sing as his final moment approached: "He made his final statement and then after the warden gave the signal, he started singing 'Silent Night.' And he got to the point, 'Round yon virgin, mother and child,' and just as he got 'child' out, was the last word."

(6) David Isay, who co-produced the documentary with Stacy Abramson, said: "It is certainly chilling to hear the process of what goes on, the ritual of the execution. The folks who do these executions are just regular, sensitive people who are doing it because it's their job. And it has an enormous impact on some of them." The Rev. Carroll Pickett, a chaplain who was present for ninety-five executions in Huntsville before he retired in 1995, told me in a telephone conversation that symptoms of some kind of distress were common among those who participated in the executions. "Sure," he

said. "It affects you. It affects anybody." I asked how it had affected him. "Well," he said, "I think it was a contributing factor to a triple bypass I had about eighteen months later. Just all of the stress, you know? I have to say that when I retired I probably had had as much as I could take." I asked Fred Allen, who suffered the breakdown, if his view on the death penalty had changed. "Yes," he said. Then after a long pause, he said, "There's nothing wrong with an individual spending the rest of his life in prison."

Here are some of the more difficult words in "Death Penalty Victims."

Vocabulary List

bombardment
(paragraph 5)

bom·bard (bäm bärd′; *for n.* bäm′bärd′) *vt.* ⟦Fr *bombarder* < *bombarde*, mortar < *bombe*, BOMB⟧ **1** to attack with or as with artillery or bombs **2** to keep attacking or pressing with questions, suggestions, etc. **3** to direct a stream of particles at (atomic nuclei) to produce nuclear transmutations —*n.* the earliest type of cannon, originally for hurling stones —*SYN.* ATTACK —**bom·bard′·ment** *n.*

chaplain
(paragraph 5)

chap·lain (chap′lən) *n.* ⟦ME *chapelain* < OFr < ML *capellanus*, orig., custodian of St. Martin's cloak: see CHAPEL⟧ **1** a clergyman attached to a chapel, as of a royal court **2** a minister, priest, or rabbi serving in a religious capacity with the armed forces, or in a prison, hospital, etc. **3** a clergyman, or sometimes a layman, appointed to perform religious functions in a public institution, club, etc. —**chap′·laincy** *n.*, *pl.* **-·cies** —**chap′·lain·ship′** *n.*

condemned
(paragraph 5)

con·demn (kən dem′) *vt.* ⟦ME *condempnen* < OFr *condemner* < L *condemnare* < *com-*, intens. + *damnare*, to harm, condemn: see DAMN⟧ **1** to pass an adverse judgment on; disapprove of strongly; censure **2** *a*) to declare to be guilty of wrongdoing; convict *b*) to pass judicial sentence on; inflict a penalty upon *c*) to doom ☆**3** to take (private property) for public use by the power of eminent domain; expropriate **4** to declare unfit for use or service [to condemn a slum tenement] —*SYN.* CRITICIZE —**con·dem′·nable** (-dem′nə bəl, -ə bəl) *adj.* —**con·demn′er** *n.*

documentary
(paragraph 2)

docu·men·tary (däk′yo͞o ment′ə rē, -yə-) *adj.* **1** consisting of, supported by, contained in, or serving as a document or documents **2** designating or of a film, TV program, etc. that dramatically shows or analyzes news events, social conditions, etc., with little or no fictionalization —*n.*, *pl.* **-·ries** a documentary film, TV show, etc.

execution
(paragraph 1)

ex·ecu·tion (ek′si kyo͞o′shən) *n.* ⟦ME *execucion* < Anglo-Fr < OFr *execution* < L *executio*, *exsecutio*: see EXECUTOR⟧ **1** the act of executing; specif., *a*) a carrying out, doing, producing, etc. *b*) a putting to death as in accordance with a legally imposed sentence **2** the manner of doing or producing something, as of performing a piece of music or a role in a play **3** [Archaic] effective action, esp. of a destructive nature **4** *Law a*) a writ or order, issued by a court, giving authority to put a judgment into effect *b*) the legal method afforded for the enforcement of a judgment of a court *c*) the act of carrying out the provisions of such a writ or order *d*) the making valid of a legal instrument, as by signing, sealing, and delivering

gurneys
(paragraph 4)

gur·ney (gʉr′nē) *n.*, *pl.* **-·neys** ⟦< ?⟧ a stretcher or cot on wheels, used in hospitals to move patients

homicide
(paragraph 5)

homi·cide (häm′ə sīd′, hō′mə-) *n.* **1** ⟦ME < OFr < LL *homicidium*, manslaughter, murder < L *homicida*, murderer < *homo*, a man (see HOMO¹) + *caedere*, to cut, kill: see -CIDE⟧ any killing of one human being by another: cf. MURDER, MANSLAUGHTER **2** ⟦ME < OFr < L *homicida*⟧ a person who kills another

horrendous
(paragraph 2)

hor·ren·dous (hô ren′dəs, hə-) *adj.* ⟦L *horrendus* < prp. of *horrere*: see HORRID⟧ horrible; frightful —**hor·ren′·dously** *adv.*

relentless
(paragraph 5)

re·lent·less (-lis) *adj.* **1** not relenting; harsh; pitiless **2** persistent; unremitting —**re·lent′·lessly** *adv.* —**re·lent′·less·ness** *n.*

sanctioned
(paragraph 5)

sanc·tion (saŋk′shən) *n.* ⟦< Fr or L: Fr < L *sanctio* < *sanctus*: see SAINT⟧ **1** the act of a recognized authority confirming or ratifying an action; authorized approval or permission **2** support; encouragement; approval **3** something that gives binding force to a law, or secures obedience to it, as the penalty for breaking it, or a reward for carrying it out **4** something, as a moral principle or influence, that makes a rule of conduct, a law, etc. binding **5** *a)* a coercive measure, as a blockade of shipping, usually taken by several nations together, for forcing a nation considered to have violated international law to end the violation *b)* a coercive measure, as a boycott, taken by a group to enforce demands: *often used in pl.* **6** [Obs.] a formal decree; law —*vt.* to give sanction to; specif., *a)* to ratify or confirm *b)* to authorize or permit; countenance —*SYN.* APPROVE —**sanc′·tion·able** *adj.*

20A VOCABULARY

Using the vocabulary words listed on pages 280–281, fill in this crossword puzzle.

Across

3. murder
4. putting to death
6. minister
8. stretchers
9. approved
10. attack

Down

1. program
2. persistent
5. declared guilty
7. horrible

Name   Date   **281**

20B   CENTRAL THEME AND MAIN IDEAS

Choose the best answer.

_____ 1. What is the central theme of "Death Penalty Victims"?
   a. Huntsville is the "prison city" of Texas.
   b. Prison chaplains play a vital role in death row executions.
   c. Media reporters are permitted to witness death row executions.
   d. Death row executions affect both participants and observers.

_____ 2. What is the main idea of paragraph 5?
   a. Death row inmates have been convicted of murder.
   b. Executing death row inmates is not easy.
   c. Death row inmates are physically healthy human beings.
   d. Executing a death row inmate takes only a few minutes.

20C   MAJOR DETAILS

Decide whether each detail is true (T), false (F), or not discussed (ND).

_____ 1. Ms. Gideon is a television reporter.

_____ 2. All of Texas's executions take place in Huntsville, Texas.

_____ 3. Death row inmates are permitted to order any food they want for their final meal.

_____ 4. Executions of death row inmates occur at 12 midnight.

_____ 5. The warden signals when the lethal injection is to start.

_____ 6. Family members of death row inmates are permitted to view the execution.

_____ 7. More men than women are on Texas' death row.

_____ 8. Texas began using the lethal injection for executions in 1982.

20D   INFERENCES

Decide whether each of the following statements can be inferred (Yes) or cannot be inferred (No) from the reading selection.

_____ 1. The death row inmate is strapped to the gurney so he will not jump up or move during the execution procedure.

_____ 2. Fred Allen misses his job as a guard at the Huntsville prison.

Name   Date

_____ 3. A lethal injection is more humane than execution by electrocution, gas, hanging, or firing squad.

_____ 4. Part of the responsibility of a chaplain is to be in the death chamber at the time of execution.

_____ 5. Major Kenneth Dean is the head of the tie-down team at the Huntsville prison.

_____ 6. Witnessing executions affects the guards more than it does the warden.

20E CRITICAL READING: FACT OR OPINION

Decide whether each statement, even if it quotes someone, contains a Fact _or an_ Opinion.

_____ 1. _From paragraph 1:_ "Nowhere in the Western world is the death penalty applied as frequently as in Texas."

_____ 2. _From paragraph 2:_ "You will never hear another sound," Ms. Gideon says, "like a mother wailing whenever she is watching her son be executed."

_____ 3. _From paragraph 5:_ "No one wants to free them [death row inmates]."

_____ 4. _From paragraph 6:_ "The Rev. Carroll Pickett [. . .] told me in a telephone conversation that symptoms of some kind of distress were common among those who participated in the executions."

_____ 5. _From paragraph 6:_ "There's nothing wrong with an individual spending the rest of his life in prison."

20F CRITICAL READING: THE AUTHOR'S STRATEGIES

Choose the best answer.

_____ 1. The main audience for "Death Penalty Victims" is
   a. people who are interested in the execution process and its effects on the participants and observers.
   b. people whose job it is to carry out executions.
   c. people who are opposed to the death penalty.
   d. people who are in favor of the death penalty.

_____ 2. The author's purpose in writing this reading is to
   a. expose.
   b. narrate.
   c. entertain.
   d. describe.

_____ 3. The author's tone in this reading is
   a. angry.
   b. solemn.
   c. forgiving.
   d. critical.

20G READER'S PROCESS: SUMMARIZING YOUR READING

_____ 1. What is the best summary of "Death Penalty Victims"?
   a. The author discusses the job of wardens on death row and the feelings they have after carrying out executions.
   b. The author discusses a documentary on the emotional and long-term effects of witnessing and carrying out executions on death row in Texas.
   c. The author discusses the reaction of a journalist and a warden who have witnessed and carried out a number of executions in Texas.
   d. The author discusses the human side of putting prisoners to death and the toll it takes on workers who are just doing their jobs.

20H READER'S RESPONSE: TO DISCUSS OR WRITE ABOUT

1. In 1976 the Supreme Court reinstated capital punishment. Today, more than 3,000 inmates sit on Death Row. At least one state, Illinois, has passed a moratorium, a legal delay, on carrying out the death penalty. Are you in favor of such a moratorium for the state where you live? Is your viewpoint based on a moral, ethical, or religious viewpoint? If so, explain in detail. If you are not in favor of a moratorium, why?

2. On the day of execution in Texas, a death row inmate is allowed five witnesses plus a spiritual advisor. The victims are allowed five witnesses. Under what conditions would you attend an execution as a witness for either the inmate or the victim? How do you think viewing an execution would affect you physically, mentally, and emotionally?

Name   Date

HOW DID YOU DO?
20 **Death Penalty Victims**

SKILL *(number of items)*	*Number Correct*		*Points for each*		*Score*
Vocabulary (10)	_____	×	2	=	_____
Central Theme and Main Ideas (2)	_____	×	7	=	_____
Major Details (8)	_____	×	3	=	_____
Inferences (6)	_____	×	3	=	_____
Critical Reading: Fact or Opinion (5)	_____	×	3	=	_____
Critical Reading: The Author's Strategies (3)	_____	×	2	=	_____
Reader's Process: Summarizing Your Reading (1)	_____	×	3	=	_____

(Possible Total: 100) *Total* _____

Should a Wife Keep Her Name?

Norman Lobsenz

LEARNING OBJECTIVES

- **Pinpoint the issues an American woman faces in keeping her maiden name after she marries.**

THINKING: GETTING STARTED

- Do you think a woman loses her identity when she takes her husband's name?

(1) Encouraged by **feminism** to maintain their separate identities, many brides have chosen to keep their maiden name* or to combine it somehow with their husband's name. Yet the emotional and technical problems that arise from this decision have made some women think twice.

(2) "I felt an obligation to carry on the family name and heritage," says Catherine Bergstrom-Katz, an actress. "But I also believed that combining our names was the fair thing to do; if I was going to take my husband's name, the least he could do was take mine." Her husband's legal name now is also Bergstrom-Katz. Though he does not use it at work, it is on all the couple's legal documents—mortgage, house deed, insurance and credit cards. Mail comes addressed to both spouses under their own names, their hyphenated name and, says Catherine, "sometimes to 'Allan Bergstrom.'" The couple's first child was named Sasha Bergstrom-Katz.

(3) Not all wives are so **adamant.** Some use their maiden name in business and their husband's name socially. And a growing number of women who once insisted on hyphenating maiden and married names have dropped the hyphen and are using the maiden name as a middle name.

(4) Despite the popular use of linked, merged or shared names, "there is still a surprising amount of opposition to the idea," says Terri Tepper, who for many years ran an information center in Barrington, Illinois, advising women who wished to retain their maiden names. Family counselors point out that it triggers highly emotional reactions, not only between the couple but also among parents and in-laws. "What about your silver and linens?" one woman asked her daughter. "How can I have them monogrammed if you and Bill have different names?"

---

*Alternate terms for "maiden name" are often preferred because they are considered less demeaning to women; such terms include "given name," "family name," and "premarriage name," although these alternatives are only beginning to come into widespread use.

Though the bride says "I do," 10 percent of all married women will keep their maiden names.

(5) While such concerns may seem relatively trivial, there are others that raise significant issues.

- *Control and commitment.* "Names have always been symbols of power," says Constance Ahrons, a therapist at the University of Southern California. "To a modern woman, keeping her name is a symbol of her independence. But a man may feel that implies a lack of **commitment** to him and to the marriage." Thus when a San Diego woman told her fiancé she had decided to keep her name, he was hurt. "Aren't you proud to be my wife?" he asked. Most men are more understanding. When Maureen Poon, a publicist, married Russell Fear, her English-Irish husband sympathized with his wife's desire to preserve her Chinese-Japanese **heritage,** especially since she was an only child. "We began married life as Poon-Fear," says Maureen. "I've since dropped the hyphen—it just confuses too many people— but Russell continues to use it when we're out together. He feels that we are 'Poon-Fear,' that we are one."
- *Cultural differences.* "Men raised in a **macho** society find it hard to accept a wife who goes by her own name," says Dr. Judith Davenport, a clinical social worker. For example, New York–born Jennifer Selvy, now a riding instructor in Denver, says her Western-rancher fiancé was horrified that she wanted to keep her name. "What will my friends say?" he protested. "Nobody will believe we're married!" His distress was so real that Selvy reluctantly yielded.

287

• *What to name the children.* When couples began hyphenating **surnames,** it was amusing to consider the tongue-twisters that might **plague** the next generation. But psychologists point out that youngsters with complex names are often teased by classmates or embarrassed if their parents have different names. And how does one explain to grandparents that their grandchild, apple of their eye, will not be carrying on the family name?

• *Technical troubles.* While there are no legal barriers in any state to a woman's keeping her maiden name—or **resuming** it in midmarriage—technology can cause complications. Hyphenated names are often too long for computers to handle; others are likely to be filed incorrectly. One reason Maureen Poon-Fear dropped the hyphen in her name was "it created a problem in consistency." She explains: "The Department of Motor Vehicles lists me as POON-FEAR. Some of my charge accounts are listed under 'P' and others under 'F,' and I was concerned about the effect on my credit rating if my payments were not properly credited."

(6) Given the difficulties of keeping one's maiden name in a society that has not yet fully adjusted to the idea, should a woman make the effort to do so?

(7) "Clearly, yes, if the name has value to her in terms of personal, family or professional identity," says Alan Loy McGinnis, co-director of the Valley Counseling Center in Glendale, California. "But if keeping one's maiden name makes either spouse feel less secure about the relationship, perhaps the couple needs to find another way to **symbolize mutual** commitment. After all, marriage today needs all the reinforcement it can get."

Here are some of the more difficult words in "Should a Wife Keep Her Name?"

Vocabulary List

adamant
(paragraph 3)

ada·mant (ad'ə mənt, -mant') *n.* [ME & OFr < L *adamas* (gen. *adamantis*), the hardest metal < Gr *adamas* (gen. *adamantos*) < a-, not + *daman*, to subdue: see TAME] **1** in ancient times, a hard stone or substance that was supposedly unbreakable **2** [Old Poet.] unbreakable hardness —*adj.* **1** too hard to be broken **2** not giving in or relenting; unyielding —*SYN.* INFLEXIBLE —**ad'a·mantly** *adv.*

commitment
(paragraph 5)

com·mit (kə mit') *vt.* ·-mit'·ted, ·-mit'·ting [ME *committen* < L *committere*, to bring together; commit < *com-*, together + *mittere*, to send: see MISSION] **1** to give in charge or trust; deliver for safekeeping; entrust; consign [we *commit* his fame to posterity] **2** to put officially in custody or confinement [*committed* to prison] **3** to hand over or set apart to be disposed of or put to some purpose [to *commit* something to the trash heap] **4** to do or perpetrate (an offense or crime) **5** to bind as by a promise; pledge; engage [*committed* to the struggle] **6** to make known the opinions or views of [to *commit* oneself on an issue] **7** to refer (a bill, etc.) to a committee to be considered —*vi.* [Informal] to make a pledge or promise: often with *to* —**commit to memory** to learn by heart; memorize — **commit to paper** (or **writing**) to write down; record —**com·mit'· table** *adj.*

SYN.—**commit**, the basic term here, implies the delivery of a person or thing into the charge or keeping of another; **entrust** implies committal based on trust and confidence; **confide** stresses the private nature of information entrusted to another and usually connotes intimacy of relationship; **consign** suggests formal action in transferring something to another's possession or control; **relegate** implies a consigning to a specific class, sphere, place, etc., esp. one of inferiority, and usually suggests the literal or figurative removal of something undesirable

com·mit·ment (-mənt) *n.* **1** a committing or being committed **2** official consignment by court order of a person as to prison or a mental hospital **3** a pledge or promise to do something **4** dedication to a long-term course of action; engagement; involvement **5** a financial liability undertaken, as an agreement to buy or sell securities **6** the act of sending proposed legislation to a committee

feminism
(paragraph 1)

fem·i·nism (fem'ə niz'əm) *n.* ⟦< L *femina*, woman + -ISM⟧ **1** [Rare] feminine qualities **2** *a*) the principle that woman should have political, economic, and social rights equal to those of men *b*) the movement to win such rights for women —**fem'i·nist** *n., adj.* —**fem'i·nis'·tic** *adj.*

heritage
(paragraph 5)

her·it·age (her'ə tij) *n.* ⟦ME < OFr < *heriter* < LL(Ec) *hereditare*, to inherit < L *hereditas*: see HEREDITY⟧ **1** property that is or can be inherited **2** *a*) something handed down from one's ancestors or the past, as a characteristic, a culture, tradition, etc. *b*) the rights, burdens, or status resulting from being born in a certain time or place; birthright

SYN.—**heritage**, the most general of these words, applies either to property passed on to an heir, or to a tradition, culture, etc. passed on to a later generation [our *heritage* of freedom]; **inheritance** applies to property, a characteristic, etc. passed on to an heir; **patrimony** strictly refers to an estate inherited from one's father, but it is also used of anything passed on from an ancestor; **birthright**, in its stricter sense, applies to the property rights of a first-born son

macho
(paragraph 5)

ma·cho (mä'chō) *n., pl.* **-chos** (-chōz, -chōs) ⟦Sp < Port., ult. < L *masculus*, MASCULINE⟧ **1** an overly assertive, virile, and domineering man **2** MACHISMO —*adj.* exhibiting or characterized by machismo; overly aggressive, virile, domineering, etc.

mutual
(paragraph 7)

mu·tual (myo͞o'cho͞o əl) *adj.* ⟦LME *mutuall* < MFr *mutuel* < L *mutuus*, mutual, reciprocal < *mutare*, to change, exchange: see MISS[1]⟧ **1** *a*) done, felt, etc. by each of two or more for or toward the other or others; reciprocal [*mutual* admiration] *b*) of, or having the same relationship toward, each other or one another [*mutual* enemies] **2** shared in common; joint [our *mutual* friend] **3** designating or of a type of insurance in which the policyholders elect the directors, share in the profits, and agree to indemnify one another against loss —**mu'·tu·al'·i·ty** (-al'ə tē) *n., pl.* **-ties** —**mu'·tu·al·ly** *adv.*

SYN.—**mutual** may be used for an interchange of feeling between two persons [John and Joe are *mutual* enemies] or may imply a sharing jointly with others [the *mutual* efforts of a group]; **reciprocal** implies a return in kind or degree by each of two sides of what is given or demonstrated by the other [a *reciprocal* trade agreement], or it may refer to any inversely corresponding relationship [the *reciprocal* functions of two machine parts]; **common** simply implies a being shared by others or by all the members of a group [our *common* interests]

plague
(paragraph 5)

plague (plāg) *n.* ⟦ME *plage* < MFr < L *plaga*, a blow, misfortune, in LL(Ec), plague < Gr *plēgē*, *plaga* < IE **plaga*, a blow < base **plag-*, to strike > FLAW[2]⟧ **1** anything that afflicts or troubles; calamity; scourge **2** any contagious epidemic disease that is deadly; esp., bubonic plague **3** [Informal] a nuisance; annoyance **4** *Bible* any of various calamities sent down as divine punishment: Ex. 9:14, Num. 16:46 —*vt.* **plagued, plagu'·ing 1** to afflict with a plague **2** to vex; harass; trouble; torment —*SYN.* ANNOY —**plagu'er** *n.*

resuming
(paragraph 5)

re·sume (ri zo͞om', -zyo͞om') *vt.* **-sumed', -sum'·ing** ⟦ME *resumen*, to assume < MFr *resumer* < L *resumere* < *re-*, again + *sumere*, to take: see CONSUME⟧ **1** *a*) to take, get, or occupy again [to resume one's seat] *b*) to take back or take on again [to *resume* a former name] **2** to begin again or go on with again after interruption [to *resume* a conversation] **3** to summarize or make a résumé of —*vi.* to begin again or go on again after interruption —**re·sum'·able** *adj.*

289

surnames
(paragraph 5)

sur·name (sur'nām') *n.* ⟦ME < *sur-* (see SUR-[1]) + *name*, infl. by earlier *surnoun* < OFr *surnom* < *sur-* + *nom* < L *nomen*, NAME⟧ **1** the family name, or last name, as distinguished from a given name **2** a name or epithet added to a person's given name (Ex.: Ivan *the Terrible*) —*vt.* **··named', ··nam'·ing** to give a surname to

symbolize
(paragraph 7)

sym·bol·ize (-līz') *vt.* **··ized', ··iz'·ing** ⟦Fr *symboliser* < ML *symbolizare*⟧ **1** to be a symbol of; typify; stand for **2** to represent by a symbol or symbols —*vi.* to use symbols —**sym'·boli·za'·tion** *n.* —**sym'·bol·iz'er** *n.*

21A   VOCABULARY

Using the vocabulary words listed on pages 288–290, fill in the blanks.

1. Adopting a child demands a tremendous emotional _____.

2. To succeed in getting into better physical shape, amateur athletes must be _____ about exercising regularly, no matter how tempted they may be to skip a workout.

3. In successful marriages, the partners realize that they share _____ rights as well as responsibilities.

4. The new owners of the house did not know that mosquitoes would _____ them each summer.

5. After working as a clown in a circus for six months, my neighbor recently returned home and is now _____ his career as a stockbroker.

6. Many forms, including employment applications, require people to give their _____ before their first names.

7. Instead of the groom's giving the bride a ring, many couples now prefer double-ring ceremonies because they want the exchange of rings to _____ their equality of partnership.

8. In recent years many people are choosing to study a foreign language, and many select the language of their grandparents as a way of preserving their _____ .

9. Little boys raised in a _____ culture may grow up to feel they are superior to women, but such an attitude is resented by many women today.

10. Over the last quarter century, the principles of _____ have encouraged many women to pursue careers that their mothers often did not have the chance to consider.

Name   Date

21B   CENTRAL THEME AND MAIN IDEAS

Choose the best answer.

_____ 1. What is the central theme of "Should a Wife Keep Her Name?"
   a. The use of hyphenated surnames causes confusion because the wife may not seem committed to the marriage, the children face ridicule, and computer errors are likely to occur.
   b. Some men are horrified by their fiancées' wish to keep their maiden names, in part because these men feel their friends will not believe a couple is married unless the woman adopts the man's name.
   c. Technical and emotional problems that sometimes arise when a woman does not take her husband's name are causing some women to think through the issues before they make a decision about their married surnames.
   d. Feminism is seen as the force behind the modern phenomenon of women keeping their maiden names after they get married.

_____ 2. What is the main idea of paragraph 5?
   a. Many concerns about women's married surnames often seem relatively trivial.
   b. The important issues about women's surnames after marriage are control and commitment, cultural differences, and what to name the children.
   c. Most men are understanding about their wives' desire to keep their maiden names or to hyphenate their maiden and married names.
   d. Some concerns about women's married surnames have raised a number of significant issues.

3. In your own words, give the main idea of paragraph 4?

   _____
   _____

21C   MAJOR DETAILS

Decide whether each detail is Major *or* Minor *based on the context of the reading selection.*

_____ 1. Many brides have chosen to keep their maiden names.

_____ 2. Catherine Bergstrom-Katz is an actress.

_____ 3. Even though her husband does not use their hyphenated name at work, Bergstrom-Katz appears on all the family's legal documents.

_____ 4. Some women have decided to use their maiden names as middle names.

_____ 5. The issue of linked names can trigger highly emotional reactions.

_____ 6. One woman is worried about what monograms to put on silver and linens that she wants to give her daughter who is keeping her maiden name.

_____ 7. Maureen Poon-Fear's husband is of English-Irish descent.

_____ 8. Russell Poon-Fear feels he and his wife are one, so he continues to use their hyphenated surnames.

_____ 9. Jennifer Selvy is now a riding instructor in Denver.

_____ 10. Psychologists point out that youngsters with complex names are often teased by classmates.

_____ 11. Jennifer Selvy's fiancé worried about what his friends would think if his wife kept her name.

_____ 12. Hyphenated surnames sometimes create problems in keeping official government and financial records consistent.

21D   INFERENCES

Choose the best answer.

_____ 1. Read paragraph 5 again. Why have names always been symbols of power?
   a. Traditionally, when a woman married and took her husband's name, he gained complete legal and financial control of her life.
   b. Many primitive tribes used to name people after animals, hoping the animals' powers would transfer to their namesakes.
   c. Traditionally, when a husband's surname is associated with great political and financial power, the man feels he is sharing that power with his wife by giving her his name.
   d. Knowing someone's name can enable anyone to look up that person's records and thereby pry into his or her life.

_____ 2. Read paragraph 5 again. What does Russell Poon-Fear think of his marriage?
   a. Because of his own background, he is glad that he has married someone of mixed heritage.
   b. He considers that through marriage his wife has become his partner in all aspects of life.
   c. He feels protective of his wife because she has no other family.
   d. He feels that without his wife he had no identity.

_____ 3. Read paragraph 7 again. Alan Loy McGinnis says "marriage today needs all the reinforcement it can get." He is implying that
   a. people often marry for the wrong reasons, so many marriages are very fragile.
   b. divorce has become too easy, so a couple has to avoid all causes for disagreements if they want their marriage to last.
   c. modern marriages face many pressures from within and from outside sources.
   d. married couples have to resist the influence of people who want to encourage the couple to get divorced.

21E CRITICAL READING: THE AUTHOR'S STRATEGIES

Choose the best answer.
_____ 1. The main audience for "Should a Wife Keep Her Name?" is
   a. husbands of women who have kept their maiden names.
   b. women who are undecided about keeping their maiden names.
   c. readers who favor the idea of women keeping their maiden names.
   d. women who prefer to keep their marriage a secret.

_____ 2. The author's purpose in writing this reading is to
   a. persuade.
   b. narrate.
   c. inform.
   d. describe.

_____ 3. The author's tone in this reading is
   a. positive.
   b. negative.
   c. objective.
   d. noncommittal.

21F READER'S PROCESS: SUMMARIZING YOUR READING

_____ 1. What is the best summary of "Should a Wife Keep Her Name?"
   a. The author discusses why using a hyphenated name after marriage can create confusion.
   b. The author discusses how some women who wanted to keep their maiden names changed their minds.

c. The author discusses the issues women face as they make the decision to use a hyphenated name or to keep their maiden name after marriage.

d. The author discusses the reactions of friends and family members when women don't take their husband's name after marriage.

21G   READER'S RESPONSE: TO DISCUSS OR WRITE ABOUT

1. Do you think that husbands of women who hyphenate their names should also hyphenate their names, as Maureen Poon-Fear's husband did? Why or why not?

2. What is the difference between being called equal and being treated as equal? Using a specific example, describe the difference.

HOW DID YOU DO?
21   Should a Wife Keep Her Name?

SKILL (number of items)	Number Correct		Points for each		Score
Vocabulary (10)	8	×	4	=	32
Central Theme and Main Ideas (3)	2	×	8	=	16
Major Details (12)	6	×	2	=	12
Inferences (3)	2	×	1	=	2
Critical Reading: The Author's Strategies (3)	_____	×	2	=	60
Reader's Process: Summarizing Your Reading (1)	_____	×	3	=	_____

(Possible Total: 100) *Total*   _____

I Became Her Target

Roger Wilkins

LEARNING OBJECTIVES

- Explain the influence a white teacher had on a black student in a Grand Rapids junior high classroom.

THINKING: GETTING STARTED

- How would you react if a teacher picked on you in class?

(1) My favorite teacher's name was "**Deadeye**" Bean. Her real name was Dorothy. She taught American history to eighth graders in the junior high section of Creston, the high school that served the north end of Grand Rapids, Michigan. It was the fall of 1944. Franklin D. Roosevelt was president; American troops were battling their way across France; Joe DiMaggio was still in the service; the Montgomery bus **boycott** was more than a decade away, and I was a 12-year-old black newcomer in a school that was otherwise all white.

(2) My mother, who had been a widow in New York, had married my stepfather, a Grand Rapids physician, the year before, and he had bought the best house he could afford for his new family. The problem for our new neighbors was that their neighborhood had previously been **pristine** (in their terms) and they were ignorant about black people. The prevailing wisdom in the neighborhood was that we were spoiling it and that we ought to go back where we belonged (or alternatively, ought not intrude where we were not wanted). There was a lot of angry talk among the adults, but nothing much came of it.

(3) But some of the kids, those first few weeks, were quite nasty. They threw stones at me, chased me home when I was on foot and spat on my bike seat when I was in class. For a time, I was a pretty lonely, friendless and sometimes frightened kid. I was just transplanted from Harlem, and here in Grand Rapids, the **dominant** culture was speaking to me **insistently.** I can see now that those youngsters were bullying and culturally disadvantaged. I knew then that they were **bigoted,** but the culture spoke to me more powerfully than my mind and I felt ashamed for being different—a nonstandard person.

(4) I now know that Dorothy Bean understood most of that and deplored it. So things began to change when I walked into her classroom. She was a pleasant-looking single woman, who looked old and wrinkled to me at the time, but who was probably about 40. Whereas my other teachers

Once a healthy student-teacher relationship is formed, it can continue to influence the child in positive ways for years to come.

approached the problem of easing in their new black pupil by ignoring him for the first few weeks, Miss Bean went right at me. On the morning after having read our first assignment, she asked me the first question. I later came to know that in Grand Rapids, she was viewed as a very liberal person who believed, among other things, that Negroes were equal.

(5) I gulped and answered her question and the follow-up. They weren't brilliant answers, but they did establish the facts that I had read the assignment and that I could speak English. Later in the hour, when one of my classmates had bungled an answer, Miss Bean came back to me with a question that required me to clean up the girl's mess and established me as a smart person.

(6) Thus, the teacher began to give me human dimensions, though not perfect ones for an eighth grader. It was somewhat better to be an **incipient** teacher's pet than merely a dark presence in the back of the room onto whose silent form my classmates could fit all the stereotypes they carried in their heads.

(7) A few days later, Miss Bean became the first teacher ever to require me to think. She asked my opinion about something Jefferson had done. In those days, all my opinions were **derivative.** I was for Roosevelt because my parents were and I was for the Yankees because my older buddy from Harlem was a Yankee fan. Besides, we didn't have opinions about historical figures like Jefferson. Like our high school building or old Mayor Welch, he just was.

(8) After I had stared at her for a few seconds, she said: "Well, should he have bought Louisiana or not?"

(9) "I guess so," I replied tentatively.

(10) "Why?" she shot back.

(11) Why! What kind of question was that, I **groused** silently. But I **ventured** an answer. Day after day, she kept doing that to me, and my answers became stronger and more confident. She was the first teacher to give me the sense that thinking was part of education and that I could form opinions that had some value.

(12) Her final service to me came on a day when my mind was wandering and I was idly digging my pencil into the writing surface on the arm of my chair. Miss Bean impulsively threw a hunk of gum eraser at me. By amazing chance, it hit my hand and sent the pencil flying. She gasped, and I crept **mortified** after my pencil as the class roared. That was the ice breaker. Afterward, kids came up to me to laugh about "Old Deadeye Bean." The incident became a legend, and I, a part of that story, became a person to talk to. So that's how I became just another kid in school and Dorothy Bean became "Old Deadeye."

Here are some of the more difficult words in "I Became Her Target."

bigoted (paragraph 3)	**bigot** (big′ət) *n.* [Fr < OFr, a term of insult used of Normans, apparently a Norman oath < ? ME *bi god,* by God] **1** a person who holds blindly and intolerantly to a particular creed, opinion, etc. **2** a narrow-minded, prejudiced person —*SYN.* ZEALOT —**big′·oted** *adj.* —**big′·ot·edly** *adv.*
boycott (paragraph 1)	**boy·cott** (boi′kät′) *vt.* [after Capt. C. C. *Boycott,* land agent ostracized by his neighbors during the Land League agitation in Ireland in 1880] **1** to join together in refusing to deal with, so as to punish, coerce, etc. **2** to refuse to buy, sell, or use [to *boycott* a newspaper] —☆*n.* an act or instance of boycotting
Deadeye (paragraph 1)	**dead·eye** (-ī′) *n.* **1** a round, flat block of wood with three holes in it for a lanyard, used in pairs on a sailing ship to hold the shrouds and stays taut **2** [Slang] an accurate marksman
derivative (paragraph 7)	**de·riva·tive** (də riv′ə tiv) *adj.* [ME *derivatif* < LL *derivativus* < L *derivatus,* pp. of *derivare:* see fol.] **1** derived **2** using or taken from other sources; not original **3** of derivation —*n.* **1** something derived **2** *Chem.* a substance derived from, or of such composition and properties that it may be considered as derived from, another substance by chemical change, esp. by the substitution of one or more elements or radicals **3** *Finance* a contract, as an option or futures contract, whose value depends on the value of the securities, commodities, etc. that form the basis of the contract **4** *Linguis.* a word formed from another or others by derivation **5** *Math.* the limiting value of a rate of change of a function with respect to a variable; the instantaneous rate of change, or slope, of a function (Ex.: the derivative of y with respect to x, often written dy/dx, is 3 when $y = 3x$) —**de·riv′a·tively** *adv.*

Vocabulary List

de·rive (di rīv′) *vt.* **·rived′, ·riv′·ing** [ME *deriven* < OFr *deriver* < L *derivare*, to divert, orig., to turn a stream from its channel < *de-*, from + *rivus*, a stream: see RIVAL] **1** to get or receive (something) *from* a source **2** to get by reasoning; deduce or infer **3** to trace from or to a source; show the derivation of **4** *Chem.* to obtain or produce (a compound) from another compound by replacing one element with one or more other elements —*vi.* to come (*from*); be derived; originate —*SYN.* RISE —**de·riv′·able** *adj.* —**de·riv′er** *n.*

dominant
(paragraph 3)

domi·nant (däm′ə nənt) *adj.* [L *dominans*, prp. of *dominari*: see fol.] **1** exercising authority or influence; dominating; ruling; prevailing **2** *Genetics* designating or relating to that one of any pair of allelic hereditary factors which, when both are present in the germ plasm, dominates over the other and appears in the organism: opposed to RECESSIVE: see MENDEL'S LAWS **3** *Music* of or based upon the fifth tone of a diatonic scale —*n.* **1** *Ecol.* that species of plant or animal most numerous in a community or exercising control over the other organisms by its influence upon the environment **2** *Genetics* a dominant character or factor **3** *Music* the fifth note of a diatonic scale —**dom′i·nantly** *adv.*

SYN.—**dominant** refers to that which dominates or controls, or has the greatest effect [*dominant* characteristics in genetics]; **predominant** refers to that which is at the moment uppermost in importance or influence [the *predominant* reason for his refusal]; **paramount** is applied to that which ranks first in importance, authority, etc. [of *paramount* interest to me]; **preeminent** implies prominence because of surpassing excellence [the *preeminent* writer of his time]; **preponderant** implies superiority in amount, weight, power, importance, etc. [the *preponderant* religion of a country]

groused
(paragraph 11)

grouse[2] (grous) [Informal] *vi.* **groused, grous′·ing** [orig. Brit army slang < ?] to complain; grumble —*n.* a complaint —**grous′er** *n.*

incipient
(paragraph 6)

in·cipi·ent (in sip′ē ənt) *adj.* [L *incipiens*, prp. of *incipere*, to begin, lit., take up < *in-*, in, on + *capere*, to take: see HAVE] in the first stage of existence; just beginning to exist or to come to notice [an *incipient* illness] —**in·cip′i·ence** *n.* or **in·cip′i·ency** —**in·cip′i·ently** *adv.*

insistently
(paragraph 3)

in·sist·ent (-tənt) *adj.* [L *insistens*] **1** insisting or demanding; persistent in demands or assertions **2** compelling the attention [an *insistent* rhythm] —**in·sist′·ently** *adv.*

mortified
(paragraph 12)

mor·tify (môrt′ə fī′) *vt.* **·fied′, ·fy′·ing** [ME *mortifien* < OFr *mortifier* < LL(Ec) *mortificare*, to kill, destroy < L *mors*, death (see MORTAL) + *facere*, to make, DO[1]] **1** to punish (one's body) or control (one's physical desires and passions) by self-denial, fasting, etc., as a means of religious or ascetic discipline **2** to cause to feel shame, humiliation, chagrin, etc.; injure the pride or self-respect of **3** [Now Rare] to cause (body tissue) to decay or become gangrenous **4** to destroy the vitality or vigor of —*vi,* **1** to practice MORTIFICATION (sense 1a) **2** [Now Rare] to decay or become gangrenous — *SYN.* ASHAMED —**mor′·ti·fi′er** *n.*

pristine
(paragraph 2)

pris·tine (pris′tēn′, -tin; pris tēn′; *chiefly Brit* pris′tīn′) *adj.* [L *pristinus*, former < OL *pri*, before: see PRIME] **1** characteristic of the earliest, or an earlier, period or condition; original ☆**2** still pure; uncorrupted; unspoiled [*pristine* beauty] —**pris′·tine·ly** *adv.*

ventured
(paragraph 11)

ven·ture (ven′chər) *n.* [ME, aphetic for *aventure*: see ADVENTURE] **1** a risky or dangerous undertaking; esp., a business enterprise in which there is danger of loss as well as chance for profit **2** something on which a risk is taken, as the merchandise in a commercial enterprise or a stake in gambling **3** chance; fortune: now only in **at a venture**, by mere chance; at random —*vt.* **·tured, ·tur·ing** **1** to expose to danger or risk [to *venture* one's life] **2** to expose (money, merchandise, etc.) to chance of loss **3** to undertake the risk of; brave [to *venture* a storm] **4** to express at the risk of criticism, objection, denial, etc. [to *venture* an opinion] —*vi.* to do or go at some risk —**ven′·turer** *n.*

22A VOCABULARY

From the context of "I Became Her Target," explain the meaning of each of the vocabulary words shown in boldface.

1. *From paragraph 1:* My favorite teacher's name was **"Deadeye"** Bean.

   _____

   _____

2. *From paragraph 1:* The Montgomery bus **boycott** was more than a decade away, and I was a 12-year-old black newcomer in a school that was otherwise all white.

   _____

   _____

3. *From paragraph 2:* The problem for our new neighbors was that their neighborhood had previously been **pristine**.

   _____

   _____

4. *From paragraph 3:* I was just transplanted from Harlem, and here in Grand Rapids, the **dominant** culture was speaking to me **insistently**.

   _____

   _____

5. *From paragraph 3:* I knew then that they were **bigoted**.

   _____

   _____

6. *From paragraph 6:* It was somewhat better to be an **incipient** teacher's pet than merely a dark presence in the back of the room.

   _____

   _____

7. *From paragraph 7:* In those days, all my opinions were **derivative**.

   _____

   _____

8. *From paragraph 11:* What kind of question was that, I **groused** silently. But I **ventured** an answer.

   _____

   _____

9. *From paragraph 12:* I crept **mortified** after my pencil as the class roared.

_____

_____

22B   CENTRAL THEME AND MAIN IDEAS

Choose the best answer.

_____ 1. What is the central theme of "I Became Her Target"?
   a. Roger Wilkins's teacher did not like him and asked him trick questions because he was black and she was a racist.
   b. Roger Wilkins's classmates had been raised by their parents to be racists, and until they were forced to be nice to Wilkins, they had no idea what black people were really like.
   c. Roger Wilkins's teacher helped him realize his worth and get the respect of the other students by challenging him to show his intelligence and answer hard questions.
   d. Roger Wilkins's classmates became his friends once they realized that he and they shared a dislike of their American history teacher.

_____ 2. What is the main idea of paragraph 7?
   a. Roger Wilkins did not like being called on to answer hard questions.
   b. Roger Wilkins did not know anything about President Jefferson.
   c. All of Roger Wilkins's opinions were derived from his parents or friends.
   d. Roger Wilkins was not used to being asked to think and form his own opinions.

_____ 3. What is the main idea of paragraph 12?
   a. Miss Bean helped Roger Wilkins gain his classmates' acceptance by throwing an eraser at him when his attention wandered.
   b. Miss Bean always looked for opportunities to embarrass her students by throwing erasers at them.
   c. Miss Bean had only pretended to be interested in Roger Wilkins's education, but she was a racist underneath.
   d. Roger Wilkins was accepted by his classmates only after he mortified Miss Bean in front of them.

22C MAJOR DETAILS

Decide whether each detail is true (T), false (F), or not discussed (ND).

_____ 1. Roger Wilkins's favorite teacher was Dorothy Bean.

_____ 2. He was in her eighth-grade American history class in 1944.

_____ 3. Before Wilkins, no black student had ever attended Creston High School in Grand Rapids, Michigan.

_____ 4. Wilkins's mother met his stepfather in New York.

_____ 5. The adults in Wilkins's new neighborhood threw stones at his house because they wanted his family to move away.

_____ 6. Miss Bean asked Roger Wilkins the very first question on the very first assignment.

_____ 7. Dorothy Bean was viewed as a very liberal person, who believed, among other things, that blacks were equal to whites.

_____ 8. Roger Wilkins had never been to Harlem.

_____ 9. Miss Bean kept asking Roger Wilkins questions day after day until his answers became increasingly confident.

_____10. It was the tradition at Creston High School to give teachers nicknames.

22D INFERENCES

Choose the best answer.

_____ 1. *Read paragraphs 1, 2, and 4 again.* Why does the author change from using the word "black" in these paragraphs to using the word "Negroes" in the last sentence of paragraph 4?
   a. By using the word "Negroes," the author shows that he is prejudiced against his own black people.
   b. The preferred, formal term for blacks was "Negroes" in 1944, and the author wants to recreate that time for the reader.
   c. The author assumes that the words "Negroes" and "blacks" are interchangeable, although today the preferred term is "blacks."
   d. The author prefers the word "Negroes," even though in 1987, when he wrote this essay, the preferred word was "blacks."

_____ 2. *Read paragraph 3 again.* What is the author implying when he calls the white students "culturally disadvantaged," a term that is usually applied to undereducated minority people?
   a. The author is not aware of how the term is usually used.
   b. The author is implying that the students at Creston High School had not gotten a good education and had not developed good study habits.
   c. The author is trying to be polite by using a nice word for "stupid."
   d. The author is being mildly sarcastic, applying a term to these students that they or their parents might have applied to him.

_____ 3. *Read paragraph 6 again.* Why did Roger Wilkins feel "it was somewhat better to be an incipient teacher's pet than merely a dark presence in the back of the room"?
   a. He preferred being liked by the teacher to being liked by no one at all.
   b. He felt that being a teacher's pet might result in his getting special privileges or a higher grade.
   c. He did not like the other students and did not care what they thought of him.
   d. He did not like sitting in the back of the room, and he hoped that Miss Bean would change his seat.

22E   CRITICAL READING: THE AUTHOR'S STRATEGIES

Choose the best answer.

_____ 1. The main audience for "I Became Her Target" is
   a. any reader who enjoys a good story.
   b. any reader who has had a bad experience in school.
   c. any reader who has fond memories of a teacher.
   d. any reader who has experienced being the "new kid."

_____ 2. The author's purpose in writing this reading is to
   a. inform.
   b. illustrate.
   c. warn.
   d. narrate.

_____ 3. The author's tone in this reading is
   a. heartfelt.
   b. serious.
   c. upset.
   d. disappointed.

Name   Date

21F   READER'S PROCESS: SUMMARIZING YOUR READING

_____ 1. What is the best summary of "I Became Her Target"?
   a. The author tells a story about a time in his childhood when he felt alone and unwanted in school.
   b. The author tells the story of an incident with a teacher that involved a flying eraser and a nickname that stuck.
   c. The author tells a story that illustrates what it's like to be the only black child in an all-white school.
   d. The author tells a story that illustrates how a teacher can influence the life of a child through the craft of teaching.

21G   READER'S RESPONSE: TO DISCUSS OR WRITE ABOUT

1. Suppose the "best house" you could "afford" (paragraph 2) were in a neighborhood where people of your race, religion, or ethnic background are not wanted. Would you move into that neighborhood? Explain your point of view fully.

2. Discuss a teacher or other adult who had a big impact on you when you were growing up. Using specific details and examples, describe the way in which he or she affected you.

HOW DID YOU DO?
22 I Became Her Target

SKILL (number of items)	Number Correct		Points for each		Score
Vocabulary (11)	_____	×	3	=	_____
Central Theme and Main Ideas (3)	_____	×	4	=	_____
Major Details (10)	_____	×	4	=	_____
Inferences (3)	_____	×	1	=	_____
Critical Reading: The Author's Strategies (3)	_____	×	3	=	_____
Reader's Process: Summarizing Your Reading (1)	_____	×	3	=	_____
	(Possible Total: 100) *Total*				_____

Guns in Kids' Bedrooms? Ohio Hunting Town Approves

Associated Press

LEARNING OBJECTIVES

- Contrast the pros and cons of children's possessing guns in a small Ohio town.

THINKING: GETTING STARTED

- Do you think we live in a gun culture society that supports romantic notions of families' learning to shoot and hunt together?

(1) The guns were kept in the boy's bedroom, resting on a rack mounted to the wall. The one investigators say was used to kill his mother—a .22-caliber rifle—was found lying on his bed. On a cold winter evening in Big Prairie, a rural hunting town, the 10-year-old boy picked up the rifle and shot his mother, 46-year-old Deborah McVay, in the head, authorities say. Relatives said mother and son had been arguing over chores: He didn't want to carry firewood into the house.

Idea (2) The notion of a 10-year-old boy keeping a **stash** of weapons in his bedroom is a jolting one to some Americans, but not so in Big Prairie, where the sound of gunshots **ricocheting** through the air is familiar—even comforting. Here, children learn to fire guns as easily as they learn to ride bicycles. The child's tender age exposes an age-old divide between **rural** and **urban** in a nation where 80 million people are registered gun owners. It also raises anew the question of whether children should have access to guns—let alone be permitted to keep loaded guns in their bedrooms.

(3) In Big Prairie, as in many other areas with deep hunting cultures, the answer is a **resounding** "yes." "You're in a rural area here, and a lot of people hunt," says Sam Crawford, a 65-year-old gas station clerk. "And we're gonna teach our kids how to hunt and how to use a gun." There's plenty of open land for hunting in Holmes County, where acres of fields and forests and swamps dominate the landscape. Seasoned hunters travel from farm to farm with the friendly **query:** "Mind if I hunt here?" It's a tradition passed down from each generation to the next. "Out here, if you don't hear a gunshot in a day's time, then something's wrong," said Ron

Approximately half the households in the United States have one or more guns. Children are not always aware of how dangerous guns are.

Martin, McVay's next-door neighbor on an isolated hill **shrouded** in trees.

(4) The weapons found in the 10-year-old's room are commonly used for hunting, although it's unclear if the boy used them to hunt. The three .22-caliber rifles would be for small game like squirrels and coyotes, the 12-gauge shotgun for deer, said Jamey Graham, a spokeswoman for the Ohio Department of Natural Resources. Sheriff's deputies did not respond when asked whether the guns were registered.

(5) State officials would not say whether the boy had a juvenile hunting license, citing privacy laws. Nearly 63,000 Ohio children, age 17 and younger, were granted hunting licenses during the current hunting season, which ends in February. In Ohio, as in many states, there is no minimum age required to earn that license. Martin had seen the boy shooting a BB gun in his backyard, like lots of children who lived nearby. "He wasn't going around threatening people or anything like that," Martin said.

(6) The boy, who has pleaded the equivalent of not guilty to a charge of murder as a juvenile, dealt with "anger issues," family members say. He was enrolled in an elementary school that specializes in children with behavioral problems and had a history of poor behavior, including one instance in which he smacked his school principal in the face with a dust pan. His parents had recently separated and were planning to divorce, said his uncle Tony Miller. The guns in his bedroom—given by his

father—were a source of conflict between the boy's parents, his uncle said. "She kept bringing the issue up about getting rid of them," Miller said, referring to the weapons. "But every time she did there was an argument about it with the father."

(7) Psychologists caution that a 10-year-old cannot fully comprehend the long-term consequences of using a gun to harm another person. Dealing with anger management is not an unusual problem for a 10-year-old boy to have—the difference in this case is that he had a weapon at his disposal, says Sherry Hamby, a gun control advocate and editor of the *Psychology of Violence*, an academic research journal. By age 5 or 6, most children understand that hitting is wrong, and a 10-year-old would most certainly know the difference between right and wrong, Hamby said. "But if you want to talk about having some sort of mature **abstract** reasoning capabilities," she said, "you're talking a minimum of 12 or 13 years old."

(8) Research shows that children are not able to process long-term consequences because connections in their brains haven't been formed, which is why their decision-making is more rash, says Anne Nurse, a **sociologist** at the College of Wooster in Wooster, Ohio. The residents of Big Prairie, though shaken by the shooting, don't see it that way. In their view, this was a parenting issue—a question of personal responsibility. Not surprisingly, gun rights **advocates** share that view. Roger James, a retiree who was born and raised near Big Prairie, says this child in particular probably shouldn't have been allowed near guns because of his behavioral issues. James says all his grandchildren hunt and were taught how to shoot a gun from an early age. As for keeping them in the bedroom: "If there's no problem, that's probably where they would keep 'em," he says.

(9) At the heart of the debate is a cultural clash between the way of life in rural America versus how people live in the cities, says Harry Wilson, a professor of political science at Roanoke College in Salem, Va., who wrote the book *Guns, Gun Control and Elections*. Wilson compared keeping guns in the home to hanging the keys to the family car on a wall hook. "Kids could decide to get the keys and figure out how to start the car, and they could figure out whatever they want to do with it," he says.

(10) Wilson, who grew up in rural Pennsylvania, remembers the loaded shotguns that his grandmother kept in various rooms of her home, used primarily for killing snakes. In some parts of this country, he says, most people don't worry about locking up their guns because "people don't go around shooting each other." "I know kids who are 10 years old who have hunted," he says. "That 10-year-old's going to understand that when you shoot something, it dies."

Here are some of the more difficult words in "Guns in Kids' Bedrooms? Ohio Town Approves."

abstract
(paragraph 7)

ab·stract *(for adj.,* ab strakt′, ab′strakt′; *for n. 1 & vt. 4,* ab′strakt′; *for n. 2,* ab′strakt′, ab strakt′; *for vt. 1, 2, & 3,* ab strakt′) *adj.* ⟦< L *abstractus,* pp. of *abstrahere,* to draw from, separate < *ab*(s)-, from + *trahere,* to DRAW⟧ **1** thought of apart from any particular instances or material objects; not concrete **2** expressing a quality thought of apart from any particular or material object [beauty is an *abstract* word] **3** not easy to understand because of being extremely complex, remote from concrete reality, etc.; abstruse **4** theoretical; not practical or applied **5** designating or of art abstracted from reality, in which designs or forms may be definite and geometric or fluid and amorphous: a generic term that encompasses various nonrealistic contemporary schools —*n.* **1** a brief statement of the essential content of a book, article, speech, court record, etc.; summary **2** an abstract thing, condition, idea, etc. —*vt.* **1** to take away; remove **2** to take dishonestly; steal **3** to think of (a quality) apart from any particular instance or material object that has it; also, to form (a general idea) from particular instances **4** to summarize; make an abstract of —*SYN.* ABRIDGMENT —**in the abstract** in theory as apart from practice —**ab·stract′er** *n.* —**ab·stract′ly** *adv.* —**ab·stract′·ness** *n.*

advocates
(paragraph 8)

ad·vo·cate (ad′və kit; *for v.,* -kāt′) *n.* ⟦ME *advocat, avocat* < L *advocatus,* a counselor < *advocare,* to summon (for aid) < *ad-,* to + *vocare,* to call⟧ **1** a person who pleads another's cause; specif., a lawyer **2** a person who speaks or writes in support of something [an *advocate* of lower taxes] —*vt.* **··cat′ed, ··cat′ing** ⟦< the *n.*⟧ to speak or write in support of; be in favor of —*SYN.* SUPPORT —**ad′·vo·ca′·tor** *n.*

query
(paragraph 3)

query (kwir′ē, kwer′ē) *n., pl.* **··ries** ⟦< L *quaere,* 2d pers. sing., imper., of *quaerere,* to ask, inquire⟧ **1** a question; inquiry **2** a doubt **3** a question mark (?) placed after a question or used to question the accuracy of written or printed matter —*vt.* **··ried, ··ry·ing 1** to call in question; ask about **2** to question (a person) **3** to mark with a QUERY (sense 3) —*vi.* to ask questions or express doubt —*SYN.* ASK

resounding
(paragraph 3)

re·sound·ing (ri zoun′diŋ) *adj.* **1** reverberating; ringing sonorously **2** thoroughgoing; complete [a *resounding* victory] **3** high-sounding —**re·sound′·ingly** *adv.*

ricocheting
(paragraph 2)

rico·chet (rik′ə shā′, rik′ə shā′; *Brit,* -shet′) *n.* ⟦Fr; used first in *fable du ricochet* (story in which the narrator constantly evades the hearers' questions) < ?⟧ **1** the oblique rebound or skipping of a bullet, stone, etc. after striking a surface at an angle **2** a bullet, etc. that ricochets —*vi.* **··cheted′** (-shād′) *or* **··chet′ted** (-shet′id), **··chet′·ing** (-shā′iŋ) *or* **··chet′·ting** (-shet′iŋ) ⟦Fr *ricocher* < the *n.*⟧ to make a ricochet motion —*SYN.* SKIP¹

rural
(paragraph 2)

ru·ral (roor′əl) *adj.* ⟦ME < MFr < LL *ruralis* < L *rus* (gen. *ruris*), the country < IE **rewos,* space < base ***rewe-,* to open, ROOM⟧ **1** of or characteristic of the country, country life, or country people; rustic **2** living in the country **3** having to do with farming; agricultural —**ru′·rally** *adv.*

SYN.—**rural** is the comprehensive, nonspecific word referring to life on the farm or in the country as distinguished from life in the city [*rural* schools]; **rustic** stresses the contrast between the supposed crudeness and unsophistication of the country and the polish and refinement of the city [*rustic* humor]; **pastoral** suggests the highly idealized primitive simplicity of rural life, originally among shepherds; **bucolic,** in contrast, suggests a down-to-earth rustic simplicity or artlessness [her *bucolic* suitor] —*ANT.* **urban**

shrouded
(paragraph 3)

shroud (shroud) *n.* ⟦ME *schroude* < OE *scrud,* akin to ON *skrud,* accouterments, cloth, OE *screade,* SHRED⟧ **1** a cloth used to wrap a corpse for burial; winding sheet **2** something that covers, protects, or screens; veil **3** any of a set of ropes or wires stretched from a ship's side to a masthead to offset lateral strain on the mast **4** any of the set of lines from the canopy of a parachute to the harness: in full **shroud line** —*vt.* **1** to wrap (a corpse) in a shroud **2** to hide from view; cover; screen **3** [Archaic] to shelter and protect —*vi.* [Archaic] to take shelter

Vocabulary List

307

Vocabulary List

sociologist
(paragraph 8)

so·ci·ol·ogy (sō'sē äl'ə jē, -shē-) *n.* [[Fr *sociologie* (coined in 1830 by Comte): see SOCIO- & -LOGY]] **1** the science of human society and of social relations, organization, and change; specif., the study of the beliefs, values, etc. of societal groups and of the processes governing social phenomena **2** SYNECOLOGY —**so'·ci·ol'o·gist** *n.*

stash
(paragraph 2)

☆**stash** (stash) [Informal] *vt.* [[< ? STOW & CACHE]] to put or hide away ☆ (money, valuables, etc.) in a secret or safe place, as for future use —*n.* **1** a place for hiding things **2** something hidden away; specif., ☆ a hidden supply of an illegal drug

urban
(paragraph 2)

ur·ban (ʉr'bən) *adj.* [[L *urbanus* < *urbs*, city]] **1** of, in, constituting, or comprising a city or town **2** characteristic of the city as distinguished from the country; citified ☆**3** in U.S. census use, designating or of an incorporated or unincorporated place with at least 50,000 inhabitants

23A   VOCABULARY

Using the vocabulary words on pages 307–308, fill in this crossword puzzle.

Name   Date

Across

1. persons who speak or write in support of something

2. in the country

3. skipping of a bullet

4. hidden away

5. a question

6. one who studies beliefs, values, etc. of societal groups

Down

3. thoroughgoing; complete

7. theoretical

8. citified

9. a collection of valuables

23B CENTRAL THEME AND MAIN IDEAS

Choose the best answer.

_____ 1. What is the central theme of "Guns in Kids' Bedrooms? Hunting Town Approves"?
a. A 10-year-old boy shoots his mother with a .22-caliber rifle after arguing with her about chores.
b. Mother and Father disagreed about their son's collection of guns in his bedroom.
c. A 10-year-old boy's access to guns used to kill his mother fuels debate over gun control.
d. Parenting issues were at the center of a 10-year-old boy's shooting his mother.

_____ 2. What is the main idea of paragraph 2?
a. A 10-year-old boy's keeping a stash of guns in his bedroom is objectionable to many Americans.
b. Permitting children to have access to guns is a controversial issue between urban and rural America.
c. The sound of gunshots' ricocheting through the air is common in Big Prairie.
d. Children learn to fire guns as easily as they learn to ride bicycles in Big Prairie.

_____ 3. What is the main idea of paragraph 4?
a. The guns found in the 10-year-old boy's room were used for hunting.
b. Whether the 10-year-old's guns were registered or not was unknown.
c. Privacy laws prevented the state officials from saying whether the 10-year-old had a juvenile hunting license.
d. Hunting for small game by juveniles in Ohio, with or without a license, is common and not considered threatening.

23C MAJOR DETAILS

Decide whether each detail is Major *or* Minor *based on the context of the reading selection.*

_____ 1. The rifle used by the 10-year-old to kill his mother was found lying on his bed.

_____ 2. Prior to the shooting, the mother and son had been arguing over chores.

_____ 3. Eighty million people are registered gun owners in the United States.

_____ 4. Nearly 63,000 Ohio children, age 17 and younger, were granted hunting licenses during the current hunting season.

_____ 5. A neighbor had seen the boy shooting a BB gun in his backyard.

_____ 6. According to an uncle, the guns in the boy's bedroom were a source of conflict between the boy's parents.

_____ 7. Psychologists say that a 10-year-old cannot realize the long-term consequences of using a gun to harm someone.

_____ 8. Residents of Big Prairie view the shooting as a parenting problem, not a problem of mature reasoning.

23D INFERENCES

*Decide whether each statement that follows can be inferred (*Yes*) or cannot be inferred (*No*).*

_____ 1. Children's storing guns in their bedrooms is uncommon in urban America.

_____ 2. The 10-year-old boy was an only child.

_____ 3. Easy accessibility to guns contributed to the boy's shooting his mother.

_____ 4. Part of the boy's behavioral problems concerned authority figures.

_____ 5. The boy would not have shot his mother if he had realized the consequences of his actions.

Name   Date

23E CRITICAL READING: FACT OR OPINION

Decide whether each statement, even if it quotes someone, contains a Fact *or an* Opinion.

_____ 1. *From paragraph 2:* "Here children learn to fire guns as easily as they learn to ride bicycles."

_____ 2. *From paragraph 3:* "Out here, if you don't hear a gunshot in a day's time, then something's wrong."

_____ 3. *From paragraph 4:* "The weapons found in the 10-year-old's room are commonly used for hunting [. . .] ."

_____ 4. *From paragraph 6:* "His parents had recently separated and were planning to divorce."

_____ 5. *From paragraph 8:* "Roger James, a retiree born and raised near Big Prairie, says this boy in particular shouldn't have been allowed near guns because of behavioral issues."

23F CRITICAL READING: THE AUTHOR'S STRATEGIES

Choose the best answer.

_____ 1. The main audience for "Guns in Kids' Bedrooms? Ohio Town Approves" is
   a. anyone who plans on moving to Ohio.
   b. anyone who has children who hunt.
   c. anyone who has children dealing with anger management.
   d. anyone who is either for or against gun control for children.

_____ 2. The author's purpose in writing this reading is to
   a. entertain.
   b. narrate.
   c. inform.
   d. describe.

_____ 3. The author's tone in this reading is
   a. fault-finding.
   b. depressing.
   c. hard-hearted.
   d. frank.

23G READER'S PROCESS: SUMMARIZING YOUR READING

_____ 1. What is the best summary of "Guns in Kids' Bedrooms? Ohio Hunting Town Approves"?
   a. A 10-year-old boy who has a stash of guns in his bedroom kills his mother out of anger about chores she wanted him to do.

b. Although residents of Big Prairie were shocked when a boy killed his mother, they attributed his actions to poor parenting, not the availability of guns used primarily for hunting.

c. Gun control is not advocated by Big Prairie residents or by gun rights supporters because Holmes County, Ohio, is a haven for hunting small game.

d. A boy with behavioral problems both at school and in the home is given guns by his father to hunt game in spite of the mother's objections.

23H   READER'S RESPONSE: TO DISCUSS OR WRITE ABOUT

1. In Big Prairie, Ohio, a 10-year-old boy shot and killed his mother with a shotgun. She had a single gunshot wound to the head. What caused a child so young to do this? Is it possible he thought that the gun was unloaded? Could the shooting have been prevented?

2. On June 26, 2008, the Supreme Court made a landmark ruling upholding the right of individuals to bear arms for hunting and for self-defense. Do you agree or disagree with this ruling? Why? Did the hunting tradition passed down from adults to children contribute in any way to the boy's shooting his mother? Explain.

HOW DID YOU DO?
23 Guns in Kids' Bedrooms? Ohio Hunting Town Approves

SKILL (number of items)	Number Correct		Points for each		Score
Vocabulary (10)	_____	×	2	=	_____
Central Theme and Main Ideas (3)	_____	×	7	=	_____
Major Details (8)	_____	×	2	=	_____
Inferences (5)	_____	×	4	=	_____
Critical Reading: Fact or Opinion (5)	_____	×	2	=	_____
Critical Reading: The Author's Strategies (3)	_____	×	3	=	_____
Reader's Process: Summarizing Your Reading (1)	_____	×	4	=	_____

(Possible Total: 100) *Total*   _____

Name   Date

Selection 24
Mute in an English-Only World

Chang-rae Lee

LEARNING OBJECTIVES

• Recount the problems a non-native speaker of English faced when she moved to the United States.

THINKING: GETTING STARTED

• Should immigrants who apply for United States citizenship be required to learn English?

(1) When I read of the trouble in Palisades Park, New Jersey, over the **proliferation** of Korean-language signs along its main commercial strip, I unexpectedly sympathized with the frustrations, resentments, and fears of the longtime residents. They clearly felt **alienated** and even unwelcome in a vital part of their community. The town, like seven others in New Jersey, has passed laws requiring that half of any commercial sign in a foreign language be in English. Now I certainly would never tolerate any exclusionary ideas about who could rightfully settle and belong in the town. But having been raised in a Korean immigrant family, I saw every day the **exacting** price and power of language, especially with my mother, who was an outsider in an English-only world.

(2) In the first years we lived in America, my mother could speak only the most basic English, and she often encountered great difficulty whenever she went out. We lived in New Rochelle, New York, in the early 1970's, and most of the local businesses were run by the **descendants** of immigrants who, generations ago, had come to the suburbs from New York City. Proudly dotting Main Street and North Avenue were Italian pastry and cheese shops, Jewish tailors and cleaners, and Polish and German butchers and bakers. If my mother's marketing couldn't wait until the weekend, when my father had free time, she would often hold off until I came home from school to buy the groceries. Though I was only six or seven years old, she insisted that I go out shopping with her and my younger sister. I mostly **loathed** the task, partly because it meant I couldn't spend the afternoon playing catch with my friends but also because I knew our errands would inevitably lead to an awkward scene, and that I would have to speak up to help my mother.

(3) I was just learning the language myself, but I was a quick study, as children are with new tongues. I had spent kindergarten in almost complete silence, hearing only the high nasality of my teacher and

A person who is not fluent in the English language would have a difficult time shopping for food in a grocery store.

comprehending little but the cranky **wails** and cries of my classmates. But soon, seemingly mere months later, I had already become a terrible ham and mimic, and I would crack up my father with impressions of teachers, his friends, and even himself. My mother scolded me for **aping** his speech, and the one time I attempted to make light of hers I rated a roundhouse smack on my bottom.

(4) For her, the English language was not very funny. It usually meant trouble and a good dose of shame, and sometimes real hurt. Although she had a good reading knowledge of the language from university classes in South Korea, she had never practiced actual conversation. So, in America she used English flashcards and phrase books and watched television with us kids. And she faithfully carried a pocket workbook illustrated with stick-figure people and compound sentences to be filled in. But none of it seemed to do her much good. Staying mostly at home to care for us, she didn't have many chances to try out **sundry** words and phrases. When she did, say, at the window of the post office, her readied speech would stall, freeze, sometimes altogether collapse.

(5) One day was unusually **harrowing.** We ventured downtown in the new Ford Country Squire my father had bought her, an enormous station wagon that seemed as long—and **deft**—as an ocean liner. We were shopping for a special meal for guests visiting that weekend, and my mother had heard that a particular butcher carried fresh oxtails, which she needed for a traditional soup. We'd never been inside the shop, but

my mother would pause before its window, which was always lined with whole hams, crown roasts, and ropes of plump handmade sausages. She greatly esteemed the **bounty** with her eyes, and my sister and I did also, but despite our desirous cries she'd turn us away and instead buy the packaged links at the Finast supermarket, where she felt comfortable looking them over and could easily spot the price. And, of course, not have to talk. But that day she was **resolved.** The butcher store was crowded, and as we stepped inside the door jingled a welcome. No one seemed to notice. We waited for some time, and people who entered after us were now being served. Finally, an old woman nudged my mother and waved a little ticket, which we hadn't taken. We patiently waited again, until one of the beefy men behind the glass display hollered our number. My mother pulled us forward and began searching the cases, but oxtails were nowhere to be found. The man, his big arms crossed, sharply said, "Come on, lady, whaddya want?" The butcher looked as if my mother had put something sour in his mouth, and he glanced back at the lighted board and called the next number.

(6) Before I knew it, she had rushed us outside and back in the wagon, which she had double-parked because of the crowd. She was furious, almost vibrating with fear and grief, and I could see she was about to cry. She wanted to go back inside but now the driver of the car we were blocking wanted to pull out. She was shooing us away. My mother, who had just earned her driver's license, started furiously working the pedals. But in her haste she must have flooded the engine, for it wouldn't turn over. The driver started honking and then another car began honking as well, and soon it seemed the entire street was shrieking at us.

(7) In the following years, my mother grew steadily more comfortable with English. In Korean, she could be fiery, stern, deeply funny and ironic; in English just slightly less so. If she was never quite fluent, she gained enough confidence to make herself clearly known to anyone, and particularly to me.

(8) Five years ago, she died of cancer, and some months after we buried her I found myself in the driveway of my father's house, washing her sedan. I liked taking care of her things; it made me feel close to her. While I was cleaning out the glove compartment, I found her pocket English workbook, the one with the silly illustrations. I had not seen it in nearly twenty years. The yellowed pages were brittle and dog-eared. She had fashioned a plain-paper wrapping for it, and I wondered whether she meant to protect the book or hide it.

(9) I doubt that she would have appreciated doing the family shopping on the new Broad Avenue of Palisades Park. But I like to think, too, that she would have understood those who now complain about the Korean-only signs. I wonder what these same people would have done if they had seen my mother studying her English workbook—or lost in a store. Would they have nodded gently at her? Would they have lent a kind word?

Here are some of the more difficult words in "Mute in an English-Only World."

alienated
(paragraph 1)

alien·ate (āl′yən āt′, āl′ē ən-) *vt.* **··at′ed, ··at′ing** [< L *alienatus,* pp. of *alienare* < *alius,* other: see ELSE] **1** to transfer the ownership of (property) to another **2** to make unfriendly; estrange [his behavior *alienated* his friends] **3** to cause to be withdrawn or detached, as from one's society **4** to cause a transference of (affection) — **al′iena′·tor** *n.*

aping
(paragraph 3)

ape (āp) *n.* [ME < OE *apa;* akin to Ger *affe* < Gmc *apan,* prob. < OSlav *opica*] **1** any gibbon or great ape **2** loosely, any Old or New World monkey **3** a person who imitates; mimic **4** a person who is uncouth, gross, clumsy, etc. —*vt.* **aped, ap′·ing** to imitate or mimic —*SYN.* IMITATE —**go ape** [Slang] to become mad; also, to become wildly enthusiastic —**ape′·like′** *adj.* —**ap′er** *n.*

bounty
(paragraph 5)

bounty (-tē) *n., pl.* **-ties** [ME *bounte* < OFr *bonte* < L *bonitas,* goodness < *bonus,* good: see BONUS] **1** generosity in giving **2** something given freely; generous gift **3** a reward, premium, or allowance, esp. one given by a government for killing certain harmful animals, raising certain crops, etc. —*SYN.* BONUS

deft
(paragraph 5)

deft (deft) *adj.* [ME *defte, dafte:* see DAFT] skillful in a quick, sure, and easy way; dexterous —*SYN.* DEXTEROUS —**deft′ly** *adv.* —**deft′·ness** *n.*

descendants
(paragraph 2)

de·scend·ant (dē sen′dənt, di-) *adj.* [ME *descendaunt* < OFr *descendant* < L *descendens,* prp. of *descendere:* see prec.] descending: also **de·scend′·ent** —*n.* **1** a person who is an offspring, however remote, of a certain ancestor, family, group, etc. **2** something that derives from an earlier form

exacting
(paragraph 1)

ex·act·ing (eg zak′tiŋ, ig-) *adj.* **1** making severe or excessive demands; not easily satisfied; strict [an *exacting* teacher] **2** demanding great care, patience, effort, etc.; arduous [an *exacting* job] —*SYN.* ONEROUS —**ex·act′·ingly** *adv.*

harrowing
(paragraph 5)

har·row[1] (har′ō) *n.* [ME *harwe* < ? OE *hearwa:* akin to ON *harfr* < IE *(s)kerp-:* see HARVEST] a frame with spikes or sharp-edged disks, drawn by a horse or tractor and used for breaking up and leveling plowed ground, covering seeds, rooting up weeds, etc. —*vt.* **1** to draw a harrow over (land) **2** to cause mental distress to; torment; vex —*vi.* to take harrowing [ground that *harrows* well] —**har′·rower** *n.* —**har′·row·ing** *adj.* —**har′·row·ingly** *adv.*

DISK HARROW

loathed
(paragraph 2)

loathe (lōth) *vt.* **loathed, loath′·ing** [ME *lothen* < OE *lathian,* to be hateful < base of *lath:* see prec.] to feel intense dislike, disgust, or hatred for; abhor; detest —*SYN.* HATE —**loath′er** *n.*

proliferation
(paragraph 1)

pro·lif·er·ate (prō lif′ə rāt′, prə-) *vt.* **··at′ed, ··at′ing** [back-form. < *proliferation* < Fr *prolifération* < *prolifère,* PROLIFEROUS + -ATION] **1** to reproduce (new parts) in quick succession **2** to produce or create in profusion —*vi.* **1** to grow by multiplying new parts, as by budding, in quick succession **2** to multiply rapidly; increase profusely —**pro·lif′·era′·tion** *n.*

resolved
(paragraph 5)

re·solved (ri zälvd′, -zôlvd′) *adj.* firm and fixed in purpose; determined; resolute —**re·solv′·edly** (-zäl′vid lē, -zôl′-) *adv.*

sundry
(paragraph 4)

sun·dry (sun′drē) *adj.* [ME *sundri* < OE *syndrig*, separate < *sundor*, apart: see SUNDER & -Y²] various; miscellaneous; divers [*sundry* items of clothing] —**pron.** [*with pl. v.*] sundry persons or things: used mainly in the phrase **all and sundry**, everybody; one and all

wails
(paragraph 3)

wail (wāl) *vi.* [ME *wailen* < ON *væla*, to lament < *væ*, WOE] **1** to express grief or pain by long, loud cries **2** to make a plaintive, sad, crying sound [the wind *wailing* in the trees] **3** [Slang] *Jazz* to play in an intense or inspired manner —*vt.* [Archaic] **1** to lament; mourn [to *wail* someone's death] **2** to cry out in mourning or lamentation —*n.* **1** a long, pitiful cry of grief and pain **2** a sound like this **3** the act of wailing —*SYN.* CRY —**wail′er** *n.*

24A   VOCABULARY

Choose the best answer.

_____ 1. An **alienated** person feels
    a. friendly.
    b. happy.
    c. withdrawn.
    d. confident.

_____ 2. **Aping** someone else's actions means
    a. accepting.
    b. ridiculing.
    c. changing.
    d. imitating.

_____ 3. A **bounty** is
    a. generous.
    b. small.
    c. level.
    d. inappropriate.

_____ 4. A surgeon needs **deft** hands, hands that are
    a. skillful.
    b. germ free.
    c. smooth.
    d. small.

_____ 5. A **descendant** is a person who is a(n) _____ of a certain ancestor, family, or group.
    a. conspirator
    b. offspring
    c. deadbeat
    d. advocate

_____ 6. The word **exacting** is closest in meaning to
    a. demanding.
    b. examining.
    c. offending.
    d. increasing.

_____ 7. A **harrowing** experience is one that causes
    a. mischief.
    b. distress.
    c. happiness
    d. inconvenience.

_____ 8. To be **loathed** is to be
    a. lost.
    b. liked.
    c. envied.
    d. hated.

_____ 9. A **proliferation** of signs suggests a(n)
    a. decrease.
    b. absence.
    c. increase.
    d. assortment.

_____ 10. Someone who is **resolved** to enter a store is
    a. determined.
    b. ready.
    c. prepared.
    d. reluctant.

_____ 11. **Sundry** as used in this essay means
    a. superb.
    b. selective.
    c. various.
    d. specific.

_____ 12. The **wail** of a grief-stricken person is best described as (a)
    a. soothing sound.
    b. whisper.
    c. lively chatter.
    d. high-pitched cry.

24B   CENTRAL THEME AND MAIN IDEAS

Choose the best answer.

_____ 1. Another title for this selection could be
    a. Shopping in Palisades, New Jersey
    b. A Mother's Difficulty with English

Name

Date

     c. Preserving English as a National Language

     d. Role Reversal in Immigrant Families

_____ 2. The main idea of paragraph 2 is

     a. As a child, Chang-rae Lee lived in New Rochelle, New York.

     b. A wide variety of shops dotted Main Street and North Avenue.

     c. Chang-rae Lee's mother had difficulty speaking English when she shopped.

     d. Chang-rae Lee and his sister sometimes accompanied their mother on shopping trips.

_____ 3. The main idea of paragraph 5 is

     a. Chang-rae Lee's mother drove downtown in the family's new Ford station wagon to shop.

     b. Chang-rae Lee's mother shopped at Finast supermarket because she could buy packaged meat.

     c. One butcher shop carried a wide selection of meat, including hams, roasts, and sausages.

     d. Shopping for oxtails in a butcher shop resulted in an upsetting experience for Chang-rae Lee's mother.

24C MAJOR DETAILS

Decide whether each detail is true (T), false (F), or not discussed (ND).

_____ 1. Eight towns in New Jersey passed laws requiring that half of any commercial sign in a foreign language be in English.

_____ 2. Chang-rae Lee's family was from Japan.

_____ 3. Chang-rae Lee did not like shopping with his mother.

_____ 4. Chang-rae Lee had difficulty learning English when he started school.

_____ 5. Most businesses in New Rochelle were run by descendants of Asian immigrants.

_____ 6. Chang-rae Lee's mother disapproved of Lee's making fun of his father's English.

_____ 7. Chang-rae Lee's mother had taken only basic English courses at the university in South Korea.

_____ 8. Chang-rae Lee's mother had a better command of reading English than speaking it.

24D   INFERENCES

Decide whether each statement below can be inferred (Yes) or cannot be inferred (No) from the reading selection.

_____ 1. In the early 1970s, Chang-rae Lee's family was the only Korean family in New Rochelle.

_____ 2. Chang-rae Lee's father resented having to give up his free time to shop with his wife.

_____ 3. Chang-rae Lee's mother watched children's cartoons on television to help her learn English.

_____ 4. Chang-rae Lee's mother had a job outside the home.

_____ 5. The butcher could not speak Korean.

_____ 6. Chang-rae Lee's mother knew it was illegal to double-park outside the butcher shop.

24E   CRITICAL READING: FACT OR OPINION

Decide whether each statement, even if it quotes someone, contains a Fact *or an* Opinion.

_____ 1. *From paragraph 1:* "But having been raised in a Korean immigrant family, I saw everyday the exacting price and power of language [. . .]"

_____ 2. *From paragraph 4:* "For her, the English language was not very funny."

_____ 3. *From paragraph 6:* "But in her haste she must have flooded the engine, for it wouldn't turn over."

_____ 4. *From paragraph 8:* "I liked taking care of her things; it made me feel close to her."

_____ 5. *From paragraph 9:* "I doubt that she would have appreciated doing the family shopping on the new Broad Avenue of Palisades Park."

24F   CRITICAL READING: THE AUTHOR'S STRATEGIES

Choose the best answer.

_____ 1. The main audience for "Mute in an English-Only World" is
   a. anyone who has lived in a bilingual community.
   b. anyone who has English as a second language.
   c. anyone who doesn't appreciate the hardships of immigrants.
   d. anyone who has ever studied a foreign language in high school.

Name   Date

_____ 2. The author's purpose in writing this reading is to
   a. describe.
   b. entertain.
   c. convince
   d. argue.

_____ 3. The author's tone in this reading is
   a. angry.
   b. reflective.
   c. calm.
   d. humorous.

24G   READER'S PROCESS: SUMMARIZING YOUR READING

Choose the best answer.

_____ 1. What is the best summary of "Mute in an English-Only World"?
   a. The author tells a story that shows how people feel when faced with a language barrier in their own community.
   b. The author tells a story about the frustration of a Korean woman who cannot speak English.
   c. The author tells a story about a community in New Jersey that became populated by Korean businesses with signs in their own language.
   d. The author tells a story that illustrates how difficult it can be to learn to speak a foreign language even after you study it in school.

24H   READER'S RESPONSE: TO DISCUSS OR WRITE ABOUT

1. The United States is a country of immigrants. Europeans began to arrive in the United States in the seventeenth century. Immigrants are still coming to the United States. Why do so many people resent the recent influx of immigrants to the United States? Be specific with your reasons.

2. Lee mentions that many of the businesses in his neighborhood were run by descendants of immigrants, many of whom had parents and grandparents who had struggled with English. Why do you think the butcher was so hateful and irritated with Lee's mother when she did not answer his question? Did Lee's mother have any other choice but to run from the store? Have you ever been treated rudely by a salesperson? If so, explain how you reacted.

HOW DID YOU DO?
24 Mute in an English-Only World

Skill (number of items)	Number Correct		Points for each		Score
Vocabulary (12)	_____	×	2	=	_____
Central Theme and Main Ideas (3)	_____	×	3	=	_____
Major Details (8)	_____	×	2	=	_____
Inferences (6)	_____	×	4	=	_____
Critical Reading: Fact or Opinion (5)	_____	×	3	=	_____
Critical Reading: The Author's Strategies (3)	_____	×	3	=	_____
Reader's Process: Summarizing Your Reading (1)	_____	×	3	=	_____

(Possible Total: 100) *Total*   _____

Name   Date

Part 6

Thinking: Getting Started

"We all have our own life to pursue, our own kind of dream to be weaving. And we all have some power to make wishes come true, as long as we keep believing."

Louisa May Alcott

The selections in Part 6 concern goals, beginning with the daughter of migrant farm workers who wants to be a doctor to that of a young man who resorts to drastic measures to win a girl's love.

"She Made Her Dream Come True" (Selection 25)—What must you have to make a dream come true?

"Yes, Top Students Reap Rich Rewards, Even as Egg Donors" (Selection 26)—Do you think prospective parents are just shopping for a commodity when they offer a high price to an intelligent egg donor?

"Long-Term Memory" (Selection 27)—What techniques do you use to remember important information?

"A Personal Stress Survival Guide" (Selection 28)—What do you do to relieve stress?

"Culture" (Selection 29)—Are there any occasions in Western culture in which cutting in line is sanctioned?

"The Chaser" (Selection 30)—Can you think of something that you wanted very badly; and then when you got it, you wished you didn't have it?

Selection 25

She Made Her Dream Come True

Michael Ryan

LEARNING OBJECTIVES

- List the obstacles the daughter of migrant farm workers overcame to become a doctor.

THINKING: GETTING STARTED

- What must you have to make a dream come true?

(1) To appreciate where Maria Vega is today, you have to understand where she was 22 years ago. "My family and I traveled up the East Coast throughout the growing season," this daughter of **migrant** workers recalled. "I went to five or six schools a year, from Florida to Pennsylvania."

(2) Maria Vega's view of life was formed in **transient** shacks with **communal** baths. In most schools she attended, Maria was placed in remedial classes, falling further behind in her studies. Homework, if any was assigned, was difficult to finish. "There was a lot of noise at night from the men who got drunk after work to forget about their troubles," she said. But every few months visitors from a different kind of world arrived. "Toward the end of the season in each state, the doctors and nurses would come," she said. These public health workers brought young Maria comfort—and relief from the frequent infections that have left a **welter** of scar tissue in her ear canals. They also brought her an idea: "I started to have this dream that I would become a doctor," she recalled. "But I never thought it was possible."

(3) Although Maria's two brothers, two sisters and parents formed a close-knit, supportive family, they had nothing in the way of financial resources. "During the holidays, my mom would sit us down and give us the same speech every year: 'There are no gifts under the tree—there is no tree,'" Maria said. What her family did give her was its support for her dream. "They told me to do what I wanted," she said, "and if it didn't work out, I could always come home to them."

(4) When Maria was in the 10th grade, her mother decided to stay in one place for a season, finding farm work around Homestead, Fla., so that Maria and her older sister could spend the year in one school. "Until that year, I had never taken a final exam," Maria told me. She worked so hard in high school that she earned a scholarship to Miami-Dade Community College. But even the basic, introductory chemistry course at Miami-Dade was difficult for her. "I had to take it twice," she said. "But I learned how to ask for help." As she recounted her story, Maria frequently talked about

Mexican migrant farm workers harvest tomatoes in Florida and load them into a trailer.

the people who helped her. "I know I didn't get here on my own," she said. Her junior college teachers provided extra assistance. They helped her get into the University of Miami, where she entered the pre-med program, supporting herself by working as a waitress and an aerobics instructor. School administrators, impressed by her effort, helped arrange scholarships and loans. Some professors even lent Maria textbooks. She graduated from Miami on time, with a Bachelor of Science in psychology.

(5) But her bachelor's degree was not an automatic ticket to medical school. Her scores on the Medical College Admissions Test, the standard medical school admissions test, were **mediocre.** "I guess I panicked when I took it the first time," she said. "Or maybe I didn't know enough." Maria applied to 20 medical schools, but she was rejected everywhere. "I didn't give up," Maria said. "I thought I'd try again next year." She took a job as a receptionist, then applied to a program at Boston University that helps prepare bright but disadvantaged students for medical school. "Her enthusiasm, and her determination to achieve her goal, showed that she is a remarkable young woman," said Dr. Kenneth Edelin, the dean who administers the program.

(6) Finally, Maria was admitted to Boston University's medical school. She is now a second-year student. "It's hard," Maria said, "but I'll do what it takes to get through." Maria isn't sure yet about her eventual medical **specialty,** but she already knows what her approach to doctoring is going to be. "I think I can relate to patients who don't live in middle-class conditions," she said. "If somebody comes in and says they don't have the

money to get medicine, I've been there. Victims of violence or alcohol or drug abuse—I grew up surrounded by that."

(7) Every September, Maria Vega's parents come to the end of their **circuit**—picking tomatoes in Pennsylvania before going back to Florida to begin the process again. Someday, Maria hopes to be able to help them to a better life. But for now, when her parents come north, she takes a bus to see them. "When I get there, my mom says, 'Here grab a bucket,' so I do," Maria said. For a few days, Maria Vega, medical student, is once again Maria Vega, migrant worker, holding on to her history and her values. As Maria's **anatomy** professor, Linda Wright, told me: "She's going to be a fantastic doctor."

Here are some of the more difficult words in "She Made Her Dream Come True."

Vocabulary List

anatomy
(paragraph 7)

anato·my (ə nat'ə mē) *n., pl.* -·mies [ME & OFr *anatomie* < LL *anatomia* < Gr *anatomia, anatomē*, a cutting up < *anatemnein* < *ana-*, up + *temnein*, to cut: see -TOMY] **1** the dissecting of an animal or plant in order to determine the position, structure, etc. of its parts **2** the science of the morphology or structure of animals or plants **3** the structure of an organism or body **4** a detailed analysis **5** [Archaic] a skeleton

circuit
(paragraph 7)

cir·cuit (sur'kit) *n.* [ME < OFr < L *circu..:us*, a going around, circuit < *circumire* < *circum* (see CIRCUM-) + *ire*, to go: see YEAR] **1** the line or the length of the line forming the boundaries of an area **2** the area bounded **3** the act of going around something; course or journey around [the moon's *circuit* of the earth] **4** *a*) the regular journey of a person performing certain duties, as of an itinerant preacher or a judge holding court at designated places *b*) the district periodically traveled through in the performance of such duties *c*) the route traveled ☆**5** the judicial district of a U.S. Court of Appeals **6** *a*) a number of associated theaters at which plays, movies, etc. are shown in turn *b*) a group of nightclubs, resorts, etc. at which entertainers appear in turn ☆*c*) a sequence of contests or matches held at various places, in which a particular group of athletes compete; also, an association or league of athletic teams [the professional bowlers' *circuit*] **7** *Elec. a*) a complete or partial path over which current may flow *b*) any hookup, wiring, etc. that is connected into this path, as for radio, television, or sound reproduction —*vi.* to go in a circuit —*vt.* to make a circuit about —*SYN.* CIRCUMFERENCE —**cir'·cuital** *adj.*

communal
(paragraph 2)

com·mu·nal (kə myōōn'əl, käm'yə nəl) *adj.* [ME & OFr < LL *communalis*] **1** of a commune or communes **2** of or belonging to the community; shared, or participated in, by all; public **3** designating or of social or economic organization in which there is common ownership of property —**com·mu·nal·i·ty** (käm'yōō nal'ə tē) *n.* —**com'·mu·nally** *adv.*

mediocre
(paragraph 5)

me·dio·cre (mē'dē ō'kər, mē'dē ō'kər) *adj.* [Fr *médiocre* < L *mediocris* < *medius*, middle (see MID¹) + *ocris*, a peak < IE base *ak-*, sharp > L *acer*] **1** neither very good nor very bad; ordinary; average **2** not good enough; inferior

migrant
(paragraph 1)

mi·grant (mī'grənt) *adj.* [L *migrans*, prp. of *migrare*] migrating; migratory —*n.* **1** a person, bird, or animal that migrates ☆**2** a farm laborer who moves from place to place to harvest seasonal crops

specialty
(paragraph 6)

spe·cialty (spesh'əl tē) *n., pl.* **-ties** ⟦ME *specialte* < OFr *especialté*⟧ **1** a special quality, feature, point, characteristic, etc. **2** a thing specialized in; special interest, field of study or professional work, etc. **3** the state of being special **4** an article or class of article characterized by special features, superior quality, novelty, etc. *[a bakery whose* specialty *is pie]* **5** *Law* a special contract, obligation, agreement, etc. under seal, or a contract by deed —*adj.* **1** designating or of a store or stores that specialize in selling certain types of goods or to certain types of customers **2** of such goods or customers

transient
(paragraph 2)

tran·sient (tran'shənt, -sē ənt; -zhənt, -zē ənt) *adj.* ⟦L *transiens*, prp. of *transire*: see TRANSIT⟧ **1** *a)* passing away with time; not permanent; temporary; transitory *b)* passing quickly or soon; fleeting; ephemeral ☆**2** staying only for a short time *[the transient population at resorts]* —*n.* ☆**1** a transient person or thing *[transients* at a hotel*]* **2** *Elec.* a temporary component of a current, resulting from a voltage surge, a change from one steady-state condition to another, etc. —**tran'·sience** *n.* or **tran'·sien·cy** —**tran'·sient·ly** *adv.*

welter
(paragraph 2)

wel·ter (wel'tər) *vi.* ⟦ME *weltren* < MDu *welteren*, freq. formation akin to OE *wealtan*, to roll, boil up: for IE base see WELL¹⟧ **1** *a)* to roll about or wallow, as a pig does in mud *b)* to be deeply or completely involved *[to* welter *in work]* **2** to be soaked, stained, or bathed *[to* welter *in blood]* **3** to tumble and toss about: said as of the sea —*n.* **1** a tossing and tumbling, as of waves **2** a confusion; turmoil

25A VOCABULARY

From the context of "She Made Her Dream Come True," explain the meaning of each vocabulary word shown in boldface.

1. *From paragraph 1:* "My family and I traveled up the East Coast throughout the growing season," this daughter of **migrant** workers recalled.

   _____

   _____

2. *From paragraph 2:* Maria Vega's view of life was formed in **transient** shacks with **communal** baths.

   _____

   _____

3. *From paragraph 2:* . . . frequent infections that left a **welter** of scar tissue in her ear canals.

   _____

   _____

4. *From paragraph 5:* Her scores on the MCAT [. . .] were **mediocre.**

   _____

   _____

5. *From paragraph 6:* Maria isn't sure yet about her eventual medical **specialty** [. . .].

_____

_____

6. *From paragraph 7:* Every September, Maria Vega's parents come to the end of their **circuit.** . . .

_____

_____

7. *From paragraph 7:* As Maria's **anatomy** professor, Linda Wright, told me: "She's going to be a fantastic doctor."

_____

_____

25B   CENTRAL THEME AND MAIN IDEAS

Choose the best answer.

_____ 1.   What is the central theme of "She Made Her Dream Come True"?
   a. Given financial support and encouragement, migrant workers can succeed in medical school.
   b. Maria Vega's overcoming problems related to finance, health, and education will help her be a sympathetic doctor.
   c. Through determination Maria Vega overcame poverty and educational disadvantages to qualify for medical school.
   d. Maria Vega plans to provide her family a better lifestyle when she becomes a doctor.

2.   In your own words, give the main idea of paragraph 4.

_____

_____

_____

_____

_____ 3.   What is the main idea of paragraph 5?
   a. Maria Vega's Bachelor of Science degree did not ensure her admission to a medical school.
   b. Twenty medical schools rejected Maria Vega's application to enroll.
   c. Maria Vega's enrolling in a Boston University program for disadvantaged students helped prepare her for medical school.
   d. Maria Vega's determination and enthusiasm helped her to achieve her goal to enroll in medical school.

Name   Date

25C MAJOR DETAILS

Decide whether each detail is Major *or* Minor *based on the context of the reading selection.*

_____ 1. Public health workers influenced Maria Vega's dream to become a doctor.

_____ 2. Maria Vega's family consisted of her parents, two brothers, and two sisters.

_____ 3. Maria Vega learned to ask for help when she had difficulties with her studies.

_____ 4. Maria Vega's college major was psychology.

_____ 5. After graduating from the University of Miami, Maria Vega worked as a receptionist.

_____ 6. Maria Vega borrowed textbooks from college professors.

_____ 7. Maria Vega's parents are migrant workers.

_____ 8. Maria Vega took her college chemistry course twice before she passed it.

_____ 9. Maria takes a bus when she goes to visit her parents.

_____ 10. Maria Vega was placed in remedial classes at most schools she attended.

25D INFERENCES

*Decide whether each of the following statements can be inferred (*Yes*) or cannot be inferred (*No*) from the reading selection.*

_____ 1. Maria Vega was 22 years old when this was written.

_____ 2. Maria Vega thought her ear infections would prevent her from becoming a doctor.

_____ 3. Frequent moves to different states negatively affected Maria Vega's academic performance in school.

_____ 4. Maria Vega resented her parents' not giving her presents at Christmas.

_____ 5. Because of Maria Vega's health problems, her mother decided to stay in one location when Maria was a sophomore.

Name   Date

_____ 6. Maria Vega's staying in one school for an entire year allowed her to make lifelong friends.

_____ 7. Maria Vega's employment as a waitress and aerobics instructor was good preparation for her becoming a doctor.

_____ 8. Maria Vega's willingness to help her family harvest crops when she visits them indicates she upholds her family's history and values.

_____ 9. Maria Vega will most likely not become wealthy when she becomes a doctor.

25E CRITICAL READING: FACT OR OPINION

Decide whether each statement, even if it quotes someone, contains a Fact *or an* Opinion.

_____ 1. *From paragraph 2:* During their visits, the health workers brought relief and comfort to Maria Vega.

_____ 2. *From paragraph 5:* "Her enthusiasm, and her determination to achieve her goal, showed that she is a remarkable woman [...]."

_____ 3. *From paragraph 7:* Maria Vega's family harvested crops from Florida to Pennsylvania.

_____ 4. *From paragraph 7:* "She's going to be a fantastic doctor."

25F CRITICAL READING: THE AUTHOR'S STRATEGIES

Choose the best answer.

_____ 1. The main audience for "She Made Her Dream Come True" is
   a. readers who are migrant workers.
   b. readers who are trying to get into medical school.
   c. readers who are inspired by stories about people who over-come hardships.
   d. readers who don't understand the lives of migrant workers.

_____ 2. The author's purpose in writing this reading is to
   a. persuade.
   b. inform.
   c. describe.
   d. entertain.

_____ 3. The author's tone in this reading is
   a. negative.
   b. concerned.
   c. sad.
   d. inspired.

25G   READER'S PROCESS: SUMMARIZING YOUR READING

Choose the best answer.

_____ 1. What is the best summary of "She Made Her Dream Come True"?
   a. The writer tells how the daughter of migrant workers achieved her goal to study medicine.
   b. The writer tells how a young woman studied hard but still had trouble getting into medical school.
   c. The writer tells how a young medical student joins her family of migrant workers in the fields each year.
   d. The writer tells how a young woman learned to ask for the help she needed to go to college and apply for medical school.

25H   READER'S RESPONSE: TO DISCUSS OR WRITE ABOUT

1. Some children have to change schools one or more times between kindergarten and the 12th grade. If this happened to you, what effect did such moving have on you? If this did not happen to you, what do you imagine the effect on you would have been?

2. Many college students are required or strongly urged to take one or more "remedial" courses (such as Developmental Reading, Basic Writing, Basic Math). If this has happened to you, what do you think are the advantages and disadvantages, both academic and social, of taking such courses? If this did not happen to you, what do you imagine would have been the academic and social advantages and disadvantages for you?

Name

Date

HOW DID YOU DO?
25 She Made Her Dream Come True

SKILL (number of items)	Number Correct		Points for each		Score
Vocabulary (8)	_____	×	2	=	_____
Central Theme and Main Ideas (3)	_____	×	5	=	_____
Major Details (10)	_____	×	3	=	_____
Inferences (9)	_____	×	3	=	_____
Critical Reading: Fact or Opinion (4)	_____	×	1	=	_____
Critical Reading: The Author's Strategies (3)	_____	×	2	=	_____
Reader's Process: Summarizing Your Reading (1)	_____	×	2	=	_____

(Possible Total: 100) *Total* _____

Yes, Top Students Reap Rich Rewards, Even as Egg Donors

Stephanie Ebbert

LEARNING OBJECTIVES

• Contrast the risks and the rewards as an egg donor.

THINKING: GETTING STARTED

• Do you think prospective parents are just shopping for a commodity when they offer a high price to an intelligent egg donor?

(1) *The Harvard Crimson* was one of three college newspapers that ran an identical classified ad seeking a woman who fit a narrow profile: younger than 29 with a GPA over 3.5 and an SAT score over 1,400. The lucky candidate stood to collect $35,000 if she donated her eggs for **harvesting.**

(2) The ad was one of 105 college newspaper ads examined by a Georgia Institute of Technology researcher who issued a report yesterday that appeared to confirm the long-held suspicion that couples who are unable to have children of their own are willing to pay more for reproductive help from someone smart. The analysis showed that higher payments offered to egg donors **correlated** with higher SAT scores. "Holding all else equal, an increase of 100 SAT points in the score of a typical incoming student increased the compensation offered to **oocyte** donors at that college or university by $2,350," wrote researcher Aaron D. Levine. The paper, published in the March-April issue of the Hastings Center Report, examined ads in 63 student newspapers in spring 2006 and was billed as the first national cross-section sample of ads for egg donors. The Hastings Center is a nonprofit, independent, nonpartisan **bioethics** research institute.

(3) **Anecdotal** reports have long depicted eager prospective parents willing to pay outrageous sums for carefully screened donors of sperm or eggs, and stories of parents offering tens of thousands of dollars for eggs from geniuses or extraordinarily talented musicians pop up regularly. The stories have alarmed some medical professionals and raised ethical questions. Concerned about eggs being treated as **commodities,** and worried that big financial rewards could **entice** women to ignore the risks of the rigorous procedures required for harvesting, the American Society for Reproductive Medicine discourages compensation based on donors' personal characteristics. The society also discourages any payments over $10,000.

(4) Levine's paper points out, however, that no outside regulator enforces those guidelines and that they are often ignored. Of the advertisements Levine examined, nearly one-quarter offered donors more than $10,000, and about one-quarter of the ads listed specific requirements, such as appearance or **ethnicity,** also in violation of guidelines that discourage greater payment for particular personal characteristics. The ads that tended to have the highest correlation between compensation and test scores in Levine's study came from hopeful parents trying to find a donor on their own and from clinics advertising on behalf of a specific set of parents. The correlation was less strong in ads taken out by clinics advertising with a specific parent in mind.

(5) The Hastings Center report, published six times a year, explores ethical, legal, and social issues in medicine, health care, public health, and the life sciences. The issue of the report containing Levine's analysis also offers a counter perspective from John A. Robertson, who chaired the ethics committee of the American Society of Reproductive Medicine. He casts doubt on the notion that it is an ethical problem to pay more for eggs from a woman with a particular ethnic background or high IQ. "After all, we allow individuals to choose their mates and sperm donors on the basis of such characteristics," Robertson wrote. "Why not choose egg donors similarly?"

(6) Carey Goldberg, coauthor of the book, "Three Wishes: A True Story of Good Friends, Crushing Heartbreak, and Astonishing Luck on Our Way to Love and Motherhood," echoed that thought, saying she realized when she chose a sperm donor 10 years ago that she could not choose most of

Young women with high SAT scores at top colleges and universities are recruited as egg donors through advertisements in college newspapers.

the personal qualities she would want her children to have. Instead, she got to examine donors' height, weight, hair color, skin color, eye color, and level of education. The donor she chose, but didn't end up using, had an SAT score higher than her own, she recalled. "Since most of the characteristics that we value in people, like kindness and creativity, aren't known to be genetically transmitted, I ended up deciding that intelligence and height are the two things I most wanted," said Goldberg, a former Globe science reporter.

(7) Fertility clinics are required by federal law to report their pregnancy success rate but not what donors are paid. Agencies involved in donations say they are not purchasing eggs but compensating donors for their time and the ordeal they must undergo. The four-month process for an egg donor involves screening—for **infectious** disease, sexually transmitted diseases, toxicology, drugs and even cigarettes—and psychological evaluations to ensure the woman is mature enough to grasp the commitment she is making. The donor must attend regular medical visits, including blood tests and ultrasounds, often requiring time off work and lost wages and childcare expenses if the donor has children of her own. Donors must give themselves nightly shots and have eggs retrieved through a **catheter.** It "is a huge undertaking and commitment," said Amy Demma, founder of Prospective Families, a Wellesley agency that matches egg donors with recipient couples. And parents are often willing to substantially increase the amounts they offer to persuade a high-test-score donor to go through with the process.

(8) Levine's paper cites the Society for Assisted Reproductive Technology, which polled its member clinics in 2006 and reported that the average compensation for egg donors was about $4,200, with steeper rates in the Northeast. The society report that 1 in 5 clinics said compensation could vary based on the donor's ethnicity or fertility history. In some cases, donors set their own rates, typically asking about $7,000, said Demma, who frowns on higher payments and said she turned down a family willing to pay a donor $15,000.

(9) "I am working with a lovely woman from MIT right now; her compensation is $7,000," said Demma. But, she said, the occasional recipient parent will say, "'I've got to pay $20,000 because I want a smarter donor parent.' Sometimes I can **dissuade** them. Sometimes they'll leave because they feel if they don't go to a Mercedes dealership, they're buying something less. What we're trying to do here is create a family."

Here are some of the more difficult words in "Yes, Top Students Reap Rich Rewards, Even as Egg Donors."

Vocabulary List

anecdotal
(paragraph 3)

an·ec·dotal (an'ik dōt'l, -ek-) *adj.* **1** of or like an anecdote **2** full of anecdotes **3** based on personal experience or reported observations unverified by controlled experiments [*anecdotal* evidence]

bioethics
(paragraph 2)

bio·eth·ics (-eth'iks) *n.* the study of the ethical problems arising from scientific advances, esp. in biology and medicine —**bi'o·eth'i·cal** *adj.*

catheter
(paragraph 7)

cath·eter (kath'ət ər) *n.* [LL < Gr *kathetēr* < *kathienai*, to let down, thrust in < *kata-*, down + *hienai*, to send: see JET¹] a slender, hollow tube, as of metal or rubber, inserted into a body passage, vessel, or cavity for passing fluids, making examinations, etc., esp. one for draining urine from the bladder

commodities
(paragraph 3)

com·mod·i·ty (kə mäd'ə tē) *n.*, *pl.* -ties [ME & OFr *commodite*, benefit, profit < L *commoditas*, fitness, adaptation < *commodus*: see COMMODE] **1** any useful thing **2** anything bought and sold; any article of commerce **3** [*pl.*] basic items or staple products, as of agriculture or mining **4** [Archaic] personal advantage

correlated
(paragraph 2)

cor·re·late (kôr'ə lāt', kär'-) *n.* [back-form. < fol.] either of two interrelated things, esp. if one implies the other —*adj.* closely and naturally related —*vi.* ··lat'ed, ··lat'ing to be mutually related (*to* or *with*) —*vt.* to bring (a thing) into mutual relation (*with* another thing); calculate or show the reciprocal relation between; specif., to bring (one of two related or interdependent quantities, sets of statistics, etc.) into contrast (*with* the other)

dissuade
(paragraph 9)

dis·suade (di swād') *vt.* ··suad'ed, ··suad'ing [L *dissuadere* < *dis-*, away, from + *suadere*, to persuade: see SWEET] **1** to turn (a person) aside (*from* a course, etc.) by persuasion or advice **2** [Obs.] to advise against (an action) —**dis·suad'er** *n.*

entice
(paragraph 3)

en·tice (en tīs', in-) *vt.* ··ticed', ··tic'ing [ME *enticen* < OFr *enticier*, to set afire, hence excite, entice, prob. < VL *intitiare* < L *in* + *titio*, a burning brand] to attract by offering hope of reward or pleasure; tempt; allure —*SYN.* LURE —**en·tice'ment** *n.* —**en·tic'ing·ly** *adv.*

ethnicity
(paragraph 4)

eth·nic (eth'nik) *adj.* [ME *ethnik* < LL(Ec) *ethnicus*, pagan < Gr *ethnikos*, national (in LGr(Ec), gentile, heathen) < *ethnos*, nation, people, *ta ethnē*, nations (in LXX, non-Jews, in N.T., gentile Christians): akin to *ēthos*: see ETHICAL] **1** [Now Rare] heathen **2** designating or of a population subgroup having a common cultural heritage or nationality, as distinguished by customs, characteristics, language, common history, etc. Also **eth'ni·cal** —*n.* a member of an ethnic group, esp. a member of a minority or nationality group that is part of a larger community —**eth'ni·cally** *adv.*

eth·nic·i·ty (eth nis'ə tē) *n.* [ETHNIC + -ITY] ethnic classification or affiliation

harvest
(paragraph 1)

har·vest (här'vist) *n.* [ME *hervest* < OE *hærfest*, akin to Ger *herbst* (OHG *herbist*) < IE *(s)kerp-* < base *(s)ker-*, to cut > SHEAR, SHORT, L *caro*, flesh, *cernere* & Gr *krinein*, to separate, *karpos*, fruit: basic sense "time of cutting"] **1** the time of the year when matured grain, fruit, vegetables, etc. are reaped and gathered in **2** a season's yield of grain, fruit, etc. when gathered in or ready to be gathered in; crop **3** the gathering in of a crop **4** the outcome or consequence of any effort or series of events [the tyrant's *harvest* of hate] —*vt.*, *vi.* **1** to gather in (a crop, etc.) **2** to gather the crop from (a field) **3** to catch, shoot, trap, etc. (fish or game), usually in an intensive, systematic way, as for commercial purposes **4** to get (something) as the result of an action or effort **5** to remove (body parts) for transplantation —**har'vest·able** *adj.*

337

Vocabulary List

infectious
(paragraph 7)

in·fec·tious (in fek′shəs) *adj.* **1** likely to cause infection; containing disease-producing organisms or matter **2** designating a disease that can be communicated by INFECTION (sense 2) **3** tending to spread or to affect others; catching *[an infectious laugh]* **4** [Obs.] infected with disease —**in·fec′·tious·ly** *adv.* —**in·fec′·tious·ness** *n.*

oocyte
(paragraph 2)

oocyte (ō′ō sīt′, ō′ə-) *n.* ⟦prec. + -CYTE⟧ *Embryology* an egg that has not yet undergone maturation

26A   VOCABULARY

Choose the best answer.

_____ 1. **Bioethics** is usually associated with ethical problems in
    a. medicine.
    b. theology.
    c. sociology.
    d. psychology.

_____ 2. **Commodities** can be described as anything that is bought and
    a. given away.
    b. sold.
    c. discarded.
    d. used up.

_____ 3. Anything that is **correlated** would be
    a. verified.
    b. suitable.
    c. protected.
    d. related.

_____ 4. To **entice** is to
    a. enlarge
    b. corrupt.
    c. attract.
    d. honor.

_____ 5. To **harvest** a woman's eggs suggests
    a. destroying.
    b. replacing.
    c. combining.
    d. gathering.

_____ 6. An **oocyte** is an egg that is not
   a. fertilized.
   b. useable.
   c. mature.
   d. harvestable.

_____ 7. An **anecdotal** report is generally based on
   a. scientific evidence.
   b. false assumptions.
   c. personal experience.
   d. undocumented research.

_____ 8. A **catheter** is a
   a. rod.
   b. pole.
   c. scanner.
   d. tube.

_____ 9. **Dissuade** is to
   a. to support.
   b. advise against.
   c. do away with.
   d. cause to disappear.

_____ 10. **Ethnicity** refers to a group's having a
   a. common cultural belief.
   b. false religious belief.
   c. similar level of education.
   d. mutual love for their country.

_____ 11. An **infectious** disease is one that is
   a. spread.
   b. unexplainable.
   c. insignificant
   d. persistent.

26B   CENTRAL THEME AND MAIN IDEAS

Choose the best answer.

_____ 1. What is the central theme of "Yes, Top Students Reap Rich Rewards, Even as Egg Donors"?
   a. Would-be parents want egg donors to have high SAT scores.
   b. College newspaper ads are a good source for would-be parents seeking egg donors.
   c. Smart students can collect sizable fees as egg donors.
   d. Egg donors ignore health risks to receive big financial rewards.

_____ 2. What is the main idea of paragraph 2?

    a. Prospective parents advertise in college newspaper for possible egg donors.

    b. Infertile couples are willing to offer higher payments to smart egg donors.

    c. A Georgia Institute of Technology researcher examined 105 college newspaper ads for egg donors.

    d. The Hastings Center is a nonprofit, independent, nonpartisan bioethics research institute.

_____ 3. What is the main idea of paragraph 7?

    a. Federal law requires fertility clinics to report pregnancy success rate but not donor compensation fees.

    b. Prospective Families is an agency that matches egg donors with recipient couples.

    c. Prospective parents often increase the compensation to entice a high-test-scorer to complete the donation process.

    d. The egg donor undergoes a rigorous physical and psychological screening to qualify as a donor.

26C   MAJOR DETAILS

Fill in the word or words that correctly complete each statement.

1. Three college newspapers ran an ad seeking egg donors who were younger than _____ with a GPA of _____ and SAT score over _____.

2. Anecdotal reports indicate prospective parents are willing to pay outrageous fees for eggs from _____ and _____ _____.

3. The stories of prospective parents willing to pay more for certain characteristics have raised _____ _____.

4. Big financial rewards could entice women to ignore the _____ of the rigorous harvesting procedure.

5. Researcher Aaron D. Levine found that nearly one-fourth of the newspaper advertisements offered payments of more than _____ to egg donors.

6. Agencies involved in donations say they are not _____ eggs but _____ donors for their time and the ordeal of harvesting eggs.

7. Screening for a potential egg donor is a _____-_____ process.

8. Donors must give themselves _____ _____ and have eggs retrieved through a _____.

Name

Date

26D CRITICAL READING: FACT OR OPINION

Decide whether each statement contains a Fact *or an* Opinion

_____ 1. *From paragraph 2:* "Holding all else equal, an increase of 100 SAT points in the score of a typical incoming student increased the compensation [. . .] by $2,350."

_____ 2. *From paragraph 5:* "After all, we allow individuals to choose their mates and sperm donors on the basis of such characteristics [. . .]. Why not choose egg donors similarly?"

_____ 3. *From paragraph 6:* "[. . .] I ended up deciding that intelligence and height are the two things that I most wanted."

_____ 4. *From paragraph 9:* "Sometimes they (recipient parents) will leave because they feel if they don't go to a Mercedes dealership, they're buying something less."

26E CRITICAL READING: THE AUTHOR'S STRATEGIES

Choose the best answer.

_____ 1. Stephanie Ebbert's main audience for "Yes, Top Students Reap Rich Rewards, Even as Egg Donors" is
   a. infertile couples interested in adoption offered by local agencies.
   b. college newspapers seeking potential egg donor advertisers.
   c. college students interested in the financial compensation and screening process as egg donors.
   d. would be parents seeking information about egg donors with high-test-scores.

_____ 2. The author's purpose in writing this reading is to
   a. inform.
   b. narrate.
   c. describe.
   d. persuade.

_____ 3. The author's tone in this reading is
   a. hostile.
   b. reflective.
   c. incredulous.
   d. pessimistic.

26F READER'S PROCESS: SUMMARIZING YOUR READING

Choose the best answer.

_____ 1. What is the best summary of "Yes, Top Students Reap Rich Rewards, Even as Egg Donors"?

a. Paying large sums of money to egg donors who are intellec-
tually gifted college students has become a bioethical issue.
b. Would-be parents are willing to pay significantly higher compensation to egg donors who are young and smart.
c. The American Society for Reproductive Health discourages
compensating egg donors with payments over $10,000.
d. Egg donor clinics in the Northeast have steeper compensation
rates, based on a poll by the Society for Assisted Reproductive
Technology.

26G READER'S PROCESS: TO DISCUSS OR WRITE ABOUT

1. Why do you think it's so important for would-be parents to seek egg
donors who can possibly provide them with "smart" children?

2. A graduate student contacted a fertility clinic at her local northern New
England teaching hospital to become an egg donor. When she added
up the time involved attending doctors' appointments, giving herself
injections, harvesting eggs and then weighing the personal risks, she
felt that the $4,000 compensation seemed ridiculously low. When the
student told the director this, the director said that she should be an
egg donor for altruistic reasons, not the money. Do you agree or disagree with the director's response? Explain your viewpoint.

HOW DID YOU DO?
26   Yes, Top Students Reap Rich Rewards,
Even as Egg Donors

SKILL (number of items)	Number Correct		Points for each		Score
Vocabulary (11)	_____	×	2	=	_____
Central Theme and Main Ideas (3)	_____	×	6	=	_____
Major Details * (13)	_____	×	2	=	_____
Critical Reading: Fact or Opinion (4)	_____	×	4	=	_____
Critical Reading: The Author's Strategies (3)	_____	×	5	=	_____
Reader Response: Summarizing Your Reading (1)	_____	×	3	=	_____

(Possible Total: 100) *Total*   _____

*Question 1 in this exercise calls for three separate answers; questions 2, 6, and 8 call for two separate
answers each. In computing your score, count each separate answer toward your number correct.

Long-Term Memory in *Fundamentals of Psychology*

Joseph Calkin and Richard S. Perrotto

LEARNING OBJECTIVES

- Clarify the differences between long- and short-term memories.

THINKING: GETTING STARTED

- What techniques do you use to remember important information?

(1) Everything you know—every word, name, fact, date, experience, definition, and skill—is contained in your long-term memory (LTM), where information is stored unconsciously for an extended period of time. How long do your memories last in LTM? No precise answer can be given. LTM **duration** can be as brief as a few minutes and as long as a lifetime. Many people believe that LTM is permanent, but the evidence is not **conclusive.** The duration of LTM depends on several factors, including the strength of the memory, its meanings, and how much it is used.

(2) How much do you know? If you started to remember everything in your LTM right now, you would probably spend the rest of your life and not finish. If short-term memory (STM) is a memory workbench where information is stored for a short period of time and in limited space, your LTM is a vast warehouse of information with no apparent limit. Surely there are millions of items stored in your LTM, but researchers have no way of estimating the maximum capacity of LTM. Although its upper limit is unknown, your everyday experience tells you that LTM holds an astounding amount of information.

THE ORGANIZATION OF LONG-TERM MEMORY

(3) The enormous LTM warehouse contains many types of knowledge, and its contents are highly organized in terms of several qualities of those memories. Four aspects of LTM have been identified and named: *semantic, episodic, procedural,* and *implicit* memory. These aspects of LTM organization are summarized in Table 1.

Table 1   Organization of Long-Term Memory

Semantic memory	Impersonal facts based on semantic, or verbal, codes
Episodic memory	Personal, autobiographical facts; flashbulb memories
Procedural memory	Skills, habits, stimulus-response associations
Implicit memory	Memories learned and retrieved without conscious effort

(4) Language is an essential part of your memory. Factual knowledge based on words, phrases, sentences, and other verbal information is contained in your **semantic memory.** Like a dictionary, semantic memory is based on *semantic codes*, representations of information in terms of the meaning of words. To appreciate the scope of semantic memory, just consider the many definitions, names, formulas, and other facts that you have learned since elementary school. Your semantic memory does not exist as thousands of independent bits of knowledge, but is organized by complex *association networks*, or groups of memories linked together on the basis of meaning.

Semantic memory
Memory for factual knowledge based on verbal information

(5) As a demonstration, start with a familiar word, *dog*, and call to mind every word association you can, for example, *pet, companion, mammal*, and so on. Then, do the same for each of those associations, and for all the associations linked to them, and so on. Before long, you will realize that the web of your word associations is almost endless. These complex semantic associations control your ability to understand and remember language-based facts. Your semantic memory is impersonal, lacking any obvious connection with specific life experiences. For instance, when you remember 2 + 2 = 4 you probably do not connect it with the situation in which you first learned it.

(6) By contrast, your **episodic memory** contains very personal, autobiographical facts—facts that are tied to episodes in your life and often ones that contain significant emotional meaning. Think of the birth of your young **siblings,** a great party you attended, a family tragedy, and other events from your personal past—these recollections reveal your episodic memory.

Episodic (epp-ee-sod-ik) memory
Memory for personal, autobiographical facts

(7) A special type of episodic memory is a *flashbulb memory*, a vivid recollection of an emotionally powerful event. Your flashbulb memories seem like moments frozen in time, and their emotional associations are thought to be responsible for their vividness. For

example, some people report flashbulb memories for January 28, 1986, the day the space shuttle *Challenger* exploded, killing the crew, while broadcast nationwide on television. Many flashbulb memories are more personal, such as the death of a close friend or the day you won the lottery. Although they seem very clear, flashbulb memories are not necessarily accurate, and people often recall with confidence false details of those events.

(8) Your memory for learned responses and action patterns is **procedural memory.** Learned skills and behaviors, as well as **stimulus-response** associations, are contained in your procedural memory. Countless everyday activities depend on procedural memory, as when you drive a car, play the piano, use a tool, or carry on a conversation. Such behavior may be acquired through conditioning and **cognitive** learning. In addition, procedural memory controls your automatic conditioned responses to stimuli. The next time you experience fear upon entering your dentist's office, you can thank your procedural memory for the reminder.

Procedural memory
Memory for learned responses and action patterns

(9) Semantic and episodic memories taken together are sometimes called *declarative memory*, which requires conscious effort to learn and **retrieve.** For example, you must exert conscious effort to memorize a new formula in math (semantic memory).

(10) Many memories, however, are acquired and remembered automatically with little or no conscious involvement. These make up your **implicit memory.** In fact, a lot of procedural memory is implicit, such as conditioned fears and other emotional responses. You do not consciously control their acquisition or activation by stimuli.

Implicit (im-pliss-it) memory
Memories learned and retrieved without conscious effort

(11) Research on the *priming effect* illustrates that implicit memory controls your unconscious retrieval of stored information. In a typical study, subjects are "primed" by exposure to some stimuli, and later their memory is tested without asking them to consciously remember the stimuli. Priming improves their memory despite the subjects' lack of awareness of learning or remembering the stimuli. Imagine that you are in such a study: You are shown some words (the priming list), which you must identify as nouns or verbs (refer to Table 2). Later, another series of words (the test list) is presented very rapidly, and you are asked simply to indicate which words you **perceive.** You are most likely to perceive the test list words that were on the priming list even though you did not try to memorize or retrieve them.

(12) Although implicit and declarative (semantic and episodic) memory have distinctive features, they are not completely independent. Rather, these aspects of LTM interact to provide you with richly integrated memories. Do you remember how to ride a bicycle? If you can describe this skill in words (semantic memory), recall yourself doing it in a specific situation (episodic memory), and show it in action (procedural memory), you are

345

Table 2   Priming Effect Study of Implicit Memory

Priming List	Test List	Primed Implicit Memory
rabbit	bird	rabbit
swim	rabbit	write
car	write	
write	house	

illustrating the integrated facets of your LTM. Recent studies suggest that declarative and implicit memory work together to create complex abilities and knowledge, such as learning the rules of language usage and classifying your experiences into organized concepts.

LONG-TERM MEMORY PROCESSES

(13) As you have learned, LTM contains many types of stored information. The complex organization of knowledge in LTM depends on a number of factors. The **depth-of-processing** model explains the strength and durability of LTM as the result of **encoding** processes. In this view, a "deep" memory is acquired by semantic codes that represent facts through language. Without semantic codes, memory is "shallow" and quite easily forgotten. A deep memory is more lasting and meaningful than a shallow one, and it is easier to recollect. This model suggests that memories based on several codes are deeper than those based on a single code.

Depth-of-processing model
View that memory strength depends on encoding processes

(14) Research on combined semantic codes and **imagery** supports this notion. This effect may be illustrated by a *paired-associates recall task*, in which you are given word pairs to remember (for example, house-pencil, fish-tree), and later you must recall one of the words when the other is presented. For instance, when shown *tree* you must say *fish*. If you use visual images along with the words to encode the paired associates, your recall is improved, especially for concrete words like those in Figure 1.

(15) In 1932, British psychologist Frederick Bartlett proposed that memories are reconstructions of events based partly on fact and partly on **schemas,** or personal beliefs about reality. In his classic study, he read a Native American folktale to his English subjects and later asked them to remember it. Their memories of the story showed changes that reflected their culture-based schemas. For instance, instead of recalling that the Indians hunted for seals in canoes, some subjects remember that they were fishing in boats.

Fish • Tree

House • Pencil

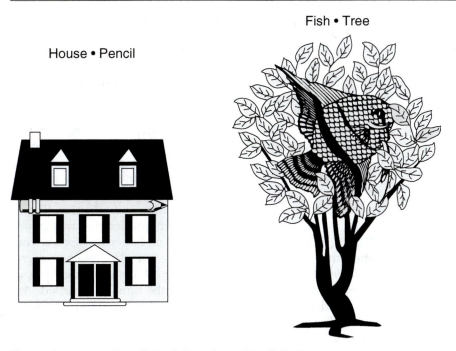

Figure 1 Imagery in a Paired-Associates Recall Task

The depth-of-processing model suggests that a combination of semantic and image codes will produce a deeper memory than will a single code. When subjects use visual images and word pairs to encode the information, their memory for the word association improves.

(16) In the tradition of Bartlett, many psychologists today consider **reconstructive memory** to be an act of remembering in which facts, personal beliefs, and inferences are all woven together. In reconstructing a past event, you often fill in the gaps with "facts" that you believe, on the basis of your personal schemas, might have occurred. In addition, you rely on familiar patterns of events stored as *memory scripts* that give you a framework for remembering. Try to remember what you did at 4:00 P.M. exactly six months ago. If it was a Wednesday during the school year, you might find yourself using your "typical-Wednesday-afternoon-at-school" script to reconstruct what you probably did. Have you ever noticed that each time you tell a story it is a little different than the last time because you add new elements or drop old details with each telling? Facts learned after a memory is formed can change it, and even the act of remembering some-times alters the memory being recalled. Reconstructive memory is also

Reconstructive memory
Remembering affected by schemas, personal beliefs, and inferences

347

open to the power of suggestion, as shown in a study by psychologists Elizabeth Loftus and John Palmer in which subjects saw a filmed car accident and were later asked how fast the cars were going. The questions were phrased either in terms of when the cars "hit" or when they "crashed." Subjects who were asked the "crashed" version recalled much higher speeds because the wording suggests that the cars were moving faster.

(17) Your ability to retrieve a memory often depends on having the proper cues at the time you try to remember. When your retrieval is influenced by stimulus cues, you show evidence of **cue-dependent memory.**

Cue-dependent memory

Memory influenced by cues in the situation or emotional state

---

Two forms of cue-dependent memory are *context-dependent memory* and *state-dependent memory*. If you try to recall some information in a situation that is similar to the one in which you learned that information, you tend to perform better than when you try in a situation that differs from the learning one. This phenomenon, called *context-dependent memory*, is the result of associations formed between situation cues and the information at the time it is learned. An example of context-dependent memory is a study of scuba divers who learned some words under water and later recalled them better when under water than on land. You can examine *context-dependent memory* in yourself by studying some material while listening to music and later testing yourself on half of the material with the same music playing and on the other half without any music. You should find that your memory is better when the music is playing.

(18) The power of situational cues may explain a curious phenomenon called déjà vu (French for "already seen") in which you feel that you recognize someone or some place with no basis for the memory in your experience. For example, on entering a house for the first time, it may seem familiar, as if you had been there before. Déjà vu is a false recognition due to **subtle** cues in the situation. Perhaps something about the house, such as an odor or room design, triggers partial memory of another place in which similar cues were present, thus giving you the feeling of familiarity.

(19) Have you ever noticed that when you are happy you remember many experiences with a similar happy feeling, or that when depressed you recall other depressing events? Such observations point to *state-dependent memory;* your state of mind influences you to retrieve memories that were formed in a similar state. Studies of state-dependent memory show that emotional states prime your retrieval of experiences with similar emotional features.

Here are some of the more difficult words in "Long-Term Memory."

cognitive
(paragraph 8)

cog·ni·tion (käg nish'ən) *n.* ⟦ME *cognicioun* < L *cognitio,* knowledge < *cognitus,* pp. of *cognoscere,* to know < *co-,* together + *gnoscere,* KNOW⟧ **1** the process of knowing in the broadest sense, including perception, memory, and judgment **2** the result of such a process; perception, conception, etc. —**cog·ni'·tional** *adj.* —**cog'·ni·tive** (-nə tiv) *adj.*

conclusive
(paragraph 1)

con·clu·sive (-siv) *adj.* ⟦LL *conclusivus* < pp. of L *concludere,* CONCLUDE⟧ that settles a question; final; decisive —**con·clu'·sively** *adv.* —**con·clu'·sive·ness** *n.*

duration
(paragraph 1)

du·ra·tion (doo rā'shən, dyoo-) *n.* ⟦ME *duracioun* < ML *duratio* < pp. of L *durare:* see DURABLE⟧ **1** continuance in time **2** the time that a thing continues or lasts

encoding
(paragraph 13)

en·code (en kōd', in-) *vt.* **··cod'ed, ··cod'·ing 1** to convert (a message, information, etc.) into code **2** to convert (data) by applying an electronic code —**en·cod'er** *n.*

imagery
(paragraph 14)

im·agery (im'ij rē, -ər ē) *n., pl.* **··ries** ⟦ME *imagerie* < OFr⟧ **1** [Now Rare] images generally; esp., statues **2** mental images, as produced by memory or imagination **3** descriptions and figures of speech

perceive
(paragraph 11)

per·ceive (pər sēv') *vt., vi.* **··ceived', ··ceiv'·ing** ⟦ME *perceyven* < OFr *perceivre* < L *percipere,* to take hold of, feel, comprehend < *per,* through + *capere,* to take: see HAVE⟧ **1** to grasp mentally; take note (of); observe **2** to become aware (of) through one of the senses, esp. through sight —*SYN.* DISCERN —**per·ceiv'·able** *adj.* —**per·ceiv'·ably** *adv.* —**per·ceiv'er** *n.*

retrieve
(paragraph 9)

re·trieve (ri trēv') *vt.* **··trieved', ··triev'·ing** ⟦ME *retreven* < inflected stem of OFr *retrouver* < *re-,* again + *trouver,* to find: see TROVER⟧ **1** to get back; recover **2** to restore; revive *[to retrieve one's spirits]* **3** to rescue or save **4** to set right or repair (a loss, error, etc.); make good **5** to recall to mind ☆**6** *Comput.* to gain access to (data) that is on a floppy disk, hard drive, etc. **7** *Hunting* to find and bring back (killed or wounded small game): said of dogs **8** *Racket Sports* to return (a ball that is hard to reach) —*vi. Hunting* to retrieve game —*n.* **1** any retrieval ☆**2** a retrieving of the ball in tennis, etc. —*SYN.* RECOVER —**re·triev'·able** *adj.*

schemas
(paragraph 15)

schema (skē'mə) *n., pl.* **··mata** (-mə tə) ⟦Gr *schēma:* see SCHEME⟧ **1** an outline, diagram, plan, or preliminary draft **2** *Psychol.* a mental image produced in response to a stimulus, that becomes a framework or basis for analyzing or responding to other related stimuli

siblings
(paragraph 6)

sib·ling (sib'liŋ) *n.* ⟦20th-c. revival of OE, a relative: see SIB & -LING¹⟧ one of two or more persons born of the same parents or, sometimes, having one parent in common; brother or sister

stimulus-response
(paragraph 8)

stimu·lus (-ləs) *n., pl.* **-u·li'** (-lī') ⟦L, a goad, sting, torment, pang, spur, incentive: see STYLE⟧ **1** something that rouses or incites to action or increased action; incentive **2** *Physiol., Psychol.* any action or agent that causes or changes an activity in an organism, organ, or part, as something that excites an end organ, starts a nerve impulse, activates a muscle, etc.

subtle
(paragraph 18)

sub·tle (sut''l) *adj.* **sub'·tler** (-lər, -'l ər), **sub'·tlest** ⟦ME *sotil* < OFr *soutil* < L *subtilis,* fine, thin, precise, orig., closely woven < *sub-* (see SUB-) + *tela,* web < *texla* < *texere,* to weave: see TECHNIC⟧ **1** thin; rare; tenuous; not dense or heavy *[a subtle gas]* **2** *a)* capable of making or noticing fine distinctions in meaning, etc. *[a subtle thinker]* *b)* marked by or requiring mental keenness *[subtle reasoning]* **3** delicately skillful or clever; deft or ingenious *[a subtle filigree]* **4** not open or direct; crafty; sly **5** delicately suggestive; not grossly obvious *[a subtle hint]* **6** working insidiously; not easily detected *[a subtle poison]* —**sub'·tle·ness** *n.* —**sub'·tly** *adv.*

27A1   VOCABULARY

From the context of "Long-Term Memory," explain the meaning of each of the vocabulary words shown in boldface.

1. *From paragraph 1:* LTM **duration** can be as brief as a few minutes and as long as a lifetime.

_____

_____

2. *From paragraph 1:* Many people believe that LTM is permanent, but the evidence is not **conclusive**.

_____

_____

3. *From paragraph 6:* Think of the birth of your young **siblings**, a great party you attended, a family tragedy. . .

_____

_____

4. *From paragraph 8:* Learned skills and behaviors, as well as **stimulus-response** associations, are contained in your procedural memory.

_____

_____

5. *From paragraph 8:* Such behavior may be acquired through conditioning and **cognitive** learning.

_____

_____

6. *From paragraph 9:* Semantic and episodic memories taken together are called declarative memory, which requires conscious effort to learn and **retrieve**.

_____

_____

7. *From paragraph 11:* You are most likely to **perceive** the test list words that were on the priming list even though you did not try to memorize or retrieve them.

_____

_____

8. *From paragraph 13:* The depth-of-processing model explains the strength and durability of LTM as the result of **encoding** processes.

_____

_____

9. *From paragraph 14:* Research on combined semantic codes and **imagery** supports this notion.

_____

_____

10. *From paragraph 15:* Their memories of the story showed changes that reflected their culture-based **schemas**.

_____

_____

11. *From paragraph 18:* Catherine devised a **subtle** scheme to get some money.

_____

_____

27A2   SPECIAL TEXTBOOK VOCABULARY

Key terms in this textbook selection are explained as they are discussed. Referring to "Long-Term Memory," fill in the blanks.

1. _____ memory contains factual knowledge based on words, phrases, sentences, and other verbal information.

2. The memory for very personal, autobiographical facts is _____.

3. A _____ memory is a vivid recollection of a more personal, emotionally powerful event.

4. Your memory for learned responses and action patterns is _____ memory.

5. _____ memory requires a conscious effort to learn and retrieve.

6. _____ memory is learned and retrieved without conscious effort.

7. The view that memory strength depends on encoding processes is the _____ model.

8. Remembering affected by schemas, personal beliefs, and inferences is _____ memory.

9. _____ memory is influenced by cues in the situation or emotional state.

10. _____ memory results from associations formed between cues and the information learned at the time.

11. Your mind's ability to retrieve memories that were formed in a similar state is _____ memory.

27B   CENTRAL THEME AND MAIN IDEAS

Choose the best answer.

_____ 1. The textbook selection "Long-Term Memory" covers a topic that could be part of a course in
   a. physics.
   b. mathematics.
   c. study skills.
   d. writing.

_____ 2. The main purpose of paragraphs 3–11 is to
   a. show the differences between long-term memory and short-term memory.
   b. name and explain how the four types of long-term memory are organized in humans.
   c. discuss the importance of language in stimulating the memory process in humans.
   d. list methods to help people retain information in long-term memory.

_____ 3. The main idea of paragraph 13 is the view that
   a. memories based on several semantic codes are deeper than those based on a single code.
   b. long-term memory contains many types of information stored in the human brain.
   c. short-term memory is "shallow" and is easy to remember.
   d. the organization of knowledge in long-term memory is complex so it is usually forgotten.

27C   MAJOR DETAILS

Decide whether each detail is true (T), false (F), or not discussed (ND).

_____ 1. Information stored in short-term memory is stored for 24 hours and then forgotten.

_____ 2. Semantic memory exists as thousands of independent bits of knowledge.

_____ 3. Flashbulb memories are not necessarily accurate.

_____ 4. Eyewitness memories are just as prone to error as other memories are.

_____ 5. According to Figure 1, a deeper memory is possible through combining semantic and visual codes.

_____ 6. Memories grow weaker over time.

_____ 7. Flashbulb memories do not involve emotions.

_____ 8. Memories are stored in both the left side and the right side of the brain.

27D   CRITICAL READING: FACT OR OPINION

Decide whether each statement contains a Fact *or an* Opinion.

_____ 1. *From paragraph 1:* "Many people believe that long-term memory is permanent [. . .]."

_____ 2. *From paragraph 5:* "Your semantic memory is impersonal [. . .]."

_____ 3. *From paragraph 8:* Everyday activities, such as driving a car or playing the piano, depend on your procedural memory.

_____ 4. *From paragraph 11:* "Research on the priming effect illustrates that implicit memory controls your unconscious retrieval of stored information."

_____ 5. *From paragraph 17:* "You should find that your memory is better when the music is playing."

27E   CRITICAL READING: THE AUTHOR'S STRATEGIES

Choose the best answer.

_____ 1. The main audience for "Long-Term Memory" in *Fundamentals of Psychology* is
   a. students studying psychology.
   b. students trying to improve their memory.
   c. students studying different types of memory.
   d. students studying long-term memory.

_____ 2. The author's purpose in writing this reading is to
   a. describe.
   b. convince.
   c. illustrate.
   d. inform.

_____ 3. The author's tone in this reading is
   a. critical.
   b. straightforward.
   c. gentle.
   d. positive.

27F   READER'S PROCESS: SUMMARIZING YOUR READING

_____ 1. What is the best summary of "Long-Term Memory" in _Fundamentals of Psychology_?
   a. The author explains the difference between long-term and short-term memory.
   b. The author explains how the mind organizes long-term memories.
   c. The author explains how the mind processes long-term memory.
   d. The author defines long-term memory and explains how it works.

27G   READER'S RESPONSE: TO DISCUSS OR WRITE ABOUT

1. Memory experts believe people can increase their ability to remember with memory aids, such as a mnemonic device. Mnemonic devices include rhymes, clues, mental pictures, and other methods. For example, many people remember the number of days in a month by using a verse that begins, "Thirty days hath September. . . " What are some mnemonic devices you use or know of to recall information?

2. If there were a drug available that claimed to improve memory, would you take it? If not, why? Should it be available to everyone? Would you support its use for victims of assault, sexual abuse, natural disaster, or terrible accidents? Why or why not?

HOW DID YOU DO?
27 Long-Term Memory

SKILL *(number of items)*	Number Correct		Points for each		Score
Vocabulary (11)	_____	×	2	=	_____
Special Textbook Vocabulary (11)	_____	×	2	=	_____
Central Theme and Main Ideas (3)	_____	×	6	=	_____
Major Details (8)	_____	×	2	=	_____
Critical Reading: Fact or Opinion (5)	_____	×	2	=	_____
Critical Reading: The Author's Strategies (3)	_____	×	3	=	_____
Reader's Process: Summarizing Your Reading (1)	_____	×	3	=	_____

(Possible *Total*: 100) *Total* _____

A Personal Stress Survival Guide in *An Invitation to Health*

Dianne Hales

LEARNING OBJECTIVES

- Name coping mechanisms and relaxation techniques used to avoid stress.

THINKING: GETTING STARTED

- What do you do to relieve stress?

(1) Although stress is a very real threat to emotional and physical well-being, its impact depends not just on what happens to you, but on how you handle it. If you tried to predict who would become ill based simply on life-change units or other stressors, you'd be correct only about 15% of the time. The inability to feel in control of stress, rather than stress itself, is often the most harmful.

(2) In studying individuals who manage stress so well that they seem "stress-resistant," researchers have observed that these individuals share many of the following traits:

- They respond actively to challenges. If a problem comes up, they look for resources, do some reading or research, and try to find a solution rather than giving up and feeling helpless. Because they've faced numerous challenges, they have confidence in their abilities to cope.
- They have personal goals, such as getting a college degree or becoming a better parent.
- They rely on a combination of planning, goal setting, problem solving, and risk taking to control stress.
- They use a minimum of substances such as nicotine, caffeine, alcohol, or drugs.
- They regularly engage in some form of relaxation, from meditation to exercise to knitting, at least fifteen minutes a day.
- They tend to seek out other people and become involved with them.

(3) In order to achieve greater control over the stress in your life, start with some self-analysis: If you're feeling overwhelmed, ask yourself: Are you taking an extra course that's draining your last ounce of energy? Are you staying up late studying every night and missing morning classes? Are you living on black coffee and jelly doughnuts? While

Stress happens when people feel they don't have the tools to manage all of the demands in their lives.

you may think that you don't have time to reduce the stress in your life, some simple changes can often ease the pressure you're under and help you achieve your long-term goals. One of the simplest, yet most effective, ways to work through stress is by putting your feelings into words that only you will read. The more honest and open you are as you write, the better. In studies at Southern Methodist University, psychologist James Pennebaker, Ph.D., found that college students who wrote in their journals about traumatic events felt much better afterward than those who wrote about **superficial** topics. Recording your experiences and feelings on paper or audiotape may help decrease stress and enhance well-being. Since the small ups and downs of daily life have an enormous impact on **psychological** and physical well-being, getting a handle on daily hassles will reduce your stress load.

Chart 1: How to Cope with Stress

A. Recognize your stress signals. Is your back bothering you more? Do you find yourself speeding or misplacing things? Force yourself to stop whenever you see these early warnings and say, "I'm under stress; I need to do something about it."

Chart 1: How to Cope with Stress, continued

B. Keep a stress journal. Focus on intense emotional experiences and "autopsy" them away to try to understand why they affected you the way they did. Rereading and thinking about your notes may help you **discern** the underlying reasons for your response and **garner** insights that can help you cope better in the future.

C. Try "stress-inoculation." Rehearse everyday situations that you find stressful, such as speaking in class. Think of how you might handle the situation, perhaps by breathing deeply before you talk, or visualizing yourself speaking with confidence.

D. Put things in proper perspective. When you're feeling hassled, stop and breathe deeply and slowly five times. Ask yourself: Will I remember what's made me so upset a month from now? If you had to rank this problem on a scale of 1 to 10, with worldwide catastrophe as 10, where would it rate? If this were the worst thing to happen to you this year, would you feel lucky?

E. Think of one simple thing that could make your life easier. What if you put up a hook to hold your keys so that you didn't spend five minutes searching for them every morning? Doing something, however small, will boost your sense of control.

POSITIVE COPING MECHANISMS

(4) After a perfectly miserable, aggravating day, a teacher comes home and yells at her children for making too much noise. Another individual, after an equally stressful day, jokes about what went wrong during the all-time most miserable moment of the month. Both of these people are using *defense mechanisms*—actions or behaviors that help protect their sense of self-worth. The first is displacing anger onto someone else; the second uses humor to **vent** frustration.

(5) Under great stress, we all may turn to negative defense mechanisms to **alleviate** anxiety and eliminate conflict. These can lead to **maladaptive** behavior, such as rationalizing overeating by explaining to yourself that you need the extra calories to cope with the extra stress in your life. *Coping mechanisms* are healthier, more mature and adaptive ways of dealing with stressful situations. While they also ward off unpleasant emotions, they usually are helpful rather than harmful. The most common are

(6) • *Sublimation,* the redirection of any drives considered unacceptable into socially acceptable channels. For example, someone who is furious with a friend or relative may go for a long run to sublimate anger.

(7) • *Religiosity,* in which one comes to terms with a painful experience, such as a child's death, by experiencing it as being in accord with God's will.

(8) • *Humor,* which counters stress by focusing on comic aspects. Medical students, for instance, often make jokes in anatomy lab as a way of dealing with their anxieties about working with cadavers.

(9) • *Altruism,* which takes a negative experience and turns it into a positive one. For example, an HIV-positive individual may talk to teenagers about AIDS (Acquired Immune Deficiency Syndrome) prevention.

MANAGING TIME

(10) Every day you make dozens of decisions, and the choices you make about how to use your time directly affect your stress level. If you have a big test on Monday and a term paper due Tuesday, you may plan to study all weekend. Then, when you're invited to a party Saturday night, you go. Although you set the alarm for 7:00 A.M. on Sunday, you don't pull yourself out of bed until noon. By the time you start studying, it's 4:00 P.M., and anxiety is building inside you. How can you tell if you've lost control of your time? The following are telltale symptoms of poor time management:

- Rushing.
- Chronic inability to make choices or decisions.
- Fatigue or listlessness.
- Constantly missed deadlines.
- Not enough time for rest or personal relationships.
- A sense of being overwhelmed by demands and details and having to do what you don't want to do most of the time.

One of the hard lessons of being on your own is that your choices and your actions have consequences. Stress is just one of them. But by thinking ahead, being realistic about your workload, and sticking to your plans, you can gain better control over your time and your stress levels.

OVERCOMING PROCRASTINATION

(11) Putting off until tomorrow what should be done today is a habit that creates a great deal of stress for many students. The three most common types of **procrastination** are putting off unpleasant things, putting off difficult tasks, and putting off tough decisions. Procrastinators are most likely to delay by wishing they didn't have to do what they must or by telling themselves they "just can't get started," which means they never do.

(12) People procrastinate, not because they're lazy, but to protect their self-esteem and make a favorable impression. "Procrastinators often perceive their worth as based solely on task ability, and their ability is determined only by how well they perform on completed tasks," notes psychologist Joseph Ferrari, Ph.D. "By never completing the tasks, they are never judged on their ability, thus allowing them to maintain an illusion of competence."

Chart 2 Breaking Out of the Procastination Trap

A. Keep track of the tasks you're most likely to put off, and try to figure why you don't want to tackle them. Think of alternative ways to get tasks done. If you put off library readings, figure out if the problem is getting to the library or the reading itself. If it's the trip to the library, arrange to walk over with a friend whose company you enjoy.

B. Keep a daily "To Do" list. Rank items according to priorities: A, B, C. Evaluate the items. Should any B's be A's? Schedule your days so the A's get accomplished.

C. Try not to fixate on half-completed projects. Divide large tasks, such as a term paper, into smaller ones, and reward yourself when you complete a part.

D. Do what you like least first. Once you have it out of the way, you can concentrate on the tasks you do enjoy.

E. Build time into your schedule for interruptions, unforeseen problems, unexpected events, and so on, so you aren't constantly racing around.

F. Beware of overcommitment. Establish ground rules for meeting your own needs (including getting enough sleep and making time for friends) before saying *yes* to any activity.

G. Learn to live according to a three-word motto: Just do it!

GOING WITH THE FLOW

(13) Americans enjoy less free time than people in many other societies—and we often don't know how to make the most of the free time we do have. According to the Americans' Use of Time Project, when we don't have to do anything else, most Americans mainly watch television: an average of 15.1 hours every week—compared with 4.9 hours visiting friends, 4.3 talking, 3.1 traveling, 2.8 reading, and 2.2 for either sports or hobbies. Yet when asked what they like to do, men and women rank playing with children, active sports, socializing and talking with family members much higher than watching TV. Three quarters of Americans believe the amount of stress in their lives is within their control. How do they prefer to handle stress? Exercise, 42%; Slowing down, 17%; Taking time off, 11%; Watching television, 7%; and Meditating, 3%.

(14) So why do we end up in front of the tube? Often it's simply because, while we carefully schedule our weekdays, we let our weekends and other free time drift. "Everybody who works looks forward to time off to do something they really enjoy, but very few do," observes psychologist Mihaly Csikszentmihalyi, Ph.D., author of *Flow: The Psychology of Optimal Experience.* "When you get home, you feel listless, so you fall into the

passive leisure trap of watching television—even though it isn't a really satisfying form of relaxation."

(15) There is an alternative, but it requires two things: prior planning and organization. "It's difficult to enjoy leisure time unless you prepare for it," says Csikszentmihalyi. "Left to themselves, things turn into a muddle; they deteriorate. To get any real psychological benefit from your free time, you have to invest some energy into it. Quality relaxation takes what I call spontaneous coordination." The first step is making leisure a priority. Too often, in our work-obsessed culture, we feel bad about simply feeling good. "We greatly undervalue relaxation," observes David Sobel, M.D., a specialist in behavioral medicine and coauthor of *Healthy Pleasures*. "It requires a certain amount of self-esteem to believe that you deserve to do something just because you enjoy it."

(16) But don't assume that the best leisure activities are expensive or elaborate. Often they're not. What they offer is flow, which Csikszentmihalyi defines as a state of altered consciousness that occurs when we are so focused, so **immersed** in what we're doing that we lose sense of time or anything else. The moment becomes everything. People find this sort of **transcendental** experience in different ways: playing chess, dancing, listening to music. Very often flow involves being outdoors—gardening, hiking, biking, sitting under a shady tree, looking for falling stars on a summer night, crunching through newly fallen snow. "Nature has a measurable restorative effect with respect to stress," says environmental psychologist Robert Ulrich, Ph.D., of Texas A&M University. Follow your own inclinations, whether or not they lead outdoors, to find your personal sources of flow.

RELAXATION TECHNIQUES

(17) Relaxation is the physical and mental state opposite that of stress. Rather than gearing up for fight or flight, our bodies and minds grow calmer and work more smoothly. We're less likely to become frazzled and more capable of staying in control. The most effective relaxation techniques include progressive relaxation, visualization, meditation, mindfulness, and biofeedback.

(18) *Progressive relaxation* works by intentionally increasing and then decreasing tension in the muscles. While sitting or lying down in a quiet, comfortable setting, you tense and release various muscles, beginning with those of the hand, for instance, and then proceeding to the arms, shoulders, neck, face, scalp, chest, stomach, buttocks, genitals, and so on, down each leg to the toes. Relaxing the muscles can quiet the mind and restore internal balance.

(19) *Visualization* or guided memory involves creating mental pictures that calm you down and focus your mind. Some people use this technique to promote healing when they are ill. The Glaser study showed that elderly

residents of retirement homes in Ohio who learned progressive relaxation and guided imagery enhanced their immune function and reported better health than did the other residents. Visualization skills require practice and, in some cases, instruction by qualified health professionals.

(20) *Meditation* has been practiced in many forms over the ages, from the yogic techniques of the Far East to the Quaker silence of more modern times. Meditation helps a person reach a state of relaxation, but with the goal of achieving inner peace and harmony. There is no one right way to meditate, and many people have discovered how to meditate on their own, without even knowing what it is they are doing. Among college students, meditation has proven especially effective in increasing relaxation. Most forms of meditation have common elements: sitting quietly for fifteen to twenty minutes once or twice a day, concentrating on a word or image, and breathing slowly and rhythmically. If you wish to try meditation, it often helps to have someone guide you through your first sessions. Or try tape recording your own voice (with or without favorite music in the background) and playing it back to yourself, freeing yourself to concentrate on the goal of turning the attention within.

(21) *Mindfulness* is a modern-day form of an ancient Asian technique that involves maintaining awareness in the present moment. You tune in to each part of your body, scanning from head to toe, noting the slightest sensation. You allow whatever you experience—an itch, an ache, a feeling of warmth—to enter your awareness. Then you open yourself to focus on all the thoughts, sensations, sounds, and feelings that enter your awareness. Mindfulness keeps you in the here-and-now, thinking about what is rather than about "what if" or "if only."

(22) *Biofeedback* is a method of obtaining feedback, or information, about some **physiological** activity occurring in the body. An electronic monitoring device attached to a person's body detects a change in an internal function and communicates it back to the person through a tone, light, or meter. By paying attention to this feedback, most people can gain some control over functions previously thought to be beyond conscious control, such as body temperature, heart rate, muscle tension, and brain waves. Biofeedback training consists of three stages:

   A. Developing increased awareness of a body state or function.
   B. Gaining control over it.
   C. Transferring this control to everyday living without use of the electronic instrument.

(23) The goal of biofeedback for stress reduction is a state of **tranquility,** usually associated with the brain's production of alpha waves (which are slower and more regular than normal waking waves). After several training sessions, most people can produce alpha waves more or less at will.

Here are some of the more difficult words in "A Personal Stress Survival Guide

alleviate
(paragraph 5)

al·le·vi·ate (ə lē'vē āt') *vt.* --at'ed, --at'·ing ⟦ME *alleviaten* < LL *alleviatus*, pp. of *alleviare*, for L *allevare* < *ad-*, to + *levis*, LIGHT²⟧ **1** to make less hard to bear; lighten or relieve (pain, suffering, etc.) **2** to reduce or decrease [*to alleviate* poverty] —*SYN.* RELIEVE —al·le'·via·tor *n.* —al·le'·via·tive *adj.* or al·le'·via·to·ry (-ə tôr'ē)

discern
(Chart 1, Item B)

dis·cern (di surn', -zurn') *vt.* ⟦ME *discernen* < OFr *discerner* < L *discernere* < *dis-*, apart + *cernere*, to separate: see HARVEST⟧ **1** to separate (a thing) mentally from another or others; recognize as separate or different **2** to perceive or recognize; make out clearly —*vi.* to perceive or recognize the difference —dis·cern'·ible *adj.* —dis·cern'·ibly *adv.*

garner
(Chart 1, Item B)

gar·ner (gär'nər) *n.* ⟦ME *gerner* < OFr *grenier* < L *granarium*, granary < *granum*, GRAIN⟧ a place for storing grain; granary —*vt.* **1** to gather up and store in or as in a granary **2** to get or earn **3** to collect or gather

immersed
(paragraph 16)

im·merse (i murs') *vt.* --mersed', --mers'·ing ⟦< L *immersus*, pp. of *immergere*, to dip, plunge into: see IN-¹ & MERGE⟧ **1** to plunge, drop, or dip into or as if into a liquid, esp. so as to cover completely **2** to baptize by submerging in water **3** to absorb deeply; engross [*immersed* in study]

maladaptive
(paragraph 5)

mal·ad·ap·ta·tion (mal'ad əp tā'shən) *n.* inadequate or faulty adaptation —mal'·adap'·tive (-ə dap'tiv) *adj.*

physiological
(paragraph 22)

physi·ol·ogy (fiz'ē äl'ə jē) *n.* ⟦Fr *physiologie* < L *physiologia* < Gr: see PHYSIO- & -LOGY⟧ **1** the branch of biology dealing with the functions and vital processes of living organisms or their parts and organs **2** the functions and vital processes, collectively (of an organism, or of an organ or system of organs) —phys'i·ol'o·gist *n.*

procrastination
(paragraph 11)

pro·cras·ti·nate (prō kras'tə nāt', prə-) *vi., vt.* --nat'ed, --nat'·ing ⟦< L *procrastinatus*, pp. of *procastinare* < *pro-*, forward (see PRO-²) + *crastinus*, belonging to the morrow < *cras*, tomorrow] to put off doing (something unpleasant or burdensome) until a future time; esp., to postpone (such actions) habitually —pro·cras'·ti·na'·tion *n.* —pro·cras'·ti·na'·tor *n.*

psychological
(paragraph 3)

psycho·logi·cal (sī'kə läj'i kəl) *adj.* **1** of psychology **2** of the mind; mental **3** affecting or intended to affect the mind Also psy'cho·log'ic —psy'cho·log'i·cally *adv.*

superficial
(paragraph 3)

su·per·fi·cial (sōō'pər fish'əl) *adj.* ⟦ME *superficyall* < L *superficialis* < *superficies*: see fol.⟧ **1** *a)* of or being on the surface [a *superficial* burn] *b)* of or limited to surface area; plane [*superficial* measurements] **2** concerned with and understanding only the easily apparent and obvious; not profound; shallow **3** quick and cursory [a *superficial* reading] **4** seeming such only at first glance; merely apparent [a *superficial* resemblance] —su'·per·fi'·ci·al'·ity (-ē al'ə tē) *n., pl.* -ties —su'·per·fi'·cially *adv.* —su'·per·fi'·cial·ness *n.*
SYN.—superficial implies concern with the obvious or surface aspects of a thing [*superficial* characteristics] and, in a derogatory sense, lack of thoroughness, profoundness, significance, etc. [*superficial* judgments]; shallow, in this connection always derogatory, implies a lack of depth of character, intellect, meaning, etc. [*shallow* writing]; cursory, which may or may not be derogatory, suggests a hasty consideration of something without pausing to note details [a *cursory* inspection] —ANT. deep, profound

tranquillity
(paragraph 23)

tran·quil·lity or **tran·quil·ity** (traŋ kwil'ə tē, tran-) *n.* the quality or state of being tranquil; calmness; serenity

Vocabulary List

transcendental
(paragraph 16)

tran·scen·den·tal (tran'sen dent''l) *adj.* ⟦ML *transcendentalis*⟧ **1** *a*) TRANSCENDENT (sense 1) *b*) SUPERNATURAL **2** abstract; metaphysical **3** of or having to do with transcendentalism **4** in Kantian philosophy, based on those elements of experience which derive not from sense data but from the inherent organizing function of the mind, and which are the necessary conditions of human knowledge; transcending sense experience but not knowledge **5** *Math. a*) not capable of being a root of any algebraic equation with rational coefficients *b*) of, pertaining to, or being a function, as a logarithm, trigonometric function, exponential, etc., that is not expressible algebraically in terms of the variables and constants (opposed to ALGEBRAIC, sense 2)) —**tran'·scen·den'·tally** *adv.*

vent
(paragraph 4)

vent[1] (vent) *n.* ⟦ME *venten* < OFr *venter,* to blow (or aphetic < OFr *esventer,* to expose to the air, let out < *es-,* out + *venter*) < VL **ventare* < L *ventus,* WIND[2]⟧ **1** [Rare] the action of escaping or passing out, or the means or opportunity to do this; issue; outlet **2** expression; release *[giving vent to emotion]* **3** *a*) a small hole or opening to permit passage or escape, as of a gas ☆*b*) a small triangular window or, now esp., an opening on or beneath the dashboard, for letting air into the passenger compartment of a motor vehicle **4** in early guns, the small hole at the breech through which a spark passes to set off the charge **5** the opening in a volcano from which gas and molten rock erupt **6** *Zool.* the excretory opening in animals; esp., the external opening of the cloaca in birds, reptiles, amphibians, and fishes —*vt.* **1** to make a vent in or provide a vent for **2** to allow (steam, gas, etc.) to escape through an opening **3** to give release or expression to **4** to relieve or unburden by giving vent to feelings *[to vent oneself in curses]*

28A1   VOCABULARY

From the context of "A Personal Stress Survival Guide," explain each of the vocabulary words shown in boldface.

1. *From paragraph 3:* . . . college students who wrote in their journals about traumatic events felt much better afterward than those who wrote about **superficial** topics.

   _____

   _____

2. *From paragraph 3:* Since the small ups and downs of daily life have an enormous impact on **psychological** and physical well-being, getting a handle on daily hassles will reduce your stress load.

   _____

   _____

3. *From Chart 1, Item B:* Rereading and thinking about your notes may help you **discern** the underlying reasons for your response and **garner** insights that can help you cope better in the future.

   _____

   _____

Name   Date

4. *From paragraph 4:* The second [person] uses humor to **vent** frustration.

   _____

   _____

5. *From paragraph 5:* Under great stress, we all may turn to negative defense mechanisms to **alleviate** anxiety and eliminate conflict.

   _____

   _____

6. *From paragraph 5:* These can lead to **maladaptive** behavior, such as overeating. . . .

   _____

   _____

7. *From paragraph 11:* The three most common types of **procrastination** are putting off unpleasant things, putting off difficult tasks, and putting off tough decisions.

   _____

   _____

8. *From paragraph 16:* What they offer is flow, which Csikszentmihalyi defines as a state of altered consciousness that occurs when we are so focused, so **immersed** in what we're doing that we lose sense of time or anything else.

   _____

   _____

9. *From paragraph 16:* People find this sort of **transcendental** experience in different ways.

   _____

   _____

10. *From paragraph 22:* Biofeedback is a method of obtaining feedback, or information, about some **physiological** activity occurring in the body.

    _____

    _____

11. *From paragraph 23:* The goal of biofeedback for stress reduction is a state of **tranquility**.

    _____

    _____

Name   Date   **365**

28A2   SPECIAL TEXTBOOK VOCABULARY

Key terms in this textbook selection are explained as they are discussed. Referring to "A Personal Stress Survival Guide," fill in the blanks.

1. _____ are actions or behaviors that people use to protect their sense of self-worth.

2. Redirecting an unacceptable drive into a socially acceptable channel is _____.

3. _____ is the practice of one's trying to accept a painful experience as being in agreement with God's will.

4. Medical students use jokes, or _____, to counteract stress they encounter during anatomy lab.

5. Turning a negative experience into a positive one is _____.

6. _____ occurs when a person intentionally increases and then decreases tension in various muscles according to a set sequence.

7. One's creating and using mental pictures to calm oneself and focus the mind is _____.

8. _____ can involve sitting quietly, concentrating, or breathing slowly and rhythmically to achieve a state of relaxation.

28B   CENTRAL THEME AND MAIN IDEAS

Choose the best answer.

_____ 1. The central theme of "A Personal Stress Survival Guide" is
   a. how unbalanced stress distribution on metal parts can cause failure of machinery resulting in serious accidents.
   b. how important is the maintenance of good mental health through all stages of life, from childhood through old age.
   c. how people can learn to handle stress: first, by learning the types of stress and, second, by using ways to minimize their effects.
   d. how to handle the trauma that can follow having almost died in a major disaster, such as a tornado, flood, or hurricane.

_____ 2. The main purpose of paragraph 2 is to
   a. describe and discuss the possible signals of stress overload.
   b. identify the common traits found in those who control stress.
   c. describe and discuss the behaviors that lead to stress.
   d. recommend involvement with other people to avoid stress.

_____ 3. The main idea of paragraph 4 is that
      a. teachers may take out their stress from work by yelling at their own children.
      b. joking about a stressful day at work can relieve stress.
      c. protecting one's sense of self-worth is necessary during stressful times.
      d. people use defense mechanisms to protect against stress.

28C MAJOR DETAILS

Fill in the word or words that correctly complete each statement.

1. The impact of stress depends not just on what _____ to you, but on how you _____ it.

2. An effective way to deal with stress is writing about your _____ in _____ that only you will read.

3. Some strategies to help you cope with stress include _____ your stress signals, _____ a stress journal, _____ "stress-inoculation," _____ things in proper perspective, and _____ of one thing to simplify your life.

4. Symptoms of _____ include rushing, the inability to make choices, fatigue, missed deadlines, and not enough time for rest.

5. The Americans' Use of Time Project showed that Americans spend the greater amount of their free time _____.

6. To make effective use of free time requires _____ and _____.

7. In our work-obsessed culture, David Sobel observes "we greatly undervalue _____."

28D INFERENCES

Decide whether each statement can be inferred (Yes) or cannot be inferred (No) from the reading selection.

_____ 1. Stress management includes striving for a personal goal because it provides reasons for choices made.

_____ 2. Stress management includes using a minimum of substances, such as nicotine and caffeine, because these stimulants can affect a person's thought processes.

_____ 3. Procrastinators have high self-esteem.

_____ 4. Stress counseling is available through many resources.

28E   CRITICAL READING: FACT OR OPINION

Decide whether each statement contains a Fact *or an* Opinion.

_____ 1. *From paragraph 1:* "The inability to feel in control of stress, rather than stress itself, is often the most harmful."

_____ 2. *From paragraph 11:* "Putting off until tomorrow what should be done today is a habit that creates a great deal of stress for many students."

_____ 3. *From paragraph 12:* "People procrastinate, not because they're lazy, but to protect their self-esteem and make a favorable impression."

_____ 4. *From paragraph 13:* "Three-quarters of Americans believe the amount of stress in their lives is within their control."

_____ 5. *From paragraph 14:* "Everybody who works looks forward to time off to do something they really enjoy but very few do [. . .]."

_____ 6. *From paragraph 19:* "The Glaser study of elderly residents of retirement homes in Ohio showed that residents who practiced progressive relaxation and guided imagery enhanced their immune function and reported better health than the other residents."

_____ 7. *From paragraph 20:* "Among college students meditation has proven especially effective in increasing relaxation."

28F   CRITICAL READING: THE AUTHOR'S STRATEGIES

Choose the best answer.

_____ 1. The main audience for "A Personal Stress Survival Guide" in *An Invitation to Health* is
   a. students studying health.
   b. students who procrastinate.
   c. students who don't know how to relax.
   d. students who need advice on handling stress.

Name   Date

_____ 2. The author's purpose in writing this reading is to
  a. persuade.
  b. expose.
  c. entertain.
  d. inform.

_____ 3. The author's tone in this reading is
  a. judgmental.
  b. critical.
  c. encouraging.
  d. objective.

28G   READER'S PROCESS: SUMMARIZING YOUR READING

Choose the best answer.

_____ 1. What is the best summary of "A Personal Stress Survival Guide"
  in *An Invitation to Health?*
  a. The author discusses why Americans watch too much
     television.
  b. The author discusses methods that can reduce stress in every-
     day life.
  c. The author discusses how students can avoid procrastinating.
  d. The author discusses how keeping a journal can help reduce
     stress.

28H   READER'S RESPONSE: TO DISCUSS OR WRITE ABOUT

1. Stress can either help or hurt a person. Good stress provides a challenge. Bad stress is harmful physically and/or psychologically. Discuss several situations that illustrate either good or bad stress in your
   life or in a friend's life.

2. Give an example of a stressful situation involving you and a family
   member, coworker, friend, or classmate. Were you able to change the
   situation? If so, explain what you did. If not, explain the coping techniques you used to handle the situation.

HOW DID YOU DO?
28 A Personal Stress Survival Guide

SKILL *(number of items)*	Number Correct		Points for each		Score
Vocabulary* (12)	_____	×	2	=	_____
Special Textbook Vocabulary (8)	_____	×	2	=	_____
Central Theme and Main Ideas (3)	_____	×	4	=	_____
Major Details** (14)	_____	×	2	=	_____
Inferences (4)	_____	×	1	=	_____
Critical Reading: Fact or Opinion (7)	_____	×	1	=	_____
Critical Reading: The Author's Strategies (3)	_____	×	2	=	_____
Reader's Process: Summarizing Your Reading (1)	_____	×	3	=	_____

(Possible Total: 100) *Total* _____

*Question 3 in this exercise calls for two separate answers. In computing your score, count each separate answer toward your number correct.

**Questions 1, 2, and 6 in this exercise call for two separate answers. Question 3 calls for five separate answers. In computing your score, count each separate answer toward your number correct.

Name   Date

Culture in *Essentials of Sociology*

James Henslin

LEARNING OBJECTIVES
- Define the term *culture shock.*

THINKING: GETTING STARTED
- Are there any instances in Western culture in which cutting in line is sanctioned?

(1) I had never felt heat like this before. This was northern Africa, and I wondered what it must be like closer to the equator. Sweat poured off me as the temperature climbed past 100 degrees Fahrenheit. As we were herded into the building—which had no air conditioning—hundreds of people lunged toward the counter at the rear of the structure. With body crushed against body, we waited as the uniformed officials behind the windows leisurely examined each passport. At times like this, I wondered what I was doing in Africa.

(2) When I first arrived in Morocco, I found the sights that greeted me exotic—not unlike the scenes in *Casablanca*, *Raiders of the Lost Ark*, and other movies. The men, women, and even the children really did wear those white robes that reached down to their feet. What was especially striking was that the women were almost totally covered. Despite the heat, they wore not only full-length gowns but also head coverings that reached down over their foreheads and veils that covered their faces from the nose down. You could see nothing but their eyes—and every eye seemed the same shade of brown.

(3) And how short everyone was! The Arab women looked to be, on average, 5 feet, and the men only about three or four inches taller. As the only blue-eyed, blond, 6-foot-plus person around, and the only one who was wearing jeans and a pullover shirt, in a world of white-robed short people I stood out like a creature from another planet. Everyone stared. No matter where I went, they stared. Wherever I looked, I found brown eyes watching me intently. Even staring back at those many dark brown eyes had no effect. It was so different from home, where, if you caught someone staring at you, that person would look embarrassed and immediately glance away.

(4) And lines? The concept apparently didn't even exist. Buying a ticket for a bus or train meant pushing and shoving toward the ticket man (always a man—no women were visible in any public position), who took the money from whichever outstretched hand he decided on.

One aspect of everyday life in Japan that would be culture shock to Westerners is the public squat toilet.

(5) And germs? That notion didn't seem to exist here either. Flies swarmed over the food in the restaurants and the unwrapped loaves of bread in the stores. Shopkeepers would considerately shoo off the flies before handing me a loaf. They also offered home delivery. I watched a bread vendor deliver a loaf to a woman who was standing on a second-floor balcony. She first threw her money to the bread vendor, and he then threw the unwrapped bread up to her. Unfortunately the throw was off. The bread bounced off the wrought-iron balcony railing and landed in the street, which was filled with people, wandering dogs, and the ever-present urinating and defecating donkeys. The vendor simply picked up the unwrapped loaf and threw it again. This certainly wasn't his day, for he missed again. But he made it on his third attempt. The woman smiled as she turned back into her apartment, apparently to prepare the noon meal for her family.

(6) As I left Morocco, I entered a crowded passport-check building on the Algerian border. With no air conditioning, the oppressive heat—about 115 degrees—was made all the worse as body crushed body. As people pushed to get to the front, tempers began to flare. When a fight broke out, a little man in uniform appeared, shouting and knocking people aside as he forced his way to a little wooden box nailed to the floor. Climbing onto

this makeshift platform, he shouted at the crowd, his arms **flailing** about him. The people fell silent. But just as soon as the man left, the shouting and shoving began again.

(7) The situation had become unbearable. His body pressed against mine, the man behind me decided that this was a good time to take a nap. Determining that I made a good support, he placed his arm against my back and leaned his head against his arm. Sweat streamed down my back at the point where his arm and head touched me. Finally, I realized that I had to abandon U.S. customs. So I pushed my way forward, forcing my frame into every cubic inch of vacant space that I could create. At the counter, I shouted in English. The official looked up at the sound of this strange tongue, and I thrust my long arms over the heads of three people, shoving my passport into his hand.

(8) What is culture? The concept is sometimes easier to grasp by description than by definition. For example, suppose you meet a young woman from India who has just arrived in the United States. That her culture is different from yours is immediately evident. You first see it in her clothing, jewelry, makeup, and hairstyle. Next you hear it in her speech. It then becomes apparent by her gestures. Later, you might hear her express unfamiliar beliefs about relationships or what is valuable in life. All of these characteristics are indicative of culture—the language, beliefs, values, norms, behaviors, and even material objects that are passed from one generation to the next.

(9) In northern Africa, I was surrounded by a culture quite different from mine. It was evident in everything I saw and heard. The material culture—such things as jewelry, art, buildings, weapons, machines, and even eating utensils, hairstyles, and clothing—provided a sharp contrast to what I was used to seeing. There is nothing inherently "natural" about material culture. That is, it is no more natural (or unnatural) to wear gowns on the street than it is to wear jeans.

(10) I also found myself immersed in an unfamiliar nonmaterial culture, that is, a group's way of thinking (its beliefs, values, and other assumptions about the world) and doing (its common patterns of behavior, including language, gestures, and other forms of interaction). North African assumptions that it is acceptable to stare at others in public and to push people aside to buy tickets are examples of nonmaterial culture. So are U.S. assumptions that it is wrong to do either of these things. Like material culture, neither custom is "right." People simply become comfortable with the customs they learn during childhood, and—as when I visited northern Africa—uncomfortable when their basic assumptions about life are challenged.

(11) To develop a sociological imagination, it is essential to understand how culture affects people's lives. If we meet someone from a different culture, the encounter may make us aware of culture's pervasive influence on all aspects of a person's life. Attaining the same level of awareness regarding our own culture, however, is quite another matter. We usually

take *our* speech, *our* gestures, *our* beliefs, and *our* customs for granted. We assume that they are "normal" or "natural," and we almost always follow them without question. As **anthropologist** Ralph Linton said, "The last thing a fish would ever notice would be water." So also with people: Except in unusual circumstances, most characteristics of our own culture remain imperceptible to us.

(12) Yet culture's significance is **profound;** it touches almost every aspect of who and what we are. We came into this life without a language; without values and morality; with no ideas about religion, war, money, love, use of space, and so on. We possessed none of these fundamental orientations that are so essential in determining the type of people we become. Yet by this point in our lives, we all have acquired them—and take them for granted. Sociologists call this *culture within us.* These learned and shared ways of believing and of doing (another definition of culture) penetrate our beings at an early age and quickly become part of our taken-for-granted assumptions about what normal behavior is. *Culture becomes the lens through which we perceive and evaluate what is going on around us.* Seldom do we question these assumptions, for like water to a fish, the lens through which we view life remains largely beyond our perception.

(13) The rare instances in which these assumptions are challenged, however, can be unsettling. Although as a sociologist I try to look at my own culture "from the outside," my trip to Africa quickly revealed how fully I had internalized my own culture. My upbringing in Western culture had given me assumptions about aspects of social life that had become rooted deeply in my being—appropriate eye contact, proper hygiene, and the use of space. But in this part of Africa these assumptions were useless in helping me navigate everyday life. No longer could I count on people to stare only **surreptitiously,** to take precautions against invisible **microbes,** or to stand in line in an orderly fashion, one behind the other.

(14) As you can tell from the opening vignette, I found these unfamiliar behaviors upsetting, for they violated my basic expectations of "the way people *ought* to be"—and I did not even realize how firmly I held these expectations until they were challenged so abruptly. When my nonmaterial culture failed me—when it no long enabled me to make sense out of the world—I experienced a disorientation known as culture shock. In the case of buying tickets, the fact that I was several inches taller than most Moroccans and thus able to outreach others helped me to adjust partially to the different ways of doing things. But I never did get used to the idea that pushing ahead of others was "right," and I always felt guilty when I used my size to receive preferential treatment.

(15) Culture shock is a two-way street, of course. You can imagine what culture shock people from a tribal society would experience if they were thrust into the United States. Imagine that you were a member of a small tribal group in the mountains of Laos. Village life and the clan were all you knew. There were no schools, and you learned everything you needed to know from your relatives. U.S. agents recruited the men of your village to

fight communists, and they gained a reputation as fierce fighters. When the U.S. forces were defeated in Vietnam, your people were moved to the United States so they wouldn't be killed in **reprisal.**

(16) Here is what happened. Keep in mind that you had never seen a television or a newspaper and that you had never gone to school. Your entire world had been the village.

- They put you in a big house with wings. It flew.
- They gave you strange food on a tray. The Sani-Wipes were hard to chew.
- After the trip you were placed in a house. This was an adventure. You had never seen locks before, as no one locked up anything in the villages. Most of the village homes didn't even have doors, much less locks.
- You found the bathroom perplexing. At first, you tried to wash rice in the bowl of water, which seemed to be provided for this purpose. But when you pressed the handle, the water and rice disappeared. After you learned what the toilet was for, you found it difficult not to slip off the little white round thing when you stood on it. In the village, you didn't need a toilet seat when you squatted in a field to **defecate.**
- When you threw water on the electric stove to put out the burner, it sparked and smoked. You became afraid to use the stove because it might explode.
- And no one liked it when you tried to plant a vegetable garden in the park.

(17) To help the Hmong **assimilate,** U.S. officials dispersed them across the nation. This, they felt, would help them to adjust to the dominant culture and prevent a Hmong subculture from developing. The dispersal brought feelings of isolation to the clan- and village-based Hmong. As soon as they had a chance, the Hmong moved from these towns scattered across the country to the same areas, the major one being in California's Central Valley. Here they renewed village relationships and helped one another adjust to the strange society suddenly thrust upon them.

(18) An important consequence of culture within us is ethnocentrism, a tendency to use our own group's way of doing things as a yardstick for judging others. All of us learn that the ways of our own group are good, right, and even superior to other ways of life. As sociologist William Sumner who developed this concept, said, "One's own group is the center of everything, and all others are scaled and rated with reference to it." Ethnocentrism has both positive and negative consequences. On the positive side, it creates in-group loyalties. On the negative side, ethnocentrism can lead to discrimination against people whose ways differ from ours.

Here are some of the more difficult words in "Culture."

anthropologist
(paragraph 11)

an·thropolo·gist (an'thrō päl'ə jist, -thrə-) *n.* a person who spe cializes in anthropology

an·thropol·ogy (an'thrō päl'ə jē, -thrə-) *n.* ⟦ANTHROPO- + -LOGY⟧ the study of humans, esp. of the variety, physical and cultural characteristics, distribution, customs, social relationships, etc. of humanity —**an'·thropo·log'i·cal** (-pō läj'i kəl, -pə-) *adj.* or **an'· thropo·log'ic** —**an'·thropo·log'i·cally** *adv.*

assimilate
(paragraph 17)

as·simi·late (ə sim'ə lāt') *vt.* --lat'ed, --lat'ing ⟦ME *assimilaten* < L *assimilatus,* pp. of *assimilare* < *ad-,* to + *similare,* make similar < *similis,* like: see SAME⟧ **1** to change (food) into a form that can be taken up by, and made part of, the body tissues; absorb into the body **2** to absorb and incorporate into one's thinking **3** to absorb (groups of different cultures) into the main cultural body **4** to make like or alike; cause to resemble: with *to* **5** [Now Rare] to compare or liken **6** *Linguis.* to cause to undergo assimilation —*vi.* **1** to become like or alike **2** to be absorbed and incorporated **3** *Linguis.* to undergo assimilation —**as·sim'i·lable** (-ə lə bəl) *adi.*

defecate
(paragraph 16)

def·e·cate (def'i kāt') *vt.* --cat'ed, --cat'ing ⟦< L *defaecatus,* pp. of *defaecare,* to cleanse from dregs, strain < *de-,* from + *faex* (gen. *faecis*), grounds, dregs⟧ to remove impurities from; refine (sugar, wine, etc.) —*vi.* **1** to become free from impurities **2** to excrete waste matter from the bowels —**def'·e·ca'·tion** *n.* —**def'·e·ca'·tor** *n.*

flailing
(paragraph 6)

flail (flāl) *n.* ⟦ME *fleil* < OFr *flaiel* & OE **flegel,* both < L *flagellum,* a whip, scourge: see FLAGELLATE⟧ a farm tool consisting of a free-swinging stick tied to the end of a long handle, used to thresh grain —*vt., vi.* **1** to thresh with a flail **2** to strike or beat as with a flail **3** to move (one's arms) about like flails

microbes
(paragraph 13)

mi·crobe (mī'krōb') *n.* ⟦Fr < Gr *mikro-* (see MICRO-) + *bios,* life (see BIO-)⟧ a microscopic organism; esp., any of the bacteria that cause disease; germ —**mi·cro'·bial** *adj.* or **mi·cro'·bic**

profound
(paragraph 12)

pro·found (prō found', prə-) *adj.* ⟦ME < OFr *profund* < L *profundus* < *pro-,* forward (see PRO-²) + *fundus,* BOTTOM⟧ **1** very deep or low [a *profound* abyss, sleep, etc.] **2** marked by intellectual depth [a *profound* discussion] **3** intensely felt [*profound* grief] **4** thoroughgoing [*profound* changes] **5** unbroken [a *profound* actions **2** designed or acting to secure conformity at any cost; drastic or ruthless

reprisal
(paragraph 15)

re·prisal (ri prī'zəl) *n.* ⟦ME *reprisail ̄ ̄ ̄ ̄ ̄ reprisaille* < It *rap-presaglia* < *riprendere,* to take back < L *reprehendere:* see REPRE-HEND⟧ **1** [Historical] the forcible seizure of property or subjects in retaliation for an injury inflicted by another country **2** the act or practice of using force, short of war, against another nation to obtain redress of grievances **3** injury done, or the doing of injury, in return for injury received; retaliation or an act of retaliation, specif. in war, as the killing of prisoners

surreptitiously
(paragraph 13)

sur·rep·ti·tious (sur'əp tish'əs) *adj.* ⟦ME *surrepticious* < L *surrep-ticius* < *surreptus,* pp. of *surripere,* to take away secretly < *sub-* (see SUB-) + *rapere,* to seize (see RAPE¹)⟧ **1** done, gotten, made, etc. in a secret, stealthy way; clandestine **2** acting in a secret, stealthy way —*SYN.* SECRET —**sur'·rep·ti'·tiously** *adv.* —**sur'·rep·ti'·tious·ness** *n.*

29A1 VOCABULARY

From the context of "Culture," explain each of the vocabulary words shown in boldface.

1. *From paragraph 6:* "[. . .] he shouted at the crowd, his arms **flailing** about him." _____

2. *From paragraph 11:* "An **anthropologist**, Ralph Linton, said, 'The last thing a fish would ever notice would be water.'"

    _____

3. *From paragraph 12:* "Yet culture's significance is **profound** [. . .]."

    _____

4. *From paragraph 13:* "No longer could I count on people to stare **surreptitiously** [. . .]. _____

5. *From paragraph 13:* " [. . .] to take precautions against invisible **microbes** [. . .]." _____

6. *From paragraph 15:* "[. . .] your people were moved to the United States so that they wouldn't be killed in **reprisal**." _____

7. *From paragraph 16:* "In the village, you didn't need a toilet seat when you went to **defecate**." _____

8. *From paragraph 17:* "To help the Hmong **assimilate**, U.S. officials dispensed them across the nation."

    _____

29A2 SPECIAL TEXTBOOK VOCABULARY

Key terms in this textbook selection are explained as they are discussed. Referring to "Culture," fill in the blanks.

1. The language, beliefs, values, norms, behaviors, and even material objects that are passed from one generation to the next are characteristics that are indicative of _____.

2. Things, such as jewelry, art, buildings, weapons, machines, and even eating utensils, hairstyles, and clothing, are indicative of

    _____.

3. A group's way of thinking (its beliefs, values, and other assumptions about the world) and doing (its common patterns of behavior, including language, gestures, and other forms of interaction) are indicative of _____.

4. _____ describes the physical and emotional discomfort a person feels when that person is exposed to a culture that is very different from one's own.

5. _____ is the tendency to believe that one's ethnic or cultural group is centrally important and that all other groups are measured in relation to one's own.

29B   CENTRAL THEME AND MAIN IDEAS

Choose the best answer.

_____ 1. The central theme of "Culture" is that
a. people from the United States who visit northern Africa will be stared at because of their clothing.
b. a people's way of thinking and acting varies significantly from one culture to another.
c. people judge one another by their manners, especially in public places.
d. people who grew up in Africa have not been taught appropriate eye contact and proper hygiene.

_____ 2. What is the main idea of paragraph 5?
a. Flies are very prevalent in Morocco.
b. A bread vendor made home deliveries.
c. Shopkeepers and customers in Morocco do not worry about germs.
d. On the third attempt at throwing bread to his customer, the vendor was successful.

3. In your own words, give the main idea of paragraph 7.

_____

_____

29C   MAJOR DETAILS

Decide whether each detail is Major *or* Minor *based on the context of the reading selection.*

_____ 1. James Henslin made a trip to Morocco in Africa.

_____ 2. The Arab women were, on the average, 5 feet, and the men only about three or four inches taller.

_____ 3. Flies swarmed over the food in restaurants and the unwrapped loaves of bread in the stores.

Name   Date

_____ 4. A fight broke out in the passport-check building.

_____ 5. James Henslin experienced culture shock when it came to buying a ticket.

29D   INFERENCES

*Decide whether each statement below can be inferred (*Yes*) or cannot be inferred (*No*) from the reading selection.*

_____ 1. Prior to going to Africa, James Henslin had studied Arab culture.

_____ 2. James Henslin believed it was wrong to push and shove to get ahead of others.

_____ 3. Fights in lines are less likely to occur when the temperature is less than 100 degrees.

_____ 4. By United States standards, restaurants in Morocco would not receive a high health rating.

_____ 5. Rather than being moved to the United States after the U.S. forces were defeated in Vietnam, the Hmong would have fared better to have remained in Laos.

29E   CRITICAL READING: FACT OR OPINION

Decide whether each statement, even if it quotes someone, contains a Fact *or* Opinion.

_____ 1. *From paragraph 3:* "Everyone stared. No matter where I went, they stared."

_____ 2. *From paragraph 5:* "This certainly wasn't his day, for he missed again."

_____ 3. *From paragraph 10:* "North African assumptions that it is acceptable to stare at others in public and to push people aside to buy tickets are examples of nonmaterial culture."

_____ 4. *From paragraph 11:* "As anthropologist Ralph Linton said, 'The last thing a fish would ever notice would be water.'"

_____ 5. *From paragraph 18:* "All of us learn that the ways of our own group are good, right, and even superior to other ways of life."

29F   CRITICAL READING: THE AUTHOR'S STRATEGIES

Choose the best answer.

_____ 1. The main audience for "Culture" is
  a. students planning to visit Africa.
  b. students studying anthropology.
  c. students studying cultural diversity.
  d. students studying good manners.

_____ 2. The author's purpose in writing this is to
  a. persuade.
  b. entertain.
  c. describe.
  d. inform.

_____ 3. The author's tone in this reading is
  a. sarcastic.
  b. envious.
  c. gentle.
  d. straightforward.

29G   READER'S PROCESS: SUMMARIZING YOUR READING

_____ 1. What is the best summary of "Culture"?
  a. James Henslin discusses the culture shock he experienced when he visited Africa and the culture shock of the Hmong when they came to the United States.
  b. James Henslin suggests that culture penetrates deeply into our thinking, becoming a taken-for-granted lens through which we see the world and our perception of reality.
  c. James Henslin defines culture, both material and nonmaterial, and shares the culture shock he experienced in Africa and the Hmong experienced in the United States.
  d. James Henslin maintains that all people are ethnocentric and use our own group's ways of doing things as a yardstick to judge everyone else.

29H   READER'S RESPONSE: TO DISCUSS OR WRITE ABOUT

1. Whatever your culture, you have developed an opinion about what is acceptable and unacceptable in social life. Explain your beliefs about the following: eye contact, hygiene, and your personal space. Be specific.

Name   Date

2. One of the most culturally diverse cities in the United States is Miami, where more than 385,000 residents have trouble speaking English. Do you think government directives, such as voting instructions, should be printed in both English and Spanish, for example? Why or why not? How about menus? Signs? Perhaps you have noticed an increase in ethnic groups in your area. What evidence do you have of this increase?

HOW DID YOU DO?
29   Culture

SKILL (number of items)	Number Correct		Points for each		Score
Vocabulary (8)	_____	×	2	=	_____
Special Textbook Vocabulary (5)	_____	×	2	=	_____
Central Theme and Main Ideas (3)	_____	×	5	=	_____
Major Details (5)	_____	×	4	=	_____
Inferences (5)	_____	×	3	=	_____
Critical Reading: Fact or Opinion (5)	_____	×	3	=	_____
Critical Reading: The Author's Strategies (3)	_____	×	2	=	_____
Reader's Process: Summarizing Your Reading (1)	_____	×	3	=	_____

The Chaser

John Collier

LEARNING OBJECTIVES

- **Point out the dangers that may result when someone becomes obsessed with or fixed upon a person for whom he or she has strong feelings.**

THINKING: GETTING STARTED

- **Can you think of something that you wanted very badly; and then when you go it, you wished you didn't have it?**

(1) Alan Austen, as nervous as a kitten, went up certain dark and creaky stairs in the neighborhood of Pell Street, and peered about for a long time on the dim landing before he found the name he wanted written **obscurely** on one of the doors.

(2) He pushed open this door, as he had been told to do, and found himself in a tiny room, which contained no furniture but a plain kitchen table, a rocking-chair, and an ordinary chair. On one of the dirty buff-colored walls were a couple of shelves, containing in all perhaps a dozen bottles and jars.

(3) An old man sat in the rocking-chair, reading a newspaper. Alan, without a word, handed him the card he had been given. "Sit down, Mr. Austen," said the man very politely. "I am glad to make your acquaintance."

(4) "Is it true," asked Alan, "that you have a certain mixture that has—er—quite extraordinary effects?"

(5) "My dear sir," replied the old man, "my stock in trade is not very large—I don't deal in laxatives and teething mixtures—but such as it is, it is varied. I think nothing I sell has effects which could be precisely described as ordinary."

(6) "Well, the fact is—" began Alan.

(7) "Here, for example," interrupted the old man, reaching for a bottle from the shelf. "Here is a liquid as colorless as water, almost tasteless, quite **imperceptible** in coffee, milk, wine, or any other beverage. It is also quite imperceptible to any known method of **autopsy**."

(8) "Do you mean it is a poison?" cried Alan, very much horrified.

THE WIZARD OF ID   Brant parker and Johnny hart

By permission of John L. Hart FLP and Creators Syndicate, Inc.

Now that medicines are available today to treat physical and emotional problems, do you think we need medicines to make people fall into love with just one person?

(9) "Call it a glove-cleaner if you like," said the old man indifferently. "Maybe it will clean gloves. I have never tried. One might call it a life-cleaner. Lives need cleaning sometimes."

(10) "I want nothing of that sort," said Alan.

(11) "Probably it is just as well," said the old man. "Do you know the price of this? For one teaspoonful, which is sufficient, I ask five thousand dollars. Never less. Not a penny less."

(12) "I hope all your mixtures are not as expensive," said Alan apprehensively.

(13) "Oh dear, no," said the old man. "It would be no good charging that sort of price for a love potion, for example. Young people who need a love potion very seldom have five thousand dollars. Otherwise they would not need a love potion."

(14) "I am glad to hear that," said Alan.

(15) "I look at it like this," said the old man. "Please a customer with one article, and he will come back when he needs another. Even if it is more costly. He will save up for it, if necessary."

(16) "So," said Alan, "you really do sell love potions?"

(17) "If I did not sell love potions," said the old man, reaching for another bottle, "I should not have mentioned the other matter to you. It is only when one is in a position to oblige that one can afford to be so **confidential.**"

(18) "And these potions," said Alan. "They are not just—just—er—"

(19) "Oh, no," said the old man. "Their effects are permanent, and extend far beyond casual impulse. But they include it. **Bountifully,** insistently. Everlastingly."

(20) "Dear me!" said Alan, attempting a look of scientific detachment. "How very interesting!"

(21) "But consider the spiritual side," said the old man.

(22) "I do, indeed," said Alan.

(23) "For indifference," said the old man, "they substitute devotion. For scorn, adoration. Give one tiny measure of this to the young lady—its flavor is imperceptible in orange juice, soup, or cocktails—and however gay and giddy she is, she will change altogether. She will want nothing but solitude, and you."

(24) "I can hardly believe it," said Alan. "She is so fond of parties."

(25) "She will not like them any more," said the old man. "She will be afraid of the pretty girls you may meet."

(26) "She will actually be jealous?" cried Alan in **rapture.** "Of me?"

(27) "Yes, she will want to be everything to you."

(28) "She is, already. Only she doesn't care about it."

(29) "She will, when she has taken this. She will care intensely. You will be her sole interest in life."

(30) "Wonderful!" cried Alan.

(31) "She will want to know all you do," said the old man. "All that has happened to you during the day. Every word of it. She will want to know what you are thinking about, why you smile suddenly, why you are looking sad."

(32) "That is love!" cried Alan.

(33) "Yes," said the old man. "How carefully she will look after you! She will never allow you to be tired, to sit in a **draught,** to neglect your food. If you are an hour late, she will be terrified. She will think you are killed, or that some **siren** has caught you."

(34) "I can hardly imagine Diana like that!" cried Alan, overwhelmed with joy.

(35) "You will not have to use your imagination," said the old man. "And, by the way, since there are always sirens, if by any chance you should, later on, slip a little, you need not worry. She will forgive you, in the end. She will be terribly hurt, of course, but she will forgive you—in the end."

(36) "That will not happen," said Alan fervently.

(37) "Of course not," said the old man. "But, if it did, you need not worry. She would never divorce you. Oh, no! And, of course, she herself will never give you the least, the very least, grounds for—uneasiness."

(38) "And how much," said Alan, "is this wonderful mixture?"

(39) "It is not as dear," said the old man, "as the glove-cleaner, or life-cleaner, as I sometimes call it. No. That is five thousand dollars, never a penny less. One has to be older than you are, to indulge in that sort of thing. One has to save up for it."

(40) "But the love potion?" said Alan.

(41) "Oh, that," said the old man, opening the drawer in the kitchen table, and taking out a tiny, rather dirty-looking **phial.** "That is just a dollar."

(42) "I can't tell you how grateful I am," said Alan, watching him fill it.

(43) "I like to oblige," said the old man. "Then customers come back, later in life, when they are rather better off, and want more expensive things. Here you are. You will find it very effective."

(44) "Thank you again," said Alan. "Good-by."

(45) "**Au revoir,**" said the old man.

Here are some of the more difficult words in "The Chaser."

Vocabulary List

au revoir
(paragraph 45)

au re·voir (ō′rə vwär′) [Fr < *au*, to the + *revoir*, seeing again < L *revidere*, see again < *re-*, again + *videre*, see: see VISION] until we meet again; goodbye: implies temporary parting

autopsy
(paragraph 7)

au·top·sy (ô′täp′sē, ôt′əp sē) *n.*, *pl.* ··sies [ML & Gr *autopsia*, a seeing with one's own eyes < Gr *autos*, self + *opsis*, a sight < *ōps*, EYE] 1 an examination and dissection of a dead body to discover the cause of death, damage done by disease, etc.; postmortem 2 a detailed critical analysis of a book, play, etc., or of some event —*vt.* ··sied, ··sy·ing to examine (a body) in this manner

bountifully
(paragraph 19)

boun·ti·ful (-tə fəl) *adj.* 1 giving freely and graciously; generous 2 provided in abundance; plentiful —**boun′·ti·fully** *adv.* —**boun′·ti·ful·ness** *n.*

chaser
(title)

chaser[1] (chā′sər) *n.* [CHASE[1] + -ER] 1 a person or thing that chases or hunts; pursuer 2 a gun formerly placed on the stern (**stern chaser**) or bow (**bow chaser**) of a ship, used during pursuit by or of another ship ☆3 a mild drink, as water, ginger ale, or beer, taken after or with whiskey, rum, etc.

confidential
(paragraph 17)

con·fi·den·tial (kän′fə den′shəl) *adj.* 1 told in confidence; imparted in secret 2 of or showing trust in another; confiding 3 entrusted with private or secret matters [a *confidential* agent] —SYN. FAMILIAR —**con′·fi·den′·ti·al′·ity** (-shē al′ə tē) *n.* or **con′·fi·den′·tial·ness** —**con′·fi·den′·tially** *adv.*

draught
(paragraph 33)

draft (draft, dräft) *n.* [ME *draught*, a drawing, pulling, stroke < base of OE *dragan*, DRAW] 1 *a)* a drawing or pulling, as of a vehicle or load *b)* the thing, quantity, or load pulled 2 *a)* a drawing in of a fish net *b)* the amount of fish caught in one draw 3 *a)* a taking of liquid into the mouth; drinking *b)* the amount taken at one drink 4 *a)* a portion of liquid for drinking; specif., a dose of medicine *b)* [Informal] a portion of beer, ale, etc. drawn from a cask 5 *a)* a drawing into the lungs, as of air or tobacco smoke *b)* the amount of air, smoke, etc., drawn in 6 a rough or preliminary sketch of a piece of writing 7 a plan or drawing of a work to be done 8 a current of air, as in a room, heating system, etc. 9 a device for regulating the current of air in a heating system 10 a written order issued by one person, bank, firm, etc., directing the payment of money to another; check 11 a demand or drain made on something

imperceptible
(paragraph 7)

im·per·cep·ti·ble (im′pər sep′tə bəl) *adj.* [Fr < ML *imperceptibilis*: see IN-[2] & PERCEPTIBLE] not plain or distinct to the senses or the mind; esp., so slight, gradual, subtle, etc. as not to be easily perceived —**im′·per·cep·ti·bil′·ity** *n.* —**im′·per·cep′·tibly** *adv.*

Vocabulary List

obscurely
(paragraph 1)

ob·scure (əb skyoor′, äb-) *adj.* 〖OFr *obscur* < L *obscurus*, lit., covered over < *ob-* (see OB-) + IE **skuro-* < base **(s)keu-*, to cover, conceal > HIDE¹, SKY〗 **1** lacking light; dim; dark; murky *[the obscure night]* **2** not easily perceived; specif., *a)* not clear or distinct; faint or undefined *[an obscure figure or sound]* *b)* not easily understood; vague; cryptic; ambiguous *[an obscure explanation]* *c)* in an inconspicuous position; hidden *[an obscure village]* **3** not well-known; not famous *[an obscure scientist]* **4** *Phonet.* pronounced as (ə) or (i) because it is not stressed; reduced; neutral: said of a vowel —*vt.* **··scured′**, **··scur′·ing** 〖L *obscurare* < the adj.〗 **1** to make obscure; specif., *a)* to darken; make dim *b)* to conceal from view; hide *c)* to make less conspicuous; overshadow *[a success that obscured earlier failures]* *d)* to make less intelligible; confuse *[testimony that obscures the issue]* **2** *Phonet.* to make (a vowel) obscure —*n.* [Rare] OBSCURITY —**ob·scure′ly** *adv.* —**ob·scure′·ness** *n.*

SYN.—**obscure** applies to that which is perceived with difficulty either because it is concealed or veiled or because of obtuseness in the perceiver *[their reasons remain obscure]*; **vague** implies such a lack of precision or exactness as to be indistinct or unclear *[a vague idea]*; **enigmatic** and **cryptic** are used of that which baffles or perplexes, the latter word implying deliberate intention to puzzle *[enigmatic behavior, a cryptic warning]*; **ambiguous** applies to that which puzzles because it allows of more than one interpretation *[an ambiguous title]*; **equivocal** is used of something ambiguous that is deliberately used to mislead or confuse *[an equivocal answer]* —**ANT.** clear, distinct, obvious

phial
(paragraph 41)

phial (fī′əl) *n.* 〖ME *fiole* < OFr < Prov *fiola* < ML < L *phiala* < Gr *phialē*, broad, shallow drinking vessel〗 a small glass bottle; vial

rapture
(paragraph 26)

rap·ture (rap′chər) *n.* 〖ML *raptura*: see RAPT & -URE〗 **1** the state of being carried away with joy, love, etc.; ecstasy **2** an expression of great joy, pleasure, etc. **3** a carrying away or being carried away in body or spirit: now rare except in theological usage —*vt.* **··tured**, **··tur·ing** [Now Rare] to enrapture; fill with ecstasy —*SYN.* ECSTASY —**the rapture** *[often* the R-*]* in some Christian theologies, the bodily ascent into heaven just before Armageddon of those who are saved (see SAVE¹, *vt.* 8) —**rap′·tur·ous** *adj.* —**rap′·tur·ously** *adv.*

siren
(paragraph 33)

si·ren (sī′rən) *n.* 〖ME *syrene* < OFr < LL *Sirena*, for L *Siren* < Gr *Seirēn* < ? *seira*, cord, rope (hence, orig. ? one who snares, entangles) < IE base **twer-*, to grasp〗 **1** *Gr. & Rom. Myth.* any of several sea nymphs, represented as part bird and part woman, who lure sailors to their death on rocky coasts by seductive singing **2** a woman who uses her sexual attractiveness to entice or allure men; a woman who is considered seductive **3** *a)* an acoustical device in which steam or air is driven against a rotating, perforated disk so as to produce sound; specif., such a device producing a loud, often wailing sound, used esp. as a warning signal *b)* an electronic device that produces a similar sound **4** any of a family (Sirenidae) of slender, eel-shaped salamanders without hind legs; esp., the mud eel

30A VOCABULARY

Using the vocabulary words listed on pages 385–386, fill in this crossword puzzle.

Across

1. an expression of great happiness and delight
3. told or divulged in secret
5. air current
8. insignificant or not easily perceived
9. not distinctly or clearly
11. a mild drink

Down

2. given freely or graciously; abundantly
4. a small glass container
6. dissection of a dead body
7. the French expression for "farewell"
10. an enchantress or seductive woman

30B CENTRAL THEME AND MAIN IDEAS

Choose the best answer.

_____ 1. The central theme of "The Chaser" is that
   a. an old man sells only two types of potions.
   b. love potions may cause distinct personality changes.
   c. "true love" may also have a dark side.
   d. there are inherent dangers involved in using potions.

_____ 2. What is the underlying assumption of "The Chaser"?

   a. The effects of love potions are permanent and irreversible.

   b. People will resort to even more drastic measures to get out of a love relationship than to get into one.

   c. Young people have less money than older people to buy what they want.

   d. A love potion may cause unfounded jealousy and unsolicited adoration.

_____ 3. The unexpected main idea of paragraph 9 is

   a. the old man's cavalier attitude toward poisoning people.

   b. the unusual names the old man chooses to disguise his poison.

   c. the philosophy that lives sometimes need to be "cleaned out."

   d. that of the two potions the old man sells, one is poison.

_____ 4. The main idea of paragraph 43 is that

   a. the old man is pleased that his customers are happy with his potions.

   b. the old man is aware that he has a tremendous service to offer his customers.

   c. the old man is willing to give his customers what they think they want now, knowing that they'll be back later for a more expensive deadly potion.

   d. the old man is anxious for his customers to return so that he can sell them more of the same potion at a higher price.

30C MAJOR DETAILS

Decide whether each detail is Major _or_ Minor _based on the context of the reading selection._

_____ 1. The potion seller's tiny room was at the top of the dark and creaky stairs.

_____ 2. There was a tremendous difference in price between the two potions.

_____ 3. The old man refers to his poison as a "life-cleaner."

_____ 4. The effects of the love potion are permanent.

_____ 5. Diana will forgive Alan's indiscretions, "in the end."

_____ 6. The potion seller is an old man.

_____ 7. The old man sells only two potions.

_____ 8. The potion seller's room contained only the barest of furniture and shelves hung on dirty buff-colored walls.

Name   Date

_____ 9. The poison is imperceptible in any autopsy.

_____10. Of his two potions, the old man tells Alan about his "life-cleaner" first.

_____11. Diana is very fond of parties.

_____12. The old man hints that all customers who purchase the first potion return later in life for the second.

30D INFERENCES

Choose the best answer.

_____ 1. The word "chaser" in the title refers to
   a. the orange juice, soup, or cocktail mixed with the love potion.
   b. the poisonous potion taken to counter the effects of the love potion.
   c. a mild drink taken following a stronger alcoholic drink.
   d the love potion purchased from the old man by young customers.

_____ 2. _Read paragraph 13 again._ The author implies that
   a. young people seldom have a need for love potions.
   b. young people in love are generally poor but are mostly indifferent to their poverty.
   c. anyone with $5,000 will have no need for a love potion because his money will make him desirable.
   d. expensive love potions would be wasted on young people, who rarely have much money anyway.

_____ 3. _Read paragraph 17 again._ The old man is implying that
   a. his potions can be very expensive and are a well-kept secret.
   b. if he did not sell love potions, Alan would not have come to see him in the first place.
   c. if he did not sell love potions, he would have no need to sell another potion to "cure" the effects of love potions.
   d. admitting to the need for a love potion is a very confidential matter.

_____ 4. _Read paragraphs 31–33 again._ Alan's exclamation of "That is love!" is answered with a flat "Yes." The old man's lack of enthusiasm is likely the result of
   a. his awareness that this love will eventually become clinging, possessive, and destructive.
   b. his belief that true love does not truly exist.
   c. his own experience with a past tragic love.
   d. his lack of interest in Alan's reaction to the potion's effects.

_____ 5. *Read paragraph 35 again.* The author uses the expression "in the end" twice, each time following the statement "She will forgive you." He does this because
   a. Alan must be persistent in asking Diana for forgiveness.
   b. Alan should be careful of these sirens and try to avoid them.
   c. Diana is likely to play the martyr first and inflict some guilt before granting forgiveness.
   d. Diana will be slow to forgive because of her confusion over Alan's unfaithfulness.

_____ 6. *Read paragraph 39 again.* The author implies that
   a. the poison is more expensive because people want it more badly than the love potion.
   b. young people have not lived long enough to have the problems associated with needing a "life-cleaner."
   c older people can expect to need "life-cleaners" and are more willing to use poisons.
   d. the poison is a precious commodity because of its inherently expensive ingredients.

_____ 7. *Read paragraphs 44–45 again.* While Alan bids the old man "goodby," the old man responds with "au revoir," implying that
   a. he is more sophisticated than Alan.
   b. he has not been in the United States long enough yet to converse easily in English.
   c. Alan is also fluent in French and understands the exchange.
   d. the parting is not permanent, and Alan will be coming back.

30E CRITICAL READING: THE AUTHOR'S STRATEGIES

Choose the best answer.

_____ 1. The main audience for "The Chaser" is
   a. anyone who wants to attract a loved one.
   b. anyone who believes in love potions.
   c. anyone who has dreamed of poisoning a lover.
   d. anyone who enjoys a love story with an ironic twist.

_____ 2. The author's purpose in writing this reading is to
   a. entertain.
   b. warn.
   c. narrate.
   d. convince.

Name   Date

_____ 3. The author's tone in this reading is
   a. ironic.
   b. dramatic.
   c. conversational.
   d. serious.

30F   READER'S PROCESS: SUMMARIZING YOUR READING

Choose the best answer.

_____ 1. What is the best summary of "The Chaser"?
   a. A young man goes to buy a love potion from an old man who sells him one for a dollar.
   b. A young man goes to buy a love potion from an old man who also sells poison.
   c. A young man goes to buy a love potion from an old man who counts on love turning to hate.
   d. A young man goes to buy a love potion and learns how it will win his lover's devotion.

30G   READER'S RESPONSE: TO DISCUSS OR WRITE ABOUT

1. Do you believe in the manufacture and distribution of a medication, such as a love potion, to affect a person's feelings for someone else? This medication might be prescribed in a situation of unrequited love. What are the advantages of such a medication? Are there any dangers? To whom would this be prescribed? Give specific support to convince your audience to consider your point of view.

2. Assume a friend came to you for advice about marriage. Would you encourage the person to marry for love, money, or some other factor? Explain fully.

HOW DID YOU DO?
30 The Chaser

SKILL (number of items)	Number Correct		Points for each		Score
Vocabulary (11)	_____	×	2	=	_____
Central Theme and Main Ideas (4)	_____	×	4	=	_____
Major Details (12)	_____	×	2	=	_____
Inferences (7)	_____	×	4	=	_____
Critical Reading: The Author's Strategies (3)	_____	×	2	=	_____
Reader's Process: Summarizing Your Reading (1)	_____	×	4	=	_____

(Possible Total: 100) *Total*   _____

Name

Date

Appendix 1

PROGRESS CHART

Total Score on Skill-Building Exercises Graph*

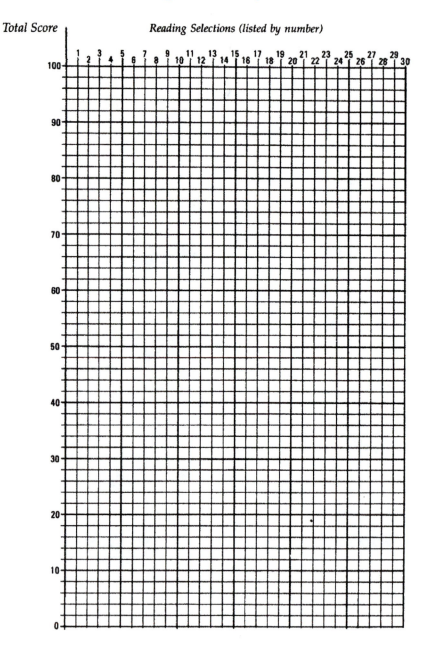

*Put a dot at your total score from the "How Did You Do?" box at the end of each reading selection. Connect the dots with a line to see your progress.

Appendix 2

GUIDE TO DICTIONARY USE[1]

With a good dictionary you can do much more than check the meanings or spellings of words. The fourth edition of *Webster's New World College Dictionary*, the dictionary featured in *Structured Reading*, is an example of a very good dictionary. The entries are clearly written, and they offer many resources of particular interest to students. This Guide to Dictionary Use can help you understand the basic features of the entries so that you can use them fully. For more details, consult the explanatory material in the front and back sections of the dictionary itself.

Main Entry Word

The technical term for each word included in the dictionary is **main entry word.** When you look up a word, the list of main entry words is what you consult. Listed alphabetically, they stand out because they are set in dark print (called *boldface*). If more than one spelling is given for a main entry word, the first spelling shown is the one more widely used. **Dictionary entry** is the technical term for the paragraph of information given for a main entry word. This textbook contains **294** entries from the fourth edition of *Webster's New World College Dictionary*.

Definitions

If a word has more than one meaning, its various **definitions** are listed in numerical order. The original meaning of the word (which is sometimes—but not always— outdated) comes first. The most recent meaning of the word appears last. Sometimes added information is given at the end of the entry, after the most recent meaning. You can tell this is happening because labels precede such information. The labels are explained here in the sections "Parts of Speech Labels," "Usage Labels," and "Field of Study Labels." For example, in the entry for *siren* (used with Selection 30 in this textbook), definition 3 gives the most recent general meaning. The first definition gives a special meaning, as the label *Gr.&Rom.Myth.* indicates.

[1]Based on "Guide to the Use of the Dictionary," *Webster's New World College Dictionary*, Fourth Edition.

si·ren (sī′rən) *n.* ⟦ME *syrene* < OFr < LL *Sirena*, for L *Siren* < Gr *Seirēn* < ? *seira*, cord, rope (hence, orig. ? one who snares, entangles) < IE base **twer-*, to grasp⟧ **1** *Gr. & Rom. Myth.* any of several sea nymphs, represented as part bird and part woman, who lure sailors to their death on rocky coasts by seductive singing **2** a woman who uses her sexual attractiveness to entice or allure men; a woman who is considered seductive **3** *a*) an acoustical device in which steam or air is driven against a rotating, perforated disk so as to produce sound; specif., such a device producing a loud, often wailing sound, used esp. as a warning signal *b*) an electronic device that produces a similar sound **4** any of a family (Sirenidae) of slender, eel-shaped salamanders without hind legs; esp., the mud eel

To decide which meaning of a word fits your situation, review the context in which the word is being used. The context can tell you whether an older or recent meaning of a word applies. Ways to figure out a word's meaning from its context are discussed in this textbook on pages 16–21.

Americanisms

An open star (★) in front of a word tells you that the word is an **Americanism.** This means that the word has its origins in the United States.

☆**avo·cado** (av′ə kä′dō, ä′və-) *n.*, *pl.* **··dos** ⟦altered (infl. by earlier Sp *avocado*, now *abogado*, advocate) < MexSp *aguacate* < Nahuatl *a:wakaλ*, avocado, lit., testicle; so named from its shape⟧ **1** a widespread, thick-skinned, pear-shaped tropical fruit, yellowish green to purplish black, with a single large seed and yellow, buttery flesh, used in salads; alligator pear **2** the tree (*Persea americana*) of the laurel family on which it grows **3** a yellowish-green color

AVOCADO

Syllabification

For pronunciation and writing purposes, words can be divided into syllables, unless a word has a single vowel sound, such as *kiss*. Each syllable represents a single vowel sound and usually its adjacent consonants. **Syllabification,** also called **word division,** becomes important for writers when space runs out at the end of a line and a word has to be carried over onto the next line. Words can be divided only at breaks for syllables.

In *Webster's New World College Dictionary,* the parts of boldface entry words are separated by a heavy centered period [•]. The heavy centered period indicates one or more places where a word can be acceptably divided at the end of a line. The entry for *proliferate* (used with Selection 24 in this book) illustrates the heavily centered period for word division.

pro·lif·er·ate (prō lif′ə rāt′, prə-) *vt.* **··at·ed, ··at′·ing** ⟦back-form. < *proliferation* < Fr *prolifèration* < *prolifère*, PROLIFEROUS + -ATION⟧ **1** to reproduce (new parts) in quick succession **2** to produce or create in profusion —*vi.* **1** to grow by multiplying new parts, as by budding, in quick succession **2** to multiply rapidly; increase profusely —**pro·lif′·era′·tion** *n.*

Pronunciation

The symbols in parentheses immediately following the main entry word show **pronunciation.** You can figure out the sound indicated by each symbol by consulting a dictionary's key to pronunciation. A "Key to Pronunciation" from *Webster's New World College Dictionary* is shown here. A more complete "Guide to Pronunciation" appears on pages xxii–xxiv of this dictionary. To get used to the key, practice first with entries for words familiar to you. Then once you are comfortable with the key, practice with entries for words that are new to you. You can practice with the sample entries in this guide and with the entries with each selection in this textbook.

PRONUNCIATION KEY

Symbol	Key Words	Symbol	Key Words
a	asp, fat, parrot	b	bed, fable, dub, ebb
ā	ape, date, play, break, fail	d	dip, beadle, had, dodder
ä	ah, car, father, cot	f	fall, after, off, phone
		g	get, haggle, dog
e	elf, ten, berry	h	he, ahead, hotel
ē	even, meet, money, flea, grieve	j	joy, agile, badge
		k	kill, tackle, bake, coat, quick
i	is, hit, mirror	l	let, yellow, ball
ī	ice, bite, high, sky	m	met, camel, trim, summer
		n	not, flannel, ton
ō	open, tone, go, boat	p	put, apple, tap
ô	all, horn, law, oar	r	red, port, dear, purr
oo	look, pull, moor, wolf	s	sell, castle, pass, nice
o͞o	ooze, tool, crew, rule	t	top, cattle, hat
yo͞o	use, cute, few	v	vat, hovel, have
yoo	cure, globule	w	will, always, swear, quick
oi	oil, point, toy	y	yet, onion, yard
ou	out, crowd, plow	z	zebra, dazzle, haze, rise
u	up, cut, color, flood	ch	chin, catcher, arch, nature
ur	urn, fur, deter, irk	sh	she, cushion, dash, machine
		th	thin, nothing, truth
ə	a in ago	*th*	then, father, lathe
	e in agent	zh	azure, leisure, beige
	i in sanity	ŋ	ring, anger, drink
	o in comply	'	[indicates that a following l
	u in focus		or n is a syllabic consonant,
ər	perhaps, murder		as in *cattle* (kat''l), *Latin*
			(lat''n); see full explanation
			on p. xiii]

Parts of Speech Labels

The first **part of speech** of a word is given after the pronunciation information in an entry. Parts of speech are abbreviated in the dictionary. They are shown in dark italic print. Here are major abbreviations and their meanings.

n.	noun
n. pl.	plural noun
vt.	transitive verb

vi.	intransitive verb
v. aux.	auxiliary verb
adj.	adjective
adv.	adverb
prep.	preposition
conj.	conjunction
pron.	pronoun
interj.	Interjection

Some words are used as more than one part of speech. If you are unsure which part of speech applies to the word in the context you are dealing with, look at all the definitions in an entry to see what works for your context. To help you work with context, use the information about using context to figure out a word's meaning, discussed in this textbook on pages 16–21.

The entry for *congruence* (used with Selection 9 in this textbook) illustrates that one word can have multiple meanings. The meanings differ as to the part of speech (noun, verb) and within a part of speech.

con·gru·ence (käŋ′grōō əns, kän′-; kən grōō′əns) *n.* ⟦ME < L *congruentia:* see fol.⟧ **1** the state or quality of being in agreement; correspondence; harmony **2** *Geom.* the property of a plane or solid figure whereby it coincides with another plane or solid figure after it is moved, rotated, or flipped over **3** *Math.* the relation between two integers each of which, when divided by a third (called the *modulus*), leaves the same remainder Also **con′·gru·ency**

Inflected Forms

The form of a word when it becomes plural or a participle or when it changes its tense is called its **inflected form.** Information about inflected forms comes after the part of speech label. Inflected forms are shown in small dark print. Information for *carcinoma* (used with Selection 13 in this textbook) illustrates the plural noun form of the word; information for *dispel* (used with Selection 12 in this textbook) illustrates letter doubling when *-ed* is added and when *-ing* is added.

car·ci·no·ma (kär′sə nō′mə) *n., pl.* ··**mas** or ··**mata** (-mə tə) ⟦L < Gr *karkinōma,* cancer < *karkinoun,* affect with a cancer < *karkinos,* crab: see CANCER⟧ any of several kinds of cancerous growths deriving from epithelial cells: see SARCOMA —**car′·ci·nom′a·tous** (-näm′ə təs, -nō′mə-) *adj.*

dis·pel (di spel′) *vt.* ··**pelled′**, ··**pel′·ling** ⟦ME *dispellen* < L *dispellere* < *dis-,* apart + *pellere,* to drive: see FELT⟧ to scatter and drive away; cause to vanish; disperse —**SYN.** SCATTER

Word History

For most main entry words, the **word history,** known as **etymology,** is given in brackets after the main entry word, its pronunciation, and any inflected forms. Abbreviations and symbols present information and origins, and words from languages other than English appear in italics.

Etymology often suggests a word's flavor. The sample dictionary entries in this guide use these frequently used symbols and abbreviations.

<	derived from
+	plus
Fr	French (MFr = Middle French; OFr = Old French)
Gr	classical Greek
IE	Indo-European
ME	Middle English
L	Latin (LL = Late Latin; VL = Vulgar Latin)
OE	Old English

Usage Labels

The customary way words are used—their **usage**—depends on many factors. The two major influences are the formality of the occasion on which the word is used and the location where the word is used. Whenever a word or sense may not be appropriate for formal writing, the dictionary entry gives usage information. Usage labels are shown in brackets following a main entry word or one of its numbered definitions. Here are the most frequently seen usage labels and their meanings.

[Brit.]	*British:* commonly accepted meaning in British English
[Informal]	*informal:* used in conversation and informal writing
[Dial.]	*dialect:* used in certain geographical areas of the United States
[Obs.]	*obsolete:* no longer in use
[Old Poet.]	*poetic:* used chiefly in earlier poetry or for poetic meaning
[Slang]	*slang:* highly informal and generally considered not standard; acceptable when used for effect or mood to convey a highly informal context

The entry for *Jim Crow* (used with Selection 16 in this textbook) indicates that it has an informal sense. The entry for *Deadeye* (used with Selection 22 in this textbook) says that one of its meanings (definition 2) is slang.

☆**Jim Crow** [[name of an early black minstrel song]] [*also* **j- c-**] [Informal] traditional discrimination against or segregation of blacks, esp. in the U.S. —**Jim′-Crow′** *vt., adj.* —**Jim Crow′·ism′**

dead·eye (-ī′) *n.* **1** a round, flat block of wood with three holes in it for a lanyard, used in pairs on a sailing ship to hold the shrouds and stays taut **2** [Slang] an accurate marksman

Field of Study Labels

Many words have special meanings when used in the context of various **fields of study.** For example, the entry for *derivative* (used in Selection 22 of this textbook) starts with its usual meanings as an adjective and then as a noun. Then come abbreviated labels that indicate special meanings from various fields of study: chemistry, linguistics, and math.

> **de·riva·tive** (də riv′ə tiv) *adj.* ⟦ME *derivatif* < LL *derivativus* < L *derivatus*, pp. of *derivare*: see fol.⟧ **1** derived **2** using or taken from other sources; not original **3** of derivation —*n.* **1** something derived **2** *Chem.* a substance derived from, or of such composition and properties that it may be considered as derived from, another substance by chemical change, esp. by the substitution of one or more elements or radicals **3** *Finance* a contract, as an option or futures contract, whose value depends on the value of the securities, commodities, etc. that form the basis of the contract **4** *Linguis.* a word formed from another or others by derivation **5** *Math.* the limiting value of a rate of change of a function with respect to a variable; the instantaneous rate of change, or slope, of a function (Ex.: the derivative of y with respect to x, often written dy/dx, is 3 when y = 3x) —**de·riv′a·tively** *adv.*

Synonyms

When a word has **synonyms** whose meanings may or may not be interchanged with it, the dictionary entry ends with the symbol **SYN,** followed by a word in small capital letters. When you look up that word, you will find at the end of its entry a **synonymy**—a list of synonyms with definitions that explain slight differences in meaning among the words listed. The synonymy is signaled by the symbol *SYN.-*. To decide which synonym fits your situation, review the context in which the word appears and match it to the definitions in the synonymy. The entry for *transform* (used with Selection 1 in this textbook) offers a synonymy of four words.

> **trans·form** (trans fôrm′; *for n.* trans′fôrm′) *vt.* ⟦ME *transformen* < L *transformare* < *trans-*, TRANS- + *formare*, to form < *forma*, FORM⟧ **1** to change the form or outward appearance of **2** to change the condition, nature, or function of; convert **3** to change the personality or character of **4** *Elec.* to change (a voltage or current value) by use of a transformer **5** *Linguis.* to change by means of a syntactic transformational rule **6** *Math.* to change (an algebraic expression or equation) to a different form having the same value **7** *Physics* to change (one form of energy) into another —*vi.* [Rare] to be or become transformed —*n. Math.* the process or result of a mathematical transformation —**trans·form′·able** *adj.* —**trans·form′a·tive** *adj.*
>
> *SYN.*—**transform,** the broadest in scope of these terms, implies a change either in external form or in inner nature, in function, etc. /she was *transformed* into a happy girl/; **transmute,** from its earlier use in alchemy, suggests a change in basic nature that seems almost miraculous /*transmuted* from a shy youth into a sophisticated man about town/; **convert** implies a change in details so as to be suitable for a new use /to *convert* an attic into an apartment/; **metamorphose** suggests a startling change produced as if by magic /a tadpole is *metamorphosed* into a frog/; **transfigure** implies a change in outward appearance which seems to exalt or glorify /his whole being was *transfigured* by love/ See also CHANGE

The following three pages show a sample dictionary page, with labels for your reference.

Cerritos / cevitamic acid   230

Cer·ri·tos (se rē′tōs) [Sp, little hills] city in SW Calif.: suburb of Los Angeles: pop. 53,000 — *American place name with etymology*

Cerro de Pasco (ser′ō dä päs′kō) mining town in the mountains of WC Peru: alt. *c.* 14,000 ft. (4,250 m): pop. 72,000

cert 1 certificate **2** certified

cer·tain (surt″n) *adj.* [ME & OFr < VL *certanus < L certus,* determined, fixed, orig. pp. of *cernere,* to distinguish, decide, orig., to sift, separate: see HARVEST] **1** fixed, settled, or determined **2** sure (to happen, etc.); inevitable **3** not to be doubted; unquestionable [*certain* evidence] **4** not failing; reliable; dependable [*a certain* cure] **5** controlled; unerring [his *certain* aim] **6** without any doubt; assured; sure; positive [*certain* of his innocence] **7** not named or described, though definite and perhaps known [*a certain* person] **8** some, but not very much; appreciable [*to a certain* extent] —*pron.* [with pl. v.] a certain indefinite number; certain ones (of) —**SYN.** SURE — **for certain** as a certainty; without doubt — *Idiomatic phrase*

cer·tain·ly (-lē) *adv.* beyond a doubt; surely

cer·tain·ty (-tē) *n.* [ME *certeinte < OFr certaineté*] **1** the quality, state, or fact of being certain **2** *pl.* **-ties** anything certain; definite act —**of a certainty** [Archaic] without a doubt; certainly

SYN.—**certainty** suggests a firm, settled belief or positiveness in the truth of something; **certitude** is sometimes distinguished from the preceding as implying an absence of objective proof, hence suggesting unassailable blind faith; **assurance** suggests confidence, but not necessarily positiveness, usually in something that is yet to happen [I have *assurance* of his continuing support]; **conviction** suggests a being convinced because of satisfactory reasons or proof and sometimes implies earlier doubt —**ANT.** doubt, skepticism — *Synonymy*

cer·tes (sur′tēz′) *adv.* [ME & OFr < VL *certas,* for L *certo,* surely < *certus:* see CERTAIN] [Archaic] certainly; verily

cer·ti·fi·a·ble (surt′ə fī′ə bəl) *adj.* that can be certified —**cer′ti·fi′a·bly** (-blē) *adv.*

cer·tif·i·cate (sər tif′i kit; *for v.,* -kāt′) *n.* [ME & OFr *certificat < ML certificatum < LL certificatus,* pp. of *certificare,* CERTIFY] a written or printed statement by which a fact is formally or officially certified or attested; specif., *a)* a document certifying that one has met specified requirements, as for teaching *b)* a document certifying ownership, a promise to pay, etc. —*vt.* **-cat′ed, -cat′ing** to attest or authorize by a certificate; issue a certificate to —**cer·tif′i·ca′tor** *n.* —**cer·tif′i·ca·to·ry** (-kə tôr′ē) *adj.* — *Part-of-speech labels* / *Derived entries*

certificate of deposit a certificate issued by a bank or a savings and loan association acknowledging the receipt of a specified sum of money in a special kind of time deposit drawing interest and requiring written notice for withdrawal

certificate of incorporation a legal document stating the name and purpose of a proposed corporation, the names of its incorporators, its stock structure, etc.

certificate of origin a certificate submitted by an exporter to those countries requiring it, listing goods to be imported and stating their place of origin

cer·ti·fi·ca·tion (surt′ə fi kā′shən) *n.* [Fr] **1** a certifying or being certified **2** a certified statement

cer·ti·fied (surt′ə fīd′) *adj.* **1** vouched for; guaranteed **2** having, or attested to by, a certificate — *Americanism*

☆certified check a check for which a bank has guaranteed payment, certifying there is enough money on deposit to cover the check

☆certified mail 1 a postal service for recording the mailing and delivery of a piece of first-class mail **2** mail recorded by this service: it is not insurable

☆certified public accountant a public accountant certified by a State examining board as having met the requirements of State law

Inflected forms

cer·ti·fy (surt'ə fī') vt. **-fied', -fy'ing** [ME *certifien* < OFr *certifier* < LL *certificare* < L *certus*, CERTAIN + -FY] **1** to declare (a thing) true, accurate, certain, etc. by formal statement, often in writing; verify; attest **2** to declare officially insane and committable to a mental institution ☆**3** to guarantee the quality or worth of (a check, document, etc.); vouch for **4** to issue a certificate or license to **5** [Archaic] to assure; make certain —vi. to testify (*to*) —*SYN.* APPROVE —**cer·ti·fi·er** *n.*

Usage label

cer·ti·o·ra·ri (sur'shē ə rer'ē) *n.* [ME < LL, lit., to be made more certain: a word in the writ] *Law* a discretionary writ from a higher court to a lower one, or to a board or official with some judicial power, requesting the record of a case for review

Field label

cer·ti·tude (surt'ə tōōd', -tyōōd') *n.* [OFr < LL(Ec) *certitudo* < L *certus*, CERTAIN] **1** a feeling of absolute sureness or conviction **2** sureness; inevitability —*SYN.* CERTAINTY

ce·ru·le·an (sə rōō'lē ən) *adj.* [L *caeruleus*; prob. < *caelulum*, dim. of *caelum*, heaven: for IE base see CESIUM] sky-blue; azure

ce·ru·men (sə rōō'mən) *n.* [< L *cera*, wax; sp. infl. by ALBUMEN] EARWAX —**ce·ru'mi·nous** (-mə nəs) *adj.*

ce·ruse (sir'ōōs', sə rōōs') *n.* [OFr < L *cerussa* < ? Gr *kēroessa*, waxlike < *kēros*, wax] **1** WHITE LEAD **2** a former cosmetic containing white lead

ce·rus·site (sir'ə sīt', sə rus'īt') *n.* [< L *cerussa* (see prec.) + -ITE[1]] native lead carbonate, PbCO₃, widely distributed in crystalline or massive form

Biographical entry

Cer·van·tes (Sa·a·ve·dra) (ther vän'tes sä'ä ved'rä; *E* sər van'tēz'), **Mi·guel de** (mē gel' the) 1547-1616; Sp. novelist, poet, & play-wright; author of *Don Quixote*

cer·ve·lat (ser və lä', -lät') *n.* [Fr] a dry, smoked sausage of beef and pork Also sp. **cer·ve·las'** (-lä')

cer·vi·cal (sur'vi kəl) *adj.* [< L *cervix* (gen. *cervicis*), the neck + -AL] *Anat.* of the neck or cervix

cer·vi·ces (sər vī'sēz', sur'və-) *n.* alt. pl. of CERVIX

cer·vi·ci·tis (sur'və sīt'is) *n.* [see -ITIS] inflammation of the cervix of the uterus

cer·vi·co- (sur'vi kō', -kə) [< L *cervix*, neck] *combining form* cervical [*cervicitis*] Also, before a vowel, **cer'vic-**

cer·vid (sur'vid') *adj.* [< ModL *Cervidae*, name of the family (< L *cervus*, stag, deer < IE *kerewos*, horned, a horned animal < base *ker-*, HORN) + -ID] of the deer family

Cer·vin (môn ser van'), **Mont** *Fr. name of the* MATTERHORN

Main entry word

cer·vine (sur'vīn', -vin) *adj.* [L *cervinus* < *cervus*: see CERVID] of or like a deer

cer·vix (sur'viks') *n.*, pl. **cer·vi·ces** (sər vī'sēz', sur'və-) or **-vix·es** [L, the neck] **1** the neck, esp. the back of the neck **2** a necklike part, as of the uterus or urinary bladder

Ce·sar·e·an or **Ce·sar·i·an** (sə zer'ā ən) *adj., n.* CAESAREAN

Etymology

ce·si·um (sē'zē əm) *n.* [ModL, orig. neut. of L *caesius*, bluish-gray (< IE base *(s)kai-*, bright > -HOOD): so named (1860) by Robert Wilhelm BUNSEN because of the blue line seen in the spectroscope] a soft, silver-white, ductile, metallic chemical element, the most electropositive of all the elements: it ignites in air, reacts vigorously with water, and is used in photoelectric cells: symbol, Cs; at. wt., 132.905; at. no., 55; sp. gr., 1.892; melt. pt., 28.64°C; boil. pt., 670°C: a radioactive isotope (**cesium-137**) with a half-life of 30.17 years is a fission product and is used in cancer research, radiation therapy, etc.

Čes·ké Bu·dě·jo·vi·ce (ches'ke bōō'de yô'vit sə) city in SW Czecho-slovakia, on the Vltava River: pop. 93,000

Čes·ko·slo·ven·sko (ches'kô slô ven'skô) *Czech name of* CZECHO-SLOVAKIA

ces·pi·tose (ses'pə tōs') *adj.* [ModL < L *caespes*, turf, grassy field + -OSE²] growing in dense, matlike clumps without creeping stems, as moss, grass, etc.

cess (ses) *n.* [prob. < ASSESS] in Ireland, an assessment; tax: now used only in bad cess to bad luck to ———————— Pronunciation

ces·sa·tion (se sā'shən) *n.* [L *cessatio* < pp. of *cessare*, CEASE] a ceasing, or stopping, either forever or for some time

ces·sion (sesh'ən) *n.* [OFr < L *cessio* < *cessus*, pp. of *cedere*, to yield: see CEDE] a ceding or giving up (of rights, property, territory, etc.) to another

ces·sion·ar·y (sesh'ə ner'ē) *n., pl.* -**ar·ies** *Law* ASSIGNEE

cess·pit (ses'pit') *n.* [< fol. + PIT²] a pit for garbage, excrement, etc.

cess·pool (-pōōl') *n.* [< ? It *cesso*, privy < L *secessus*, place of retirement (in LL, privy, drain): see SECEDE] **1** a deep hole or pit in the ground, usually covered, to receive drainage or sewage from the sinks, toilets, etc. of a house **2** a center of moral filth and corruption ———————— Definitions

ces·ta (ses'tə) *n.* [Sp, basket < L *cista*: see CHEST] in jai alai, the narrow, curved, basketlike racket strapped to the forearm, in which the ball is caught and hurled against a wall

c'est la vie (se lä vē') [Fr] that's life; such is life

ces·tode (ses'tōd') *n.* [CEST(US)¹ + -ODE²] any of a class (Cestoda) ———————— Scientific name
of parasitic flatworms, with a ribbonlike body and no intestinal canal; tapeworm —*adj.* of such a worm

ces·toid (-toid') *adj.* ribbonlike, as a tapeworm

ces·tus¹ (-təs) *n.* [L < Gr *kestos*, a girdle; akin to *kentein*, to stitch: see CENTER] in ancient times, a woman's belt or girdle

ces·tus² (-təs) *n.* [L *caestus* < *caedere*, to strike, cut down: see -CIDE] a contrivance of leather straps, often weighted with metal, worn on the hand by boxers in ancient Rome

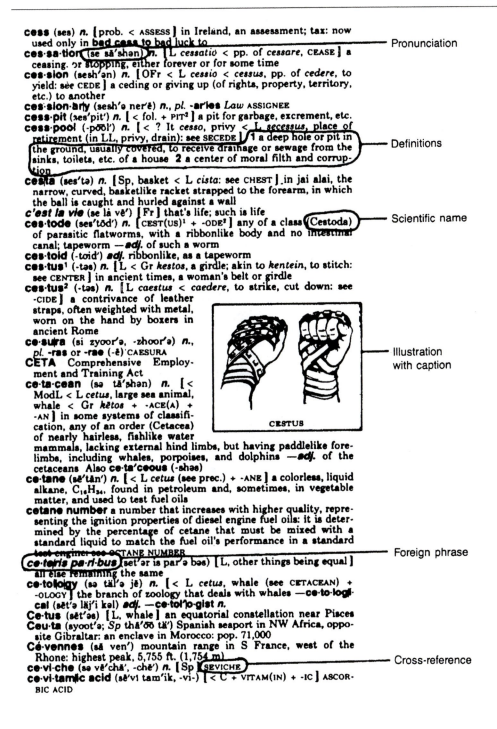

CESTUS

————— Illustration with caption

ce·su·ra (si zyoor'ə, -zhoor'ə) *n., pl.* -**ras** or -**rae** (-ē) CAESURA

CETA Comprehensive Employment and Training Act

ce·ta·cean (sə tā'shən) *n.* [< ModL < L *cetus*, large sea animal, whale < Gr *kētos* + -ACE(A) + -AN] in some systems of classification, any of an order (Cetacea) of nearly hairless, fishlike water mammals, lacking external hind limbs, but having paddlelike forelimbs, including whales, porpoises, and dolphins —*adj.* of the cetaceans Also **ce·ta'ceous** (-shəs)

ce·tane (sē'tān') *n.* [< L *cetus* (see prec.) + -ANE] a colorless, liquid alkane, $C_{16}H_{34}$, found in petroleum and, sometimes, in vegetable matter, and used to test fuel oils

cetane number a number that increases with higher quality, representing the ignition properties of diesel engine fuel oils: it is determined by the percentage of cetane that must be mixed with a standard liquid to match the fuel oil's performance in a standard test engine: see OCTANE NUMBER ———————— Foreign phrase

ce·te·ris pa·ri·bus (set'ər is par'ə bəs) [L, other things being equal] all else remaining the same

ce·tol·o·gy (sə täl'ə jē) *n.* [< L *cetus*, whale (see CETACEAN) + -OLOGY] the branch of zoology that deals with whales —**ce·to·log·i·cal** (sēt'ə läj'i kəl) *adj.* —**ce·tol'o·gist** *n.*

Ce·tus (sēt'əs) [L, whale] an equatorial constellation near Pisces

Ceu·ta (syōōt'ə; *Sp* thä'ōō tä') Spanish seaport in NW Africa, opposite Gibraltar: an enclave in Morocco: pop. 71,000

Cé·vennes (sā ven') mountain range in S France, west of the Rhone: highest peak, 5,755 ft. (1,754 m) ———————— Cross-reference

ce·vi·che (sə vē'chä', -chē') *n.* [Sp SEVICHE]

ce·vi·tam·ic acid (sē'vi tam'ik, -vi-) [< C + VITAM(IN) + -IC] ASCORBIC ACID

Credits

Vocabulary Index

411

General Index

Note: Page numbers with *f* indicate figures; those with *t* indicate tables.